Complex Organizations
A Critical Essay

THIRD EDITION

Complex Organizations
A Critical Essay

THIRD EDITION

CHARLES PERROW
YALE UNIVERSITY

Academic Consultants
ALBERT J. REISS, JR.
HAROLD L. WILENSKY

McGraw-Hill, Inc.
New York   St. Louis   San Francisco   Auckland   Bogotá
Caracas   Lisbon   London   Madrid   Mexico City   Milan
Montreal   New Delhi   San Juan   Singapore
Sydney   Tokyo   Toronto

This book is printed on acid-free paper.

COMPLEX ORGANIZATIONS

Third Edition

19 20 DOC/DOC 0 9 8 7 6 5 4 3 2

Library of Congress Cataloging-in-Publication Data
Perrow, Charles.
    Complex organizations: a critical essay / Charles Perrow. — 3rd
ed.
        p. cm.
    Originally published: New York: Random House, c1986.
    Includes bibliographical references and index.
    ISBN 0–07–554799–6 (alk. paper)
    1. Complex organizations. I. Title.
HM131.P382 1993
302.3'5--dc20   93–44202
ISBN 0–07–554799–6

Cover: "Structure Q," by Oi Sawa, 1984. Courtesy of Viridian Gallery, New York.

Permissions Acknowledgements

21–22: Quote from EXPLORATION IN MANAGEMENT by Wilfred Brown. Copyright © 1960 by Wilfred Brown. Reprinted by permission of John Wiley & Sons, Inc.

53–54, 56–61: Quotes and table from Reinhard Bendix, WORK AND AUTHORITY IN INDUSTRY: IDEOLOGIES OF MANAGEMENT IN THE COURSE OF INDUSTRI-ALIZATION. Berkeley: University of California Press, 1974, pp. 69, 254, 267, 271–274, 280, 296, 298, and 315.

74–75: Quotes from THE FUNCTIONS OF THE EXECUTIVE by Chester I. Barnard. Copyright 1938 and © 1968 by the President and Fellows of Harvard College. Copyright © 1966 by Grace F. Noera Barnard. Reprinted by permission of Harvard University Press, publisher.

93–94: Quote from LEADERSHIP AND ORGANIZATION: A BEHAVIORAL SCI-ENCE APPROACH by Robert Tannenbaum, I. R. Weschler, and F. Massarik. Copyright © 1961 by McGraw-Hill, Inc. Reprinted by permission of The McGraw-Hill Book Company.

107–110: Quotes from MANAGEMENT BY PARTICIPATION by Alfred J. Marrow, David G. Bowers, and Stanley E. Seashore. Copyright © 1967 by Alfred J. Marrow. Re-printed by permission of Harper & Row, Publishers, Inc.

149–150: Figures from NORMAL ACCIDENTS: LIVING WITH HIGH-RISK TECH-NOLOGIES, by Charles Perrow. Copyright © 1984 by Basic Books, Inc. Reprinted by permission of the publisher.

Preface

It is an honor to prepare the third edition of a book that is less a text than an essay, selective rather than encompassing, exploratory rather than definitive, and irreverent and critical rather than academic and admiring. While I have been immensely gratified by readers' appreciative comments on the two other editions, the honor really goes to the field as a whole.

Organizational analysis has grown in depth, breadth, self-criticism, and sophistication over the twenty-five years that I have observed it. In 1960 most of the important topics for the field came from other, more well-developed fields. Today I believe the reverse is true: we are exporting ideas, data, and topics to psychology, social psychology, political science, and even economics more than we are importing them. In 1960 there were few of us in organizational analysis. Now there are many, scattered throughout many disciplines and professions. Certainly in key areas of sociology—stratification, political processes, social psychology, social movements, social change, and others—organizations, and thus organizational analysis, are now seen as the key. Twenty-five years ago the following statement would have been considered preposterous: all important social processes either have their origin in formal organizations or are strongly mediated by them; the study of organizations must be at the core of all social science. Today the first part of the statement is generally accepted, and I expect that within two decades the second part will also be accepted. Thus, a third edition is a tribute to the vitality and importance of this field.

This edition intensifies the strategy of the earlier editions: to provide a developmental overview of the major schools of thought and a close examination of the most interesting recent approaches. I have made more explicit the development of the field and have added some very new theories. All the material retained from the previous editions has been edited for improvements in style, references have been updated when useful, and more contemporary illustrations have been provided in some cases. The "beyond bureaucracy" section has been deleted because I think the points once made in that section are more apparent today and the question of new organizational forms is too unsettled to be treated with assurance as yet. The section on "ethno-Marxism" has also been dropped; both ethnomethodology and Marxism are incorporated in developments discussed throughout the book.

Among the new materials are an extensive discussion of the historical development of organizations, including the paths that the United States might have taken but didn't, at the beginning of Chapter 2 ("Managerial Ideologies and the Origins of the Human Relations Movement"); a more substantial discussion of bounded rationality and "garbage can" theory, including an attempt to relate their appearance to the larger movement of "deconstructionism" in social science and the humanities, in Chapter 4 ("The Neo-Weberian Model"); a section summarizing the implications for organizational theory of my recent book, *Normal Accidents: Living with High-Risk Technologies,* at the end of Chapter 4; and a discussion of recent developments in population-ecology models and of an evolutionary model of routine, at the end of Chapter 6 ("The Environment").

In addition two new chapters are included. Chapter 7 discusses two economic models of organizations—agency theory and transaction-costs economics. These models are getting a great deal of attention, and it is time to critically evaluate them. They force us to be more explicit about the conditions that favor narrowly self-interested behavior in organizations and those that favor other-regarding behavior. I try to make a start on this task. The final chapter provides a summary of the book, especially the theme running throughout it: the importance of a power perspective in organizational analysis. Utilizing this perspective, I examine two additional new theoretical positions: the cultural view, featuring the role of myths and symbols, and an evolutionary historical account of the origins of bureaucracy. Both have much to recommend them, but as always, I have my criticisms.

Thus, as this third edition demonstrates, an astounding wealth of research, ideas, theories, and material for analysis is afloat in our subject area, ranging from labor control by Josiah Wedgwood in 1750 to deregulation under President Reagan; and from cognitive psychology to the vast networks of international capitalism. I ended the first edition on the baleful note that somehow the institutional school and the neo-Weberian model should inform one another. That was in 1971. By 1978, in preparing the second edition, I was enthusiastic about all the new work, especially on environmental and bounded rationality models. Now, in 1985, I don't believe there is another area of social science as productive, exciting, inventive, and above all, as relevant to our daily trials as the field of organizational analysis. I hope the scope and complexity of topics that go with this development do not daunt the post-1985 reader, but rather stimulate her or him to join the field and contribute to our understanding.

Harold Wilensky once again provided valuable and trenchant criticisms of all the new material for this edition. Paul DiMaggio and Walter Powell improved the last chapter with judicious comments. But my greatest debt is owed to four scholars—DiMaggio, Powell, Greg Dow, and Robert Eccles—for very careful and detailed comments on and ideas for Chapter 7, which deals with economic theories of organizations. Valuable help on this chapter also came from Lee Clarke, Mark Granovetter, Richard Nelson, Marshall Meyer, Harold Wilensky, and Oliver Williamson. Rebecca Friedkin, Susan Kelley, and Ronald Jepperson were constructively critical of earlier versions, as were other members of the COSI seminar at Yale University.

As before, and even more so if that were possible, I owe this book to Edith.

Charles Perrow
Guilford, Conn.

Contents

Complex Organizations
A Critical Essay

THIRD EDITION

Why Bureaucracy?

Several miles from a medium-sized city near one of the Great Lakes, there was a plant that mined gypsum rock, crushed it, mixed it with bonding and foaming agents, spread it out on a wide sheet of paper, covered it with another sheet, let it set a bit, sliced it into large but inedible sandwiches, and then dried them. The resulting material was sold as wallboard, used for insulation and for dividing up rooms in buildings. Plants such as this were scattered about the country, some of them owned, as was this one, by General Gypsum Corporation (a pseudonym). A book by Alvin Gouldner, *Patterns of Industrial Bureaucracy,* described the plant and the surrounding communities as they existed in 1950.[1]

The towns around the plant were small and had been settled about a century before. The people in the area generally knew one another well and regarded strangers with considerable misgiving. They led a peaceful, semirural life, with an emphasis upon farming, hunting, and fishing. They were conservative in their outlook, strait-laced in their behavior, and, according to one member, "thrifty, religious, God-fearing, and anti-Semitic."[2]

The gypsum plant fitted comfortably into the style of life in the area. Most of the men working at the plant, some 225 including the miners, had worked there for many years. They knew one another well on the job and visited outside the plant in the surrounding hamlets. Indeed, perhaps as many as one-half of the workers were related to others employed in the plant. The personnel man who hired and fired people argued that it was good to learn something about a prospective employee by asking others in the plant or community about him and his family. He did not want hostile employees or troublemakers. He also preferred farm boys over city boys. The former worked harder, he thought, and took greater pride in their work. The personnel man had few other rules for hiring, firing, or other matters with which he had to deal, however. He disliked paperwork and, as one employee said, "He regarded everything that happened as an exception to the rule." He had only an eighth-grade education, but since he relied so heavily on the community norms and

[1] Alvin Gouldner, *Patterns of Industrial Bureaucracy* (New York: Free Press, 1954).
[2] Ibid., p. 35.

his own rule-of-thumb methods, not much education seemed to be required. Apparently, hardly anyone was ever fired from the plant. Even those who left during the war years to work in defense plants paying much higher wages were welcomed back when those plants closed. A city boy, however, or a stranger laid off by a defense plant in the city had a hard time getting a job from this man.

In the plant itself, the workers had considerable leeway. The men were able to try different jobs until they found one that they liked, as long as they did so within the general limits of their union regulations. Moreover, they stretched out their lunch hours, were allowed to arrive late as long as they had some excuse, and were not required to keep busy. As long as their work was done, their time was their own. Production records were kept informally. The trouble was that the company management felt that not enough work was being done.

Further, the rhythm of the plant was, to some degree, determined by the men. During hunting season fewer showed up; the same thing sometimes occurred during planting season, since many employees farmed in their spare time. In cold weather more of them complained of sprains or other ailments so they could be transferred to the "sample room," where the work was light and the room was warm, until they were feeling better. This was preferable to staying at home and using up sick leave or to living off unemployment compensation. Mining operations fell off considerably on Mondays because of hangovers among the heavy-drinking miners. As a mill foreman explained, "You can't ride the men very hard when they are your neighbors. Lots of these men grew up together."[3]

Many employees used the plant materials and services freely. Men took dynamite home with them to explode in ponds (an easy way to fish) and for construction. They appropriated quantities of wallboard, even truckloads, for their personal use. They brought in broken items such as furniture to be fixed by the carpenters. And both employees and farmers in the area brought in broken parts for free welding.

For the workers, the plant was a pleasant and comfortable operation. One could hardly "get ahead," but few desired to go wherever "ahead" was. Those who showed a desire to advance in the company got transfers to company plants in different areas. Others left for the big city.

But for other interested parties, the plant was not all that satisfying. A job seeker found it difficult to get work if he was not well known, did not have relatives in the plant, or did not measure up to the vague standards of the personnel man —which had little to do with the ability to do the job. Customers found deliveries erratic. They might have suspected that if all gypsum plants were run this way, they would be paying a surcharge to cover the purloined materials, free repair work, and general slack. Top managers in the company headquarters, faced with postwar competition from other companies and competing products, were apparently climbing the walls.

When the plant manager died ("Old Doug," he was affectionately called), headquarters sent in an aggressive new manager with orders to tighten things up— increase productivity and cut costs. According to Gouldner's account, this man was not blessed with bountiful tact and insight, even though he was otherwise efficient.

[3]Ibid., p. 65.

He cracked down rather hard and accumulated much ill will. He activated dormant rules, instituted new ones, demoted the personnel man, and brought in one who applied a "universalistic" standard—the only thing that counted was a person's ability to do the job. The new manager successfully "bureaucratized" the surface plant. (He was unable to bureaucratize the more dangerous mine, for there was too much uncertainty and unpredictability in the work, and teamwork was extremely important.) However, some time later he was faced with a wildcat strike.

What had been a "traditional" form of organization, or in the terms of Max Weber,[4] a "traditional bureaucracy," became a "rational-legal bureaucracy." A rational-legal bureaucracy is based on rational principles (rational in terms of management's interests, not necessarily the worker's), is backed by legal sanctions, and exists in a legal framework. A miner fired for taking a case of dynamite, for example, was unsuccessful in his appeal that "everyone did it" and that the foreman "told him he could." Tradition or precedent was not binding; the material belonged to the company, not to the miner or the foreman.

Most of the key elements of the rational-legal bureaucracy are represented in this brief case history. They include:

1. Equal treatment for all employees.
2. Reliance on expertise, skills, and experience relevant to the position.
3. No extraorganizational prerogatives of the position (such as taking dynamite, wallboard, etc.); that is, the position is seen as belonging to the organization, not the person. The employee cannot use it for personal ends.
4. Specific standards of work and output.
5. Extensive record keeping dealing with the work and output.
6. Establishment and enforcement of rules and regulations that serve the interests of the organization.
7. Recognition that rules and regulations bind managers as well as employees; thus employees can hold management to the terms of the employment contract.

The rational-legal form of bureaucracy developed over many centuries of Western civilization. It grew slowly and erratically, beginning in the Middle Ages, and reached its full form on a widespread basis only in the twentieth century.[5] Nearly all large, complex organizations in the United States, for example, are best classified as bureaucracies, though the degree and forms of bureaucratization vary.

Its "ideal" form, however, is never realized for at least three reasons. First, it

[4]The famous German sociologist, writing in the early decades of this century, laid out the model of bureaucracy and described and explained its origins. Weber's writings on bureaucracy appear in two different parts of an uncompleted draft of his opus, *Economy and Society*. The first part is presented in Max Weber, *The Theory of Social and Economic Organization*, trans. A. M. Henderson and Talcott Parsons (New York: Oxford University Press, 1947), pp. 324–340. The second part, which was actually written first and is a more discursive section, appears in Max Weber, *From Max Weber, Essays in Sociology*, trans. and ed. by Hans Gerth and C. Wright Mills (New York: Oxford University Press, 1946), pp. 196–244. The corresponding pages in the 1968 translation of Weber's work, *Economy and Society*, ed. Guenther Roth and Claus Wittich (New York: Irvington Publications, 1968), are vol. 1, pp. 212–225 and vol. 3, pp. 956–1001.

[5]See Reinhard Bendix, "Bureaucracy," in *International Encyclopedia of the Social Sciences* (New York: Free Press, 1977).

tries to do what must be (hopefully) forever impossible—to eliminate all unwanted extraorganizational influences on the behavior of members. Ideally, members should act only in the organization's interests. The problem is that even if the interest of the organization is unambiguous, people do not exist just for organizations. They track all kinds of mud from the rest of their lives into the organization, and they have all kinds of interests that are independent of the organization.

Second, the ideal form also falls short of realization when rapid changes in some of the organizational tasks are required. *Bureaucracies are set up to deal with stable, routine tasks; that is the basis of organizational efficiency.* Without stable tasks there cannot be a stable division of labor, a prescribed acquisition of skills and experience, formal planning and coordination, and so on. But when changes come along, organizations must alter their programs; when such changes are frequent and rapid, the form of organization becomes so temporary that the efficiencies of bureaucracy cannot be realized. (The price of the product it delivers then goes up.) The gypsum mine could not be bureaucratized to the degree that the surface plant was because the unpredictability of the seams and the dangers and variability of the raw material made continual change and improvisation necessary.

Third, bureaucracy in its ideal form falls short of its expectations because people are only indifferently intelligent, prescient, all-knowing, and energetic. All organizations must be designed for the "average" person one is likely to find in each position, not the superhuman.

While bureaucracy always falls short of the ideal model that Weber outlined, neither Weber in his time nor many people today would be comfortable with the ideal. In fact, much can be said for the placid, community-oriented gypsum-plant organization before the owners decided it was not making enough money for them. There was job rotation and variability, consideration for special problems such as minor illnesses, and trust among the workers and between workers and management. Furthermore, to a small extent, workers could consider the resources of the organization (wallboard, the carpentry shop) to be theirs. Perhaps above all, they could farm and hunt and thus avoid complete dependence on wages paid by the gypsum plant. If all gypsum companies were like this, some of the "social costs" of bureaucracy —dependence on a wage, dull work, and inflexible demands—would be spread over all consumers of the product. But all companies are not like this, so this one could not compete and survive. In this sense, where all organizations strive toward efficiency as defined by the owners, the rational-legal form of bureaucracy is the most efficient form of administration known in industrial societies.

Weber claimed that all else is dilettantism, but the verdict is not yet in. Alternative forms of organization are being tried. Nevertheless, they have yet to do more than to humanize rigid bureaucracies and make them more adaptive to changes. They have not seriously challenged the wage system, which takes in about 85 percent of the gainfully employed who must work for someone else. Nor have they fully rejected the notion that the resources of the organization belong to the owners of private firms or the officials of state and voluntary organizations, rather than to all members. Without fundamental changes in the wage system and ideas of ownership, alternative forms of bureaucracy are likely to be expensive, unstable, brief, and rare.

In the rest of this chapter, I am going to illustrate the essentials of bureaucracy by showing what happens when they are violated (as they constantly are). The chapter will give us all an appreciation for bureaucracy as a remarkable product of gradual, halting, and often unwitting social engineering. As we shall see, many of the "sins" of bureaucracy really reveal the failure to bureaucratize sufficiently. But while I will defend bureaucracy from many of the attacks we all are prone to make, I will attack it much more severely on quite different grounds, grounds that social scientists have been reluctant to explore. Let me explain my puzzling position briefly.

Critics usually attack bureaucracy for two reasons—it is unadaptive, and it stifles the humanity of employees. Both are legitimate criticisms to a degree. But what the first avoids noticing is that another description of unadaptiveness might be stability, steadfastness, and predictability. If we want a particular change and fail to get it, we blame the unadaptive bureaucracy. If it changes in ways we do not like, though, we call for stability. The second criticism—that bureaucracies stifle spontaneity, freedom, and self-realization—is certainly true for many employees, but unfortunately, since they do not own what they produce and must work for someone else, expressions of spontaneity and self-realization are not likely to result in better goods and services for consumers. We have constructed a society where the satisfaction of our wants as consumers largely depends on restricting the employees who do the producing. Bureaucracy cannot be faulted for society's demands; if blame is to be placed, it should fall on those elites who constructed bureaucracy over many generations and offered us no alternatives, a subject we will return to at the end of the book.

Most social scientists (almost all of them until the mid-1970s) have offered these two criticisms of bureaucracy—rigidity and employee discipline—if they have offered any. I would offer a third: bureaucracy has become a means, both in capitalist and noncapitalist countries, of centralizing power in society and legitimating or disguising that centralization. A full defense of this thesis is impossible here. But this book will sketch, through a critical review of historical and recent thought on organizational analysis, how social scientists have, until recently, avoided the "big" question of unregulated and unperceived power through bureaucratic organizations, even though the research that has been done points in this direction.

Bureaucracy is a tool, a social tool that legitimizes control of the many by the few, despite the formal apparatus of democracy, and this control has generated unregulated and unperceived social power. This power includes much more than just control of employees. As bureaucracies satisfy, delight, pollute, and satiate us with their output of goods and services, they also shape our ideas, our very way of conceiving of ourselves, control our life chances, and even define our humanity. As employees, whether we see ourselves as exploited or as pursuing "careers," we may dimly perceive this fact; as citizens in a society of organizations, where large organizations have absorbed all that used to be small, independent, personal, communitarian, religious, or ethnic, it is rarely perceived. We grow up in organizations; to stand outside them is to see their effect on what we believe, what we value, and, more important, how we think and reason. Throughout this book I will attempt to stand outside them.

At present, without huge, disruptive, and perilous changes, we cannot survive without large organizations. Organizations mobilize social resources for ends that are often essential and even desirable. But organizations also concentrate those resources in the hands of a few who are prone to use them for ends we do not approve of, for ends we may not even be aware of, and, more frightening still, for ends we are led to accept because we are not in a position to conceive alternative ones. The investigation of these fearful possibilities has too long been left to writers, journalists, and radical political leaders. It is time that organizational theorists began to use their expertise to uncover the true nature of bureaucracy. This will require a better understanding both of the virtues of bureaucracy and its largely unexplored dangers.

This chapter will examine the customary view of the sins of bureaucracy and then argue that these sins result largely from a failure to bureaucratize properly. If we must have bureaucracy, we must understand its many strengths. The rest of the book roughly follows the historical development of bureaucratic theory. Chapter 2 briefly examines how we came to be a society of organizations and what the initial justifications were for the authority of the manager and owner over the new employee class. These justifications formed the basis for the human relations school, or the organizational behavior school, still the largest one in the field of organizational analysis. Chapter 3 looks at the school critically. Chapter 4 discusses several modifications of the bureaucracy Weber described and ends with an application of the resulting "neo-Weberian" model to the problem of running risky systems. These four chapters provide a rough synthesis of much of the theory of internal organizational processes from a structural point of view.

The remaining chapters look outward to the environment. The institutional school is examined in Chapter 5; it was the first to raise rather timid questions about the effect organizations have on society, and it emphasized creative leadership as the solution. Chapter 6 turns to more complex models, starting with rock music to illustrate how organizations define and control environments whenever they can. The chapter then examines two models in detail—network analysis and population ecology. Chapter 7 looks at a new contender for theoretical preeminence: economic models of organizations. The two models discussed there present fundamental challenges to most organizational theory, and while some weaknesses of noneconomic models are exposed, I hope I am able to thrust the challenge aside. The final chapter sums up the dominant theme of the book: a power perspective on organizations.

PURGING PARTICULARISM

One of the many dilemmas of organizations is that they attempt to be efficient in producing their output of steel, court convictions, reformed delinquents, legislation, or whatever, and yet they seek to be quite particular about who shall enjoy the pay and the honor of doing the work. *Particularism* means that criteria irrelevant for efficient production (e.g., only relatives of the boss have a chance at top positions), in contrast to universalistic criteria (e.g., competence is all that counts), are used to choose employees. The criteria of efficiency and particularism are likely to clash, since the most efficient workers may lack the particular social characteristics desired. For example, few Jews ever rise very high in such industries as steel;[6] few blacks have thus far been able to break into many skilled trades in the construction industry. In a study of one manufacturing firm, Melville Dalton found that membership in the Masons was a prerequisite to advancement in management. Even though it is hard to imagine what there is about Masonic membership that would increase managerial efficiency,[7] ambitious managers were smart enough to join the fraternal order. Some levels in organizations, some work groups, and even whole plants are uni-ethnic— that is, all Irish or all Polish. One of the distinctive characteristics of voluntary associations such as patriotic societies or clubs is that they often specify membership criteria openly, while economic or governmental organizations can only do so informally. The Daughters of the American Revolution was founded at a time when many native-born Anglo-Saxons had parents who had lived during the days of the Revolution; the unqualified, then, were conveniently all immigrants.

The development of bureaucracy has been in part an attempt to purge organizations of particularism. This has been difficult, because organizations are profoundly "social," in the sense that all kinds of social characteristics affect their operation *by intent.* Take the relatively trivial matters of nepotism (giving preferred treatment to relatives) and personal favoritism. Both are very common—and very annoying, unless you are a favored relative or friend of the boss. But both reflect social solutions to the organizational problems of members. One of the things that you can do with the power that a decent position in an organization gives you is to reward people whom you like or are related to you or who will help you in return. Families, for example, are a major resource in society; relatives who work for you can be expected to hide your mistakes and incompetence, warn you about threats to your position, and support you in conflicts with others. Similarly, subordinates are well advised to defer to their superior because they will be protected and rewarded for covering for their boss, warning her, and lightening her workload. Two or three levels above the boss, the higher-ups will try to measure objective competence, but it is both hard to determine competence and easy to disguise incompetence. Since the subordinate's career and even comfort are always at risk in organizations, we can hardly expect them always to put the abstract "interests of the organization" ahead of their own interests and those of the bosses who control their fate.

The social character of organizations goes deeper. In a society where organizations provide the livelihood of eight out of ten of the "economically active" and where organizations are necessary for most other interests, merely being allowed to be a member of an organization is critical for well-being, if not survival. Assiduous efforts are made to restrict access to this resource; organizations discriminate on social, rather than objective, grounds in letting people in.

We view these particularistic criteria with suspicion partly because of our

[6]And not just steel, of course. In Detroit, only two-thirds of 1 percent of the white-collar jobs at the three major auto companies are filled by Jews. A 1960 study of 1,500 U.S. corporations showed that although Jews made up 8 percent of all college graduates and, even more important, 15 percent of the graduates of professional and business schools, they account for only 0.5 percent of management. See "Has Bias Locked Up the Room at the Top?" *Business Week*, January 24, 1970.

[7]Melville Dalton, *Men Who Manage* (New York: Wiley, 1959).

democratic ideals of equality. But we also view them with suspicion because we dimly recognize that organizations draw on resources provided by society in general and thus are beholden to all of society. In spite of this fact, though, there is, for example, a flourishing and byzantine structure of courts, laws, and law-enforcement facilities that is available to organizations to protect their interests. We support this structure through taxes. On campus, fraternities and sororities have special access to university facilities, receive special protection—and are tax-exempt. And private clubs that discriminate get quiet subsidies in one form or another. For example, in 1984 a county judge in Maryland ruled that an elite golf club, the Burning Tree Club, would lose its $186,000 real estate tax exemption because it would not admit women as members; indeed, even the kitchen staff had to be male. How could a club that charged an initiation fee of $12,000 and annual dues of $1,700 justify a yearly tax break of $186,000? Because the huge grounds preserved open spaces (in a suburb where the least expensive homes cost $400,000). The Burning Tree officials said they would appeal, cited the constitutional guarantee of freedom of association, and charged that the necessary increase in dues—about $292 per member—would turn the club into "a rich man's club."[8]

The factory is fairly free to pollute the air and water, to enforce its law through its own police force and its access to the courts, to hire and fire (and thus provide or deny livelihood), to utilize the services of the local chamber of commerce (which is tax-exempt and may even receive local tax support), and to draw upon tax-supported services of many state and federal agencies. These things cost all of us money. No matter that the factory pays taxes in return, or that the sorority provides housing and surveillance that the university might otherwise have to build and provide. Common resources are drawn from society, whatever the specific products returned. Thus, we feel the services should be common to all who desire them. Particularism or discrimination is frowned upon.

But these are political rather than bureaucratic reasons for distrusting particularism. The bureaucratic reason for frowning on particularism is that efficiency is forgone if recruitment or access is decided upon grounds that are not related to the members' performance in the organization. For most organizational goals or roles, social origins (race, ethnicity, and class) are not likely to be a measure of competence. The steel company or bank that bars Jews from middle management is possibly depriving itself of talent at the higher levels. The appointment of a large political campaign donor to the position of Ambassador to the Court of St. James suggests that the criteria are not knowledge of foreign affairs and skill in foreign diplomacy, but party loyalty and personal wealth. The son of the president of a corporation may well start out on the shop floor or as a sales trainee, but it is not his competence that moves him quickly to a vice-presidency. Moreover, the frequent practice of a professional person hiring staff members from the same university he or she attended suggests something other than universalistic criteria. One finds this in university departments ("only Eastern schools have a chance there," or "that's where Michigan sends its run-of-the-mill Ph.D.'s"), research and development labs ("someone from MIT doesn't stand a chance in that company"), social agencies ("they only

[8]*New York Times*, September 14, 1984, p. 1.

give supervisory positions to Chicago graduates" [University of Chicago School of Social Work]), and hospital medical staffs ("that's a Johns Hopkins shop").

The problem with these practices is not only that there is little relationship between the social criteria for hiring or promoting people and the characteristics that affect performance in the organization. More serious, the particularistic criteria are likely to be *negatively* related to performance—the more these particularistic criteria are used, the poorer the performance. By hiring only Chicago graduates, one may have to take some who were among the poorer students, missing out on the good Michigan graduates. More serious still, one may end up with only one way of seeing the world and only one way of approaching a problem. By using broad or universalistic hiring criteria, the chances of getting different perspectives, and thus more ideas, are increased.

That particularistic criteria are often equivalent to favoritism also means that corruption is a likely accompaniment. The agency head who hires or favors primarily people from her own region, state, or university may get subtle returns in the bargain. She may be favored as a consultant to her former university or to the state government and receive handsome fees; she may place herself at the head of the line for bigger and better appointments. Competence is hard to judge, so we rely on familiarity. The corruption may be less discreet, as in the political spoils system, whereby the elected official hires only people who are willing to contribute to his election campaign or to provide him with kickbacks.

Tenure and the Career Concept

Political patronage reached such a corrupting extreme in the late nineteenth century that the merit system and civil service examinations were instituted in the federal and most state governments. We now pay a price for that sweeping change, since merit systems may have little to do with merit. Once a civil service appointee receives "tenure," it is very hard to remove that employee for lack of competence. Over the years, as the organization changes and the demand for new skills increases, the person who may have once been a very competent employee may turn out to be quite incompetent. But the organization is stuck with him or her. One need look no further, for example, than university departments where skills change quickly, promise does not materialize into productivity, or people simply pass their prime. If research-oriented universities changed to the extent that teaching ability became a prime criterion for competence, rather than a secondary one, many tenured people might be found incompetent.

It is a tenet of the bureaucratic model of organizations that an employee is expected to pursue a "career" in the organization. Thus, if the person burns out too quickly or, more likely, if the skills demanded of the position change without the occupant changing (e.g., more emphasis on teaching and less on research), the organization is expected to retain him or her. The employee has tenure. Despite the frequency with which this annoyance is met in organizations, the career principle is a sound one. People would not be likely to master sets of skills through long technical training or experience in an organization if they knew they could not perpetually draw on the capital of their investment. There must be some guarantee that if the demands of the job change radically in the future, a person will still be credited with having met them in the present. Otherwise, personnel might be less willing to make large investments in skills.

In short, the benefits of universalistic standards clearly appear to exceed the costs; tenure may be a necessary inducement for mastering obscure skills and a necessary protection against arbitrary rulers. There are costs, but the alternatives are worse.

Universalism and Organizational Goals

Universalistic criteria, then, would appear to be a proper goal in organizations, and few would fault the bureaucratic model in this respect. But the situation is not that simple. To establish the standards, one has to know the real goals of the organization. Suppose a manufacturing firm favors members of a certain fraternal organization when it hires and promotes its managers. On the face of it, this sounds particularistic. Closer examination, though, might well reveal that the manufacturing organization receives a variety of tax benefits from the local government, and the local government is heavily loaded with Masons, Lions, Legionnaires, or whatever. If the firm gives preference to Masons, should they be the dominant group in the city government, it may avoid paying its fair share of the sewage system; it may get special arrangements for power supplies; zoning ordinances may be drafted so that it does not have to pay a heavy school tax; it may be able to get certain city streets closed to permit convenient expansion; and a good share of its security protection may come from the city's police department, rather than from plant guards. Furthermore, the local authorities may see that other plants are discouraged from coming in, through zoning ordinances or restrictions on transportation or available power supplies. Competing industry, particularly, would up the demand for skilled labor in one field and drive up wages. Moreover, the city planning commission may ensure that a new superhighway comes close to the front gate of the plant, even at the expense of cutting a residential district in two.

Showing favoritism within the manufacturing company to this fraternal organization is hardly, then, a particularistic criterion from the *company's* point of view. Any loss in managerial competence that may result from using selective criteria is more than offset by the gain of having sympathetic friends in the city administration. For similar reasons, defense industries have a disproportionate number of former military officers in their top echelons, even though it is questionable whether former procurement or inspection officers are particularly good managers of large aerospace firms or conglomerates. For defense industries, political ties to the Pentagon are a universalistic criterion. Similarly, experience in the major corporations and investment houses is often crucial for top civilian positions in the State Department, the Defense Department, the CIA, and the Atomic Energy Commission; Richard Barnet found that seventy of the ninety-one top men in those agencies from 1940 to 1967 had such backgrounds.[9] The Polish foreman who favors Polish workers under him is acting no differently.

[9]Richard Barnet, *Economy of Death* (New York: Atheneum House, 1969).

This reasoning also applies to voluntary associations such as fraternities and sororities. If the "real" goals of the Greek-letter societies were auxiliary support for the university, good fellowship, recreation, character building, and efficient housing, then discrimination against Jews and blacks would be unwarranted. However, if the goal of the fraternity or sorority also includes promoting social class and ethnic solidarity, ties that will lead to business or marital advantages, and reinforcement of religious, ethnic, and class sentiments, then the discrimination is certainly efficient. The Jew or the black is deemed an inappropriate resource for the organization; he or she does nothing for the group.

We may deplore the particularism of the Greek-letter society or the manufacturing firm and call for the universalism that is explicit in the bureaucratic model. There, at least, bureaucracy is virtuous in its impersonality. But to deplore particularism is only to advance an ideal and to neglect the reality of organizational affairs. The real cause for concern is not just the failure to apply universalism; rather it involves the uses the leaders make of the organization; these determine just what are universalistic or particularistic criteria. We are being naive when we deplore patronage, collusion, and snobbery in our political, economic, and voluntary organizations, as if those traits stemmed from a failure to apply sound organizational principles or even general moral principles. A more realistic view would question the uses to which owners and managers put these organizations, for these uses define what is efficient for those in control. Organizations are tools. The bureaucratic ideal assumes the uses are legitimate—that is, in society's interests. In doing so, it disguises some of the purposes to which people put organizations. Still, bureaucracy— with its ideals of clearly stated goals and rational instrumentation of legitimate purposes—is a clear advance over ancient satrapies, feudal domains, family dynasties, warlords and their retinues, and the autocracies of the past. At the least, since official goals are proclaimed, unofficial, unpublicized, and unlegitimated uses can be held up to scrutiny when they are found, and action can be taken. The hidden uses of organizations, always present, can be exposed and addressed.

The Contest for Control

Organizations generate power; control and use of that power are vital organizational issues. Particularism is a strategy to control and use that power, and it is not easily purged. It is a central theme of this book that organizations must be seen as tools, as having bundles of all sorts of resources that people inside and outside can make use of and try to control. Organizations are multipurpose tools because they can do many things for many people.

For example, regardless of their goals, organizations offer employment opportunities for friends and relatives, as well as for oneself. They also provide prestige and status for their members, as well as chances to make contacts and to strengthen social class ties. Obviously, there are opportunities for graft and corruption through organizations. But most important of all, *organizations are tools for shaping the world as one wishes it to be shaped.* They provide the means for imposing one's own definition of the proper affairs of humankind on others. The person who controls an organization has power that goes far beyond that of those lacking such control.

The power of the rich lies not in their ability to buy goods and services, but in their capacity to control the ends toward which the vast resources of large organizations are directed.

Such power is naturally contested. People attempt to achieve control of organizations or even parts of an organization in order to gain that power. "If I were in charge I would do it this way." "We really should be doing such and such." "Top management should never let the union [or suppliers, or customers, or medical staff, or the prison guards, or the government, or middle management, or whatever] get away with this." "The trouble with top management is that it is only interested in immediate profits and not in long-term growth; I want to see this organization strong over the long run." "This agency should be serving lower-class people, not the middle class." "Top management is too tied to the industry way of doing things; it is preoccupied with traditions that are no longer relevant, and it does not want to rock the boat." "We should be revolutionizing things in this industry." "We don't want people of *that sort* in our company." "Business has a responsibility to protect the American way of life. We should make it clear to these groups that they can't get away with this." These are statements about power and the uses to which it can be put.

Retaining or gaining power is difficult because it is almost always contested, and the contest is not decided by measuring the "efficiency" or "productivity" of the contenders. The criterion is not narrow and testable, but general and vague. The principles of bureaucracy have little to do with the contest. One decidedly unbureaucratic principle is crucial—personal loyalty or loyalty to a superior rather than to the organization and its goals. One of the best ways to seize or retain control is to surround oneself with loyal people. If a person has a certain charisma or force of personality, the loyalty may be freely given by strangers and acquaintances. If one lacks this rare quality, there are other means of ensuring loyalty. The most powerful is dependence. The subordinate who is a relative of a superior or a friend of the family is more dependent than one who is not; his or her superior has privileged access to "significant others" in the subordinate's social world. The marginally competent manager who is promoted over others is vulnerable and thus had better be loyal.

Of course, one purchases some inefficiency along with this loyalty. Inefficiency means that the costs of doing business are increased. But the difference between a small increase in the operating cost and a threat to losing control of all or some of the resources of the organization is enormous. In most cases, the exchange of loyalty for competence is in the executive's interest.

Even less-than-exemplary subordinates can perform very well for their superiors. A man may lack good judgment in setting policies, be inefficient in organizing his work and his staff, and even spend an excessive amount of time on the golf course or traveling at company expense. However, if he manages to sniff out potential sources of opposition within the organization, nominate loyal subordinates and identify those who cannot be trusted, and generally keep track of the activities of "internal enemies," he is worth a great deal to his boss. Such functions are commonplace in organizations of all types. As we have said, organizations are tools; they mobilize resources that can be used for a variety of ends. These resources and the goals of the organization are up for grabs, and people grab for them continually. Internecine warfare, often involving lawsuits, is a very prominent news item in the business press; it generally concerns the uses to which organizational power is to be put.

Viewing organizations as tools should reduce our tendency to cry incompetence when they do not do what we think they should. Incompetence certainly exists; organizations must contend with the distribution of incompetence in the general population, as well as the distribution of tendencies toward venality, stupidity, sycophancy, and so on, since they must draw upon the general population for employees. But a tool view alerts us to the possibility that what we see as incompetent performance or policy really reflects what some leaders wanted all along. A president will not announce that he or she intends to discipline labor and reduce inflation by creating a recession; it will be announced instead that the economy is not competitive enough. If an acquired firm goes downhill in performance, the new leaders need not be charged with incompetence in running the acquisition; they may have decided to appropriate its available cash and other liquid assets, its unused tax credits, and its best personnel and use them where they will provide greater returns. The acquired firm may then be sold, or even scrapped, possibly with significant tax breaks. Before assuming that an outcome was unintended, it is best to see if someone in top management might not have had reason to have intended the outcome. Bureaucracy is not the breeder of incompetence, as we often would like to believe. Instead, bureaucratic organization allows leaders to achieve goals, some of which are unannounced and costly for the rest of us and are only *attributed* to incompetence.

In conclusion, we have explored particularism in organizations, indicating the desirability of the bureaucratic ideal of universalism—hiring and promoting on the basis of performance ability (skills, competence, diligence, etc.) rather than on agreement to support the goals of the organization. We deplore particularism for several reasons. It goes against the values of a liberal society—that is, it yields racial or religious discrimination; it involves using public resources for the advantage of specific groups; it promotes inefficiency in organizations. But we also have been suggesting that much of the particularism we frown on is particularistic only if we think the goals of an organization should be other than what they are; from the point of view of those who control the organization, the criteria may really be universalistic and promote the efficiency of the organization. Better personnel practices, or standards, or screening criteria are irrelevant when only changes in the uses to which the organization is put would meet the criticisms. This is because organizations are tools designed to perform work for their masters, and particularism or universalism is relative to the goals of the masters. Because organizations generate power to get a variety of things done, people contend for that power, and favoritism and nepotism help to ensure loyalty to the contenders.

We also briefly touched on one other characteristic of bureaucracy—tenure, or the career principle; we argued that the costs of this principle, as seen in the frustration of dealing with incompetent personnel who have civil service protection or incompetent tenured professors, are more than made up for by its advantages. These include freedom from arbitrary authority, protection from changes in skill demands and declining ability, and assurance that one's investment in skills and experience will be secure. The bureaucratic model emphasizes efficiency in the long run, not the short run.

It is a tribute to the bureaucratic model as it developed since the Middle Ages that it has at least partially answered the problem of particularism and pursued it with vigor. Loyalty to the king or lord or chief was once everything; incompetence counted for little. With the rise of the university-educated scribes, jurists, and mathematicians, a class of presumably professional, neutral, and loyal personnel arose, the business administration students of yore.[10] The kings and chiefs could use these and get both competence and loyalty (through dependence) in their administration. The eunuch in the harem is the prototype of the modern professional; he can be trusted with everything except that which really counts—the uses to which the masters put the organization. We have come so far from the particularism of medieval days that nepotism and favoritism today are frowned on as both subversive and inefficient. A substantial residue of these practices remains in organizations simply because organizations, then as now, are tools in the hands of their masters; thus, control over them is a prize that many people seek. Particularism is one weapon in that struggle, but its use must be masked.

FEATHERING THE NEST

Organizations generate a great deal of power and leverage in the social world, power and leverage far beyond their ostensible goals. But one problem of organizations is that they are very leaky vessels. It is quite easy for a member of one to use some of his or her power and leverage for personal ends rather than for the ends of the organization. (The ends of the organization, we may say for the present, are those of a small group at the top of the organization or, in many cases, a small group outside the organization that controls those at the top.) In the ideal world of the ideal bureaucracy, it should be possible to calculate neatly, and thus control, the relationship between a person's contribution to an organization and the rewards he or she receives. Theoretically, too, the rewards the organization has to pay should not exceed the contribution of the person. In practice, this is very difficult because it is hard to control people so closely and because organizations have permeable boundaries. People tend to act as if they own their positions; they use them to generate income, status, and other things that rightfully belong to the organization. Bureaucracy has made great strides in reducing the discrepancy between people's contributions, on the one hand, and the inducements necessary to keep them in the organization and make them work, on the other.[11] During the

---

[10]As Lewis Coser notes in *Greedy Institutions* (New York: Free Press, 1974), slaves, Jews, and others excluded from society could also be used because they owed to their lord their promotion from nonpersons to quasipersons.

[11]The contributions-inducements theory of organizations was first formulated by Chester Barnard in the late 1930s and subsequently greatly refined by James G. March and Herbert A. Simon in their book, *Organizations* (New York: Wiley, 1958). Their contributions are cited as landmarks in organizational theory, despite the simplicity of the idea or perhaps because of it. We shall take them up later.

period when bureaucracies were just beginning to form, this problem was most acute.

During the late Middle Ages, the king who wanted revenues from the land and from the people he controlled would sell a tax franchise to someone, generally a nobleman. This official would agree to pay the king a set fee; he was then free to collect as much money as he could from the people and keep anything beyond the set fee. The king benefited because he did not have to organize and maintain a large bureaucracy to collect taxes. However, the collector might extract such a heavy toll that the subjects would revolt. Or the basis of the economy might be ruined so that fewer and fewer taxes could be collected. Or the collector might become so rich that he could challenge the power of the king. Eventually, the king or the state took control of taxation, centralized it, hired personnel on a salaried basis to run the system, and used the army to back up the collectors. In this way, the imbalance between the effort and reward of the tax collector was markedly reduced. The tax collectors were paid what they were worth on the labor market at that time.

Today, we do not find tax collectors paying a franchise fee to the state to collect as much as they can, but problems still remain because government units are empowered to force people to pay taxes. This power is a source of leverage for the officeholder. For example, local assessors (who determine the value of property for taxation purposes) have been known to make deals with business firms or other interests such that certain property is assessed at a lower value than it would normally be. Then the assessors receive a percentage of the reduction from the organization that is being assessed. Internal revenue agents have been known to make deals with taxpayers whereby the latter's taxes are reduced and the agents get a portion of the savings. The Internal Revenue Service spends a good deal of money on various forms of surveillance to minimize this practice and to keep the agent from using the power of that organization for his or her private purposes.

The medieval system of selling franchises is still legally practiced in some of the less-organized areas of our economy. For example, small businesspeople, particularly doctors and dentists, "sell" delinquent accounts to a tax-collecting firm; the tax-collecting firm gives the businessperson, say, 40 percent of the value of the account and then keeps anything above that amount, if it is able to collect. Most businesses are wary of using all the powers legally or illegally at hand to collect debts because they do not want to alienate people who might be future customers or clients. For the tax-collecting firm, however, this is not a constraint, so their methods of extracting money from debtors are more severe.[12] Of course, the agencies also do not care whether the debtors feel that the debt is unjust or not. It is irrelevant to the agency if the debtors failed to pay their full bill because they were overcharged or because they did not receive the goods or services. Furthermore, agencies stand

---

[12] One of the most frequent consumer fraud devices is for a collection agency to send a fake social survey questionnaire out. Along with the usual attitude questions ("How do you feel about law and order?"), unsuspecting debtors are asked about their place of employment, the value of their car and other property, and whether their spouse works or not. The agencies also send letters on official-looking stationery saying that a heavily insured package is being held for them by the post office, and they should fill out the identification papers and mail them in to receive the package. Debtors thus disclose the information that the collection agency can use as leverage. Both practices are forbidden by law but are very hard to police.

to gain a great deal by collecting all or 70 percent of the debt rather than 40 percent, so they pursue their task with vigor. Agencies also find it easier to extract money from the poorer and less well-educated strata of society since those with few resources are more easily intimidated.

Another example of ancient practices in the less well-organized and rationalized sectors of our economy is the selling of professional services. Normally, one thinks that a client goes to a doctor, dentist, or lawyer on a voluntary basis. However, for a number of reasons, clients do not have effective choice in these matters. In varying degrees, professionals have captive clients. There is not much competition among doctors, for example, because clients have few ways to judge doctors and have to consider geographical accessibility; also, doctors have restricted entry to their profession to keep the numbers low. If the patient has been going to a particular doctor for any period of time at all, she has a "sunk cost" in this relationship—the doctor knows her and has X rays and other records. What happens, then, when a doctor or lawyer or dentist retires or moves away? If it is a sizable practice at all, it will be "sold" to another professional. Indeed, if the professional dies, his or her beneficiaries can sell the practice. Patients are not literally sold to the new buyer, of course, but in fact the new buyer has quite privileged access to them. Practices are put up for competitive bidding and go to the highest bidder. Of course, there is no guarantee of any relationship between ability and reward, since an incompetent doctor, for example, may be able to pay more for a practice than a good one. Given the highly entrepreneurial, even medieval, character of our independent professions, little was done until recently to rationalize or bureaucratize them in order to control the relationship between effort and reward.

However, rationalization of medical and legal services is beginning to appear as the demand for service has increased. Walk-in storefront medical clinics and law offices are opening; psychological counselors have formal ties with medical and legal professionals. Shopping-center emporiums with doctors, dentists, opticians, lawyers, accountants, tax experts, counselors, chaplains, chiropractors, and fitness experts will probably soon provide one-stop service for every conceivable personal need. We seem to have survived the loss of a personal relationship with our grocer or barber; we will probably accept, though not welcome, taking a number and standing in line for the next available professional. This is an efficient use of work power for the organizers of such groups, as for-profit hospital chains and franchises have learned. (The Kentucky Fried Chicken organization, for instance, has branched off into hospital franchises.)

The rationalization of professional services also reduces the occasions for the individual professional to feather his or her nest, though very likely at the expense of individualized service. The relationship between the effort the professional puts in and the reward he or she receives, open to abuse before such rationalization, is greatly controlled. But note that the consumer's definitions of effort and reward are no longer as potent; it is the entrepreneur who runs the service or the emporium who now sets the definition. Bureaucracy requires standardized inputs and outputs; after taking your number and waiting your turn for whichever professional is free, the professional will take note of your need and sort it into the nearest appropriate box for standard treatment, no exceptions please, in the interest of low fees and quick turnover. The relationship between effort and reward for the employée may be very rational, but for the consumer, an individualized, personal definition is lost. Why bureaucracy in the area of personalized services? Because most of us cannot afford the personalized attention, and our key needs would remain untended. We should not blame bureaucracy for not providing the personal services available only to the wealthy.

Once professionals have been bureaucratized, they will, like everyone else, seek to feather their nests from the copious amounts of down floating around in most organizations. Generally, such uses are simply taken for granted, as if they were fringe benefits written into the employment contract. No professor in his right mind (and they all have right minds in this regard) would think of buying his own paper, pencils, carbon paper, and so on to write a book from which he hopes to gain substantial income in the form of royalty. It does not occur to many professors that they should pay for the privilege of using a huge library that caters to their exotic tastes and allows them to keep books out for months or years without paying fines. Nor do many universities question a professor's use of secretarial time that is officially budgeted as an educational expense. When pressed, professors may insist that while they draw royalties on their books (which range from a few dollars a year to over $100,000), they are really contributing to the educational resources of society and that this is an inexpensive way to produce knowledge and teaching materials. This is true enough, but it is still remarkable that very few universities have attempted to require professors to pay back to the school some percentage of any outside income that comes from exploiting resources that are tax exempt or derived from students and, in public universities, from the taxpayers. A few have tried, and fewer actually do it; it meets with considerable resistance. In addition to royalties from books, there are the matters of lecture engagements and consulting jobs. A professor at a prestigious university is able to demand very high fees for consulting and lecturing and will get many opportunities to do these things. Since few prepare for these tasks only on Saturdays and Sundays, spending the other five days of the week busily teaching, these activities undoubtedly divert one from teaching duties.

Virtually all organizations offer opportunities to feather one's nest. Recall the dynamite that was readily taken from the gypsum mine described at the opening of this chapter. A more dramatic example is the scandals in the Chicago police department and other police departments in the early 1960s that were referred to as the "cops and/or robbers" syndrome. These scandals involved police officers who, by knowing when people were going to be away and when on-duty officers were not likely to be around, were able to burglarize stores and homes.

We may not expect a great deal of rectitude in police departments, but we might in voluntary hospitals supported by government funds, private donations, community chest funds, and, of course, patient fees. Nevertheless, I was not surprised to find that in some voluntary hospitals it was the custom for top-level administrators, physicians, and surgeons to receive expensive filets and other food from the hospital kitchens for use at home. Also, the maintenance staff occasionally remodeled or maintained the private houses of key executives, doctors, or board members. These illustrations may be trivial, but the principle is not. Organizations generate surpluses and leverage in our world, and those who have any power in them can use these for their own ends. The device of bureaucracy was designed to prevent *any but the masters* of the organization from doing this.

We might think that the more bureaucratized and rationalized the organization is, the less nest feathering will occur. This may be so, at least at the lower levels, but we have no research on the subject. However, to the extent that business and industrial organizations are among the most bureaucratized and rationalized, the generalization probably would not stand. Highly placed executives of business and industrial firms sometimes profit handsomely from giving lucrative contracts to suppliers in which they have invested their personal funds. These arrangements rarely become public because it is very difficult to gain such information. One did become public in 1960, when an aggressive stockholder pursued the matter with the Chrysler Corporation. Eventually, the president of Chrysler resigned, and, after being sued by the corporation, returned $450,000 to the company. He allegedly favored suppliers in whose firm he had a personal financial interest. (It is not often, however, that a stockholder with only a pittance of stock can bring down the administrative head of a large corporation.) Perhaps the reason that such an "unbureaucratic" practice could occur in a highly bureaucratized firm is that, as Max Weber noted long ago, the top of an organization is never bureaucratized. It always belongs to somebody. In this case, though, the board of directors and stockholders insisted that the organization was also theirs; it did not belong just to the president.

The practice of feathering one's nest in large part reflects the problem of separating the interests of the person from the interests of the organization. In our organizational society, this becomes increasingly difficult. For example, to whom does the experience of an employee belong? Does it belong to him or her or to the organization in which that experience was acquired? The growth of bureaucracy was equivalent to putting a label of "company property" on the skills, experience, and creativity of the employee. It is a measure of our socialization into a society of bureaucratic organizations that we no longer question this extraction at all in the case of blue-collar workers and most white-collar ones. But consider industry at the turn of the century. Most of the work in the large, mass-producing factories and mills (except textiles, which had been "rationalized" long before) was done by work crews that were recruited, organized, and paid by independent contractors.[13] They used the company's facilities, supplies, and tools but worked under yearly contracts to produce so many rifle barrels or parts of sewing machines or whatever. The contractors sometimes made very large profits and paid their workers presumably what the market would bear, or more likely, what the local custom dictated. The system was apparently quite efficient—technological changes were rapidly introduced and were in the interests of the contractors. It flourished in factories producing highly engineered products on a mass basis. Owners supplied the capital and organized the final assembly and marketing.

The genius of F. W. Taylor and others in the scientific management movement

---

[13]Dan Clawson, *Bureaucracy and the Labor Process: The Transformation of U.S. Industry: 1860–1920* (New York: Monthly Review Press, 1980). See also the more general discussion of this issue in Harry Braverman, *Labor and Monopoly Capital* (New York: Monthly Review Press, 1975).

(see Chapter 2) was to convince the owners that they should employ engineers to go around and find out how the men and women drilled the rifle barrels or made the gears for machine tools or cast the locomotive parts, centralize this information and study it, then break the tasks down into small parts so as to remove as much of the skill and accumulated experience as possible, hire a foreman who would supervise the crew for a wage, and assign the highly specialized "deskilled" tasks to the workers and pay them at a much lower wage rate. The owners "expropriated" the craft skills and craft system and designated as company property the ingenuity, experience, and creativity of the workers. Only now are we beginning to painfully rediscover and recommend giving back to the workers a small part of what had been their own property, in the form of such schemes as job enlargement, workers' participation, workers' autonomy, and group incentives.

What was settled for workers and most managers long ago (sometimes through bloody strikes)[14] still appears for top executives and scientists in new fields today. What happens when a team of researchers, or an executive and three or four subordinates who have been working together for a long time, leave the organization? At least two issues are involved. One is the charge that the leader raided the company by taking the subordinates along, since they had been trained by the organization; the other is the knowledge of the technology, business operations, market strategies, and so forth developed within the organization and now taken elsewhere. In both cases, the organization loses heavily. Such incidents have become frequent enough to produce a number of court rulings. The principles are still obscure, but in general the court has been ruling in favor of the former firm in requiring, for example, that the departing manager or scientist not work in the same product area for a period of five years. If he or she goes to work for firm B, after having worked in firm A, and firm B comes out with a product that is similar to the one he or she was working on in firm A, firm A can sue firm B on the grounds that the person left A with specific knowledge and gave it to B.

The executive and the subordinates need not go to another established firm, taking with them the fruit of years of experimentation, trial, gestation, and stimulation. They may start their own company. In one case, an engineer for IBM took thirty-six people with him and started a competing company that made integrated circuits for memory cores for large computers. IBM sued. Even if a large firm had little hope of winning such a suit, it could help persuade other employees that it is not wise to leave with so many company-provided resources in their hands. It is a measure of our organizational society that the courts are able to rule in favor of the organization rather than the creative individual [15]

The case of the scientist who decides that what she has in her head belongs

[14]Katherine Stone, "The Origins of Job Structures in the Steel Industry," *Radical America* 7, no. 6 (November/December 1973): 19–64, describes the process and conflicts for the steel industry. See also the seminal piece by Steven Marglin, "What Do Bosses Do?" *Review of Radical Political Economics* 6, no. 2 (Summer 1974): 33–60, and the book by Richard Edwards, *Contested Terrain: The Transformation of the Workplace in the Twentieth Century* (New York: Basic Books, 1979).

[15]But on the other hand, it is striking that few creative individuals appear to start on their own, forming their own companies. Generally, they work first for a large firm. Only then can they attract the necessary capital from those arbitrators of the business scene, the banks.

to her and not to the organization, even though organizational resources were used to develop it, is a borderline case in the basic question of who owns the office. As such it is illuminating. For there is no intrinsic difference between such a case and one in which an executive makes sure that the supplier in which he has a financial interest gets contracts from his company, even though that supplier's products may be inferior. In both cases, the organization provides a resource, which is then exploited by the individual for his or her own benefit and to the disadvantage of the organization. It does not matter whether the organization is considered a socially valuable one or whether the individual is moral or immoral. We are stuck with the organizational logic of our time; the official does not own his or her office—as Weber put it, and as the gypsum-plant employees and countless other workers discovered. The organization takes precedence over the individual.

Stated thusly, we are likely to deplore this concept. But as consumers of the goods and services of many organizations, we are likely to applaud it. Why bureaucracy if it takes precedence over the individual? Because our society has developed no alternative method of flooding us with goods and services just as cheaply.

"THERE OUGHT TO BE A RULE"

We have looked at several criticisms of bureaucracy and argued that some of its supposed sins have more to do with the uses to which organizations are put than any inherent evil and others are only abuses from the point of view of special interests, not the organization as a whole. But the weaknesses of bureaucracy considered so far are rather minor. Rules and red tape, hierarchy, and conservatism are more frequently identified as sins and considered more serious. First let us take the criticism that bureaucracies have too many rules.

A multitude of rules and regulations appears to be the very essence of a bureaucracy. The term "red tape" adequately conveys the problem. Rules govern everything; one cannot make a move unless one does it by the book or, to use military slang, by the numbers. Every office in every department has seen to it that its autonomy is protected by rules. An attempt to change one rule immediately runs into the problem that half a dozen other rules are connected to it; to change these, a geometric proportion of additional rules will be affected, and so on.

While it is obvious that some rules are needed in organizations, it is generally felt that most organizations have far too many rules. How might these be eliminated?

Reducing Rules

There are a number of ways to reduce the number of rules. One way is to mechanize as much as possible. A typewriter eliminates the need for rules about the size and clarity of script and the way letters will be formed. Rules on these matters were common before the appearance of typewriters. Any machine is a complex bundle of rules that are built into the machine itself. Machines ensure standardized products, thus eliminating rules regarding dimensional characteristics. They ensure even output time; they also indicate precisely what kind of material can be fed into them. The larger the machine, the more people it presumably replaces, and this eliminates rules about how workers are to interact, cooperate, and coordinate their activities. The thoroughly automated factory, of which we have none as yet, would be one with few or no written rules or regulations.

Another way to cut down on the number of rules is to insist on near uniformity of personnel in an organization. If we could hire people with the same physical characteristics, intelligence, amount of self-discipline, personality traits, and so on, we would need far fewer rules to govern the range of differences that we usually observe among personnel. If none of them had families, ever got sick, or needed vacations, and if all were thoroughly trained before they arrived at the office, plant, or agency, matters would also be simplified greatly. But, for the lack of a robot, we have people and thus rules.

If we could seal the organization off from its environment so that nothing ever affected it, we would need very few rules regarding relationships with the environment. We would also need few or no rules regarding changes in procedures— because nothing would change. Once things were started in the proper manner, they could run that way forever. Finally, if we could produce only simple products in our organizations, rather than complex ones in various sizes, shapes, and colors and with a lot of custom-made attributes, this would eliminate the need for a lot of rules.

As these comments suggest, we might not care for organizations that eliminate the need for rules—they would be rather dull, mechanized, and inflexible. Rules are needed in organizations when complexity increases due to variability in personnel, customers, environment, techniques of producing the goods and services, and so on. When these matters are complex, it is not possible to allow personnel to "do their own thing," no matter how much we might prefer that. And every time variability in handling personnel is introduced by these complexities, rules are required to limit the discretion of those with power to handle people under them. There will be rules about favoritism and nepotism and discrimination on irrelevant grounds, rules about transferring people, rules about expectations regarding pay, promotion, accrued leave, and so on.

Of course, rules in the sense of formal written procedures can be essentially eliminated, thus giving the impression of a place that operates with few rules, even though the impression is bound to be mistaken. Wilfred Brown, an experienced and successful manager, discussed this matter at some length in connection with the English industrial firm of which he was president:

> Many managers feel that "freedom" lies in the sort of situation where their supervisor says to them: "There are not many regulations in this place. You will understand the job in a month or two, and you make your own decisions. No red tape—you are expected to take command; make the decisions off your own bat as they arise. I am against a lot of rules or regulations, and we do not commit too much to paper." In my experience a manager in such a situation has virtually no "freedom to act" at all. He starts making decisions and his boss sends for him to say: "Look here, Jones, I am sorry to tell you that you have made two rather serious mistakes in the course of reorganizing your work. You have promoted one man to supervisor who is not the next man due for promotion

in the factory, and you have engaged five additional machinists, a decision you should have referred to me because we have some surplus men in this category in an adjacent factory." Now Jones might well say: "You said there were no regulations but, in fact, you have already mentioned the existence of two; one concerned with promotion and the other with increase of establishment. Please detail these regulations to me precisely, so that I can work to them in future, and let me know now of any further regulations which bear upon my work."

In practice, Jones probably says nothing of the kind, because he does not think in this way; to him regulations are stumbling blocks in the path of those wishing to display initiative. He will proceed, over the years, to learn, by making mistakes, of the whole array of regulations which, by the very nature of Executive Systems, do in fact exist. His boss will have to say to him frequently: "Yes, Jones, freedom for subordinates to act on their own is the policy here, but surely it must have been obvious that you should have seen me before doing *that.*" Jones is thus in a situation where he does not know what decisions he can or cannot make, and when in doubt he is likely to follow a course of doing nothing at all. In three years he will have got through this difficult period; he will know when he can or cannot act, because he has learn[ed] by testing what his boss was unable to give him in writing—*the prescribed component of his job.* Thereafter, Jones will be a staunch supporter of the "no-red-tape" policy, and so the situation will continue.

It is much more efficient to delineate as precisely as possible to a new subordinate all of the regulations he must observe and then say: "You must take all the decisions that seem to you to be required, so long as you keep within the bounds of that policy. If, keeping within those bounds, you take decisions which I think you should have referred to me, then I cannot criticize; for such a happening implies that some part of the policy [by] which I wish you to operate has not been disclosed to you. I must, then, formulate that policy and add it to the prescribed content of your job." If, in addition, the manager can give his subordinate a rounded idea of the discretionary component of his job by stating the types of decisions which he must make, then that subordinate is in a real position to act on his own initiative in the prescribed area.

I have found, however, particularly in discussing jobs with external applicants, that the array of policy represented by our Policy Document, Standing Orders and Directives, causes people to assume the precise opposite of the real situation, i.e., that this extant written policy will deprive them of the right to make decisions. In fact, it is only by delineating the area of "freedom" in this way that a subordinate knows when he can make decisions. The absence of written policy leaves him in a position where any decision he takes, however apparently trivial, may infringe [upon] an unstated policy and produce a reprimand.[16]

Professionalization and Rules.   Buying and installing machines, as indicated above, is one way to reduce the number of rules in an organization. The rules are built into the machine itself, and the organization pays for those rules when it buys the machine. A quite similar means to reduce the number of written rules is to "buy" personnel who have complex rules built into them. We generally call these people professionals. Professionals, such as engineers and scientists, psychiatrists, doctors, social workers, teachers, and professors, are trained on the outside, usually at great

---

[16]Wilfred Brown, *Exploration in Management* (New York: Wiley, 1960), pp. 97–98.

public expense, and a large number of rules are inculcated into them. They bring these to the organization and are expected to act on them without further reference to their skills. While accounting practices differ more widely than some might expect, accountants in general are expected to be familiar with the rules and techniques of accounting. Doctors know when they should give certain drugs or what kinds of drugs should not be given to certain kinds of people; medicine is a complex body of rather imperfect rules. Professors, through long, arduous, and heroic training, learn rules about plagiarism in their writing, truth in their teaching, and deference to their more senior colleagues.

Professionals, like machines, cost a lot of money. There is a high initial investment in training that someone must pay, and the care and feeding of machines and professionals is expensive. Therefore, we tend to use them only when the economies are apparent or when there is no real choice. We charge more for services produced by complex machines or professionals than simple ones—other things, such as volume of production, being equal. It costs more to go to Harvard or to an outstanding hospital than it does to attend a city college or go to a substandard hospital. Were we able to thoroughly routinize the tasks performed by professionals and get around the restrictions that professionals are able to place on their positions, we would substitute machines for them. We are trying, for better or worse, with computerized teaching.

Expressive Groups. One other example of a way to avoid rules in an organization is rare but interesting. This involves organizations where all members agree on the goals of the organization (or, to put it more accurately, where the goals of the individual members are identical) and the techniques for achieving these goals are within the ability of all members. In such cases, few or no rules are required. Each will do his or her own thing, but this will fit with the thing of all other members. Such organizations are generally quite small and usually oriented around expressive needs. Few organizations have members solely on this basis. Most of the so-called voluntary associations rely on services to the members for which members pay in one form or another through dues, allowing their name to be used, or doing some work.[17] Since most voluntary associations provide services to members, they, like other organizations, also have a proliferation of rules and regulations.

Interdepartmental Regulations

So far, we have been talking about rules with respect to the whole organization. A quite different dimension of rules appears when we examine the relationships among units in an organization. Here many rules are clearly the basis of self-protection, predictability, and autonomy. Take the matter of distribution requirements in a university. The rule that students shall take a certain number of credits in various departments exists because students are not homogeneous when they enter the university; all cannot be expected to "know their own best interests."

[17]Charles Perrow, "Members as a Resource in Voluntary Organization," in *Organizations and Clients*, ed. W. Rosengren and M. Lefton (Columbus, Ohio: Charles E. Merrill, 1970), pp. 93–116.

Only some would be motivated enough, the argument goes, to sample the sciences if they are majoring in the humanities or to sample the humanities if they are in the sciences, so a rule is promulgated. However, the matter does not end there. Departments, knowing there will be a big influx of students into their courses, want to control which courses the students come into. So they set rules regarding which courses are to be utilized for distribution requirements. This protects departmental autonomy and provides scheduling benefits and staffing economies. To change these rules when the characteristics of students or advances of knowledge have changed may prove to be quite difficult because a host of other practices have grown up in the department that depend on the designation of certain courses appropriate for distribution requirements. For example, perhaps only instructors and assistant professors are assigned to teach these courses. Also, majors may be steered into more high-level courses where enrollment is kept down. A dean who attempts to force the department to make what seems to be eminently sensible changes from her point of view, or the point of view of the students or other departments, may run into serious opposition from the department. The change would threaten the department's whole fragile structure of work assignments and course requirements. The department might turn around in retaliation and change some of its rules on its own. For example, it might limit the enrollment in certain courses. Soon, if not immediately, a first-class *political* situation has evolved that has little to do with the original problem and can be solved only by bargaining. But bargaining threatens the status quo, involves other departments, and ramifies the changes. Because rules protect interests, and groups are interdependent, changing the rules is difficult.

Rules are like an invisible skein that bundles together all the technological and social aspects of organizations. As such, rules stem from past adjustments and seek to stabilize the present and future. When things are different in the future, an attempt to change these tough, invisible threads means that all kinds of practices, bargains, agreements, and payoffs will tumble out of the web and must be stuffed back in again. As a result of these kinds of interdependencies, changes in organizational rules (which go on continuously, if only informally)[18] are generally incremental—a little bit here and there. The hope is that somehow the whole structure of the organization will gradually, painlessly, and, most of all, *covertly* change over time. It generally does.

In sum, rules protect those who are subject to them. Rules are means of preserving group autonomy and freedom; to reduce the number of rules in an organization generally means to make it more impersonal, more inflexible, more standardized. But even given this, rules are still a bore. We would all prefer to be free of them, or so it would seem. Actually, only *some* rules are bores. The good, effective rules are rarely noticed; the bad ones stand out. Bad rules are inevitable. Some merely reflect the fact that people make rules, and people are not generally geniuses. The problem is not rules in general, but particular ones that need changing.

[18]Peter M. Blau, *The Dynamics of Bureaucracy,* 2nd rev. ed. (Chicago: University of Chicago Press, 1973).

Rules as Scapegoats

Rules are the scapegoats for a variety of organizational problems. Complaints about excessive rules or bad rules generally are symptomatic of more deep-seated problems that cannot be solved by changing rules. During the unhappy days of the breakdown in telephone service in New York in 1969–1970, a number of "stupid" rules surfaced and were held to have caused the difficulties. Actually, the difficulties appeared to be that the system was designed so that it would operate with a good deal of inefficiency and slack. Such an operation is easy when an organization has a monopoly and, despite the lack of risk, a guaranteed high rate of return. Savings from technical advances need not result in significant rate decreases, but simply in more inefficient ways of doing business—which is, after all, the easiest route. No one in the company gets upset, and since the public is uninformed and the rate-setting agencies are weak and generally captives of the utilities, the lack of rate reduction is not noticed. (The same appears to be true for the gas and electric utilities, which also are very profitable, inefficiently regulated monopolies.) When greater demands were made on the company than it could fulfill, it became apparent that, for example, the business-office side of the company in the New York area was not talking to the plant or operations side; both hid under a complex set of rules and regulations that governed their interrelationship and the operations within each of the divisions. As long as there was sufficient "fat," or surplus, in the system, it did not matter; when more efficiency was needed to meet demand for services, these inefficiencies surfaced, and rules got the blame. The rules were not bad in themselves. For example, they probably reduced contact and thus antagonisms between the operations and customer-service branches. A more efficient operation would require more contact, however, and under these situations the rules were inappropriate. But the whole premise on which the system operated would have to be changed; rules would be only one aspect that would be changed.

In a similar fashion, hidebound government bureaucracies are not unresponsive to their clients because of their rules but because of the premises they operate on and the system designed around those premises. The New York public school system[19] and the Bureau of Indian Affairs are two outstanding examples. In both cases, professionals have captured the organization and made it too difficult or expensive for policy makers—board members, staff of the Secretary of the Interior, politicians, and the like—to wrest control and change practices. The incredible rules of these agencies are only by-products and symptoms of a commonplace fact of organization life: those who can will seize control of an organization and use it for their own ends—in these cases security, power, and expansion.

As we noted above, good rules are often those that are rarely noticed. They may be written down or just a matter of custom, but they are rarely challenged. They simply make sense. Some other good rules are those that cut the Gordian knots that inevitably bind organized endeavors of any complexity. Frequently, there is no clear ground for doing A instead of B; both will have unpleasant outcomes. Rather than agonize over a decision, a rule cuts the knot. Another function of good rules is to

---

[19]David Rogers, *110 Livingstone Street* (New York: Random House, 1968).

justify unpleasant decisions or actions: "Sorry, old boy, but I will have to discipline you for that." "I know it's not fair, from your point of view, but it's the rule." "It took a lot of extra work, and I made some enemies in the agency, but the rule is that these kinds of clients are entitled to more service." Without the rules, these necessary but unpleasant actions might not be taken.

The greatest problem with rules is that organizations and their environments change faster than the rules. Most bad rules were once good, designed for a situation that no longer exists. Nepotism was apparently a problem in university departments of the past, when they were dominated by one man who made all the decisions as to what the courses would be, what texts would be used, who was to be hired and who promoted. It was easy to extend this power by putting one's wife on the staff. Today, departmental chairpersons have much less power, and there are more finely graded criteria for performance. Yet, as more women once again come into the academic job market and have husbands who are also teachers, the nepotism rule becomes more burdensome and discriminatory. It is often stoutly defended, though, by those who resent women professors anyway, since they are a threat to male hegemony.

In sum, "there ought to be a rule" is as valid as saying "there are too damn many rules around here." Rules do a lot of things in organizations: they protect as well as restrict; coordinate as well as block; channel effort as well as limit it; permit universalism as well as provide sanctuary for the inept; maintain stability as well as retard change; permit diversity as well as restrict it. They constitute the organizational memory and the means for change. As such, rules in themselves are neither good nor bad, nor even that important. It is only because they are easy scapegoats for other problems that are more difficult to divine and analyze that we have to spend this much time on them. Social scientists, no less than the person in the street, love to denounce them and to propose ruleless organizations. But ruleless organizations are likely to be either completely automated, if they are efficient and have much output, or completely professionalized, turning out expensive and exotic services. Only a tiny fraction of organizations fit either case.

"WHO'S IN CHARGE AROUND HERE?"

For many social scientists, rules are a nuisance, but the existence of a hierarchical ordering of offices and authority is a barely tolerable evil. The principle of hierarchical ordering of offices and authority says that for every person there shall be one person above to whom he or she primarily reports and from whom he or she primarily receives direction. The organization is structured in the form of a pyramid, with the top controlling everything. Power is centralized. Though all aspects of bureaucracy —rules, universalism, impersonality, tenure, and stability—are criticized, hierarchy, the most characteristic aspect of bureaucracy, is judged its worst. It is the negation of individual autonomy, freedom, spontaneity, creativity, dignity, and independence.

The Collegial University

When we think of organizations with elaborate hierarchies, we often have the government and its bureaus in mind, or perhaps the large corporation. Professional organizations, according to theory, are not so arranged—colleagues are at more or less the same level.[20] I would probably be considered a professional, being a full professor of sociology in a university, so let us see what I might have had to go through at the University of Wisconsin in 1970 in order to make a suggestion, take up an issue, make a complaint, or whatever, if I wished to touch all bases. Theoretically, I would first go to the assistant chairman of my department, who would send the matter on to the chairman. The chairman might wish to consult with the departmental executive committee to be on "solid ground" before proceeding. The departmental chairman would then take it up with one of the appropriate assistant deans (there were eight to choose from) in the College of Letters and Science, who would refer it to one of the associate deans (there were four of them), who would take it up with the dean of the College of Letters and Science (there are Colleges of Agriculture, Engineering, etc., each of which has its dean and associate and assistant deans). If the matter involved the graduate program at all, it would next go to one of the two assistant deans, and then to one of the five associate deans of the Graduate School; then it would be taken up with the dean of the Graduate School (who would, of course, confer with the dean of the pertinent college). The Graduate School dean might consult with a student-faculty committee in the process. After that, it would be taken up by one of the two assistants to the chancellor, who would refer it to one of the two vice-chancellors, who would take it up with the chancellor of the Madison campus (there are other campuses—Milwaukee, Green Bay, and Parkside among them). The chancellor of the Madison campus would send it along to one of the vice-presidents of the university (he had seven to choose from), who would take it up with the president of the university. If the matter were still unresolved and had not lost its power of ascent, the president would take it up with the university's regents. They, in turn, might have to refer to the State Coordinating Council for Higher Education (which has several staff layers of its own). It, though, receives its power from the legislature, whose actions can be vetoed by the governor. Were the matter important enough to go as far as the Coordinating Council, it would have gone through five major levels of authority, each with about three internal levels of authority, for a total of at least fifteen steps in the staircase.

Of course, it is not that simple. We have assumed that the matter did not involve any of the numerous other fiefdoms in the university, which is highly unlikely. There are numerous councils, committees, divisional organizations (e.g., a chairman of social studies), administrative units (such as the admissions office with its director, associate director, and four assistant directors), the libraries (an Egyptian-sized pyramid in itself), a jumble of business offices, the computing center, counseling services, and offices concerned with public relations, parking, physical plant, protection and security, purchasing, registration, student affairs, and so on—

[20]Talcott Parsons, "Introduction," in Max Weber, *The Theory of Social and Economic Organization,* pp. 58–60. Amitai Etzioni, *A Comparative Analysis of Complex Organizations* (New York: Free Press, 1961), pp. 218–261.

each of which could be involved. A professor has occasion to deal with all of these at times. In addition, much power is exercised by the campus university committee, the senate, the all-university faculty assembly, the university faculty council, the course committee, the divisional executive committee, the social studies committee of the graduate school, the research committee, the honors committee, various student-faculty committees (at the time an area of exponential growth in form, though with little substance), and various all-university committees. These committees plug the interstitial areas of the fifteen levels above me very effectively and relieve all the assistant deans or whatever of their backbreaking loads.

Of course, even with fifteen levels of authority and a tropical jungle of committee growth to go through to get to the top, I would not be at the bottom of the heap. Below me are strung out the associate professors, assistant professors, instructors, lecturers, teaching assistants, graduate students, and, somewhere down there, undergraduates. This is not a chain of command; undergraduates have been known to talk directly to full professors without going through a teaching assistant, for example. But these levels come into operation in numerous ways. For example, if two full professors desire the same office, the one who has been "in rank" longer will generally get it. We cannot really add six more levels below a full professor in terms of authority, though we can in terms of status.

In addition, I might have a secretary, research assistant, undergraduate work-study assistants, and graduate student trainees in a training program—that is, another little empire. (I have left out the enormous informal power of the head secretary of the department, other directors of training programs or of the graduate program, renowned colleagues, and those who somehow just manage to amass power.) Just to grasp this social structure intellectually, let alone maneuver in it, is a demanding task.[21]

So much for the myth that the university is a collegial body having a minimum of hierarchy and status difference. Nor should one assume that other professional bodies, such as the medical staff of a hospital or the U.S. Senate, also enjoy the advantages of lack of hierarchy. The medical personnel in hospitals are generally highly organized in a structure that parallels that of the administrative staff of the hospital. The medical staff has its own nursing committee, outpatient department committee, pharmacy committee, and so forth, and in between the major ranks of junior and senior attending staff are several clear distinctions in grade, with appropriate powers and entrance criteria.[22] The U.S. Senate is also more highly structured than one would expect on the basis of the contrast between bureaucratic and

[21]I wish to thank Robert Taylor, former vice-president of the University of Wisconsin, for constructive comments on this material. As he points out, the chain of command works in a variety of ways, depending on who or what is involved. "Very little (maybe no) 'traffic' moves up or down this chain in this fashion. The fact is that most of it moves as your letter [to me] did—from professor to vice-president and back with all the other levels left in blessed ignorance. And, of course, no modern student would countenance such a chain for a moment—he'd pick up the phone and call the president or the president of the board of regents, if he thought either of these officials capable of acting on his request." (Private correspondence.) This is true, but in a crunch, the chain is there for those higher up to use it. As we shall see, much short-circuiting of the chain occurs in organizations that are not made up of "professionals."

[22]Charles Perrow, "Goals and Power Structures: A Historical Case Study," and Mary E. W. Goss, "Patterns of Bureaucracy Among Hospital Staff Physicians," in *The Hospital in Modern Society*, ed. Eliot Freidson (New York: Free Press, 1963).

professional organizations, and it takes a new senator a long time to learn all the aspects of this structure. Even law firms are highly structured.[23] Indeed, any group with a division of labor, professional or not, will be hierarchically structured.

The Sins of Hierarchy

What is the consequence of this ubiquitous structuring of even "professional" organizations? For the critics of bureaucracy, the consequence is that the bulk of people in the lower and middle levels are prevented from really giving their all for goal achievement; they turn, instead, into infantile, fearful robots. The argument runs like this:

The hierarchy promotes rigidity and timidity. Subordinates are afraid of passing bad news up the ladder[24] or of suggesting changes.[25] (Such an action would imply that their superiors should have thought of the changes and did not.) They also are more afraid of new situations than of familiar ones, since with the new situations, those above them might introduce new evils, while the old ones are sufficient. The hierarchy promotes delays and sluggishness; everything must be kicked upstairs for a decision either because the boss insists or because the subordinate does not want to risk making a poor decision. All this indecision exists at the same time that superiors are being authoritarian, dictatorial, and rigid, making snap judgments that they refuse to reconsider, implementing on-the-spot decisions without consulting their subordinates, and generally stifling any independence or creativity at the subordinate levels. Subordinates are under constant surveillance from superiors; thus they often give up trying to exercise initiative or imagination and instead suppress or distort information. Finally, since everything must go through channels, and these are vertical, two people at the same level in two different departments cannot work things out themselves but must involve long lines of superiors.

At this point one may wonder how organizations can function at all, but it becomes even more alarming when we consider a contrasting series of complaints frequently made by members of a hierarchy. These are complaints about people in one department making decisions that affect other units without checking first with their respective superiors, and about the *lack* of clear lines of authority, the *failure* to exercise authority or to be decisive, and the *lack* of accountability. Some typical complaints:

1. Who's in charge here? Who am I supposed to take this matter to?
2. That bureau gets away with murder; no one will exercise authority over it, and it is not clear what their authority is supposed to be.
3. Some technician in engineering went ahead and made these design changes in conjunction with a department head in production, but they never bothered to check with the sales manager or the account supervisor in finance.

[23]Erwin O. Smigel, *Wall Street Lawyer*, rev. ed. (Bloomington, Ind.: Indiana University Press, 1970).

[24]Harold L. Wilensky, *Organizational Intelligence: Knowledge and Policy in Government and Industry* (New York: Basic Books, 1969), pp. 42–48.

[25]Victor A. Thompson, *Modern Organization*, 2nd ed. (University, Ala.: Univ. of Alabama Press, 1977), Chapter 8.

4. We make changes, and before we can see how well they are working out, we are making more changes.
5. What this place lacks is decisive leadership.
6. No one told me.

In such cases we hear of too much flexibility, too little attention to the hierarchy, too little forceful decision making. According to one survey,[26] managers in industrial firms are decidedly in favor of more, rather than less, clarity in lines of authority, rules, duties, specification of procedures, and so on. Only when the structure is clear can authority be delegated, they indicate, as did Wilfred Brown (see pp. 21–22).

If both the presence and the absence of hierarchy can be faulted, and if authority can be both excessive and absent, change too rapid and too infrequent, employees both fearful and aggressive, gutless and crafty, and flexible and rigid, the problem may not lie in hierarchy per se. Some degree of hierarchy is needed in any organized endeavor, but how much and in what kinds of endeavors? We are only beginning to phrase the problem in this fashion, and to get a glimpse of how hierarchies actually work.

Research on Span of Control

Take the matter of "span of control"—the number of subordinates whom a superior directly controls. This is the building block of hierarchy. If each superior controls few people—has a narrow span of control—there will be many levels in the organization; if he or she controls many, there will be few. For twenty to thirty years, social scientists and management theorists debated regarding the optimum span of control —was it four, six, eight, or what? If only we knew, we could design our organizations properly. Embedded in this discussion was the assumption that if a manager had many people under her, she could not supervise them closely, and thus they would have more autonomy.[27] This assumption was furthered in an influential piece of reporting by a personnel officer with Sears Roebuck who described how morale and efficiency improved when the number of levels in the organization was reduced.[28]

Of course, as is true of most "principles" of organization, there was an alternative view—rarely stated as a principle, but acted on by management consulting firms. This principle said that if a manager had a lot of people reporting to him, he was centralizing power and would not want to give it up. Such a manager should establish an intermediate level in order to give his subordinates some leeway. A wide span of control meant reluctance to delegate, rather than delegation.

Few theorists took the rule-of-thumb wisdom of the management consultants seriously, however. One of the best theorists, for example, is Peter Blau. He and his associates conducted a study of 156 public personnel agencies, starting with "a few

[26]Charles Perrow, "Working Paper on Technology and Structure," mimeographed, February 1970.

[27]William F. Whyte, "Human Relations—A Progress Report," in *Complex Organizations, A Sociological Reader*, ed. Amitai Etzioni (New York: Holt, Rinehart & Winston, 1962), pp. 100–112.

[28]James C. Worthy, "Organizational Structure and Employee Morale," *American Sociological Review* 15 (1950): 169–179.

plausible considerations" that led to inferences "which appeared straightforward and perhaps even self-evident." They reasoned that if a person was well trained, he or she would need little supervision. The span of control would be wide. If personnel were not well trained, they would need more supervision, and the span of control would be narrow and the hierarchy higher. (In the language of journal articles, it reads like this: The inferences suggested, "as an initial hypothesis, that expert requirements decrease the ratio of managerial to nonsupervisory personnel in organizations, which widens the average span of control."[29])

To the admitted surprise of Blau and associates, the hypothesis was found to be incorrect. The more qualified the people, the *less* the span of control. They then suggested that the explanation might be that a narrow span of control—only two or three subordinates per superior—allows easy consultation on difficult problems and permits common problem solving. Though they did not state it directly, this would suggest that wide spans of control could mean close supervision but little consultation.

Actually, as is so true in much of organizational research, the resolution of the dilemma lies in distinguishing different types of organizations or situations. In some cases, a span of control of ten can mean close supervision through highly routinized controls over people performing routine tasks; in others, it can mean very little supervision, with the ten subordinates working out things with each other and only occasionally seeking the advice or direction of the boss.[30] The span of control, then, can be independent of the closeness of supervision. Supervision can be direct or indirect with either a wide or a narrow span of control.

The span of control, in turn, affects the degree of hierarchy, or the number of levels of supervision in an organization. Where spans of control are wide, the organization tends to be "squat"—there are not many levels of authority. Where spans of control are narrow, the organization tends to have a narrow, "tall" hierarchy, with many levels of authority. But we have argued that a squat organization does not necessarily mean either close or distant supervision. There are a number of factors that might affect the closeness of supervision (beyond, of course, the personality and leadership style of a manager), and they are worth listing to indicate the complexity of the matter:

1. The degree to which tasks are routine or nonroutine.
2. The difference between the expertise of the manager and that of his or her subordinates; the amount of interdependence among tasks under one manager; and the interdependence of these tasks with those performed under different managers.

[29]Peter Blau, "The Hierarchy of Authority in Organizations," *American Journal of Sociology* 73 (January 1968): 453–457.

[30]See, for example, the various discussions by Joan Woodward, *Industrial Organization: Theory and Practice* (London: Oxford University Press, 1965). In discussing span of control, Jay Lorsch generally finds a broad span is associated with nonroutine tasks, contrary to Blau. But on the other hand, in the routine production department of one of his companies, Lorsch also finds a broad span of control. See Jay W. Lorsch, *Product Innovation and Organization* (New York: Macmillan, 1965), p. 53. For a good discussion and additional evidence supporting Blau's view see Gerald Bell, "Determinants of Span of Control," *American Journal of Sociology* 73, no. 1 (July 1967): 90–101.

3. The interdependence of the department as a whole with other departments in the organization, and the varying kinds of routine and nonroutine mixes of the departments.
4. The degree to which written rules and regulations or machines can reduce the need for personal supervision.
5. The extent to which flexibility and rapid response is necessary to the organization.

Given these relevant sources of variation, it remains to be seen whether, as Blau maintains, the relationship they suggested between span of control and supervision is likely to hold in all organizations.

Using the same data, Marshall Meyer concludes that there are two strategies available to organizations—control through direct supervision, utilizing a wide span of control, which promotes flexibility of response since the manager can change things quickly; and control through rules, regulations, and professional expertise, utilizing a greater number of hierarchical levels with a narrow span of control, which promotes more "rational" administration and more stable operations.[31] Blau also concludes that there are two types of organizations, but he labels the first the "old-fashioned bureaucracy." It has a "squat hierarchy with authority centralized at the top," little automation, and personnel rules that emphasize managerial discretion, seniority, and personal judgment. The second he calls the "modern organization" with a "tall, slim hierarchy with decentralized authority," relying upon experts, automation, and universalistic personnel procedures (objective merit standards).[32]

Meyer's data show only weak support for Blau's conclusions; the differences between the two types of strategies are in the predicted direction but are quite small. The important thing, however, is that they are *not* in the *opposite* direction; that is, the usual view of hierarchy would indicate that the higher the degree of hierarchy the greater the centralized control.[33] But that does not hold here. If anything, the greater hierarchy is associated with decentralization. Blau handles his data somewhat differently and finds somewhat stronger relationships, but more important, he finds the relationships consistent over three types of organizations: personnel departments, finance departments, and state employment agencies. Thus, even though the differences may not be large in any one sample, the consistency over the three is impressive.

Furthermore, a quite independent and large study in England, generally referred to as the Aston study because the team, headed by Derek Pugh, was then at the University of Aston in Birmingham, came to very similar conclu-

[31]Marshall Meyer, "Two Authority Structures of Bureaucratic Organizations," *Administrative Science Quarterly* 13 (September 1968): 211–228.

[32]Blau, "Hierarchy." There are complex problems here of different degrees of "tallness" in different units of an organization that are not relevant for these agencies, but would be for most organizations.

[33]See, for example, Worthy, "Employee Morale." It is noteworthy that in a study of school teachers that used, by and large, unloaded questions to tap bureaucracy, it was found that, quite contrary to the authors' expectations, "Teachers in highly bureaucratic systems had a significantly higher, not lower, sense of power than those in less bureaucratic systems." See Gerald H. Moeller and W. W. Charters, "Relation of Bureaucratization to Sense of Power Among Teachers," *Administrative Science Quarterly* 10, no. 4 (March 1966): 457. These authors were as surprised as Blau and his associates but fell back upon the influence of other factors that might have clouded or reversed a relationship predicted by most schools of thought.

sions.[34] In the Blau and the Aston studies, the gap between the indicators used and the concepts these indicators were supposed to represent is often very large. For example, the items that are used to measure the degree of delegation of authority, or decentralization, refer only to decisions that are visible, binary (either-or), and capable of clear statement in official rules, such as the level at which a certain amount of money can be spent without prior authorization. More subtle, basic, and certainly more powerful decisions are not measured; these may be quite centralized. We refer to this as the problem of "operationalization," or making the measurement of concepts operational. The operationalization of the concept of hierarchy in the Aston study was particularly controversial. Nevertheless, one can have some confidence in the findings of the Blau and Aston studies for three important reasons: (1) they are independently arrived at, using different measures; (2) they were unexpected by both research teams; and (3) they are counterintuitive.

In short, we cannot assume that the more hierarchical the organization, the more centralized it is. If the limited data show anything, they indicate an inverse relationship. More important, the very characteristics that both Blau and Meyer ascribe to their tall, hierarchical, and decentralized organizations are those that Weber stressed in his bureaucratic model: expertise, written rules and regulations, clear ordering of positions, and hierarchy. The characteristics of the squat centralized organization are personal rule, personal evaluations, and low expertise. These are closer to the traditional model, which the development of bureaucracy attempted to supplant.

Hierarchy and Timidity

Another attribute often associated with tall hierarchies is timidity and caution on the part of subordinates who fear criticism from superiors and thus hesitate to pass unpleasant information up the line. That such an attitude exists in bureaucracies is clear, but that it is an inevitable concomitant of hierarchy, and thus its product, is far from evident. Timidity and caution appear to vary greatly among bureaucracies, on the basis of casual impressions. Peter Blau, in his study of two government agencies, commented that he found little evidence of this behavior.[35] It certainly does not show up among the more successful managers in Dalton's study,[36] nor among all managers in Gouldner's study.[37] Why, then, the variation?

It would seem that tendencies toward conservatism and self-protective behavior

[34]The best summary and introduction to these studies is that of John Child, "Predicting and Understanding Organization Structure," *Administrative Science Quarterly* 18, no. 2 (June 1973): 168–185. For a sample of the criticisms of this important survey see Howard Aldrich, "Technology and Organizational Structure: A Reexamination of the Findings of the Aston Group," *Administrative Science Quarterly* 17, no. 1 (March 1972): 26–43; Sergio E. Mindlin and Howard Aldrich, "Interorganizational Dependence: A Review of the Concepts and Reexamination of the Findings of the Aston Group," *Administrative Science Quarterly* 20, no. 3 (September 1975): 382–392; and especially William Starbuck, "A Trip to View the Elephants and Rattlesnakes in the Garden of Aston," in *Perspectives on Organization Design and Behavior,* ed. Andrew H. Van de Ven and William F. Joyce (New York: Wiley, 1981), pp. 167–199.

[35]Blau, *Dynamics.*

[36]Dalton, *Men Who Manage.*

[37]Gouldner, *Industrial Bureaucracy.*

are natural outcomes of all organized activity that is not spontaneously coordinated and based on wholehearted cooperation. But it also would appear that organizations have mechanisms to minimize the danger and even reverse these tendencies. For example, people can be rewarded for passing critical items of information up the hierarchy; the reward may have to be high if it reflects on one's superior, but if it is that important to the organization it can be done. Actually, the opposite is sometimes a problem—a person gets ahead by showing up the superior. Between these two stances—timidity and cunning—there is the far more usual situation in which constructive criticisms are encouraged and rewarded because the boss can take the credit. Accounting departments are generally rewarded for critical information, which is why, in the organization Dalton studied, it was so essential for aggressive managers to neutralize or bribe the accountants. Innovative and risk-taking behavior may be harder to reward than conservative behavior, but it is possible to do it.

Timidity and caution appear to be functions of the technology and market of organizations, rather than of their degree of hierarchy. In some market situations —for example, Social Security administration, aid to dependent children, railroads, public utilities, mining (especially in such oligopolistic situations as sulfur mining) —there is little perceived need for risk taking. In other large and equally bureaucratic organizations—the Agency for International Development in its golden days of the late 1950s and early 1960s, the federal rehabilitation agencies during the 1950s and early 1960s, which used the money dumped on them by an uncomprehending Congress to upgrade physically healthy but untrained blacks, and the electronics and chemical industries—risk taking is much more in evidence. There is no evidence that these organizations had fewer levels of authority than more conservative organizations.

Still, problems remain. Some officials do insist that a great many minor matters be brought to their attention before action is taken. The explanation may be that they are poor or insecure administrators or have incompetent subordinates. This happens all the time, but it can hardly be attributed to hierarchy alone. Sometimes it is impossible to get an answer out of a higher officer; the explanation may simply be that he does not know and unfortunately will not admit it, or that he is still searching, or that he is perhaps hoping that the lower officer will go ahead and make the decision (and take the blame if it is wrong). But someone has to decide, and the principle of hierarchy at least specifies *who* should decide if ambiguity exists. Wilfred Brown observes that the principal function of a hierarchy is to resolve disputes or uncertainties; things go on well enough without slavishly going through channels if there is no dispute and no uncertainty.[38]

The Official and the Unofficial Hierarchical Order

One of the true delights of the organizational expert is to indicate to the uninitiated the wide discrepancy between the official hierarchy (or rules, for that matter) and the unofficial one. It is a remarkable phenomenon in many cases and well known

[38]Wilfred Brown, *Exploration in Management.*

to most people who spend their working lives as managers in organizations. Departmental secretaries in many universities have power far beyond their status. David Mechanic's well-known essay, "Sources of Power of Lower Participants in Complex Organization," touches on this and other examples.[39] Melville Dalton, in his excruciatingly unsettling study of a manufacturing plant, reveals top people with no power and those three or four levels below with extensive power.[40] Sociologists have been particularly fond of the contrast between the official and the unofficial because it indicates that organizations are natural systems rather than artificial or mechanistic ones—living things that the people within them create out of their own needs, rather than rational tools in the hands of a master. They are right, of course: between the conception and the reality, as the poet tells us, falls the shadow. The first thing the new employee should learn is who is really in charge, who has the goods on whom, what are the major debts and dependencies—all things that are not reflected by the neat boxes in the organization chart. With this knowledge he or she can navigate with more skill and ease.

For the organizational theorists, however, a different kind of question is required: What are the systematic bases for the deviations? We should not expect the official map to be completely accurate because:

1. It is never up-to-date—it does not reflect the growing power of a subordinate who will be promoted over his or her boss in a year or two, or the waning power of a boss who has been passed by because of changes in technology or markets.
2. It does not pretend to make the finely graded distinctions that operating personnel have to live by—for example, three departments may be on the same official level, but one of them is three times the size of the other two and may carry commensurately more power.
3. It does not reflect all transactions in the organization, but primarily those disputes that can be settled formally.
4. Most important, the hierarchy functions primarily for routine situations; when new ones come along, someone two levels down may have more say for this or that situation, but unless the new situation itself becomes the persistent or frequent one, his or her authority will only be temporary. If it persists, that person may well move up fast.
5. Finally, hierarchical principles are sometimes violated intentionally. When, for example, the head office cannot get enough information about a division's operation, it sends in a spy. Dalton describes such a case. The man involved had a relatively unimportant job of manager of industrial relations, but his power over many other aspects of the organization was substantial because everyone knew that he was there to find out what was going on.

Few organizations keep an official chart of offices ranked by authority for very long or, if they do, such charts are rarely referred to. (Some organizations even refuse to draw them up.) Positions and units move up and down in authority over time, and the lag with the official chart is always there. Thus, we should not be surprised

---

[39]David Mechanic, "Sources of Power of Lower Participants in Complex Organization," *Administrative Science Quarterly* 7, no. 4 (December 1962): 349–364.
[40]Dalton, *Men Who Manage*, Chapter 2.

at the discrepancy, nor should we assume that the unofficial is necessarily a more accurate rendition than the official. The two are just different and only briefly join hands in their mutual evolution. While the "natural" or "living" system is impor- tant, it may only be a wistful and touching part of a rather mechanical and impera- tive whole. The fact that the dean and I (or the chancellor and I, or the president and I) are both professors in a collegial body of equals is as much a romance of the actual situation as the view that only the yeasty, vital, living, informal system counts in an organization. The official hierarchy is there, and no one who has both eyes open forgets it. One must know the hierarchy to survive it.

THREE USES OF HIERARCHY

Perhaps the most common criticism of hierarchy (and related aspects of bureaucrati- zation, such as the emphasis on rules) results from the failure to attribute to hierarchy the successes that it enjoys. If things are going well, we talk of cooperation; if they are going badly, we speak of the "emphasis on hierarchy" or this "goddamned bureaucracy" with all its red tape and gutless or overbearing people. Three semific- tional examples of problem solving in organizations will illustrate this. (These are composites of situations I observed while studying industrial firms.)

Example A: Task Specialization

A foreman in the rolling mill of a steel company (where hot strips of steel are passed between heavy rollers to reduce their width, lengthen them, and change their molecular structure) is having difficulty with cracks in the ends of steel bars. The ends must be cut off, his scrap rate rises, and longer bars than are necessary must be rolled. He is not held personally accountable for the waste, but it is an annoyance, requires explanations, and offends his sense of craftsmanship. He decides on the basis of past experience that the problem may be due to the length of time the bar spends in the annealing furnace (which gives it a slow bake) before it reaches him. If the baking time were longer, he feels, the bars would not crack. He asks his supervisor to request the annealing unit to leave them in longer. His supervisor says, "We'd better check with the metallurgical department in Research to see if this will make it more difficult to grind and shape the bars for the customer. I will call the director of metallurgy; he will know who to ask." (Note that the supervisor thereby skips a level in the hierarchy *and* crosses departmental lines. See the accompanying chart, which presents a simplified version of an official chart, omitting many depart- ments and functions not relevant here. The level is noted at certain points in my narrative as an aid in judging the fit between hierarchy and interaction.) The metallurgy director (Level III) says, "I'll have Charley check it, and he will let you know." Charley is a technician (VI) in Research and Development (R&D) and happens to be more or less at the foreman's level. (It is difficult to compare the levels of authority in departments like R&D or Sales with those in Production.) But he knows these problems better than his own immediate supervisor of Research Group A (V), who is new, or the superintendent of Process Research (IV), who coordinates

Figure 1   Simplified Chart for Examples of Hierarchy

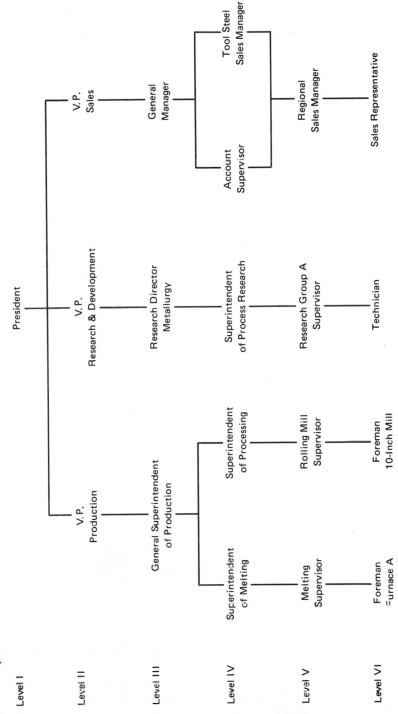

several groups and is out of touch with detailed problems. (Note, then, that the research director [III] has skipped two levels of authority in his own organization.)

At this point, Charley might say to the rolling mill supervisor, "We don't know. It very well might, and it is a good thing you checked. But it will take a week of research to find out, and since we have all these other projects it will have to be spread out over a month or two. To get this entered into our schedule will require the authorization of the Group A supervisor, and I know that he will have to check with the superintendent of Process Research because things are tight right now. The latter is away for a week visiting customer plants, but we could estimate the amount of delay to other projects and call him." If this were the response, the cry of "bureaucracy" or "hierarchy" might go up, and the foreman would think twice about making another suggestion. Nevertheless, the response would be perfectly proper and in the interests of the organization.

To simplify matters, though, let us assume that Charley says, "I doubt that it would have any effect on machineability. But if this steel is being used to make cutting tools for numerically controlled machining tools [highly automated devices], it might affect their cutting life because of the heat generated. Someone should check to see what this grade is used for." So the supervisor of the rolling mill calls the account supervisor in Sales to find out who handles this particular account. The account supervisor gives him the name of a sales representative (VI). The sales rep is out, but he is finally located on the other side of the country. He does not know what the customer is using this grade for, but he will check. In a couple of days he finds out. "It would be all right, though we should probably let them know about the change so they can do a tool-life check; they are a big customer and are quite particular about these things. But the main problem is that there are some touchy negotiations going on with that company. I am not affected by them; they concern stainless steel. But I picked it up from the secretary of the vice-president of Sales. You had better check with the manager of Tool Steel Sales (IV)."

Parenthetically, to have information about the touchy negotiations is not part of this sales representative's responsibility, but it is an important bit of gossip for him to have picked up. If he had not picked it up, the minor change in steel characteristics would endanger a large order, as we shall see. But any manager in any organization picks up all the rumors he can about these sorts of things; the official lines of communication, strung up and down the official hierarchy, are designed less to inform than to record action, less to initiate than to justify and protect action. "Do it first, and let the paperwork and official authorizations follow" is a frequent injunction when time is at a premium or novel events are being dealt with. On the other hand, much communication outside the official lines, such as this bit of gossip, is only occasionally important and utilized. To design a communications system to handle all the informal bits of information formally would create a monster.

The matter now goes to the tool steel manager who says, "Yes, we are trying to negotiate a contract with Universal to buy our new type of stainless steel. It involves a different part of the organization than tool steel, of course, but the purchasing agent who is in on these negotiations also handles tool steel purchases. I (IV) will check with the vice-president of Sales (II) about the status of the negotiations, or even with the president (I) if the V.P. is not around this week. We cannot, of course, put anything in writing, and we better stay off the phone, too." (That is, they cannot call the V.P. at a customer's plant because the customer probably had bugged the line; industrial espionage is a very big and serious business.)

The whole thing might fall apart at this point because the negotiations have been touchy, and if word got to the purchasing agent that the customer would be subjected to the nuisance of a tool-life check, he might be a little more cool than he already is to the deal. He is already cool because the steel firm did the very unusual thing of refusing to rehire his college-going, hell-raising son for a plush summer job. Purchasing agents do not expect such treatment. But the lad was so unreliable and stirred up so much trouble that the steel company gave him a company car and told him to stay away the rest of the summer. Putting this aside, however, let us say that the vice-president of Sales (II) tells the tool steel manager (IV): "The purchasing agent hasn't got a thing to say about this. It is up to their vice-president of Production, and we can promise better deliveries than the competition. Anyway, I hate the purchasing agent's guts. Tell production to go ahead if they want." (He then mumbles to himself, "Why do they have to bring every little thing to me? What is the V.P. of Production doing anyway?")

The foreman of the 10-inch rolling mill, who has been wondering what has been holding up such a simple matter for two or three weeks, finally gets his go-ahead, providing the annealing department will agree. The sales rep has to be informed so that he can tell the customer when a slightly different type of steel will be coming through. (He decides to tell the customer that this constitutes a minor breakthrough in increasing quality, since he suspects that if the customer views it in this light, the tool-life checks are more likely to be positive—a sound judgment that conforms to social science experimental evidence on perception and "experimenter effect.") The foreman then tries the new method out and finds that it makes no difference at all in terms of the degree to which ends of the bars crack and have to be scrapped.

We have just described a moderately hierarchical organization. But our remarks about hierarchy were asides. We also described a series of specialized functions, tasks, and sequences—which we could have done without reference to the hierarchy. The V.P. of Sales (II) knew about some negotiations; the lowly sales rep (VI) knew about product usage. The V.P. of Production (II) probably will never hear of the event, and would not even if the technique had worked. (If it might have resulted in large savings, the superintendent of Production [III] would have heard about it from the superintendent of Processing [IV], who would have been told by the rolling mill supervisor [V], so that all could claim credit. The V.P. of Production, then, of course, would have kept the president [I] informed at all stages. The hierarchy is always involved when rewards are at stake.) Had anything gone wrong at any point, it might have occasioned curses about the hierarchical aspects of the company. ("Everything has to go up to the manager of metallurgy, and he is so scared of his position that he refuses to approve anything"—a doubtful, if useful, generalization, since he probably would not last long if that were true, or else he would be ignored and someone else would make the decision.) But the hierarchy was important, if only implicit, in this example. The supervisor relied on the metallurgy manager to decide who in his group would know about the consequences of annealing times; the tool steel manager had to buck a decision about relationships with the customer up to his superior, the V.P. of Sales. The hierarchy established routes of communication where information was needed and levels where certain kinds of decisions could be made. The foreman could not undertake all these inquiries himself, since he did not have the access to the hierarchy that his supervisor did, and also because he was too busy rolling steel. His supervisor exists to handle such communications. Thus, in this commonplace example of organizational problem solving, we find specialized tasks and hierarchies merged; one could not function without the other. Though the hierarchy was crucial because it identified knowledge sources and decision powers, the participants would never think to praise its existence. Most of the times that it serves its function, it is unnoticed.

Example B: Hierarchy

Let us imagine another situation, however, where this hierarchy and division of labor would not function well. Let us assume that the impetus for change comes from outside. The aforementioned customer, along with other customers, has installed new machinery, and the type of steel the firm had used before for drills and routers no longer works very well. The customers thus need tougher steel and longer bits, but there is no economical grade they can shift to. They leave it to their suppliers. (They undoubtedly buy from more than one supplier to hedge against poor deliveries or changes in quality.) Whoever supplies the steel first will have a substantial competitive edge for some time. They tell the sales representative (VI) and the tool steel manager (IV). This creates a crisis in the supplying organization—a crash program is needed to develop a steel with somewhat different characteristics. In a highly structured, hierarchical organization the sequence would be something as follows:

The tool steel manager (IV) would contact the general manager of Sales (III) who would tell the V.P. of Sales (II), since this is an important matter. The latter would contact his opposite number in Research—the V.P. of Research (II). He, in turn, would bring in the manager of metallurgy (III) and others on his staff and order a research program. Other projects would have to be dropped or slowed up, so the head of Research or his metallurgy manager would contact other parts of Sales and Production, telling them of the impending delays. The research program would then go ahead, and after a few weeks, or even months, Research would come up with a likely steel. The V.P. of Research (II) would take this to the V.P. of Production (II), who would pass it on down the line of his organization until, after a few days, it got to the melting, cogging, and rolling work stations. The melters would try out the new recipe, no doubt running into trouble, send the message of "trouble" up the production hierarchy to the V.P., who would inform the V.P. of Research, who would send it down his side. After the trouble is corrected, the cogging mill might find that the new steel is too hard to shape on the press usually used for this purpose, so they must get permission from Production to put it on the larger press (which means delaying other work). After all this is settled, rolling will probably run into problems and will inform the plant superintendent or the V.P. of Production, through channels, who will take the matter up again with his counterpart in Research. And so on.

The hierarchy is involved at almost every step, on the grounds of task specialization. But, in fact, the manager of metallurgy or the V.P. of Production may not need to make all the decisions he does, since all he decides is that the usual, official lines of communication and authority shall be utilized. If so, this is a misuse of the hierarchy. Once the decision has been made to go ahead with the program—a decision that must move up the proper channels for authorization—it should be defined as a matter for the experts involved. Their superiors must be informed of what they are doing so they can monitor the task, but they do not need to make any further decisions unless, of course, the budget is to be exceeded or there is a clash with other priorities that cannot be settled at a lower level. Why, then, would the managers behave as they did in example B, treating a novel event as if it could traverse the hierarchy in the same manner as a routine one? There might be many reasons. Unfamiliarity with an event like this (lack of precedent) can cause insecurity. A struggle for power or prestige may turn on the failure of one or another group to do its job well, so that constant surveillance is required, and since lower-level managers do not want to get blamed for something when the stakes are so high, they seek unnecessary authorization. Or it might be simple job insecurity or even ineptitude on the part of someone in the hierarchy, which forces all to play his game.

Example C: The Task Group

In contrast, let us say that after receiving the signal from the customer, the manager of Tool Steel Sales (IV), perhaps familiar with this sort of problem, suggests to the director of metallurgy (III) and the superintendent of Production (III) that a special task force be set up. They decide who should be on it, what its mission should be, and probably set up at this time two or three other groups to be activated later on. Research starts to work on the problem but while doing so consults with the superintendent of Melting, the superintendent of Processing, and someone from Sales who knows about the various other schedules that might be disrupted. Research, rather than pushing to a final elegant solution, gets Melting to try out a variety of plausible mixes in one of the small melting furnaces when they are not in heavy use. A few of these are tried out in the intermediate press and other cogging and rolling operations. These decisions are made without reference to anyone higher in the hierarchy than the members of the task force, and in most cases they are made by people considerably lower—for example, the foreman of the 10-inch rolling mill, whom we met before, is brought into the matter, and he tells the melters that if they add a little sulfur it might help; and the research technician, whom we also met before, says that that would louse everything up, but if you cooled it faster it might work; and so on. Meanwhile, when normal production runs are about to be slowed up by these special efforts, the representative of Sales finds out what would be the least costly way to handle it and talks to people—perhaps two levels above him in the sales hierarchy—so they know why things will be delayed and why they will have to do a little extra selling to keep their customers happy. Back and forth the experimentation goes on, with the metallurgical lab and research people in continual contact with those on the shop floor, until a steel that meets the customer's requirements and can be made on the firm's equipment at a reasonable price emerges. Only then do people from levels II and III need to be contacted.

Discussion

In our first example, a fairly routine change in procedure was made, and hierarchy and task specialization merged easily; they were coterminous. The organization was set up to handle just such events. In the second example, the hierarchy took precedence over task specialization and expertise. A routine, noncrisis solution was applied to a nonroutine crisis situation. At the same time, the hierarchy was made to bear the load of insecurity or mistrust or ineptitude. This meant that the volume of official communication was high (e.g., things had to go back and forth from Production to Research) and efforts were wasted (e.g., a solution from Research would be scrapped because it would not work in Melting, and a new one started). But everyone did what he was trained to do and, presumably, quite efficiently. In the third case, hierarchy was de-emphasized, and task specialization was emphasized. This was defined as a special event; a new temporary unit was set up to deal with it, and it was designed to interfere as little as possible with the routine flow of events that went on around it. The organizational structure for handling routine events was not changed or affected. Indeed, the official hierarchy could not be abandoned since it serviced routine work. Thus, hierarchy itself is not the problem; indeed it is essential. The problem is using it when it should be side-stepped temporarily.

PROFESSIONALISM AND DISCIPLINE

The final criticism of bureaucracy that we shall consider is one of the most widespread. It concerns the discrepancy between the expertise of the subordinate and that of the superior. That is to say, it involves the manager or official who knows less about things than the people that work for him or her yet who exercises authority over them. Virtually every discussion of bureaucracy mentions this point. It is an attractive criticism because we all resent, more or less, those who have authority over us when we suspect that we know more about life on the firing line than they do. The outstanding example of this concerns professionals in organizations. The manager of professionals often simply cannot be as well informed as highly trained subordinates. Social scientists have always been preoccupied with the plight of professionals and have defended their interests extensively.

This whole line of thought started with a footnote in Talcott Parsons' introduction to his translation of parts of Weber's *Economy and Society.* Weber, Parsons said, confused two types of authority in his discussion—the authority that is based on "technical competence," and the authority based on "incumbency of a legally defined office."[41] Could there not be a discrepancy between the two? Could there not be officials who were not experts but who directed the work of those who were? Indeed, there were examples, asserted Parsons. Unfortunately, his main example had little to do with organizations, and his second example was something less than relevant. But since this is possibly the most important footnote in the history of organizational theory, it is worth digging into at some length.

[41]Parsons, "Introduction," in Weber, *The Theory of Social and Economic Organizations*, p. 59.

Parsons's main example was the physician whose "authority rests fundamentally on the belief on the part of the patient that the physician has and will employ for his benefit a technical competence adequate to help him in his illness." The trouble with the example is that in this role the physician does not function in an organization. Parsons recognizes this, but adds that where the physician does function in an organization, "instead of a rigid hierarchy of status and authority [hierarchies are always rigid, one gathers] there tends to be what is roughly, in formal status, a 'company of equals,' an equalization of status which ignores the inevitable gradation of distinction and achievement to be found in any considerable group of technically competent persons."[42] However, the evidence from studies of hospitals indicates that medical staffs are quite bureaucratic in their organizational functioning, with hierarchies that are apparent; moreover, they are quite sensitive to "inevitable gradations of distinction and achievement."[43]

His other example concerns "powers of coercion in case of recalcitrance." It is not logically essential, he says, that the person with this power "should have either superior knowledge or superior skill as compared to those subject to his orders. Thus, the treasurer of a corporation is empowered to sign checks disbursing large funds. There is no implication in this 'power' that he is a more competent signer of checks than the bank clerks or tellers who cash or deposit them for the recipient."[44] The example is irrelevant because the power of the treasurer rests in his knowledge that certain checks should be made out and sent, not in his ability to sign his name.

Nevertheless, despite these two quite weak illustrations, the idea took immediate root. (Many earlier writers had noted the possible discrepancy between authority and expertise, of course, but Parsons made it famous.) Everyone, it appears, could think of superiors who were less competent than their subordinates, and the bureaucratic dilemma of expertise and discipline was firmly established. Alvin Gouldner used it as the organizing basis for his previously mentioned study of a gypsum plant, *Patterns of Industrial Bureaucracy.*[45] In his hands, it became the explanation for two contrasting bureaucratic patterns—representative bureaucracy, which relied on expertise "based on rules established by agreement, rules which are technically justified and administered by specially qualified personnel, and to which consent is given voluntarily," and punishment-centered bureaucracy, "based on the imposition of rules, and on obedience for its own sake."[46] He, too, thought that Weber saw things two ways; in one, administration was based on expertise, and in the other "Weber held that bureaucracy was a mode of administration in which obedience was an end in itself."[47] (That Weber held nothing of the sort regarding obedience is not important here; it is the distinction that is. Gouldner's representative pattern, incidentally, is based on the slim reed of a safety rule.)

Stanley Udy, studying records of organizations in primitive societies, and Ar-

[42]Ibid., p. 60.

[43]Perrow and Goss in *The Hospital in Modern Society.*

[44]Parsons, "Introduction," in Weber, *The Theory of Social and Economic Organizations,* p. 60.

[45]Gouldner, *Industrial Bureaucracy.*

[46]Ibid., p. 24.

[47]Ibid., p. 22.

thur Stinchcombe, in his discussion of the organization of the construction industry, come to much the same conclusion—that there are two fundamentally different forms of organizations, rational or professional organizations and bureaucratic ones.[48] But data on primitive organizations, and the statistics from the construction industry, have dubious relevance for modern large-scale organizations, though both of these studies are excellent for other purposes. The next use of the distinction is by Peter Blau in the article cited above, where it sets the stage for his analysis.[49] But it is apparent that the professionalized (and more hierarchical) organizations are the closest to the Weberian ideal, as we have seen. Blau's data thus support the opposite conclusion—professionalism is consistent with bureaucracy. While Weber asserted the importance of strict discipline, he was much more emphatic about the critical importance of expertise.[50]

But the most extensive use of this distinction has been in the voluminous literature on professionals in organizations; it was the hottest single topic in the field of organizational analysis during the early 1960s and continues to be discussed. With the increasing importance of university-trained scientists and engineers in organizations, the expense of these people, and the need to keep their morale high in a highly competitive employment market, a number of social scientists began to study their adjustment to industrial organizations. Some of these studies were concerned mostly with research laboratories, where the work was complex, innovative, unstructured, and unpredictable. These were truly new organizations that were difficult to cut to the bureaucratic pattern. Some sense of the enormous importance of charismatic leadership, individual autonomy, and serendipity can be gleaned from the fascinating account of the way J. Robert Oppenheimer directed the large Los Alamos laboratory, where the first atomic bombs were built, during World War II.[51] The

[48]Stanley H. Udy, Jr., "'Bureaucracy' and 'Rationality' in Weber's Organization Theory," *American Sociological Review* 24 (1959): 591–595; Arthur L. Stinchcombe, "Bureaucratic and Craft Administration of Production," *Administrative Science Quarterly* 4 (1959): 168–187.

[49]Blau, "Hierarchy."

[50]See Weber, *The Theory of Social and Economic Organizations,* pp. 337–339, for the following: "The primary source of bureaucratic administration lies in the role of technical knowledge. . . . Bureaucratic administration means fundamentally the exercise of control on the basis of knowledge. This is the feature of it which makes it specifically rational. . . . Bureaucracy is superior in knowledge, including both technical knowledge and knowledge of the concrete fact."

[51]Nuel Pharr Davis, *Lawrence and Oppenheimer* (New York: Simon & Schuster, 1968), Chapters 6 and 7. General Groves is reported to have said, "Here at great expense the government has assembled the world's largest collection of crackpots" (pp. 173–174). He proceeded to run it like an asylum as well as a factory. Group leaders were required to turn in reports on the daily hours worked by Nobel laureates and other top scientists. The purpose, which they did not know, was to keep down absenteeism. "The payroll office did not know what to do with work reports ranging up to a preposterous and unreimbursable eighteen hours a day." The military police closed up the labs at five o'clock every afternoon. Said a physicist, "Apparently they didn't have orders to throw us out, but they did have orders to lock up the supplies. We sawed around the locks on the stockroom doors and just stayed and worked. We kept a refrigerator full of sandwich stuff because everybody was pretty hungry by four in the morning, our usual quitting time. After a while, whoever was directing the M.P.'s caught the spirit of the thing and stopped replacing the locks" (p. 181). Another scientist contrasted the University of California lab at Berkeley, run by Ernest Lawrence, with the Los Alamos complex. They were similar only in the long hours put in. "The difference was the atmosphere. There you did whatever task they assigned you and learned not to ask why. Here (Los Alamos) you asked what you liked and at least thought you did what you liked. There the pressure came from outside. Here there didn't seem to be any pressure" (pp. 181–182).

efforts of General Groves (under whom Oppenheimer worked) to bureaucratize the enterprise—to treat it as if it were turning out Sherman tanks—had disastrous effects on morale and productivity. This example is more pertinent for understanding professionals than, say, studies of such research labs as Bell Laboratories or the DuPont experimental station, since in the Los Alamos case a single product was turned out—a bomb. In the labs, the administrative organization is an umbrella over scores of individual or small-group projects that produce diverse outputs unrelated to one another. To generalize from this highly decentralized type of operation to the usual case of large groups of professionals working on various aspects of one problem or product is misleading.

Many of the studies of scientists in industry, however, did deal with actual industrial organizations with a common problem focus rather than with university-like basic research labs. They revealed, in keeping with antibureaucratic views, that scientists did indeed resent the constraints placed on them by the organization in general, and by their superiors in particular, and preferred the luxuries of academic life such as flexible schedules, few deadlines, uninhibited bull sessions, conference going, freedom to publish, and so on. This is not surprising. If you present yourself as a sociologist or a psychologist from a university and ask if these things are not valued more than profits, production deadlines, and restrictions on publications and inability to study whatever problem one is interested in, the answer is very likely to be yes. The hypothesis is confirmed: there is a conflict between professional values and bureaucratic ones.

However, if one asked a question such as the following, the answer might be quite different: "Would you sooner spend most of your time working on a basic problem that might result in an academic journal publication, but be of little value to the company, or on a problem the company is interested in which might bring you a handsome bonus and a promotion?" Such a question has not been asked, but it poses the dilemma in realistic terms. I suspect that the majority of scientists and engineers in industry would choose the profitable project. The reasons are close at hand. The education these people receive in a university is from departments that are vocationally oriented.[52] Engineering departments and such science departments as chemistry and geology are designed to meet industrial needs, at least at the undergraduate level, and in many places at the graduate levels. Professors in these departments judge the quality of their teaching by the status of the companies in which their students obtain jobs. The professors also consult with industrial firms. The curriculum is designed to be relevant to industrial employment. The large majority of the students go into industry. Once there, they find that the route to power, prestige, and money is through serving the company and, in particular, through getting out of technical work and into management. Dalton has observed that the action and the rewards are in line positions rather than in staff (professional) positions.[53] A study by Fred Goldner and R. R. Ritti of recent engineering gradu-

[52]See Harold L. Wilensky, "The Professionalization of Everyone?" *American Journal of Sociology* 70 (September 1964): 137–158, for a discussion of the role of the training institution in the process of professionalization.

[53]Dalton, *Men Who Manage;* see also "Conflicts Between Staff and Line Managerial Officers," *American Sociological Review* 15 (1950): 342–351.

ates, conceived without a bias in favor of a conflict between scientists and managers, found that "from the start of their business careers many engineers have personal goals that coincide with the business goals of the corporations."[54] Business-oriented goals, dealing with power and participation in the affairs of the company, were ranked far above professional goals.

Furthermore, although it is rarely noted, managers also are usually college-trained—for example in law, business administration, and economics. Are they not professionals, too? Presumably they would prefer to work in a universitylike atmosphere if they could have the power and the income provided by industry at the same time. They, too, resent supervision and discipline and if asked the proper questions would probably question the profit goal of business even as do scientists. In fact, the student with a master's degree in business administration will hear more about the "social responsibilities" of business than the scientist.

Finally, the distinction made by Parsons and invoked by so many since then fails to recognize the *technical* character of administration. That is, though the scientist promoted to a supervisory position will soon lose some of her *scientific* technical competence (she cannot keep up with the field; the new graduates know the latest things in some cases; she loses touch with the practical, daily problems), she is probably promoted on, and expected to exercise and increase, her *administrative* technical competence. The job of the scientific manager is to manage, not to do research. It is a very common observation in industry that the best scientists do not make the best managers; the skills required are quite different, even though the manager of scientists must know a good bit about the technical work of these specialists. The same is true of the manager in marketing, finance, personnel, and even production. By assuming that official incumbency of a supervisory role has no relationship to expertise (expertise in management, in this case), it is possible for critics of the bureaucratic model to suggest a hiatus between expertise and occupancy of an official position. It was Weber's simple but enduring insight to see how crucial expertise was as a requirement for holding office throughout the hierarchy. The critics of bureaucracy have failed to utilize that simple insight when they propose that the official is not an expert in anything but survival. Far more damning would be the criticism that bureaucracy, by enfeebling so many workers, has made management a specialized skill demanding expertise.

SUMMARY

When we attribute the ills of organizations and those of our society to the bureaucratization of large-scale organizations, as we are so wont to do, we may be only fooling ourselves. We may be talking about specific instances of maladministration, of which there will naturally be many since people are more or less imperfect, or

---

[54]Fred Goldner and R. R. Ritti, "Professionalization as Career Immobility," *American Journal of Sociology* 73 (March 1967): 491. This article contains a good discussion of the issues raised here, as well as citations and review of the literature that views the goals of professionals and managers (or the company) as in conflict. See also the critical review of the literature in Norman Kaplan, "Professional Scientists in Industry," *Social Problems* 13 (Summer 1965): 88–97.

we are talking about the uses to which the power generated by organizations is put. The presence of hierarchy, rules, division of labor, tenure provisions, and so on can hardly be blamed for maladministration or abuses of social power. Indeed, the bureaucratic model provides a greater check on these problems than do nonbureaucratic or traditional alternatives once you have managerial capitalism. Critics, then, of our organizational society, whether they are the radicals of the Left emphasizing spontaneity and freedom, the New Right demanding their own form of radical decentralization, or the liberals in between speaking of the inability of organizations to be responsive to community values, had best turn to the key issue of who controls the varied forms of power generated by organizations, rather than flail away at the windmills of bureaucracy. If we want our material civilization to continue as it is and are not ready to change the economic system drastically, we will have to have large-scale bureaucratic enterprises in the economic, social, and governmental areas. The development of industrialization has made this the most efficient way to get the routine work of a society done. If we were prepared to engineer a modest change in our economy, we could even reap more of the advantages of bureaucracy. Our present system of huge, inflexible firms dominating markets in highly concentrated industries costs us dearly. Large size distorts bureaucracy, encouraging the problems of outdated rules, improperly invoked hierarchies, particularism, and favoritism. If all but the few industries where capital investment must be enormous were limited to modest-sized firms of, say, less than 1,000 employees, they could be efficient, flexible, and limited in their market power.

In this chapter, we have, in effect, ranged over the model of bureaucracy drawn up by Weber, extending it in many places but rarely if ever modifying it greatly. Since the next two chapters deal with the attack on bureaucracy as a mechanistic, unfeeling, authoritarian system, I will summarize the basic Weberian model here. In Chapters 4 and 5 we will extend it.

Weber's model of bureaucracy contains three groups of characteristics: those that relate to the structure and function of organization, those that deal with means of rewarding effort, and those that deal with protections for the individuals.

Regarding the structure and functioning of the organization, Weber specified that the business of the organization be conducted on a continuous basis; that there be a hierarchy of offices, with each office under the control of a higher one; that this hierarchy entail a systematic division of labor based on specialized training and expertise; and that the division of labor specify the area of action for which the official is competent, the responsibilities he or she has in this regard, and the amount of his or her power or authority. The performance of duties is to be governed by written rules, imposed or enacted, and by written records (files) of acts and decisions already taken. This cluster of characteristics did two things for Weber's model: (a) it provided mechanisms for control over performance of individuals, and (b) it provided means for specialization and expertise and means for coordinating roles and preventing them from interfering with each other.

The second group of characteristics, dealing with rewards, specified that officials receive fixed salaries, graded by rank; and that officials did not own the means of production or administration, could not appropriate their offices, had to separate their private affairs and property from the organization's affairs and property, had to render an accounting of the use of organizational property, and had to consider their offices as their sole or primary occupation. The provision of salary rather than other forms of reward and the clear role separation contrasted sharply with charismatic and traditional forms of administration, but charismatic and traditional forms of rewards still linger in bureaucracies.

Finally, in contrast to other forms of administration, the rights of individuals are protected in the Weberian bureaucratic model. This is necessary not only to ensure a source of personnel but also to prevent the arbitrary use of power in the service of nonorganizational or antiorganizational goals. Officials serve voluntarily and are appointed; service constitutes a career with promotions according to seniority or achievement; obedience is owed to the officeholder, not to the person; officials are subject to authority only with respect to their official obligations; compulsion can be exercised only under definite conditions; and there is the right of appeal of decisions and statements of grievances.

Managerial Ideologies and the Origins of the Human Relations Movement

What Weber observed so perceptively in the first decade of this century was really quite revolutionary. While rules and regulations and clerks and managers had been around for centuries—building the pyramids in ancient Egypt, making ship's tackle on assembly lines in medieval Venice, counting the profits of the East India Company in post-Renaissance England, insuring the risky but fabulously profitable shippers of Holland in Rembrandt's time—something new had been wrought in the nineteenth century: "factory bureaucracy." We are only beginning to understand its profound importance.

As Weber clearly saw, but as we have failed to keep clearly in view, modern bureaucracy depends on a particular social structure: a citizen must not be able to survive on his or her own but has to work for someone else. All else follows from this. The employee must produce more than he or she is paid, to make it worthwhile for a boss to hire the employee. But without employees there would be little or no bureaucracy. It was not easy to get people to work for others and receive wages in return. Since the eighteenth century, when the system began, people have preferred either to be self-employed or to pay back a portion of their output to the person providing the land, seed, or tools and keep the surplus themselves. In nineteenth-century America the system of wage labor was so despised and novel that it was called "wage slavery."

The term is significant. Slavery was the closest thing to factory bureaucracy that people could conceive of; it was the closest precedent in history. (Another precedent was also invoked—the military—and people referred to the "industrial army" in attempting to describe the new situation.) In England, where the factory system began, the unnaturalness of working for someone else's profit twelve hours a day, seven days a week was so pronounced that the early factories had to rely on criminals and paupers to do the work. Nearly everyone else farmed and kept part of their output, while giving the rest to the landholder (who had the land on consignment from the Crown). The first mass of "free labor" (workers not tied by law and custom to the land of the nobles) was created by the enclosure acts. Noblemen found that by forcing their peasants off the farms and turning the farms into grazing land for sheep, they could make large profits from the burgeoning wool trade. The peasants resisted being dispossessed, but the state upheld the right of the nobles to breach the traditional arrangements. These peasants were the first large "labor supply" for the new factories.[1] Similar problems appeared in the nineteenth century in the United States; people preferred to farm, and factory owners turned to Europe for immigrants to work in the factories, actually sending recruiters abroad in some cases and providing transportation that the indentured servants or "wage slaves" would gradually pay for out of their wages.

Now we give it no thought at all. Only about 15 percent of our working population is able to get by without working for someone else. High schools, colleges, and universities train us to accept wage slavery. People continuously, and ruinously, try to go into business for themselves; some of the traditional professionals succeed in remaining independent, and of course the owners of businesses are self-employed, even while they employ others. The rest of us go to work for someone else.

The first factories did not need large numbers of wage slaves for any technological reasons; they were created by bringing people under one roof to do what they could do, and usually did do, on their own in their homes. Under one roof they could be controlled better, made to work longer hours and for lower rates of pay. They had no choice. Either they had been forced off the farms, or, if they were already producing goods in their cottages on their own, they could not compete with the factory owners who got dependent people to work harder and longer for less. Once owners had large groups of dependent workers, machinery was designed to take advantage of this favorable state of affairs, and specialization and standardization proceeded apace. Without wage slaves there would be no point to huge steam-powered factories.[2]

The system was so notorious that legislation was enacted in nineteenth-century Britain to protect the factory workers a mite, and the founders of the first textile mills in the United States at first attempted to deliberately avoid the poverty, degradation, and exploitation they saw in the British textile mills. (Their enormous profits soon overwhelmed these noble impulses, though, and once they started importing Irish laborers, Lowell, Massachusetts, began to go the way of Manchester, England.)

By 1830 Britain was threatened with insurrection. The army was sent to the areas of unrest—the largest deployment of military force in the island's history—and police forces were created to put down worker revolts. Resistance to the factory in the United States was less (and conditions were probably better because of the labor shortage that even massive immigration could not meet), but our cities and towns are dotted with armories. These were not built in quaint castlelike designs to train the national guard. Rather, they were built as fortresses to put down a militant population that resisted factory work, poor working conditions, and perhaps above all, lack of independence.[3]

[1]See Francis Hearn, *Domination, Legitimization, and Resistance: The Incorporation of the Nineteenth-Century English Working Class* (Westport, Conn.: Greenwood Press, 1978).

[2]See David Montgomery, *Workers' Control in America: Studies in the History of Work, Technology, and Labor Struggles* (New York: Cambridge University Press, 1980), for an excellent study in the burgeoning field of working conditions in the nineteenth century.

[3]This was recognized in the early 1800s by Charles Babbage and Andrew Ure, who wrote about emerging industrial processes, but aside from Karl Marx, it was not noted again up until 1965 in Sidney Pollard,

In the middle and late nineteenth century, it was uncertain as to which way factory bureaucracy would develop in the United States. One path was pursued some decades later by Soviet Russia with Lenin's New Economic Plan of 1919, which embraced fierce labor control and Taylorism, and precisedly planned and timed the worker's every movement, removing all discretion from the job. It it is still in effect in most Soviet-bloc countries—and most inefficient for all concerned. It was tried in the United States, but labor and community resistance, aided by a roughly democratic form of government and an open and weak class system, made it impossible. Workers, for instance, fought pitched battles over the issue of fierce labor control. A second possible path took the form of a system of inside contracting, where capitalists supplied the building, materials, steam power, and major machinery, and contractors within the organization hired their own workers, made a yearly contract with the capitalist owner of the firm, and kept the surplus profits.[4]

This system had much to recommend it. Innovation was high, because the contractor reaped the rewards. Labor control was more communitarian, since contractors used relatives, friends, and ethnic and religious associates. (It was particularism on a grand scale, but so is "community.") Historians have sought, found, and emphasized the exploitation of workers by contractors, but even these selected cases do not exceed the exploitation practiced by owners in firms without subcontractors. The historical record is scanty, but one expects that the primary-group ties in the work group limited exploitation and encouraged group self-interest over the self-interest of the contractor. A final advantage was that the inside contracting system spread the wealth. Indeed, it was to appropriate the financial rewards that the contractors received that owners began to substitute salaried foremen for the contractors. Owners then reaped the profits that the contractors once earned. To a feeble extent, we are trying to recapture the advantages of this system today with group incentives, self-management, stock options for workers, and profit centers in our firms. It was in place in the largest and most technologically advanced firms in the middle and late nineteenth century.

A third path, which we actually took, was a middle course between the rigid control of Taylorism and the more open system of inside contractors. Employee rights were fought for and built into labor contracts; supervisory control was moderate, not extreme, in most organizations; wage bargaining limited to a small extent the extraction of maximum possible profits from the work of employees; and much later, government protections in the form of Social Security, unemployment insurance, health benefits, and the like were finally forthcoming.

The Genesis of Modern Management: A Study of the Industrial Revolution in Great Britain (New York: Cambridge University Press, 1965). Its implications were first exploited by Steven Marglin, "What Do Bosses Do?" *Review of Radical Political Economics* 6, no. 2 (Summer 1974): 33–60.

[4]The best work on inside contracting, Taylorism, and the organizational-control (rather than technological-efficiency) basis of what I call "factory bureaucracy" is Dan Clawson, *Bureaucracy and the Labor Process* (New York: Monthly Review Press, 1980). The literature in this area is burgeoning. Other key works are a seminal, but rather romantic, book by Harry Braverman, *Labor and Monopoly Capital* (New York: Monthly Review Press, 1974), as well as David Nobel, *America by Design* (New York: Knopf, 1977); and Richard Edwards, *Contested Terrain: The Transformation of the Workplace in the Twentieth Century* (New York: Basic Books, 1979).

By 1900 the revolution in the United States was over; bureaucracy was accepted as the normal human condition, and specialization, formalization, and hierarchy spread from the factory to the farm, government agency, research lab, hospital, university, and church. It was "efficient" (for the owners or the state). Wealth became increasingly concentrated at the top of society, but there was enough to trickle down and raise the standard of living of the middle and lower classes. The economic system has been enormously stable; the largest corporations of, say, 1910 are still the largest in their respective industries; the distribution of wealth in society has remained essentially the same since 1900 (highly concentrated); the principles of organizations, while more sophisticated and detailed today, are essentially those of Max Weber's time. We became a stable society of organizations, accepting our lot as wage earners toiling for large organizations, directly or indirectly. Organizational theory was among the first to accept the change and, indeed, as we shall see, to glorify the "imperative coordination" Weber identified as its key.

CLASSICAL MANAGEMENT THEORY

Max Weber's actual writings on bureaucracy did not reach either social scientists or those concerned with business administration in the United States until the 1940s. The material was not translated, and there was not much social science interest in the matter. Meanwhile, a theory of industrial and business management was being developed by practicing managers and professors in the growing business schools of the United States, drawing at times upon some influential European authors such as Henry Fayol. We will not discuss this body of literature, which is referred to as classical management theory or, sometimes, as the literature of the scientific management school; it is well summarized by Joseph Massie.[5] Two points need mentioning, however, since this school of thought is scorned by social scientists today. First, though the classical theory was derided for presenting "principles" that were really only proverbs,[6] all the resources of organizational research and theory today have not managed to substitute better principles (or proverbs) for those ridiculed. We have more now, but they are no more scientific or useful than the classical ones. Second, the principles, which amount to pious directives to "plan ahead," pay attention to coordination, refrain from wasting executive time on established routine functions and instead to deal with the exceptional cases that come up, served management very well. As obvious as "plan ahead" sounds, it took a lot of saying back in the 1920s, for business rarely did any planning.[7] (Today the injunctions parade under the name of "Management by Objectives," and in more mathematical terms, PERT.) It was also quite a struggle to separate the chief

[5]Joseph Massie, "Management Theory," in *The Handbook of Organizations*, ed. James March (Chicago: Rand McNally, 1965), pp. 387–422.

[6]See the slashing criticism by Herbert Simon in his *Administrative Behavior*, 3rd ed. (New York: Free Press, 1976).

[7]For an account of how little they did and how much shock was required to force planning, see Harold Wilensky, "Intelligence in Industry," *Annals, American Academy of Social Science* 388 (March 1970): 46–58.

executive (often the founder or his relative) from routine affairs—to get him to delegate authority and deal only with the exceptions. It still is. Finally, a successful and durable business of management consulting and an endless series of successful books rest on the basic principles of the classical management school. These principles have worked and are still working, for they addressed themselves to very real problems of management, problems more pressing for managers than those discussed by social science.

The problems advanced by social scientists have been primarily the problems of human relations in an authoritarian setting. The how, when, and why of these concerns form one of the most fascinating stories in the field of organizational analysis and industrial sociology. Why did management to some extent, and social science to an overwhelming extent, become so preoccupied with human relations in the workplace, with treating the worker well and trying to construct a nonauthoritarian environment in an authoritarian setting? Reinhard Bendix, in a fascinating book on the topic of management's justification for ruling in a variety of countries and times, provides the answer for the United States in one of his chapters.[8] His account is the indispensable background for the dominant strand of organizational theory today. I have summarized it here. (All page numbers listed below are references to pages in the Bendix book.)

FROM SURVIVAL OF THE FITTEST TO COOPERATION IN SIXTY YEARS

Classical management theorists, and Weber himself, had little to say about workers in industry or nonsalaried personnel in government. It was not until workers forced themselves on the consciousness of management by developing unions, or until a scarcity of labor occurred (due in part to the end of massive immigration), that those concerned with either organizational theory or principles of management practice began to include the worker within their purview. Workers had been simply another resource, like the machines that began to replace them in increasing numbers. They were docile, without effective organization, needed jobs, and were remarkably content to suffer extensive hardships in the workplace and in the marketplace. Extensive, lasting unionization did not appear in the United States until the 1910s, in contrast to other industrializing countries where it began to develop fifty years earlier.

In this country, there was a special problem facing management—namely, ideology. On the one hand, democracy stressed liberty and equality for all. On the other hand, large masses of workers and nonsalaried personnel had to submit to apparently arbitrary authority, backed up by local and national police forces and legal power, for ten to twelve hours a day, six days a week. Their right to combine into organizations of their own was severely limited or simply prohibited. How, asks Bendix, could entrepreneurs justify the "privilege of voluntary action and association for themselves, while imposing upon all subordinates the duty of obedience and the

[8]Reinhard Bendix, *Work and Authority in Industry* (New York: Wiley, 1956).

obligation to serve their employers to the best of their ability?" *(xxi)* This is the most crucial question a social science of organizations could ask, yet it has rarely been raised by students of organizations.

Social Darwinism

Bendix picks up the story in the 1880s, when the United States was lagging behind Britain, Germany, and France in industrialization. From about 1880 to 1910 "the United States underwent the most rapid economic expansion of any industrialized country for a comparable period of time." *(254)* The rapid expansion was accompanied by ruthless treatment of workers; the United States lagged far behind Britain in social reforms and unionization. Perhaps for this reason, the doctrine of Social Darwinism—the theory of survival of the fittest applied to social life rather than to animals—found more ready reception here than in Britain. Success and riches were regarded both as signs of progress for the nation, to be honored and cherished, and as the reward for those who had proved themselves in the struggle for survival. The struggle was a human battle; the "captains of industry" were better fighters than most of us, wrote sociologist C. R. Henderson in the *American Journal of Sociology* in 1896. *(256)* They fought on "the battlefield where the 'struggle for existence' is defining the industrially 'fittest to survive.' " Some saw success as the sign of virtue in the Christian mission of business enterprise ("What is the true conception of life but divine ownership and human administration?" asked a man of God); *(257)* some were more ruthless, stressing the role that the "lowest passions of mankind" played in human progress, since civilization would not advance if such evils were always avoided. But all agreed that success entitled a man to command; failure indicated the lack of the requisite personal qualities. And success was only for the few in the struggle for existence. "Many a man is entirely incapable of assuming responsibility," wrote N. C. Fowler in *The Boy, How to Help Him Succeed* in 1902. "He is a success as the led, but not as the leader. He lacks the courage of willingness to assume responsibility and the ability of handling others." *(259)*

For those who failed the test, so much the worse; they would be weeded out. Elbert Hubbard, whose book *A Message to Garcia* was extremely popular at the turn of the century, made the message clear (the title refers to a lieutenant who carried an important message to General Garcia in Cuba in spite of overwhelming odds):

> We have recently been hearing much maudlin sympathy expressed for the "downtrodden denizen of the sweatshop" and the "homeless wanderer searching for honest employment," and with it all often go many hard words for the men in power.
> Nothing is said about the employer who grows old before his time in a vain attempt to get frowsy ne'er-do-wells to do intelligent work; and his long patient striving with "help" that does nothing but loaf when his back is turned. In every store and factory there is a constant weeding-out process going on. No matter how good times are, this sorting continues, only if times are hard and work is scarce, the sorting is done finer—but out, and forever out, the incompetent and unworthy go. It is the survival of the

fittest. Self-interest prompts every employer to keep the best—those who can carry a message to Garcia. *(264–265)*

(Modernize the language and we have this ever popular message in the mathematical equations of that branch of modern economics called "agency theory"; see Chapter 7.)

But what if success eluded you? What was needed to ensure it? One answer was provided by the New Thought Movement of the late nineteenth and early twentieth centuries, designed to appeal to the ever hopeful and providing a more civilized explanation than the law of the jungle. The answer was mental power— the power of positive thinking. (It is still very much with us, providing hope for those who cannot accept luck, opportunity, or inferiority as the explanation for their failure.) According to the author of *Thought Force in Business*, "Business success is due to certain qualities of mind. Anything is yours, if you only want it hard enough. Just think of that. *Anything!* Try it. Try it in earnest and you will succeed. It is the operation of a mighty law."*(260)* The book titles tell the story: every backyard, even the lowliest, is strewn with *Acres of Diamonds* if you will only gather them. Just learn about *Your Forces and How to Use Them;* it is the key to *Mastery of Fate,* and *The Culture of Courage.* By 1925 Orison Sweet Marden had sold some 3 million copies of his various books, and unfortunate babies were named after him. One 1894 title: *Pushing to the Front, or Success Under Difficulties.*

The ethic was an individual one and the message for workers was clear. It was not circumstances, the chance of birth, opportunities provided by wealth and education, nor even luck that guided your fate; it was failure to try. But at least it was not that they were biologically unfit, as in Social Darwinism. The New Thought Movement did not directly challenge Social Darwinism, however, and one even finds the two in an uneasy blend.

The Collective Response of Unions

Meanwhile, workers were constructing their own explanations for the inequities of power and treasure in industry. In 1897 American trade unions had 487,000 members; seven years later they had 2,072,700. This enormous increase was accompanied by considerable violence on both sides, in the true form of the struggle for survival. But, in management's hands, the doctrine had not meant that workers *too* could struggle for existence; *that* would not serve society. As the president of the National Association of Manufacturers said in 1903:

> Organized labor knows but one law and that is the law of physical force—the law of the Huns and Vandals, the law of the savage. All its purposes are accomplished either by actual force or by the threat of force. . . . It is, in all essential features, a mob power knowing no master except its own will. Its history is stained with blood and ruin. . . . It extends its tactics of coercion and intimidation over all classes, dictating to the press and to the politicians and strangling independence of thought and American manhood. *(266)*

One of the objections to labor unions was that they represented collective action, not reflecting individual strength or individual will power. But that objection soon was overtaken by events, for employers found they could not fight trade unions individually; regardless of the ethic of individual responsibility, they had to band together. They had cooperated before with regard to problems of markets and government, but never to solve a problem within their own firms. Management's response was the "right to work" philosophy of the early part of the century—the "open shop" (no union) movement. Bendix analyzes the situation as follows:

> The rising tide of trade unionism forced American employers to acknowledge, however implicitly, that their own individual authority in the enterprise no longer sufficed. It is necessary to appreciate the novelty of this theme. American businessmen and industrialists were the recognized elite of society. Their great wealth was accepted as a well-earned reward for their outstanding fitness in the struggle for survival. And when these ideas were applied to the relations between capital and labor, the workers were merely admonished to struggle for survival on the terms acceptable to their employers. Yet at this pinnacle of their social recognition, American businessmen were challenged by the trade unions. And they were challenged in the employer's central activity, the management of his "own" plant, where his authority was supposedly absolute. It is not surprising that the ideology of the open shop, the employers' response to this challenge, came to embody all the sacred symbols by which their own fortunes could be identified with the foundation of the social order. *(267)*

One of the important consequences of the challenge was that the nature of the employers' authority was in doubt. If it had been absolute, there would have been no labor problem; the offending worker would have been dismissed. If a labor problem was admitted, authority was not adequate to deal with it; otherwise, the problem would not have existed. The sad fact was that authority was being questioned by the unions. One article compared the machine tool with the "human machine" and found the latter regretfully lacking. The machine tool was "never obstinate, perverse, discouraged," and if something went wrong it could be corrected. "If the human machine could be controlled by the set rules that govern machine tool operation, the world would be a much different place."

But since it could not, and because labor had become a problem, this tended "to eat the heart out of the glorification of success," as Bendix puts it. A change in ideology was in the making, and a 1910 article admitted that it was not only hard work and the goal of success that mattered, but the employee should also gain the "confidence, respect, and cooperation of his employer." *(271–274)* This was significant because it recognized that the employer could prescribe the conditions of success or failure; it was not just a question of hard work, jungle laws, or positive thinking.

Enter Science

Even more destructive of the Social Darwinist struggle for survival as an ideology of management was the rise of "Scientific Management," founded by Frederick W. Taylor early in the twentieth century. Briefly, the goal of Scientific Management was to analyze jobs very carefully into their smallest aspects, scrutinize the capabilities of the human machine just as carefully, and then fit the two together to achieve the greatest economy. Job techniques would be redesigned to make maximum use of human abilities; humans would be trained to perform the jobs optimally.

It is difficult to think of this as a breakthrough, since it seems so obvious; but it was a breakthrough for several reasons. Most important, it took skills from the hands of the workers and gave them to engineers, decreasing the owners' dependency upon workers. As mentioned earlier in this chapter, under the prevalent inside contracting system, workers were responsible for many technological innovations, and through the contractor they presumably reaped some of the rewards. Now, under the deskilling program of Taylor, they found their wages reduced and their ranks split into finely graded distinctions that helped crush collective action. Deskilling labor saved costs. This was the crucial benefit to the owners (which Bendix hardly deals with). In terms of justification of authority, Taylorism had three advantages for management. First, it applied research (stopwatch clocking of the smallest movements) to work, rather than letting tradition guide it or letting each work group set its pace. Time-study specialists and industrial engineers continue this work today in most sophisticated factories. Second, it made some bow, at least, to the interests of the workers, arguing that such research permitted management to explore the possibilities for the workers' development, allowing them to advance to the highest level that their natural abilities would allow. In this view the struggle for survival is irrelevant if everyone works up to his or her own abilities; positive thinking will not affect the outcome of scientific research.

Third, this theory suggested that it is *cooperation* between labor and capital that brings success. In Taylor's view, this was the most important message, for it should take the eyes of labor and management off the *division* of the surplus (higher wages or higher profits) and instead turn them toward the problem of increasing the *size* of the surplus; in this fashion there could be both higher wages and higher profits. Indeed, under this enlightened system there would be no need for unions. Bendix argues that it meant the end of arbitrary power on the part of management; science would decide. The personal exercise of authority would cease. It hasn't, and whatever science exists is not neutral but pro-management. But Bendix is correct that the image of the employer was transformed in the process. "From a man whose success in the world made him the natural leader of the industrial order, he had become a leader of men whose success depended in part upon a science which would place each man in 'the highest class of work for which his natural abilities fit him.'" *(280)*

Employers, however, did not at first embrace the ideology of Taylorism, even though deskilling, bureaucratization, and control were proceeding apace. For one thing, Taylorism "questioned their good judgment and superior ability which had been the subject of public celebration for many years." *(280)* It reduced their discretion, placing it in the hands of technicians; it implied that management's failure to utilize the skills of workers was the reason for workers' inefficiencies and restiveness. Indeed, Congress conducted hearings on Taylorism, so lively was the debate and so suspicious were employers. But the effect was to break the hold of the old ideologies. Indeed, the ideal of cooperation appeared to many to be a more useful ideological underpinning than Social Darwinism. It was apparent that sheer initiative or a fighting spirit was not appropriate in increasingly large, complex, bureaucratized firms. Also, the union movement, while subsiding after World War I, was a permanent fixture, and employers would have to fight its expansion and its encroachments on managerial prerogatives with more subtle ideological weapons— even as they continued to use violence. Company unions (plantwide organizations of workers set up and controlled by management) were established, and welfare schemes were introduced to counter social unrest and the threat of socialism. Management as a class became separate from ownership, and by 1920 there were three partners, not just two—capitalists, managers, and labor. Workers now were not expected to emulate their superiors and achieve success, but to accept the modest rewards and inherent satisfactions of good work. *(285)* By 1928, conversely, a management journal urged: "Treat workers as human beings. Show your interest in their personal success and welfare." *(294)*

The Responsibility to Lead

By 1935 a completely new note was sounding, one that was to figure heavily in the more theoretical works of two grandparents of present-day organizational theorists, Elton Mayo and Chester Barnard: "People are tractable, docile, gullible, uncritical —and wanting to be led. But far more than this is deeply true of them. They want to feel united, tied, bound to something, some cause, bigger than they, commanding them yet worthy of them, summoning them to significance in living." *(296)* This observation is, of course, an ancient justification for leadership (and especially totalitarianism), but it signified a clean break from the previous ideologies. Workers would realize fulfillment through working hard to maximize the profit of owners; large-scale, hierarchical industrial organizations were plainly good for people. Left to themselves, people are not of much use; in organizations they can be "summoned to significance in living." This was a far cry from the beliefs of a century earlier, when to work in a large organization was to be a "wage slave."

One implication of the changing emphasis was that employers were now enjoined to do something about or for the workers. Bendix notes:

> As long as they had regarded success itself as the sign of virtue and of superior qualities, no further justification of industrial leadership had been necessary. The counterpart of this belief had been that failure was the sign of vice and incapacity. And since success and failure resulted from the struggle for survival, it was beyond the reach of human interference. Now employers and managers proposed to do something about workers who failed to produce efficiently and to cooperate fully. Apparently they were no longer satisfied to regard such failure as the unavoidable outcome of the competitive struggle. Instead they would investigate the causes of failure and prevent their recurrence by the development of appropriate managerial policies. The qualities of leadership needed for this purpose were necessarily different from, and less self-evident than, those required for success in the struggle for survival. Among American employers the superiority of industrial leaders was as unquestioned as ever, but it had become the subject of discussion as well as of celebration. *(298)*

This meant that, as stated in *American Management Review* in 1924, "The study of the employee's mind alone will not solve, and often confuses, the problem. The mind of management is also an integral part of human relationships in industry." *(299)*

Along with the increasing responsibility of management for the character of the workplace went a change in the qualities managers were expected to have in order to succeed. In the mid-nineteenth century, those qualities were "industry, arrangement, calculation, prudence, punctuality, and perseverance." These are the moral traits of a person acting alone. They do not deal with interpersonal relations, leadership, or even competence. But industry was not very complex at the time, and such things as prudence and punctuality perhaps needed emphasis and may have even been decisive. A list from the year 1918 provides a dramatic contrast: intelligence, ability, enthusiasm, honesty, and fairness. Ten years later the lists had gone even farther: the leader should be worthy of his authority, eager to acquire new information, willing to learn from subordinates, anxious to see them develop, able to take criticism and acknowledge mistakes. Furthermore, these qualities were not inherited but could be developed through training. *(301)* That managers might submit to training in itself shows how great the change was. This last list, emphasizing leadership, interpersonal relations, and competence, would do very nicely today, sixty years later, and could be duplicated in a casual reading of management journals.

It was in such an environment that Dale Carnegie's *Public Speaking and Influencing Men in Business* could flourish. (It was later titled *How to Win Friends and Influence People,* suggesting a more universalistic application.) Emphasizing will power but also manipulative techniques that induce the cooperation of subordinates, Dale Carnegie Institutes have become a permanent fixture among the services available to business and are still widely used. The 1926 volume became the "official text" of many progressive organizations, such as American Telephone and Telegraph (AT&T), and management associations. As with the leadership list, the concerns were interpersonal relations and the handling of people.

Persuasion and Cooperation

The next major change in the ideologies of management was the assertion of the basic identity of the nature of managers and workers, even though the one, naturally, had developed some aspects of their nature more fully than the other. This came about with the social philosophy of Elton Mayo as applied to industrial cooperation. Unlike Taylor, Mayo broke with the tradition of regarding each worker as a wage-maximizing individual in isolation. He attacked what he called the "rabble hypothesis" of economic theory that was being used in industry and that still guides much of economics. There were three tenets to that hypothesis, said Mayo, and he took exception to all three: society consisted of unorganized individuals—discrete atoms rather than natural social groups; each individual acts according to calculations of his or her own self-interest, rather than being swayed by group norms; and each individual thinks logically, rather than being swayed by emotions and sentiments.

It was a brilliant criticism, heralding much modern organizational theory. Today we emphasize the group context of behavior and the way in which context shapes the individual's goals, which are not solely self-interested. And by denying that behavior is always logical or rational, Mayo anticipated the powerful influence of Herbert Simon's notion of bounded (limited) rationality. But as we shall see in Chapter 7, economists who now study the internal processes of organizations still expound a modified version of the "rabble hypothesis" that Mayo assailed.

Mayo's alternative is not as fully developed as today's social psychological and sociological theories of organizational processes; it strikes one as quite romantic and primitive in its conceptualization. But as an alternative to the theories of the 1920s and 1930s it was dramatic. (The best summary is his 1945 book *The Social Problems of an Industrial Civilization.*) He emphasized the desire to be in good standing with one's fellows, the role of emotions, and the instincts of human association. Economic self-interest was the exception rather than the rule. This held for all people, whether owners, managers, or workers. They must all cooperate if civilization were to survive. But, almost inevitably, the distinction between workers and others crept back in Mayo's writing. The administrative elite of owners and managers had more capacity to engage in logical thinking and calculation than the workers. It was a capacity born of the necessity of guiding complex organizations. Therefore, the elite had a greater responsibility for providing an organizational environment in which employees could fulfill their "eager human desire for cooperative activity." *(315)* People found themselves in organizations.

After analyzing the functioning of the most extensive human relations programs in the 1950s, Bendix concludes that Mayo's contribution found only limited acceptance in managerial practices but that its influence upon management ideology was pervasive. *(319)* A new vocabulary of motives was constructed out of his view of humankind as preeminently social and cooperative; it would offer new justifications for management authority and worker obedience.

Mayo's philosophy was severely criticized by many social scientists. His statements about "spontaneous" cooperation and his longing for a medieval past where each person knew his or her place in a cooperative endeavor made him an easy target, especially in the late 1930s and the 1940s, when labor's chances of gaining power in industry rested not on spontaneous cooperation but on the legitimization of industrial conflict through collective bargaining and strikes. Mayo's critics felt that his view of cooperation was espoused at the expense of labor and on the terms of management and other legitimate and exploitative segments of society.

Summary

The ideologies of management had gone from Social Darwinism to social cooperation in about half a century. Table 1 suggests the radical nature of this change. For example, the explanations for employee failure or problems with employees run from biological unfitness to incorrect handling. The changes in ideology, of course, went hand in hand with the changes in the structure and technology of industry. As it became more bureaucratized, large, and mechanized, interpersonal problems loomed larger and those of the sheer force of will, inventiveness, or effort declined. As responsibility for costly machinery and breakdowns in assembly lines became greater, even deskilled workers needed to be retained because of their experience,

Table 1 Managerial Ideologies[9]

What is the justification for management rule and worker obedience?

EXPLANATORY DOCTRINE	CHARACTERIZATION OF OWNERS OR MANAGERS	PERIOD AND DOCTRINE	POSITIVE CHARACTERIZATION OF EMPLOYEES	EXPLANATIONS OF EMPLOYEE FAILURE
Survival of the fittest	Superior individuals	1870: Social Darwinism	Independence, initiative, aggressiveness	Biologically unfit
Survival of the best	Moral superiority and will power	1895–1915: New Thought Movement	Proper thoughts; will power	Will not try
The fit dictate conditions of success	Power by virtue of position and success	(Unionization)	Compliance, worthiness of management's respect	Insubordinate, unworthy
Scientific determination	Skillful utilization of labor, efficiency	1915—, Scientific Management	Trainability, utilization of capabilities to the fullest	Will not work or learn
Manipulation	Personality skills	Post–World War I: Dale Carnegie	Cooperation by inducement, stable expectations and rewards	Will not cooperate as a partner
Natural cooperation, rational assessment of whole person	Personality skills, statesmanship, rationality, and logic	Mid-1930s: Elton Mayo	Nonlogicality, desire for security and recognition	Not handled correctly

[9]Largely based on Bendix, *Work and Authority in Industry.*

and specialized craft jobs grew. As immigration dried up and capital investments increased (making work stoppages more costly for management), unionization became a more potent weapon. Attitudes of the public and of public officials also changed, of course, making Social Darwinism a less acceptable explanation.[10]

The new ideologies of management, however, rested not on fixed qualities of managers or the system; instead, they stressed things that management had to *do*, such as discovering a common purpose or making a deliberate effort to structure a cooperative system. The eager desire for cooperation was there; it was up to management to give it rein. At the same time as this ideology was born, the instruments for its expression were being created in the business schools and social science departments of the nation. Workers could be studied not only by time and motion engineers, but by psychologists, social psychologists, and sociologists. The vast amount of empirical work undertaken by these academicians in industrial (and military) studies was eventually to culminate in our present-day theories of organizations. The first to construct the theoretical outlines of the major theory of organizations existing today was the businessman Chester Barnard.

BARNARD'S COMPANY TOWN

When Barnard was writing *The Functions of the Executive*[11] in the late 1930s, hardly anything around qualified as an academic theory of organizations in the United States. As Bendix indicated,[12] there was a growing emphasis on the cooperative nature of business enterprises—a vague and uncomfortable ideology that capital, management, and labor somehow had to unite for the good of all. From the Social Darwinism of the late 19th century, management ideology had moved through a

[10]For a good general survey of the social problems of the Industrial Revolution and the conflicting schools of thought, see Part 1 of Harold L. Wilensky and Charles N. Lebeaux, *Industrial Society and Social Welfare*, rev. ed. (New York: Free Press, 1965). Wilensky's introduction to this edition is as pertinent as it was twenty years ago. It includes, for example, material on the lack of support for working women. This subject should become explosive in the 1980s, but since the feminist movement has sadly given a low priority to the problem of child rearing while women work full time and instead has emphasized equal rights, the injustice may continue. "Why can't a woman be like a man?" asks Henry Higgins in George Bernard Shaw's *Pygmalion*. She can, say the feminists. But as the careful surveys of Alfred Kahn and Sheila Kamerman show—for example, Kamerman, Kahn, and Paul Kingston, *Maternity Policies and Working Women* (New York: Columbia University Press, 1983)—and as Sylvia Ann Hewlett brilliantly analyzes in her *Paper Tigers* (New York: Morrow, 1985), she will have a very hard time in the United States if she tried to both work full-time and bear and rear children. Yet about 40 percent of women have to try. Women have entered the labor force in large numbers with several strikes against them. First, because of household and child-caring duties that men generally refuse to share, they have no time to spend on union-organizing activity, at a time when unions are declining and seeking to preserve the gains for the elite workers in high-wage industries. Second, employment growth is limited overwhelmingly to low-skilled jobs in low-paid service industries. Third, today's conservative political environment emphasizes individualism and free markets, while working women need protective legislation because of their dual burden. Finally, the feminist movement is also unresponsive to women's dual burden. In Europe, in contrast, child rearing is treated as something socially necessary, similar to military service, and women's jobs are protected, maternity benefits are provided, careers are not interrupted, day care is provided, and the individual burden of child rearing is shared with the whole society.

[11]Chester Barnard, *The Functions of the Executive* (Cambridge, Mass.: Harvard University Press, 1938).

[12]Bendix, *Work and Authority in Industry*, Chapter 5.

number of doctrines that progressively weakened management's justification for authoritarian rule and led management to the uneasy position that it had a responsibility to join hands with labor in a common enterprise. Classical management theory was hardly adequate as a theory of organizations, since it relied on "plan ahead" proverbs and assumed that management was there to control the enterprise, divide the work rationally, pay minimum wages to ensure profit, and take advantage of a large and dependent labor market. It did not speak to the issues of unionism and industrial unrest. The Weberian model of bureaucracy would have been adequate because it was more complete, systematic, and theoretical than anything turned out by the management theorists. But this had not even been translated from the German by the 1930s and it would only begin to have an impact upon organizational theory at the end of the next decade. Besides, it was inconsistent with the growing concern with cooperation. The sweeping generalizations of Elton Mayo, offering a medieval order in the midst of a rapidly changing and expanding industrial civilization, were not appropriate. Parts of Mayo as well as classical management theory could be used, of course, but there was no coherent unified theory to encompass the new view of organizations.

The void was filled by Barnard's 1938 volume. This enormously influential and remarkable book contains within it the seeds of three distinct trends of organizational theory that were to dominate the field for the next three decades. One was the institutional school as represented by Philip Selznick (see Chapter 5); another was the decision-making school as represented by Herbert Simon (see Chapter 4); the third was the human relations school (see Chapter 3). The leading theorists of these schools freely acknowledged their debt to Barnard. It would not be much of an exaggeration to say that the field of organizational theory is dominated by Max Weber and Chester Barnard, each presenting different models, and that the followers of Barnard hold numerical superiority. All those simplified, dramatic dichotomies —such as mechanical systems versus organic systems; production-centered versus employee-centered organizations; rigid, inflexible versus adaptive, responsive organizations; and authoritarian versus democratic organizations—stem from the contrast of the Weberian and the Barnardian models.[13]

The Barnardian model went beyond the pious statements that labor and management should cooperate and that cooperation would reduce conflict or raise productivity. Barnard was the first to insist, at length, that organizations *by their very nature* are cooperative systems and cannot fail to be so.

In a sense this is true. People do cooperate with one another in organizations, or in any enduring social group for that matter. In organizations, the cooperation goes beyond formal rules, is not precisely calculated to conform to the amount of wages or salary, is frequently spontaneous and generous, and, by and large, is in the interests of the goals of the organization. But, in the Weberian view, this is hardly the essence of organizations, since people are basically constrained to cooperate because of hierarchy of authority, separation of office and person, and so on. As we

---

[13]Terence K. Hopkins, "Bureaucratic Authority: The Convergence of Weber and Barnard," in Amitai Etzioni, *Complex Organizations* (New York: Holt, Rinehart & Winston, 1962), pp. 159–167, attempts to reconcile the two but himself comes to the conclusion that only on the most general level—organizations are both coordinated and imperative systems—is this really possible.

say today, these are "structural" sources of cooperation, and creating the best structure for a particular organization is difficult and never fully realized. For Barnard, however, cooperation is the essence of organizations. He emphasized cooperation almost to the exclusion of such things as conflict, imperative coordination, and financial inducements. His position is somewhat extreme, but because it underlies so much of organizational theory today, the remainder of this chapter will be devoted to rather close criticism of it.

To read Barnard today is a chore, and I do not recommend it except for historical analysis. Barnard knew he was breaking new ground, and as a careful executive (he was president of New Jersey Bell Telephone Company, a part of the Bell Telephone System that breeds and honors careful executives), he may have felt compelled to examine and classify every lump of soil in tedious detail. The first sixty-one pages of his book consist of an attempt to ground his work in some kind of theory of human interaction, complete with epistemological discussions; this section is most notable for the endless presentation of categories on categories and the relentless analysis of workers moving a stone. Yet to unravel this semiphilosophical treatise is to gain an insight into a basic posture of a good part of organizational theory.

The Setting

Barnard was confronted with a difficult problem. The United States was only beginning to cope with the Great Depression; it did not know that a war around the corner would increase productivity as twentieth-century capitalism itself had not. The prospects were grim indeed around 1936 and 1937, when Barnard was writing. Throughout the 1930s social unrest had been high, and the legitimacy of established organizations was being questioned. Radical ideologies were strong among the intelligentsia, and direct and often violent action was apparent among the working classes. Yet to respond to this perilous situation with an authoritarian model harking back to the days of Social Darwinism was not appropriate for a subtle and highly intelligent social philosopher in those years.

The Bell System, that until recently giant web of organizations, was one of the first to adopt the principles of treating workers decently and considering them as partners in a triumvirate of capital, management, and labor. The president of AT&T wrote in a business journal in 1926 of the cooperative nature of the company and its obligations to investors, employees, and patrons. In testimony before the Federal Communications Commission in 1936, he re-emphasized this and said that his loyalties were divided as equally as possible among the three parties. The question was raised as to whether labor was not bearing the brunt of the Depression rather than the investors, thus making the partnership hardly equal, since throughout the Depression AT&T had managed to adhere to the principle of the $9 dividend on each share of stock while the number of employees had been reduced by nearly 40 percent.[14] As president of a subsidiary of AT&T, Barnard was of course aware of

---

[14]The reduction in workers had begun before the Depression hit AT&T and could not be accounted for by the level of business that the firm had. At the end of 1937 it was doing more business than in

such issues. In fact, in an earlier position he had performed an essentially political role in dealing with the federal government.[15] Given these kinds of challenges, the state of the nation in the mid-1930s, and the state of organizational theory, what was Barnard's response?

The Moral Organization

First, organizations per se had to be defended and even sanctified. It is significant that the opening sentence of Barnard's book reads as follows: "With all the thought that has been turned upon the unrest of the present day in the literature of social reform, one finds practically no reference to formal organization as the concrete social process by which social action is largely accomplished."[16] That formal organizations were largely responsible for the Depression and the social unrest is, of course, not mentioned. Rather, belief in the power of individual action is alluded to as a basic cause of the trouble. Organizations, Barnard tells us, cannot fail to have a moral purpose. Society itself finds its form, its "structure and process," through formal organizations. The only goal of business, he says, can be service. It is not profit nor power nor political ideology and certainly not personal gain. The common purpose of an organization must always be a moral purpose, and to inculcate this moral purpose into the very fiber of the organization and its members is the only meaningful task of the executive.

This view is important; it is not a mere publicity handout by a corporation executive. Years later a similar position was set forth by one of the three or four leading organizational theorists, Philip Selznick, in his book *Leadership in Administration,* though Selznick wrote in far more sophisticated terms. The idea that power can exist or survive only if it is legitimate, which is found in the writings of Talcott Parsons,[17] represents a similar view. If organizations exist and have power, that power must be legitimized by society and therefore given the mantle of morality. To question this would be to question the very "structure and process" of modern society.

Why were organizations moral for Barnard? Not simply because of the key role of the executive inculcating moral purpose, though that is important, but because organizations are cooperative systems. People cooperate in organizations. They join organizations voluntarily. They cooperate toward a goal, the goal of the organization. Therefore, the goal must be a common goal, a goal of all participants. Such a goal could not fail to be moral, because morality emerges from cooperative endeavors. Society could not exist without cooperation, and the clearest form of cooperation may be seen in organizations. Thus, in this view, if people cooperate in the pursuit

---

1929, but it still had about 30 percent fewer employees. Part of this was due to technological change, but a good part of it was due to the "speed-up" on the production line. See the discussion in N. R. Danielian, *AT&T, The Story of Industrial Conquest* (New York: Vanguard Press, 1939), pp. 200–221.

[15]Ibid., pp. 259, 260, 270.

[16]Barnard, *The Functions of the Executive*, p. 1.

[17]Talcott Parsons, *Structure and Process in Modern Societies* (New York: Free Press, 1960), p. 121.

of common goals, there can be no problem with the output of organizations; they must be moral institutions.

The Organization and the Individual

There are a number of thorny problems with Barnard's view. First, if the emphasis is on the collectivity—the organization or the cooperative *system*—how does one handle the individual? Barnard was worried about philosophies that emphasized the individual and his or her decisions or acts, since morality was a collective phenomenon. It is the Bell System that counted, not President Gifford of AT&T or President Barnard of New Jersey Bell. But how do you separate the individual from the organization? How can you talk about organizations without talking about individuals? This is a basic and enduring problem for all organizational theory. The "field" theory of Kurt Lewin, developed after Barnard's book was published, drew its strength from Lewin's attempt to discuss fields of forces rather than individuals. The interminable debate in the 1940s and 1950s over the old question of whether the group was more than the sum of its parts, and the almost inevitable but shaky answer of yes, is a similar illustration of this ontological problem. The current faddish term "synergism," indicating that something unique emerges from the interaction of discrete inputs of energy, is a reaffirmation of the reality (and superiority) of the collective character of a system. The persistent and unsatisfactory debate over whether there are such things as organizational goals, when only individuals would appear to be goal-directed sources of energy,[18] is another manifestation.

Barnard was the first, I believe, to confront this problem systematically and head-on in terms of formal organizations (though Emile Durkheim had done so for groups or society in general). It was essential for Barnard's ideology that the group win out. Therefore, he defined organizations as "nonpersonal." They do not consist of persons, or things such as machinery, or ideas such as technology, or even what he vaguely referred to as "social situations." Instead, the organization consists of "forces." These are emitted by persons, but persons themselves are not, strictly speaking, members of the organization. They are part of the environment of the organization, part of a larger cooperative system that includes the organization. He insists throughout the book that organizational actions are nonpersonal in character; even executive decisions do not reflect personal choice. It is because the activities of humans are *coordinated* to make a *system* "that their significant aspects are nonpersonal."[19]

This is an awkward position to hold, and even though Barnard does maintain it throughout the book, he is forced to distinguish between the organizational aspects of people and the personal aspects. He suggests "that every participant in an organization may be regarded as having a dual personality—an organization personality and an individual personality."[20] This is somewhat similar to the concept

---

[18]For a statement on this, see Herbert A. Simon, "On the Concept of Organizational Goal," *Administrative Science Quarterly* 9 (June 1964): 1–22.

[19]Barnard, *Functions of the Executive*, p. 77.

[20]Ibid., p. 88.

of an organizational "office," but the difference is important. The concept of office or social position pertains to prescribed duties and responsibilities. The person holds or "fills" the office. But he or she does not, except in exaggerated cases which are subjects of ridicule and humor, *become* the office, nor is the office an equivalent (except in exaggerated cases) of a personality. For Barnard, the identification is much stronger; the organizational personality is all-pervasive for the person acting as a member of an organization. For the five men moving a stone, he notes, it is not important what this means to each man personally once they have agreed to cooperate; what is important is what each thinks it means to the organization as a whole.[21] The extreme situation is, for Barnard, the best illustration of the concept: "In military action, individual conduct may be so dominated by organization personality that it is utterly contradictory of what personal motivation would require."[22]

This position allows Barnard not only to reify the organization (something that all organization theorists are forced to do to some extent) but to minimize the importance of personal choice. The executive makes decisions and thus chooses among alternatives, but these do not reflect personal choice. These actions are nonpersonal in character because the executive is part of a system of "consciously coordinated activities or forces of two or more persons,"[23] which is Barnard's definition of a formal organization. This allows him to speak contemptuously of "the exaggeration in some connections of the power and of the meaning of personal choice." The "connections" undoubtedly referred to some of the radical ideologies that were circulating during the Depression. These exaggerations of the power and meaning of personal choice, Barnard says, are "vicious roots, not merely of misunderstanding but of false and abortive effort."[24] True and productive effort will be performed through organizations.

The consequences of extolling the organization over the person are clear when we examine Barnard's insistence that organizations are superior to individuals. Organizations are rational; individuals are not. Or, in Barnard's terms, logicality emerges from the interaction of organizational personalities or the field of forces given off by people. Persons themselves, or individual actions, are likely to be nonlogical in character. Thus, one cannot define organizations as consisting of people, for then they would be nonlogical and by implication nonrational. He speaks of the "superlative degree to which logical processes *must* and *can* characterize organization action as contrasted with individual action."[25] Logic is not a characteristic of the individual but only of the coordinated relationship of individuals acting in terms of their organizational personality. Only in organization can we have the "deliberate adoption of means and ends" since this is the "essence of formal organization."[26]

This view is held by many organizational theorists. But the solution of Weber

---

[21]Ibid.
[22]Ibid.
[23]Ibid., p. 73
[24]Ibid., p. 15.
[25]Ibid., p. 186. (Italics added.)
[26]Ibid.

and classical management theorists is to see in the organization a means of control-ling individuals in the interests of the goals of the leaders of the organization. The organization is more rational than the individuals because order is imposed on members by those who control the organization, and the order is in the interests of goals or purposes established and guarded by those in charge. It is rationality only in the *leaders'* terms. For Barnard, the organization is more rational than the individuals because the organization is nonpersonal, or supraindividual; it is some-thing that extracts from individual behavior the logic based on common goals and willing cooperation. The duality that pervades Weber is that of the ruler and the ruled; the duality that pervades Barnard is that of the organizational personality and the individual personality.[27]

THE PROCESSES OF ORGANIZATION

Executive Decision Making

How, then, do organizations actually function? First, there is the key role of execu-tive decision making. Not only are leaders supposed to inculcate moral purpose into every member of the organization, but their main activity is to make the key, or, as Selznick put it years later, the "critical" decisions. As obvious as this may seem today, it was not so clear forty years ago. The role of the executive in the literature of that time was analyzed in much more general, vague, and moralistic terms. Barnard was groping his way toward an essentially behavioral analysis of leadership by singling out the importance of rational analysis of alternatives and selection of the best one. He felt that the direction an organization takes hangs on one or two major decisions made by an executive in a year. Possibly what Barnard had in mind were such things as Eddie Rickenbacker's decision, while he was president of Eastern Airlines, to emphasize cost reduction while competitive airlines were em-phasizing customer comforts and expansion of service. Rickenbacker's decision made a lot of money for Eastern for a number of years, but it proved to be the wrong one as the competitors overtook the company.[28] Sewell Avery's decision to sit on millions in Montgomery Ward cash and securities in anticipation of a post–World War II depression and to stick with small stores gave Sears a permanent lead, since the latter expanded by building large suburban stores as quickly as possible. And the decision of General William Westmoreland to engage in search-and-destroy activi-

[27]Only in some forms of conflict theory of organizations is the matter of rationality handled in such a way as to avoid these two positions. If different sets of actors are rationally pursuing different interests and goals, the question of organizational rationality is moot. It is the value, for example, of Erving Goffman's inconoclastic work on mental hospitals that he insists that presumably irrational patients, ruled over by rational staff members, are indeed quite rational in their perceptions and interests. The staff members, in the patients' view, appear quite irrational. In emphasizing this, Goffman tends to describe the hospital as irrational as an organization, but it is in reality only ineffectual. See Erving Goffman, *Asylums* (New York: Doubleday, 1961); and Charles Perrow, "Hospitals: Technology, Structure, and Goals," in *The Handbook of Organizations,* ed. James March, pp. 910–971.

[28]For this and other examples of critical decisions as to goals, see Charles Perrow, *Organizational Analysis: A Sociological View* (Belmont, Calif.: Wadsworth, 1970), Chapter 5.

ties in Vietnam, seeking out the enemy wherever he might be, was a critical executive decision that was reversed by his replacement, General Creighton Abrams. Barnard not only saw the significance of such key decisions but he saw the need to analyze executive behavior in these terms, rather than merely in moralistic ones.

Indoctrination

Despite his analysis of executive decision making, Barnard could not see the organization as the shadow of one person. He believed that all people must share the goals that the key decisions both reflect and shape. But if organizations are cooperative systems with all people working toward a common goal, how does one explain the fact that there is conflict in organizations, recalcitrance on the part of some members, lack of cooperation, and so forth? Barnard does admit that sometimes the ends of the person and the ends of the organization are not the same; indeed, he grants, they may be in opposition. He indicates that such opposition is most likely to occur among the lower-ranking participants in an organization. When faced with such opposition, the answer is not to buy off the opponents with inducements of higher wages, nor to threaten them with loss of employment, nor to let them participate in changing the goals of the organization. The answer is indoctrination.

When common purposes do not exist, the answer is to manufacture them. "The most important inherent difficulty in the operation of cooperative systems" is "the necessity for indoctrinating those at the lower levels with general purposes. . . ."[29] This may actually involve deception:

> We may say, then, that a purpose can serve as an element of a cooperative system only so long as the participants do not recognize that there are serious divergences of their understanding of that purpose as the object of cooperation. . . . Hence, an objective purpose that can serve as the basis for a cooperative system is one that is *believed* by the contributors (or potential contributors) to it to be the determined purpose of the organization. The inculcation of belief in the real existence of a common purpose is an essential executive function.[30]

Thus we have an inconsistency. Organizations consist of forces generated by people acting in concert to achieve common goals, but it turns out that the goals are not indeed always shared or common. And it is even difficult to identify goals that all would hold in common with the leaders once the leaders' aims are understood. So propaganda and indoctrination are necessary. The leaders apparently set the goals and then try to make sure that they are commonly held.

Inducements and Contributions

Another idea that does not fit with Barnard's cooperative view is that of the balance between "inducements and contributions." Only in recent years has it become

[29]Barnard, *Functions of the Executive*, p. 233.
[30]Ibid., p. 87.

fashionable to conceive of organizations as systems with inputs and outputs. Barnard was way ahead of his time when he did so in 1938. Each individual makes an input to the organization (a contribution) and receives some part of the output (an inducement). Work and loyalty are contributions. Wages, prestige, and the like are inducements. If there is an excess of inducements over contributions—if people do not give enough for what they get—the organization will fail. If the two are in balance, the organization will survive and will be in equilibrium.

The distinction between contributions and inducements was utilized extensively by Herbert Simon in his work ten years later.[31] Neither Simon nor Barnard, however, deals with the situation in which contributions exceed inducements. This accounts for profits. Presumably, it is in the interest of the organization, and certainly was in the interest of the Bell Telephone System during Barnard's reign, to make sure that people give more than they receive. Otherwise, the organization could not prosper, grow, and gather power. It is on precisely this analysis that unions make their case for a bigger share of the profits in the form of wage increases. There are other problems with the contributions-inducements theory. It is hard to escape the impression that it is obvious and tautological. If a worker leaves an organization, we say that the balance was upset for her; if she does not, it was not upset. But was it wages that caused her to leave, or other job opportunities, or dissatisfaction with the common purpose, or excess travel time, or the weather in that part of the country, or what? The theory does not tell us; presumably, something must have happened, but this is hardly enlightening.

There is a more serious problem. Why would the employees have to make elaborate calculations of inducements and contributions if the crux of the matter were cooperation in a *common purpose?* The inducements-contributions theory rests more easily with Weber or with the classical management school than with the cooperative school. (The human relations theorists have emphasized cooperation and neglected the inducements-contributions idea; Simon does just the reverse.) However, Barnard appears to minimize this contradiction by listing eight inducements,[32] only one of which is material in character. The other seven include such terms as "the condition of communion" and "associational attractiveness." Furthermore, he repeatedly denies that material inducements are very important to organizations. Thus, the calculations of inducements and contributions can be made in terms of whether employees rank the making of cars, butter, and guns as important common goals or not. One might well wonder whether Barnard seriously believed that the employees' acceptance of the purpose of General Motors, whether that might be profit, producing cars, or whatever, was "essential" for all members. Is such a purpose an important inducement? However, much of organizational theory, especially as encompassed in the human relations approach, appears to share his view.

It is essential to Barnard's view of organizations that the importance of economic incentives be consistently played down. It is striking to find him repeatedly

---

[31] Herbert Simon, *Administrative Behavior*, 3rd ed. (New York: Free Press, 1976): and James G. March and Herbert A. Simon, *Organizations* (New York: Wiley, 1958).

[32] Barnard, *Functions of the Executive*, p. 142.

asserting, during the Depression, "the almost negligible" role of material incentives " beyond the level of the bare physiological necessities."[33] He seems to be saying that workers will work for the wage that will just keep them alive, and they will derive their real satisfaction from such things as the condition of communion. Even the bare physiological necessities, this corporation president and major organizational theorist continues, "are so limited that they are satisfied with small quantities." Though the Depression is not mentioned in this book (social unrest is), in another volume Barnard notes that the food allowance for a person on relief was 6 cents a meal. Nevertheless, it is "wholesale general persuasion in the form of salesmanship and advertising" that has persuaded employees that money is important.[34] (He does not note that it is organizations that advertise; that would suggest an immoral output.) The logical organization is separated from the nonlogical environment as well as from the nonlogical individual.

Authority

A plain fact about organizations is that the people at the top have a lot more authority than those at the bottom. Authority to give orders, fire, fine, and otherwise control individuals is an essential part of organizations. This presents something of a problem for those who believe in a cooperative system. Barnard's solution, widely cited and firmly embraced by many theorists, is that authority comes from the bottom. The subordinate makes a decision to grant authority to the person above him or her. If a subordinate does not accept the legitimacy of an order, the person giving it has no authority.[35] The idea is an old one, probably extending back to the Greeks. Barnard himself quotes Roberto Michels, a friend of Max Weber, to the effect that even when authority rests on physical force, and is accepted because of fear or force, it is still *accepted.* Weber made much the same point, but he stated it as a limiting case, noting that there is always an irreducible element of voluntary compliance in an authoritarian relationship. But what was a limiting case for Weber is the basic nature of the phenomenon for Barnard. Barnard quotes a "notable business executive" who had been an army officer in World War I to the effect that the army is the "greatest of all democracies" because when the order to move forward is given, it is the enlisted man who has to decide on his own to accept that order.[36]

Barnard also speaks of the "fiction of the superior authority," but it is hardly a fiction if one can be fired for disobeying orders or shot for not moving ahead on orders. And organizations do fire people, Barnard admits, but he prefers to refer to

[33]Ibid., p. 143.

[34]Ibid., p. 144.

[35]Ibid., pp. 163–164.

[36]Ibid., p. 164. This view of authority is not consistent with Barnard's concept of the "organizational personality." As noted earlier, he uses heroic military behavior to illustrate the predominance of the organizational personality. The person who decides on his own to move forward is using his organizational personality, not his individual personality. Since the organizational personality can be based on indoctrination or propaganda, authority can be a top-down phenomenon. In the present example, authority is considered a bottom-up phenomenon.

voluntary resignation or to "terminating the connection" when the "attitude of the individual indicates in advance likelihood of disobedience."[37] Indeed, he says at one point that "to fail in an obligation intentionally is an act of hostility. This no organization can permit; and it must respond with punitive action if it can, even to the point of incarcerating or executing the culprit."[38] There is no "fiction" involved in these exercises of superior authority. But to define authority differently would be to weaken the emphasis on cooperation. If organizations are primarily or even exclusively cooperative in nature, there is no room for a definition of authority that includes imposed rules and coercion as important aspects.[39]

Informal Groups

One of the most celebrated discussions in Barnard's work is that of the role of informal groups within organizations. Weber and the classical management theorists were, of course, aware of informal relations in organizations, but they saw them as problems to be overcome in the interest of complete control. It was the merit of Barnard's discussion that he saw the functional aspects of informal groups. Such groups are necessary, so to speak, to "oil the wheels" of the formal organization, to provide understanding and motivation in those areas where the formal organization is deficient. Barnard notes that they are responsible for establishing attitudes, understandings, customs, habits, and institutions. They are necessary to the operation of the formal organization as a means of communication, of cohesion, and of protecting the integrity of the individual.

To Barnard's discredit, however, he completely neglected the possibility of negative aspects of informal relations. This had been extensively documented in the Hawthorne study, with which he was familiar.[40] For F. J. Roethlisberger and W. J. Dickson, the informal organization could and did have disruptive and dysfunctional aspects, such as setting standards for what was considered a fair day's output that were below those of management, or supporting systematic rule violation. But Barnard denied that the informal organization could have common purposes; for him, the purposes, such as they were, were only personal.[41] This would make agreements on a fair day's production, arrived at among workers and policed by them, fall into the category of unorganized activity. Why would this be important for Barnard? Because for him, only the formal organization can be rational. Informal organizations are not; they "correspond to the unconscious or nonintellectual actions and habits of individuals," whereas formal organizations correspond "to their reasoned and calculated actions and policies."[42] Barnard comes close here to joining

[37]Ibid., pp. 166–167.

[38]Ibid., p. 171.

[39]For Weber, authority in bureaucracies was rational-legal authority, a type of domination based on legally enacted, rational rules that were held to be legitimate by all members. The rules were either agreed on or imposed. The fact that members accepted the legitimacy of the authority in no way altered the facts that rules could be imposed and that coercion lay behind them.

[40]F. J. Roethlisberger and William J. Dickson, *Management and the Worker* (Cambridge, Mass.: Harvard University Press, 1947).

[41]Barnard, *Functions of the Executive*, p. 115.

[42]Ibid., p. 116.

Roethlisberger and Dickson in their assumption that management behavior is mainly rational and workers' behavior nonrational.

The Fulminating Executive

Finally, as we have noted, the executive is the key to the organization of society. It is he or she who bears the moral freight of organizations in society. True, all personnel are important in an organization. "The work of cooperation is not the work of leadership, but of organization as a whole." Cooperation is an attribute of organizations, for the force is given off by all. But, Barnard continues.:

> These structures do not remain in existence, they usually do not come into being, the vitality is lacking, there is no enduring cooperation, without the creation of faith, the catalyst by which the living system of human effort is enabled to continue its incessant interchanges of energies and satisfactions. Cooperation, not leadership, is the creative process; but leadership is the indispensable fulminator of its forces.[43]

Of course, for such a superhuman leader, material incentives are irrelevant. The most important single contribution required of the executive is loyalty, or "domination by the organization personality."[44] But since this is also the least susceptible to tangible inducements, material incentives play an "incidental and superficial role" in the case of the executive. One wonders why, then, their salaries are high. The functionalist Barnard tells us. In a statement altogether remarkable, especially in 1938, he says that income becomes significant enough to be "an important secondary factor to individuals [top executives] in many cases, because prestige and official responsibilities impose heavy burdens on them." But, he adds, even though they need material incentives to meet the burdens of prestige, these incentives are still not only insufficient but are "often abortive."[45]

THE THEORY IN PRACTICE

Barnard was an operating executive. He knew organizations thoroughly. He spent his working life in the telephone company, and he rose to one of its highest positions. He was a man who, unlike most social scientists, could "tell it like it is"; could give the illuminating example or detail; could use his own experience to convince us of the merit of his model. Illustrations from experience or from events recorded by others do not prove anything about a theory but, in the absence of empirical research, the quality of examples and illustrations is important. If, as in Barnard's book, one finds simple illustrations (workers rolling a stone or, in his longest one, five men engaged in woodcutting) coexisting with complex and subtle theory, one is likely to ask which should be believed. Theory illuminates the real world; examples lend cogency to untested theory.

[43]Ibid., p. 259.
[44]Ibid., p. 220.
[45]Ibid., p. 221.

There are practically no illustrations in his book of actual organizations functioning in a situation. In fact, only three references to the telephone company occur. Two of them are trivial and incidental (all the decisions that go into moving a telephone pole, and the height of switchboards). The third is an account of a telephone operator so devoted to her ill mother that she took an inferior post in an isolated area so that, while working, she might watch the house she shared with the mother. The house burned down one day, but despite her commitment to her mother, she stayed at the switchboard, watching it burn. Her "organizational personality" won out. Says Barnard, "She showed extraordinary 'moral courage,' we would say, in conforming to a code of her organization—the *moral* necessity of uninterrupted service."[46]

Aside from this curious example, real-life organizations with their conflicts, multiple goals, cliques, and ambiguities are absent from this book. The answer, I believe, lies in Barnard's determination to purge the organization of unseemly, nonmoral, or nonlogical human behavior and to uphold the cooperative model.

Fortunately, in another volume of essays, Barnard has given us a concrete example of organizational behavior and particularly of his own behavior. He first wrote it up for a seminar at the Harvard Business School.[47]

Barnard in Action

For eighteen months at the beginning of the Great Depression, Barnard was the Director of Emergency Relief in New Jersey, and then in 1935 he served as chairman of the Relief Council in Trenton, where there had been especially severe problems of unemployment and relief administration. Here, indeed, was a nonroutine situation and an obvious clash of interests. In fact, one key meeting between Barnard and a delegation of workers was abruptly terminated when a large crowd of over 2,000 demonstrators, supporting the workers, was broken up by the police. A second meeting was scheduled and took place; the purpose was to hear the grievances of the unemployed. Barnard rejected their demand to meet with the whole Relief Council and instead insisted that only he and eight of the workers' representatives meet. Barnard analyzed the situation for a seminar in sociology conducted by L. J. Henderson and later published the analysis in a collection of papers.[48]

He stressed that the complaints of the workers, to which he listened for two hours, were, with few exceptions, "either trivial or related to past history no longer relevant to the existing conditions. As a whole, they were utterly inadequate to explain or justify the organization of the relief recipients, their mass meeting, or the time and effort of the representatives, some of whom could certainly have employed

[46]Ibid., p. 269.

[47]The Bell System has had a long and cozy relationship with the Harvard Business School. N. R. Danielian describes the company's overtures to professors who teach—and influence—public utility law and regulation, and the thinly disguised propaganda addresses by executives of the company that are given at the school at the suggestion of the company. (See Danielian, *AT&T*, pp. 297–302.) Barnard himself spent a good deal of time at Harvard talking with L. J. Henderson and others.

[48]Chester Barnard, *Organization and Management* (Cambridge, Mass.: Harvard University Press, 1948), pp. 51–79.

themselves to better advantage materially in the endeavor to obtain jobs or create places for themselves."[49] Rather than attempting to make real complaints about relief provisions during a period of severe unemployment in an industrial city, "what these men wanted was opportunity for self-expression and recognition. . . . To have dismissed the grievances as trivial, however, would have been to destroy the opportunity that was literally more important to these personalities than more or less food for themselves or families."[50] So much for one view of the realities of the situation, more or less food. Really at stake were nonlogical sentiments; why else would they not be out looking for work? Indeed, the problem with relief was obvious; it was not the well-to-do and those who ran the state and city who were opposed to higher payments. (Barnard agreed the payments of 6 cents per meal per person were "insufficient.")[51] "The well-to-do," he told the workers' committee, "have lost plenty and are grumbling much about taxes and this or that, and lots of them have lost their nerve. But they're not the people who are opposed to you. . . . The people who are most opposed to you and whom you and I must pay most attention to are those nearest you—those just one jump ahead of the bread line."[52] This made the problem one of educating the marginally employed, not deficit spending or higher taxes for the well-off and moderately well-off (such as those with large holdings of telephone stock, which continued to pay its $9 dividend). Education, of course, would take time.

Unimpeded by nonlogical sentiments, Barnard drove his point home. "What ought to be done either in the way of correction of faults or increases of allowances, I will do if I can, because they ought to be done." Then, pounding the table for emphasis, he continued: "But one thing I want to make clear. I'll be god-damned if I will do anything for you on the basis that you ought to have it just because you want it, or because you organize mass meetings, or what you will. I'll do my best to do what ought to be done, but I won't give you a nickel on any other basis." He would decide what "ought to be done." He added that his position was "based more on your own interest than on anything else. For the kind of behavior which you have been exhibiting is alienating from you the very people upon whom you or I depend to get the money for relief, and I assure you there are many who object to giving it now."[53] So much for cooperation. They were wrong in their method—they would get satisfaction only on Barnard's terms and not theirs—and they were wrong about the source of the difficulty. After another hour's discussion, they left, leaving it all in Barnard's hands. "As I look back on it, I do not think I had ever before made a purely personal accomplishment the equal of this," said Barnard.[54] Presumably Mayo would have applauded too. Characteristically, Barnard never indicated what decision he took about what should be done; it was simply not relevant. This little cameo, concrete and descriptive, of actual organizational behavior and organiza-

[49]Ibid., p. 71.

[50]Ibid.

[51]Ibid., p. 72.

[52]Ibid., pp. 74–75.

[53]Ibid., pp. 73–74.

[54]Ibid., p. 75.

tional problems bears little resemblance to the cooperative systems analyzed in his classic volume. Once again, we find Barnard violating his cooperative model when the realities of organizational life must be considered.

SUMMARY

What can we learn, then, from this analysis of the cooperative view of organizations as laid out by its most distinguished proponent? First, there is the separation of organization and person that cuts through all his major concepts. He glorifies the organization and minimizes the person, as in his contrasts of decision making (decisions are nonpersonal if they are constructive); of the formal and the informal organization; of the logical processes of the organization and the nonlogical processes of the individual; of authority that is accepted willingly and authority that does not exist if it is not accepted; of ideal motives and incentives versus material ones. In all these contrasts, the second half of the coin—the potentially disruptive, the impediments to organizational functioning—is either seen in solely positive terms (as in the case of informal groups) or minimized to the point of extinction. In this fashion the problem areas of organizations—power, conflict, individual goals, and so on—are outside of his model, to be dealt with summarily by the authoritarian executive.

In their place is the moral organization. Organizations are logical; their common purpose is the purpose of all, and they exist in ever-widening circles of cooperative systems. If the army is the greatest of all democracies, we have little to fear from organizations; if they exist in a cooperative system, we need not fear conflict between organizations; if they are oriented toward a common purpose, we need not fear conflict within organizations. Organizations are legitimized by their very definition. They are cooperative and pursue a moral purpose. That which is evil comes from without—even as advertising stimulates artificial desires for economic incentives.

Because of the nonrationality of individuals and their desires, indoctrination, propaganda, inducements, and so forth are needed. Executive leadership will shape these in the proper manner. The organization is not merely made up of persons; it is something greater than that, and personal decisions and personal power are not, or at least should not be, relevant. When the person comes into Barnard's scheme, it is as the slave voluntarily giving legitimacy to the authority of the master. A manufactured consensus and harmony and the dominance of the organizational personality, even as the house burns down while the operator watches helplessly, are what Barnard has to offer. (He mercifully tells us in a footnote that the mother was rescued.)

The basic weakness of Barnard's model lies in its extreme functionalism—that is, the uncritical acceptance of organizations as functional for all concerned and the moralism that follows from this view. Barnard's central concepts, which are so widely used today, combine to legitimize and justify what should remain forever problematic—the value of imperatively coordinated systems of human effort. Bureaucracy, with all its technical superiority, scared Weber, for here was a powerful tool in the hands of the state and the private corporation that was based on domination, legalized and rationalized. For Barnard, organizations were the measure of human cooperative instincts and were essentially democratic in nature and benign in their influence.[55]

The road from Barnard's company town, which we will follow in the next three chapters, went primarily in three directions:

1. The institutional view of the executive and the organization. This is elaborated and refined primarily by Philip Selznick in his *Leadership in Administration,* [56] where the interpenetration of the organization and the community is stressed, with the organization having responsibility to protect and reflect the values of the larger society and with the leader-statesman as the catalyst of that process. That the community might have conflicting views from which the organization can select, or that the organization is capable of creating and defining values that are then imposed on the community, is barely considered.

2. The idea that decision making is the primordial organizational act and the idea of equilibrium. These are refined and developed primarily by Herbert Simon in parts of *Administrative Behavior* [57] and the first half of James March and Herbert Simon's *Organizations.* [58] It results in an essentially psychological view of organizations, an emphasis on rational cognition at the expense of structure, and a neglect of the degree to which the nature of the equilibrium is manufactured by the organization as a consequence of the latter's enormous power.[59]

3. The human relations tradition. While this tradition, following the impressive documentation of Roethlisberger and Dickson (see Chapter 3), has to deal with the negative effects of informal groups, negative effects are seen as aberrant and pathological; they can be reversed and the true nature of informal groups allowed to assert itself and thus serve the organization. This brings this view into line with that of Barnard. Conflict is also not ignored but is treated in a similar fashion. Bottom-up authority flourishes in the participative management viewpoint. Wages and material incentives have little place in this (or any other) current organizational theory, though no one takes the extreme position of Barnard. The uncritical emphasis on communication as a manipulative device is maintained. The superiority of group over individual cognition and rationality is acclaimed, even while much human relations theory is dedicated to individual-level phenomena.

[55] It is quite possible to cite passages from Barnard that indicate a highly structural, even Weberian, point of view (e.g., the sections on communication); that show considerable concern with bases of conflict; and that show that he was sometimes less concerned with cooperation than with coordination by the leader. Perhaps for this reason, some find Barnard insightful and valuable even today. However, this is to argue that when he contradicts himself, he is useful. His legacy was not a structural view of conflict and centrifugal forces in organizations, for then we might have a model of authoritarian organizations. Instead, he is cited for his position that organizations are cooperative systems. The value of his story about the relief agency is not that it reveals Barnard the man, but that this description of a real organization so contradicts his theory. So do his discussions of handling conflict, engineering consent, and so on.

[56] Philip Selznick, *Leadership in Administration* (New York: Harper & Row, 1957).

[57] Simon, *Administrative Behavior.*

[58] March and Simon, *Organizations.*

[59] As we will see in Chapter 4, a quite different orientation can be found in both of these books, especially in the last half of *Organizations,* where a limited-rationality view of behavior is utilized and an essentially bureaucratic structure is fleshed out by analyzing the way the premises of decisions are controlled by unobtrusive means. This alternative view of organizations greatly enhances the skeletal model of Weber and constitutes a major advance in theory. It owes little to Barnard, however.

Yet, it is ironic that Barnard's extreme position with regard to the cooperative nature of the system "solves" many of the problems the human relations theorists labor over by denying they exist. There is no word in Barnard's book suggesting that organizations should be changed to allow more participation from subordinates, nor that people should be treated more decently than they are. (Indeed, he decries such attempts as insincere.) How could this be a problem in organizations, when authority is derived only from the subordinate? The only real problem lies in establishing a common purpose, and even the status of that problem is ambiguous since if organizations consist of people cooperating in terms of their economy of incentives, the common purpose must emerge without help; indeed, it would be immoral to be anything but a midwife to it, or it would not then be genuine. Of course, the executive must also make the right decisions and lay out the proper channels of communication, but Barnard tells us nothing concrete about these matters. In short, Barnard is a more extreme apologist for management than the human relations theorists. He continues in the tradition of Elton Mayo, as described by Bendix,[60] though he is far more subtle and insightful than most, and far more respected.

[60]Bendix, *Work and Authority in Industry.*

The Human Relations Model

HAWTHORNE AND ALL THAT

In another part of the AT&T forest, another dramatic event was taking shape in the late 1920s and 1930s, and it would enrich organizational theory and fill the texts with references to such terms as the "bank wiring group," the "Hawthorne effect," and the "Mica-splitting Test Room."[1]

Picture a grimy factory in Cicero, outside of Chicago, in the late 1920s, where electrical apparatus for the Bell System was turned out. This was the Hawthorne plant of Western Electric, a wholly owned and very profitable subsidiary of AT&T that produced all of the latter's equipment. As we have seen, AT&T management was progressive for its time, and it was looking for ways to increase productivity among the workers. Strong reliance on simply speeding up the production lines and changing piecework rates was to start in about 1928–1929. But between 1924 and 1927, managers experimented with environmental conditions such as lighting. These experiments were remarkably frustrating.

The researchers at Western Electric took two groups of workers doing the same kinds of jobs, put them into separate rooms, and kept careful records of their productivity. One group (the test group) had the intensity of its lighting increased. Its productivity went up. For the other group (the control group), there was no change in lighting. But, to the amazement of the researchers, its productivity went

---

[1] F. J. Roethlisberger and W. J. Dickson, *Management and the Worker* (Cambridge, Mass.: Harvard University Press, 1947). The story of the book has been told many times. I have relied primarily on Henry Landsberger's sympathetic account, *Hawthorne Revisited* (Ithaca, N.Y.: Cornell University Press, 1958), and with regard to the early history of the research, I have called upon the critical account of Loren Baritz, *The Servants of Power* (Westport, Conn.: Greenwood Press, 1974). Baritz devotes several chapters to the emergence of psychological testing and morale studies, which preceded the Hawthorne research, in an attempt to show how the social sciences were co-opted from the outset by the industrial elite. It is a one-sided account that neglects the degree to which social scientists were interested in improving conditions in factories and learning about human behavior in general, and it fails to indicate the mechanisms by which so many of them supposedly sold out to business interests. Nevertheless, it is a useful documentary. The most famous (and literate) summary of the major experiments is found in George Homans' *The Human Group* (New York: Harcourt Brace Jovanovich, 1950), but it is a highly colored account that I find inaccurate.

up also. Even more puzzling, when the degree of illumination in the test group was gradually lowered back to the original level, it was found that output still continued to go up. Output also continued to increase in the control group. The researchers continued to drop the illumination of the test group, but it was not until the workers were working under conditions of bright moonlight that productivity stopped rising and fell off sharply.

Patiently, the researchers set out to vary the types of groups they studied and the types of work the groups did. They ran the experiments again. The productivity of both test and control groups increased. Doggedly, the researchers stuck to their initial hypotheses and decided that the increase was caused by the combination of artificial lighting and natural illumination. Next, they used only artificial lighting, but again the results were similar.

It was not until several years later that this phenomenon was explained and labeled the "Hawthorne effect." Lighting had been changed in one group and not the other group, but the researchers had neglected a more important change that had occurred for both groups—namely, that management had put them into special rooms to control the lighting and thus had segregated them from the rest of the workers and treated them as something special. In short, the real change had been that management had taken an interest in the two groups of workers. They were given special treatment and special status as compared to the rest of the workers. The attention apparently raised morale, and morale raised productivity. It was a happy thought.

But that was realized much later. Meanwhile, puzzled by the results, the researchers (an industrial psychologist from Harvard, F. J. Roethlisberger, and a member of Western Electric management, W. J. Dickson) turned to other variables. Elton Mayo had been called in by this time, since he was also on the faculty of the Harvard Business School. Aside from his writings about the crisis of industrial civilization, he had done work on the effects of rest pauses and on "negative reverie" among workers as an impediment to higher productivity. (Jobs were so dull that workers daydreamed about things and did not pay attention to their work; hence Mayo called the reverie, but not the work, "negative.") The new round of experiments introduced rest pauses and altered the length of the working day.

Several women assembling electrical relays were selected on the basis of friendship choices and put to work in a special room, where an observer recorded their conversations and interactions. They were removed from direct supervision and also placed under a modified group-incentive pay rate (each woman's pay depending in part on the productivity of the group). They knew they were the subjects of an experiment and apparently tried hard to do well. Again, as rests were introduced, productivity went up, and the effect persisted whether rests were increased or decreased, the length of the day increased or decreased. The women developed close friendships, and an uncooperative member was replaced by one they chose. The authors exhaustively examined all the traditional variables of industrial psychology —methods, fatigue, monotony, and the wage incentive system—and then started two new experiments, the "Second Relay Assembly Group" and the "Mica-splitting Test Room" to further examine the effect of incentives and rest changes. These results were quite ambiguous. Output no longer soared. There were too many variables to control—the Mica group was on individual piecework, and the women were preoccupied with the increasing layoffs at the plant occasioned by the Great Depression, so perhaps this was why their output did not increase. Moreover, the Second Relay Assembly Group did not do as well as the first and various explanations were offered.

Norms and Sentiments

But in general, the researchers were confused and admitted it. (Their book is a model of frank reporting on the step-by-step stages of the research.) The variations in results seemed to have something to do with the vague factor of employee "attitudes and preoccupations." So they did an analysis on "what's on the worker's mind," a favorite topic of the 1920s and 1930s. They hired a number of people to interview workers throughout the plant, asking very general questions designed to get the employees to talk.

As Henry Landsberger points out in his book *Hawthorne Revisited,* this was possibly the first attempt at what is now called nondirective counseling. Later, just before *Management and the Worker* was published, management implemented the recommendations of Roethlisberger and Dickson and established a formal interviewing program at the Hawthorne works. Large numbers of personnel—some 300 or so—were employed to wander about the plant encouraging workers to tell them their complaints in confidence. Management did not act upon the complaints (and were not even told of them), but the workers supposedly felt much better after having blown off steam and having concluded that management was interested.

The interviews conducted during the research led to the analysis of the nonlogical or nonrational (but not necessarily irrational) character of the workers' "sentiments." It also led to the discovery that workers restricted output and penalized those who produced more than the group had informally agreed to; that some supervisors were rated as better leaders than others because they treated the employees decently; and that there were cliques and informal groups. (That these findings should be labeled "discoveries" indicated how little members of management and industrial psychologists—and indeed, industrial sociologists in general, if there were any at that time—knew about actual organizations.)

The researchers decided to return to the study of groups, since this appeared to be more important than an analysis of individual attitudes. They set up the Bank Wiring Observation Room, in which they established an already existing group of workers and inspectors to wire banks of equipment. They observed this group carefully for seven months, until the lack of work in the section ended the experiment. The observations disclosed that there was deliberate and controlled restriction of output by the workers. A "fair day's rate" was established informally and policed by the group; "rate busters" were subject to ostracism, sabotage, and physical reprisals. There was also a political system of falsifying records (to a rather trivial extent as far as the company was concerned; the company was quite satisfied with the productivity of the group). These techniques were used to retaliate against supervisors and inspectors who played favorites, to cover up for certain workers, and to discipline others. (Other studies have supported these findings in a variety of settings.)

The sordid picture of group pressures, individual competition, falsification, and reprisals hardly supported the view that productivity was related to rest pauses or, for that matter, that this was a cooperative system in Barnard's terms or Mayo's. (Mayo's own writings on the experiment seem to miss the point.[2]) But the hostilities and survival techniques of workers were not stressed; instead, the finding that workers formed social groups with elaborate norms and customs was stressed. Underlying this view of groups were the omnipresent explanations of "sentiments": nonrational behavior, lack of cooperation with (rational) management, and lack of identification with the (rational) goals of the company. It was not the fear of producing too much, which could mean that some would be laid off, that led to worker restriction of output (though, honest reporters that they were, the authors noted that the company was laying off workers). Such explanations, they explicitly say, were merely rationalizations. It was group norms and the sentiments of the individuals, rather than objective conditions, that formed the bases for explaining this behavior. The sociological tradition of Comte, Pareto, Durkheim, and Sumner that emphasized nonrational norms and sentiments never received a better press.[3]

The Critics

The Roethlisberger and Dickson volume is firmly established as a classic; indeed, it was obvious from the first that this was to be an extremely influential book. But as soon as it appeared, it was also heavily and widely criticized. The *American Journal of Sociology* gave it a critical review,[4] and Robert S. Lynd (of *Middletown* fame, the first of the modern American community studies) wrote a scathing review, published in the *Political Science Quarterly*, of an earlier volume by T. N. Whitehead, *Leadership in a Free Society*, that incorporated some of the same material.[5] As Landsberger put it in 1958, "a most spectacular academic battle has raged since then—or perhaps it would be more accurate to say that a limited number of gunners has kept up a steady barrage, reusing the same ammunition."[6] It was a splendid group of marksmen, including Reinhard Bendix, Clark Kerr (much later to be the embattled head of the University of California during the Free Speech Movement of the 1960s), Herbert Blumer, C. Wright Mills, Wilbert E. Moore, Harold Wilensky, and Daniel Bell. As Landsberger points out, many of the criticisms are actually directed at Elton Mayo, rather than at Roethlisberger and Dickson's *Management and the Worker*, which was primarily a research monograph. But while one

[2]Elton Mayo, *The Social Problems of an Industrial Civilization* (Cambridge, Mass.: Harvard University Press, 1945).

[3]Only Pareto is mentioned in the book; Mayo knew of him through L. J. Henderson, the Harvard natural scientist. Though any sociologist aware of Emile Durkheim's *Division of Labor in Society* (New York: Free Press, 1947, first published in French in 1893) would have been prepared for the discovery of group norms and sentiments in industry, no sociologists were looking at the time. The biggest sociological find of the decade was thus left to people in the field of business administration.

[4]*American Journal of Sociology* 46 (1940): 98–101.

[5]*Political Science Quarterly* 52 (1937): 590–592; T. N. Whitehead, *Leadership in a Free Society* (Cambridge, Mass.: Harvard University Press, 1936).

[6]Landsberger, *Hawthorne Revisited*, pp. 1–2.

can find, here and there in the volume, recognition of matters that Mayo neglected, or recognition of contrary evidence and viewpoints, it still seems fair to say that the volume in general is cast in the Mayo framework and reflects his values.

As might be expected, some of the most common criticisms hit at the exclusively negative role assigned to conflict by the authors and their concern with cooperation and equilibrium. Cooperation, say the critics, is to be on management's terms and in management's image. There are no legitimate grounds given for conflict of interests between, say, labor and management. A related criticism is that management is seen as rational, while the worker is seen as nonrational. Kerr stated, "We cannot accept the view that rationality and initiative are vouchsafed only to the elite, and that the common man is left only the virtues of faith and obedience."[7]

Another strong criticism was that, in their search for causes of negative attitudes on the part of workers, the researchers gave primary emphasis to the social groups in the workplace. As Bell pointed out, "There is no view of the larger institutional framework of our economic system within which these relationships arise and have their meaning."[8] Those who took into consideration the larger framework stressed the natural, inevitable, and even healthy conflict between the divergent interests of management and workers, the progressive rationalization and depersonalization of industrial technology, the insecurity that violent business cycles implied for workers, and the unequal power of the two groups. That such conflicts of interests and inequalities of power might be solved by better face-to-face relations between workers and management, or by the famous counseling system, seemed doubtful. Furthermore, the critics felt, the volume, as well as Mayo's ideology, pointed the way toward manipulation of the worker, who was seen as a child or primitive whose self-protective mechanisms and efforts to reduce monotony and boredom were not in the interests of a cooperative social system. Mayo compared the industrial researchers to physicians, administering to the ills of workers, but it is not at all clear that the efficiency of industrial organization is in the same category as individual good health.

It is both revealing and ironic that the major critics of *Management and the Worker* did not challenge it on empirical grounds, asking whether the evidence was properly gathered and correctly interpreted. The "steady barrage" by the limited number of gunners was restricted to the ideology implicit in the study. Doubtless, that ideology was more pernicious to them than the scientific standards of the study. The social sciences, at least in the area of complex organizations, have been desperate for *ideas*, not data. The practitioners seize on concepts that will make sense of the world; if the concepts make sense, the social scientists do not inquire too carefully into the empirical support for these ideas or concepts. For those who find the ideas repugnant, the most pressing thing to do is to respond on ideological grounds; only later do some have the "luxury" of patiently reexamining the empirical documentation of the new idea.

The first critical examination of the actual data and the interpretations of Roethlisberger and Dickson that I am aware of was published fifteen years after the

---

[7]Quoted in ibid., p. 31.
[8]Quoted in ibid., p. 33.

original study.[9] The author, Michael Argyle, flatly announced in a later paper that "despite a widespread belief to the contrary, 'social' factors have never been shown to be of very great significance as determinants of productivity differences between otherwise similar departments," and he cited the Hawthorne studies as a case in point.[10] In 1967 Alex Carey came to a similar conclusion: "The results of these studies, far from supporting the various components of the 'human relations approach,' are surprisingly consistent with a rather old-world view about the value of monetary incentives, driving leadership, and discipline."[11]

Carey then asks why social scientists have continued to neglect the discrepancy between the evidence and the conclusions contained in this seminal work. The answer is probably rather simple. After the Hawthorne studies were published, a small-scale social movement got under way—financed by government agencies, business organizations, universities, and business-supported foundations—which sought to find ways to increase productivity by manipulating social factors. Conducting more or less careful, scientific studies of the relationship between such attitudes as morale and such behaviors as productivity, the members of what came to be called the "human relations movement" increasingly suffered setbacks. The relationship between morale and productivity, and that between good leadership and productivity, proved to be less than clear and less than substantial. Since their own sophisticated studies of the influence of social factors on production were in serious trouble, the human relations theorists did not have much incentive to make a searching critique of the first major study.[12]

We will turn in a moment to the thirty-year history of the effort to link morale and leadership to productivity. Much has been learned about individual and group behavior as a result of the effort, but most of the acquired knowledge, unfortunately, tells us little about *organizations* as such. Why spend, then, the better part of a chapter on something that has been generally unproductive in shedding light on organizations? For one thing, this is the most voluminous and substantial part of the literature on organizations. Just as one must know something about the Hawthorne studies, one must also know something about current human relations models. Second, the premises of the movement are so sensible, and even compelling, that it is necessary to examine them in detail to see where they might go wrong. Why

[9]Michael Argyle, "The Relay Assembly Test Room in Retrospect," *Occupational Psychology 27* (1953): 98–103.

[10]Michael Argyle, Godfrey Gardner, and Frank Cioffi, "Supervisory Methods Related to Productivity, Absenteeism, and Labour Turnover," *Human Relations* 11 (1958): 24.

[11]Alex Carey, "The Hawthorne Studies: A Radical Criticism," *American Sociological Review* 32 (June 1967): 416. See also the methodological criticism of A. J. Sykes in "Economic Interest and the Hawthorne Researches: A Comment," *Human Relations 18* (1965): 253–263. It is interesting that all of these critics are British. The criticisms cover a host of complicated issues and cannot be easily summarized; the reader is directed to the actual articles and to the original study itself. Inadequate controls, failure to assess the impact of such things as replacement of slow workers by fast ones, changes in incentives, and ignoring the contrary evidence the authors themselves present are frequent themes.

[12]The dispute about the Hawthorne studies continues and has even increased in intensity. See Richard Herbert Francke and James D. Kaul, "The Hawthorne Experiments: First Statistical Interpretation," *American Sociological Review* 43 (1978): 623–643; and Dana Bramel and Ronald Friend, "Hawthorne, the Myth of the Docile Worker, and Class Bias in Psychology," *American Psychologist* 36 (1981): 867–878.

would happy workers not produce more? Why not allow workers to participate in decisions? Third, we learn a great deal about the complexity of *human* behavior by taking this tour; it should give us some pause when we try, in later chapters, to deal with *organizational* behavior. There are no simple keys to unlock the secrets of organizations; an examination of the "obvious" truths of human relations research will make this clear. In a sense, if truly sociological studies of organizations were as numerous, well done, and well criticized as the social psychological studies, we, too, might be more overwhelmed than we are by the complexities of organizational analysis.

I wish to emphasize the above points because my criticism of the human relations movement will be rather scathing. I think there are more productive paths for understanding organizations and for gaining some control over the way they shape our lives than those provided by this movement. But the structural or sociological analysis, it must be said, has not been tested by forty years of accumulated studies bearing on its central theses. Indeed, one is not quite sure what the central theses of the structural school are, while those of the human relations school are clear.

Finally, the work of those who are generally associated with the human relations school has produced some promising lines of inquiry that constitute departures from the central tenets of the school. The work of Stanley Seashore and Ephraim Yuchtman on organizational goals and, especially, the first part of the volume by Daniel Katz and Robert Kahn, which uses a sophisticated "open-system" or "social-system" approach, are two examples.[13] We won't go into them here because we are dealing with the main schools of thought and the basic conceptions of organizations that have been well researched or thought through. The work of these people, such as Arnold Tannenbaum, whom we will briefly consider, is a product of the human relations movement, but it goes far beyond the output of that school.

We will arbitrarily divide our discussion of the human relations school into two branches. The first is concerned with morale, leadership, and productivity. The second, more sophisticated, branch is concerned with the structuring of groups; it builds on the premises of the first but applies them to the organization as a whole.

LEADERSHIP AND PRODUCTIVITY MODELS

The general thesis of this branch of human relations theory is that good leadership will lead to increased productivity on the part of employees. "Good leadership" is generally described as democratic rather than authoritarian, employee-centered rather than production-centered, concerned with human relations rather than with bureaucratic rules, and so on. It is hypothesized that good leadership will lead to high morale, and high morale will lead to increased effort, resulting in higher production.

[13]Stanley E. Seashore and Ephraim Yuchtman, "Factorial Analysis of Organizational Performance," *Administrative Science Quarterly* 12, no. 3 (December 1967): 377–395. Daniel Katz and Robert Kahn, *Social Psychology of Organizations* (New York: Wiley, 1966).

It will also reduce turnover (leaving one organization for another) and absenteeism, thus raising productivity by minimizing both training time and the disruption caused by absent workers.

The history of research in this area is one of progressive disenchantment with the above theses and progressive awareness of the complexities of human behavior and human situations. As a result of forty years of intensive research, we have a large body of information on what does *not* clearly and simply affect productivity (or the intervening variable, morale) and a growing list of qualifiers and conditions that have to be taken into account. The size of this list threatens to overwhelm us before we can, with confidence, either advise managers as to what they should do to increase productivity or develop theories that have much explanatory power.

Attitudes and Performance

One of the early systematic studies in the field of industrial psychology was conducted in 1930. The investigators used questionnaires and interviews to determine the attitudes of 200–300 young girls tending machines in a mill.[14] They concluded that the girls' productivity had no relationship to their attitudes toward their work, their supervisors, personnel policies, and so on. The researchers also examined a number of other variables, such as age, intelligence, education, and emotional adjustment, and found that even when these were taken into account, there was no such relationship. It all might have ended there with this negative finding, except that the result was so hard to believe. Happy employees should be productive employees; that was the sermon that was increasingly preached in the management journals and by social scientists. Starting in the 1940s, study after study sought to prove the relationship.

By 1954 there had been about fifty studies of the relationship between attitudes and performance, and two psychologists, Arthur Brayfield and Walter Crockett, paused to survey the studies carefully. The conclusion of the 1930 study was upheld; there was little evidence that attitudes bore any "simple or even appreciative relationship to performance."[15] Personnel who were satisfied with their network of interpersonal relationships were not necessarily highly motivated to produce; indeed, the worker had many goals, and productivity was at best a peripheral one. Satisfactions were related, however, to absenteeism and turnover. This should not surprise us. If anyone is going to leave or be absent, it is likely to be that person who is the most dissatisfied. Staying home on Monday or getting another job is of direct benefit to that worker. Increasing his or her effort on the job is not.

After the Brayfield and Crockett articles in 1955, the work in this area began to slack off, though studies continued to appear. A review of the literature, published in 1964 by Victor Vroom, concluded that there was a small and fairly consistent

[14]Arthur Kornhauser and A. Sharp, "Employee Attitudes, Suggestions from a Study in a Factory," *Personnel Journal* 10 (1932): 393–401.

[15]Arthur H. Brayfield and Walter H. Crockett, "Employee Attitudes and Employee Performance," *Psychological Bulletin* 52, no. 5 (1955): 396–424. Many of the references we will be citing in this section are conveniently included in L. L. Cummings and W. E. Scott, *Readings in Organizational Behavior and Human Performance,* rev. ed. (Homewood, Ill.: Irwin, 1973).

relationship between satisfaction and performance.[16] He cited twenty-three correlations from the literature, and in twenty there was a positive relationship, even though the median correlation was only .14 (which explains only about 2 percent of the relationship between satisfaction and productivity). If there is so little a relationship, it would hardly behoove managers to try to increase the work satisfaction and morale of workers, except to reduce turnover and absenteeism.

But the matter has not rested there. Edward Lawler and Lyman Porter reviewed thirty studies considering the relationship between satisfaction and performance, and they decided that the problem might simply be that the causal relationship should be reversed.[17] Satisfaction might result from high performance, rather than being a cause of it, *if* the employee is rewarded for high performance. The cause of high performance might be any number of things, including good equipment and authoritarian leadership. Lawler and Porter tested their hypothesis using data from 148 lower- and middle-level managers in 5 organizations, and they found support for it. They concluded that instead of trying to maximize satisfaction in organizations, organizations should pay attention to the requirement that high performance be rewarded by satisfying such higher-order needs as "self-actualization" and "autonomy."[18]

This viewpoint shows considerably more imagination than the standard one of high morale leading to high productivity, but it fails to give enough weight to a much neglected aspect of organizational life: in many jobs there is no room for high performance. Assembly-line workers can only do an adequate or a poor job, not a good one, for they do not control the pace of the work or make any decisions that might increase productivity. They may fail to make an adequate weld, but making one that indicates great skill and craftsmanship will bring them no recognition. In fact, it may bring a reprimand for wasting energy and metal when only an adequate weld is required. I suspect that many managerial and white-collar workers are in the same position. An adequate level of productivity is determined by the volume of input received and the volume of output absorbed. These depend on other units of the organization. A worker or a manager and her staff may not receive an increase in inputs, or other groups may not be able to handle an increase in outputs. If so, an increase in productivity is impossible, and superior quality is likely to be wasted.[19] The so-called pride of craftsmanship is systematically excluded from as many jobs as possible because it is difficult for management to control this variable. Productivity, it is safe to say, depends much more on such things as technological changes or economies of scale than on human effort.[20]

[16]Victor Vroom, *Work and Motivation* (New York: Wiley, 1964).

[17]Edward E. Lawler, III and Lyman W. Porter, "The Effect of Performance on Job Satisfaction," *Industrial Relations* 7, no. 1 (October 1967): 20–28.

[18]Recently Dornbush and Scott have examined the role of rewards very thoroughly, and indicate that the role of evaluation by superiors is not only a key factor in all kinds of organizations, but a neglected one. Sanford Dornbush and W. Richard Scott, *Evaluation and the Exercise of Authority* (San Francisco: Jossey-Bass, 1975).

[19]For a classic example of this, see the account of the toy painters in William F. Whyte, *Money and Motivation* (Westport, Conn.: Greenwood Press, 1977), pp. 90–99.

[20]See, for example, Robert Dubin, "Supervision and Productivity," in Robert Dubin et al., *Leadership and Productivity* (San Francisco: Chandler, 1965), p. 50.

Leadership and Performance

The relationship between attitudes and performance is a simple statement of the productivity problem. More sophisticated is the attempt to determine the effect of leadership behavior on human performance. The reasoning here is that if one can find out what makes a good leader, and if one can then teach people to be good leaders, or at least find ways to select good leaders, then presumably most of our organizational problems would be solved. Indeed, we could solve our national and even our international problems, for, as everyone knows, "what we need is good leadership." The results of this quest, still going on, have been as disillusioning as the more simple attempt to show that good attitudes result in good performance. As we shall see, the result might be summed up as saying "it all depends. . . ."

Furthermore, the human relations tradition has viewed managerial or supervisory behavior as consisting primarily of leading workers and not of making good decisions about such nonpersonal, mundane factors as the market, technology, competition, or organizational structure. But the nonpersonal decisions appear to have far more effect than decisions as to how to lead people. There is some confusion here, since we are prone to say that an organization has done well because of exceptional leadership. What we generally mean is that the decisions made with regard to organizational structure, type of product or service, quality control, new technologies, and so on have been good decisions, not just that the leaders have summoned an extra ounce of cooperation and motivation from the followers or been helpful in planning the workers' tasks or in teaching them skills. Of course, one can handle followers so poorly as to negate the advantages of organizational resources and opportunities, or one can have such an extraordinary personality as to compel loyalty, devotion, and hard work even without superior resources and opportunities. But these are exceptional cases. For most organizations, the impact of moderately good or bad relations with subordinates appears to be small and difficult to separate from other considerations.

For all practical purposes, the leadership studies began in earnest in about 1945 with a ten-year research project at Ohio State University. The researchers, mainly psychologists, started out in a practical and empirical manner characteristic of much of the post–World War II social science research. They sought to find and catalogue all of the traits that might affect leadership ability and to see which were the most important. Literally hundreds of traits were examined. The focus was on the leader, not on the members of the group. Most any leader of any group would do. Little attention was paid, at least initially, to the situation the group found itself in or to the type of organization or task.

After several years of research and with increasingly sophisticated data analysis techniques, two dimensions or "factors" emerged that appeared to account for most of the variation between leadership style and group performance.[21] One, called "initiating structure," referred to structuring and defining the roles of both leader and subordinates. A high-scoring leader would be active in planning, communicating

[21]See the studies reported in R. M. Stogdill and A. E. Coons, eds., *Leader Behavior: Its Description and Measurement* (Columbus, Ohio: Bureau of Business Research, 1957).

information, scheduling activities, trying out new ideas, and so on. The other factor was called "consideration"—consideration for the feelings of subordinates, respect for their ideas, and mutual trust. A high-scoring individual promoted rapport and two-way communication. (Two other factors were dropped.)

A leader could be high on both of these; they were not viewed as opposite poles on a continuum. This conceptualization represented an advance, for it eschewed the simple dichotomy characteristic of early human relations research—the dichotomy between leaders who practiced good human relations and those who did not. In this earlier view, it was sufficient to contrast the democratic leader with the authoritarian one, sometimes conceiving of a third position, laissez faire.[22] The Ohio State studies indicated that "structural" or "task-oriented" expertise—planning work, eliciting ideas, scheduling, and so on—was as important as good interpersonal relations.

At about the same time, another set of studies began to appear from the Survey Research Center at the University of Michigan. Initially, they conceptualized two styles, employee orientation and production orientation,[23] which were thought to be at the opposite poles of a continuum. The first represented good human relations practices; the second, an emphasis on the technical aspects of the job. Several years later, it was decided that these were not the opposite poles of a continuum, but independent. Thus, a leader could be high on both. Still other conceptualizations appeared, one of which added the dimension of "modifying employee goals," described as "behavior that influences the actual personal goals of subordinates in organizationally useful directions,"[24] just in case subordinates had the wrong ideas. Recently, Floyd Mann emphasized three skills: human relations skills, technical skills, and "administrative skills."[25] In this case, technical skills are confined to the methods and techniques for getting a task done, while administrative skills include such structural aspects as planning, organizing, task assignment, inspection, coordination, and making sure that the group goals mesh with the goals of the total organization.

David Bowers and Stanley Seashore came up with a four-factor theory of leadership, something of a modification of an earlier five-dimension theory proposed by Rensis Likert in his *New Patterns of Management* (see p. 99).[26] Traditional human relations theory was covered by two aspects—giving support and interaction facilitation; a third factor recognized the importance of "enthusiasm" for achieving goals; and the last was a work facilitation factor (combining Mann's technical and administrative skills). Others proposed other factors. All of them were more or less

[22]This trio was the product of the single most influential study of leadership, conducted in 1938 by Kurt Lewin, R. Lippett, and R. White. See R. K. White, *Autocracy and Democracy* (Westport, Conn.: Greenwood Press, 1972).

[23]Daniel Katz, N. Maccoby, and Nancy C. Morse, *Productivity, Supervision, and Morale in an Office Situation* (Detroit, Mich.: Darel Press, 1950).

[24]Robert L. Kahn, "Human Relations on the Shop Floor," in *Human Relations and Modern Management,* ed. E. M. Hugh-Jones (Amsterdam: North-Holland, 1958), pp. 43–74.

[25]Mann, in Dubin et al., *Leadership and Productivity,* pp. 68–103.

[26]David G. Bowers and Stanley E. Seashore, "Predicting Organizational Effectiveness with a Four-Factor Theory of Leadership,"*Administrative Science Quarterly* 11, no. 2 (September 1966): 238–263.

compatible with the initiating structure and consideration dimensions discovered in the Ohio State studies, but most offered elaborations and recombinations of elaborations. None dealt with the content of actual decisions—for example, to change production methods.

Unfortunately, despite these many variations on a common theme, enthusiasm has often outrun careful research. In 1966 Abraham Korman published a sober review of a large number of studies that related the various measures of consideration and initiating structure to measures of organizational effectiveness. He concluded that although the concepts had become bywords in industrial psychology, "it seems apparent that very little is now known as to how these variables may predict work-group performance and the conditions which affect such predictions. At the current time, we cannot even say whether they have any predictive significance at all."[27]

Many of the reported correlations were insignificant; the correlation between consideration and performance was better than that between initiating structure and performance (the latter was sometimes negative); the research did not take into account the situations of the groups or the possibility of important intervening variables; some correlations for consideration were the opposite of those predicted; and so on. "The piecemeal accumulation of 'two-variable' studies . . . does not provide the kinds of direction needed."[28] The influence of the size of a group (in one case, the more authoritarian leaders were more effective in large groups than the less authoritarian ones), urban versus semirural environments, the role of the wishes and expectations of subordinates, the self-esteem of subordinates, and so on were all held to complicate the relationship.

Such pessimistic conclusions have greeted other articles of faith about the way to increase productivity or organizational effectiveness. In addition to the importance of leadership, most human relations theorists have held that "job enlargement" will increase both satisfactions and productivity. According to the theory, the essence of bureaucracy is the minute division of tasks in order to increase predictability and skills, reduce training time, and make surveillance and evaluation more effective. This division of labor results in simplified, low-skill-level, short-cycle jobs. This in turn produces monotony, boredom, and dissatisfaction, which results in absenteeism, turnover, and restriction of output. In 1968 Charles Hulin and Milton Blood reviewed a large number of studies concerned with job enlargement and concluded as follows: "Those which have used acceptable methodology, control groups, appropriate analysis, and multivariate designs have generally not yielded evidence which could be considered as supporting the job-enlargement thesis. Those studies which do appear to support such a thesis frequently contain a number of deviations from normally acceptable research practices."[29] The latter group of studies is the larger, however, and has "generated the greatest favor and [has] been

[27]Abraham K. Korman, "Consideration,' 'Initiating Structure,' and Organizational Criteria—A Review," *Personnel Psychology* 19, no. 4 (1966): 349–361. (Quote is from p. 361.)

[28]Ibid., p. 360.

[29]Charles L. Hulin and Milton R. Blood, "Job Enlargement, Individual Differences, and Worker Responses," *Psychological Bulletin* 69, no. 1 (1968): 41–55.

accepted as gospel by a large number of psychologists and human relations theorists." Nevertheless, the case for job enlargement has been "drastically overstated and overgeneralized."[30] Hulin and Blood note studies that argue that not all workers are satisfied when they are allowed to take part in decision making, and they suggest that some prefer routine, repetitious, and specified work methods.

Theories of leadership and productivity more complex than the two-factor theory of consideration and initiating structure, or the comparable three-, four-, and five-factor models, have been offered. Frederick Herzberg's two-factor theory, for example, holds that people have two independent sets of needs—the need to avoid pain and the need to grow psychologically.[31] Avoidance of pain can be accomplished without necessarily producing happiness. Thus Herzberg made the intriguing suggestion that some aspects of work, such as company policy, administration, technical supervision, and salary, are "hygienic" factors that, if personnel are not content with them, will lead to dissatisfaction. But, if employees are content with them, these things will not *contribute* to satisfaction. Other aspects, such as the nature of the work itself and intrinsic rewards of the work, are motivators. If they are perceived positively, they will lead to satisfaction; but their absence will not lead to dissatisfaction.

This theory attracted much attention, perhaps partly because of the potentially powerful suggestion that factors contributing to satisfaction and those contributing to dissatisfaction are independent. If this were so, it could open up a complex area of research and perhaps rescue some of the previous theories. The theory also makes intuitive sense. However, it has been subjected to harsh criticism on methodological and other grounds. For example, only if one adopts the questionable empirical methods of Herzberg and his students does one find support for it. Robert House and Lawrence Wigdor, in their review, find considerable evidence that what causes job satisfaction for one person need not cause it for another. Job satisfaction is relative to a large number of alternatives available to the individual and affected by job level, age, sex, education, culture, job cycle time, and the respondent's standing in his or her group.[32] Thus, once more, the number of variables mount.

A far more sophisticated study of leadership, Fred Fiedler's "contingency" theory,[33] is the last we shall consider. Pondering several decades of research on leadership, Fiedler increased the complexity of the problem geometrically when he demonstrated that the "climate" of the group has a substantial impact upon the effectiveness of leadership styles. If the group situation is either highly favorable or highly unfavorable for the leader, a task-oriented leader does best; if it is in between, a leader skilled in interpersonal relations is best. By a favorable situation, Fiedler meant the extent to which relationships between the leader and the member are good, tasks can be easily programmed, and the position of the leader is clearly

[30]Ibid.

[31]Frederick Herzberg, *Work and the Nature of Man* (New York: Crowell, 1966). The theory was first put forth in F. Herzberg, B. Mausner, and B. Snyderman, *The Motivation to Work,* 2nd ed. (New York: Wiley, 1959).

[32]Robert J. House and Lawrence A. Wigdor, "Herzberg's Dual-Factor Theory of Job Satisfaction and Motivation: A Review of the Evidence and a Criticism," *Personnel Psychology* 20 (1967): 369–389.

[33]Fred E. Fiedler, *A Theory of Leadership Effectiveness* (New York: McGraw-Hill, 1967).

established. Apparently, if all these exist to a substantial degree, the best leader is the one who provides task direction and gets on with the work of the group. Interpersonal relations are not problematic and will take care of themselves. If the relationships between the leader and members are bad, tasks are unclear, and the position of the leader is not clearly established (what Fiedler calls "low position power"), then attention to interpersonal relations will be wasted; strong direction is needed. But if the situation is in between, then interpersonal leadership or something close to consideration is critical. Fiedler calls this a contingency theory of leadership—it is contingent on some nonleadership variables. If true—and he has considerable supporting data from a variety of groups in different countries, though some of these data are less convincing than others—this represents an increase in sophistication and complexity over the prevailing views.

Unfortunately, the matter does not end with the complex interaction of leadership style, group structure, tasks, and relationships in the group. There are still other factors that influence leadership effectiveness. First, Fiedler's findings are more relevant to interacting groups than to those that "counteract" (such as committees that represent different viewpoints) or those that require little member interdependence ("co-acting" groups, such as machine operators working side by side). Second, the degree of stress is important since the findings do not appear to hold where group stress is minimal.[34] Another reservation concerns the timing of the leadership style. At what point in the group situation does the leader emphasize task performance or interpersonal relations?[35] (Someone could work on that particular complication alone for five years.) Furthermore, Fiedler notes that other variables—such as member abilities and motivation, group heterogeneity, expertness of the leader, the leader's familiarity with the task, and his or her familiarity with the group—are likely to be important. No doubt others would turn up when research is conducted on still more groups. If so, what are we left with?

One is tempted to say that the research on leadership has left us with the clear view that things are far more complicated and "contingent" than we initially believed and that, in fact, they are so complicated and contingent that it may not be worth our while to spin out more and more categories and qualifications. Already, the task of either training leaders to fit the jobs or designing jobs to fit the leaders, a position Fiedler is led to advocate,[36] appears to be monumental. If leadership techniques must change with every change in group personnel, task, timing, experience, and so on, then either leaders or jobs must constantly change, and this will make predictions difficult. At the extremes, we can be fairly confident in identifying good or bad leaders; but for most situations we will probably have little to say. We may learn a great deal about interpersonal relations but not much about organizations.[37]

[34]Ibid., pp. 189–195.

[35]W. K. Graham, "Description of Leader Behavior and Evaluation of Leaders as a Function of LPC," *Personnel Psychology* 21 (Winter 1968): 457–464.

[36]Fred Fiedler, "Engineer the Job to Fit the Manager," *Harvard Business Review* 43, no. 5 (1965): 115–122.

[37]This is not true of the Vroom-Yetton model; they find that leaders do not have one dominant style. Rather, they use different ones, depending on the situation, and shift easily. Once this point is made

Training Leaders

Finally, even if we have vague hunches that good leaders are those who practice good human relations, that most leaders do not, and that we have an idea of what good human relations are, can we train leaders to perform better? A whole industry has evolved around the assumption that we can. Academic social scientists make handsome outside incomes from participating in training programs for management; independent corporations have been set up to do this; business schools derive no small part of their income from conducting training programs. The most famous and financially successful of these programs have been dubbed T-group programs, with the T standing for training. These sessions seek to expand interpersonal consciousness, develop authenticity in interpersonal relations and spontaneous behavior, eliminate behavior that stems from hierarchical positions and substitute collaborative behavior, and develop ability to solve conflicts through problem solving rather than through bargaining, coercion, or power manipulation. Since this training technique has become so widespread and important in the organizational world, extending to noneconomic organizations and being incorporated into business school curricula, it is worth quoting from one account to give the flavor of these sessions, which can be both illuminating and devastating for the individuals involved.

> At the fifth meeting the group's feelings about its own progress became the initial focus of discussion. The "talkers" participated as usual, conversation shifting rapidly from one point to another. Dissatisfaction was mounting, expressed through loud, snide remarks by some and through apathy by others.
>
> George Franklin appeared particularly disturbed. Finally pounding the table, he exclaimed, "I don't know what is going on here! I should be paid for listening to this drivel? I'm getting just a bit sick of wasting my time here. If the profs don't put out —I quit!" George was pleased; he was angry, and he had said so. As he sat back in his chair, he felt he had the group behind him. He felt he had the guts to say what most of the others were thinking! Some members of the group applauded loudly, but others showed obvious disapproval. They wondered why George was excited over so insignificant an issue, why he hadn't done something constructive rather than just sounding off as usual. Why, they wondered, did he say their comments were "drivel"?
>
> George Franklin became the focus of discussion. "What do you mean, George, by saying this nonsense?" "What do you expect, a neat set of rules to meet all your problems?" George was getting uncomfortable. These were questions difficult for him to answer. Gradually he began to realize that a large part of the group disagreed with him; then he began to wonder why. He was learning something about people he hadn't known before." . . . How does it feel, George, to have people disagree with you when you thought you had them behind you? . . ."

---

it appears obvious. Our strong inclination to believe in a dominant style rather than contextual variations in style may be an attribution we make to convince ourselves of order in a world of supervision that is at least very flexible, if not actually disorderly. The Vroom-Yetton model clearly points to the importance of context—that is, structure—and as such it tells us about organizations rather than interpersonal relations. See Victor H. Vroom and Arthur G. Jago, "On the Validity of the Vroom-Yetton Model," *Journal of Applied Psychology* 63, no. 2 (1978), 151–162.

Bob White was first annoyed with George and now with the discussion. He was getting tense, a bit shaky perhaps. Bob didn't like anybody to get a raw deal, and he felt that George was getting it. At first Bob tried to minimize George's outburst, and then he suggested that the group get on to the real issues; but the group continued to focus on George. Finally Bob said, "Why don't you leave George alone and stop picking on him? We're not getting anywhere this way."

With the help of the leaders, the group focused on Bob. "What do you mean, 'picking' on him?" "Why, Bob, have you tried to change the discussion?" "Why are you so protective of George?" Bob began to realize that the group wanted to focus on George; he also saw that George didn't think he was being picked on but felt he was learning something about himself and how others reacted to him. "Why do I always get upset," Bob began to wonder, "when people start to look at each other? Why do I feel sort of sick when people get angry at each other?" . . . Now Bob was learning something about how people saw him, while gaining some insight into his own behavior.[38]

In 1968 John Campbell and Marvin Dunnette conducted a thorough review of the evidence for the effectiveness of T-group training, and their conclusion is melancholy.[39] "To sum up, the assumption that T-group training has positive utility for organizations must necessarily rest on shaky ground. It has been neither confirmed nor disconfirmed. The authors wish to emphasize again that utility for the organization is not necessarily the same as utility for the individual."[40]

Their last point deserves elaboration. As they carefully note in an addendum to their review, many people have enthusiastically testified to the benefits of the experience—for themselves, as persons. The cold scientific criteria that Campbell and Dunnette use to judge the effectiveness of something so "life enhancing" to participants must surely be irrelevant to participants. Their enthusiasm is frequently great. If the effects are not found to carry over into actual organizational situations, it may be the problem of the research, not of the T-group training.

There is something to this posture, though Campbell and Dunnette are correct that it is also quite inappropriate to make claims for the effectiveness of these techniques merely on the enthusiastic response of some or most participants. One suspects that most managers live drab and muted lives in some respects and rarely enjoy those life-enhancing, self-actualizing experiences and encounters that others realize through cultural and aesthetic activities. If so, or even if everyone needs more of these experiences, the returns to the individual may be high, and the costs to him or her and the organization may be quite trivial. We should, then, bless T-groups because they do for managers what pot and other drugs, rock concerts, and music videos do for the younger generation. The search for authenticity and spontaneity should be never-ending, and if it must occur in the guise of better productivity in

---

[38]Robert Tannenbaum, I. R. Weschler, and F. Massarik, *Leadership and Organization: A Behavioral Science Approach* (New York: McGraw-Hill, 1961), p. 123.

[39]John P. Campbell and Marvin D. Dunnette, "Effectiveness of T-Group Experiences in Managerial Training and Development," *Psychological Bulletin* 70, no. 2 (August 1968): 73–104.

[40]Ibid., p. 98. For a spirited exchange between these authors and Chris Argyris on the topic, see Marvin Dunnette, John Campbell, and Chris Argyris, "A Symposium: Laboratory Training," *Industrial Relations* 8, no. 1 (October 1968): 1–46.

organizations, let it. The trainees will return refreshed to a world of hierarchies, conflict, authority, stupidity, and brilliance, but the hierarchies and the like probably will not fade away. Most organizations remain highly authoritarian systems; some even use T-groups to hide that essential fact.

Summary of the Research

This completes our review of the research dealing primarily with leadership and productivity models. Most of that research is psychological in theory and orientation. In sheer volume, it constitutes the largest group of empirical studies within the human relations tradition, and perhaps in organizational analysis in general. The research has generally been carried out with more sophistication with regard to control groups, multivariate analysis, replication studies, and so on than any other branch of organizational research. A great deal has been learned about individuals and small groups in the process, but what we have learned about organizations is primarily that our simple models do not hold in all or most cases, nor do they account for much of the variance when they do hold. The models have become increasingly complex, with something like the following progression: high morale leades to high productivity; good leadership ("democratic" leadership, good human relations, consideration, etc.) leads to high morale (and thus to high productivity); effective leadership (combining a concern for people with a concern for task effectiveness) leads to high morale and/or high productivity; effective leadership has to be tailored to the group situation (e.g., group task, structure, member relationship, timing, stress, etc.). With few exceptions there is little recognition that leaders can vary their styles to fit the demands of the situation.

The increase in complexity has resulted in a decrease in applicability and in theoretical power. We are now in a situation where the variables are so numerous and complex that we can hardly generalize about organizations or even types of organizations. Only in extreme cases of very poor leadership or very good leadership can we say much with confidence, except that most situations fall between these extremes.

A similar fate may await the more general theories of sociologists when they, too, amass a large number of sophisticated studies. Or it may be, one hopes, that any theory that has the power to explain a good deal of organizational behavior will have to deal with more general variables than leadership and small-group behavior. It will have to deal with such variables as types of structure, group interrelationships, character of resources, technology, and environmental influences, where the more specific variables of leader behavior and small-group characteristics are held to be randomly distributed and thus have little effect when a large number of organizations are the object of study. The conclusion reached by Harold Wilensky almost thirty years ago still stands:

> All this suggests that, at minimum, the practitioner who wants to apply the human relations research has no clear directive as to what to do—and this is true not only of the findings on size of immediate work group, the character of informal work group

solidarity, degree of identification with company goals, and type of leadership style as related to productivity; it applies also to the findings on the relation of "morale" (i.e., satisfaction with job and with company) to all of these variables. The evidence is typically inconclusive, the interpretations sometimes contradictory.[41]

Perhaps in reaction to this mounting complexity, psychologists have tried to cut the Gordian knot in another manner—with the blunt edge of stimulus-response theory. The idea goes back to the Russian scientist Ivan Pavlov who taught dogs to salivate at the sound of a bell. It became entwined with more sophisticated learning theory (behavior is a learned response, not an expression of complex inner drives, fixed traits, or need satisfactions) and emerged in the 1950s and 1960s as "operant conditioning" theory, associated with psychologist B. F. Skinner.[42] Its simplicity exceeds that of the leadership-morale-productivity model. Behavior is a function of its consequences, runs the dictum. If you are rewarded for "emitting" a type of behavior, you will repeat it; if the behavior is ignored or punished, the behavior will be "extinguished." Rewards are more powerful than punishments; therefore, managers should emphasize "reinforcers" rather than demotivators. Reinforcements should come immediately after the behavior that one wishes to reinforce, but if repetitive acts are to be rewarded, it is best to reward random, intermittent instances of the behavior; otherwise the person can become satiated with the reward and not connect it to the behavior. Despite the fact that the human relations tradition strongly believes in rewards, the operant conditioning formulation is regarded with suspicion and distaste. It sounds mechanical, dehumanizing, overly manipulative, and treats employees as if they were pigeons, rats in a maze, or at best, children. Operant conditioning advocates deny all this, of course.

For a variety of reasons it has been difficult to apply this theory to organizations in any scientific way. (There are the usual highly publicized cures, based on quite ambiguous situations where a variety of uncontrolled factors could be operating to produce the effects, much as in the leadership area.) Fred Luthans and Robert Kreitner devoted a book to the subject of organizational applications, but the examples concern such relatively trivial or simple situations as being late to work.[43] But it is too early to rule this approach out of court. At the least it supports the growing emphasis on evaluating and rewarding performance,[44] conforms to what we know skilled leaders often do (try to praise good behavior immediately, and avoid punishing bad behavior with immobilizing global assertions such as "you are always doing that"), and, finally, agrees with the growing emphasis on the plasticity of behavior and the de-emphasis of basic character traits, values, and norms. I expect it will eventually have a large audience.

[41]Harold L. Wilensky, "Human Relations in the Workplace," in Conrad Arensberg et al., *Research in Industrial Human Relations: A Critical Appraisal* (New York: Harper & Row, 1957), p. 34.

[42]B. F. Skinner, *Beyond Freedom and Dignity* (New York: Bantam Books, 1971).

[43]Fred Luthans and Robert Kreitner, *Organizational Behavior Modification* (Glenview, Ill.: Scott, Foresman, 1975).

[44]Dornbush and Scott, *Evaluation and the Exercise of Authority.*

THE GROUP RELATIONS MODELS

The second branch of the human relations movement incorporates the assumptions of the first—the importance of leadership, and so forth—but is more concerned with changing the total organizational climate than the practices of individual leaders. The assumptions of the psychological model are generalized to larger units, and there is more concern with the interaction of groups, the role of top management in setting a proper climate, minimizing hierarchical differences throughout the organization, and increasing the influence of all groups. The distinction between the two branches is more academic than real, but it will serve our expository purposes.

Whereas the psychological model sometimes views good human relations techniques as only a hygienic device (it is better to treat people decently than poorly), designed to minimize opposition and to encourage cooperation with the superior, it is characteristic of the group-oriented branch to stress the creative aspects of good organizational climates. That is, using the terms proposed by Raymond Miles, the former is concerned with "human relations" while the latter is concerned with "human resources."[45] All organizational members constitute valuable resources, and we should learn to develop, tap, and free these resources. Humans are assumed to desire to participate fully, to solve their "higher needs" of autonomy and self-actualization, and to wish to identify with the goals of the organization. They will do so if the leadership and structure of the organization will permit it.

Miles implies that one reason it was not possible to clearly establish that high morale led to high productivity is that the relationship often goes in the opposite direction: high morale may be *due to* high productivity, rather than the reverse. He argues somewhat as follows: increased productivity comes from the release of the individuals' creative energies; the way to ensure this release is to create a climate that allows members to participate fully. When they participate fully, they realize their higher needs and thus have increased morale. But increased morale is a by-product of the "human resources model" rather than a means to higher productivity as in the "human relations model." In the human relations model, participation is seen as the "least-cost method of obtaining cooperation and getting . . . decisions accepted," but in the human resources model it is a means of moving the level of decision making down to where those most informed make the decision, are able to utilize their experience, and are encouraged to search for novel solutions to problems. Finally, in this more expansive view of cooperation, people not only want to belong, be liked, and be respected, as in the more limited human relations model, but they want to "contribute effectively and creatively to the accomplishment of worthwhile objectives."[46]

This view seems to resemble those of the human relations pioneers, such as Barnard and Mayo, who wished to summon people to higher fulfillments (and company profits). But I think Miles means something more prosaic, a perhaps romantic view that I share. Simply stated, people do not like to do apparently

---

[45]Raymond E. Miles, "Human Relations or Human Resources," *Harvard Business Review* 43, no. 4 (July/August 1965): 148–155.
[46]Ibid., p. 151.

meaningless work; they prefer something that seems to do some good, even if it is for the company. An effective degradation technique in prisons and concentration camps is to force inmates to work hard at stacking things perfectly, then unstacking them, then restacking, and so on. Though this is an extreme example, meaningless jobs—and annoying ones, such as undoing a superior's error ("If they would only get things right in the first place")—sap one's sense of personal worth in organizations. If one must work for someone else's profit or credit, let it at least be socially constructive work.

The expansive view of human nature explicit in the second branch of human relations theory finds its theoretical justification in the work of psychologist Abraham Maslow.[47] Several members of this school cite his work in this connection. Maslow held that there is a hierarchy of needs in the individual. Once the lower-order needs, such as physiological and safety needs, are satisfied, the higher-order needs, such as self-actualization and autonomy, come into play. Each higher-order need is not activated until the one below it is reasonably satisfied.

Despite the lack of solid research evidence (possibly because vague needs cannot be measured) and the existence of circumstantial evidence that there is no clear hierarchical ordering of the needs, Maslow's theory has proved very useful for the human relations (or human resources) movement. It justifies extensive involvement in, and identification with, the organization. A person who participates in an organization only to the extent of the contract, or to the extent of giving what she considers to be a fair degree of effort for the return she receives, is considered to be a stunted individual—even though she may be self-actualizing outside the organization. Chris Argyris, for example, posits a fundamental conflict between the individual and the organization, finding that the organization generally demands dependent, childish behavior from its members and makes it difficult for them to grow and achieve or maintain "maturity."[48] The assumption here is that the organizational context is the principal one for individuals, and if they are not capable of self-actualizing behavior in the organization, they are immature. Therefore Argyris calls for radical restructuring of organizations and extensive T-group therapy to permit all those capable of maturity to behave maturely; indeed, it is the responsibility of the organization to develop maturity in individuals.

Such maturity, it would seem, would be on organizational terms. Though Argyris and others note the creative aspect of conflict, little in their work suggests that a proper form of self-actualization might be to organize employees for better working conditions, to advocate more ethical advertising practices, or to expose the cover-up of unjustified expenses in government contracts. Nor, presumably, would it be mature to oppose the development of chemical warfare techniques in a chemical firm or a nonprofit research laboratory,[49] to be in favor of mass transit rather

---

[47]Abraham Maslow, *Motivation and Personality*, 2nd ed. (New York: Harper & Row, 1970); and Maslow, *Toward a Psychology of Being*, 2nd ed. (New York: Van Nostrand Reinhold, 1968).

[48]Chris Argyris, *Interpersonal Competence and Organizational Effectiveness* (Homewood, Ill.: Dorsey Press, 1962). He argues that a great service the industrial world can offer to our society is to develop "fully functioning human beings who aspire to excellence." See p. 5.

[49]For example, when the president of the Stanford Research Institute (SRI) said that no one was forced to work on a project he found morally objectionable, one SRI physicist objected that he was pressured

than private automobiles at General Motors, to oppose price-fixing techniques at General Electric, or to call for better testing of drugs and more accurate advertising in a pharmaceutical firm.

In contrast, one might argue that people may disagree with some or all of the goals of an organization (including the goal of profit maximization) but still find that they can best be reimbursed for their efforts, training, and skills in this rather than other organizations, and so can remain members without being immature. Probably most employees, at both the managerial and blue-collar level, do not seriously inquire into the objectives and tactics of the organizations that employ them. If so, to "contribute effectively and creatively to the accomplishment of worthwhile objectives" is not an important element in organizational analysis. But for the human relations theorists, such self-actualization, *on organizational terms,* is crucial.

The Likert Model

The two most influential models that represent the second branch of human relations theory are those of Douglas McGregor and Rensis Likert. The McGregor model is the less developed.[50] He simply contrasted "Theory X"—which represented a caricature of bureaucratic theory wherein management is supposed to believe that workers hate their work, will do anything to avoid it, are "indifferent to organizational needs," and can only be made to cooperate through the application of heavy negative sanctions—with "Theory Y"—wherein managers assume that such things as the capacity for assuming responsibility, the potential for development, and the readiness to direct behavior toward organizational goals are all present in people. The essential task of management, in this view, is to arrange things so people achieve their own goals by accomplishing those of the organization.

The Likert model also rests simply on a contrast between the exploitative and authoritative and the "participative management" models, with intermediate points.[51] However, it is more complex than McGregor's model since it specifies more variables and is more concerned with the interaction of groups. Furthermore, a vast amount of research conducted by those associated with the Institute for Social Research at the University of Michigan is cited in connection with it. (The Institute, a highly productive organization that Likert headed until his retirement, conducts both basic and applied research on organizations and groups. It is financed by contracts from business organizations and grants from various branches of the federal government and foundations.)

We will limit our attention to the Likert model. It is the best known of the human relations models, and Likert's first major book, *New Patterns of Management,* published in 1961, received three management awards and a great deal of

---

into doing chemical warfare research. He was fired, and the executive vice-president of SRI said: "People like that have a decision to make—do they want to support the organization or not." "The University Arsenal," *Look,* August 26, 1969, p. 34.

[50]Douglas McGregor, *The Human Side of Enterprise* (New York: McGraw-Hill, 1960).

[51]Rensis Likert, *New Patterns of Management* (New York: McGraw-Hill, 1961).

critical acclaim. A second book, *The Human Organization*, published in 1967, carried the work somewhat farther by reporting on some further studies and refining the basic indicators. A third book repeats the basic characterization.[52]

Likert's "science-based theory," as he calls it, is summarized by a lengthy table that appears at the end of each of his books; he compares this to a periodic table in chemistry.[53] Across the top of the version appearing in the 1961 book are four "systems" of organizations, called exploitative authoritative (which corresponds to the Weberian model of bureaucracy or to McGregor's Theory X), benevolent authoritative, consultative, and finally, participative group. He then lists forty-two aspects of organizations, and for each he indicates the values it has under each of the four systems. For example, the first aspect listed is the nature of the underlying motives that are tapped in organizations. For the exploitative authoritative system these are "physical security, economic security, and some use of the desire for status."[54] The organization in this system depends on these underlying motives. As one moves from this system to the participative group system, more motives are added—for example, the desire for new experience and motivational forces arising from group processes. The next aspect concerns the manner in which motives are used. At one extreme, this is through "fear, threats, punishment, and occasional rewards." At the other, motives are used by means of "economic rewards based on a compensation system developed through participation, group participation and involvement in setting goals, improving methods, appraising progress toward goals, etc."[55]

Likert proceeds through the forty-two aspects, specifying the differences between the four systems. In the 1967 book the list is slightly revised and expanded to fifty-one aspects. Also, the names of the four systems are dropped, and he labels them only System 1 through System 4. Since the list is used as a research tool, with managers checking where their organization falls on each aspect, he felt it was advisable not to influence the answers by labeling the systems as exploitative authoritative, and so on. (In later uses of this research tool, even the headings, System 1, etc., were dropped, and the order of some of the aspects was reversed, going from good to bad, in order to avoid "response set behavior.")

There are several interesting things to note about Likert's list. First, the theory does not depend on leadership alone. The fifty-one aspects are divided into eight groups, only one of which deals with leadership processes. There are groups concerned with the character of motivational forces, communication processes, interac-

---

[52]Rensis Likert, *The Human Organization* (New York: McGraw-Hill, 1967); and Likert, *New Ways of Managing Conflict* (New York: McGraw-Hill, 1975).

[53]Likert, *New Patterns*, p. 234. Three other major aspects of his theory will not be dealt with here. One is a useful statement of the causal links among his groups of variables (*Human Organization*, p. 137); a second is a convincing statement of the need for accounting procedures that reflect human resources (ibid., chapters 5, 6, and 9); the third is a discussion of "organizational families" and the "linking pin function" (ibid., Chapter 10). The last constitutes an assertion that the relationships between a superior and, say four subordinates should not consist of four separate superior-subordinate contacts, but all five should interact as a group, with the superior linking this group to other groups. To the extent that tasks performed by the subordinates are at all interdependent, the need for this is obvious in all organizational theory.

[54]Likert, *New Patterns*, p. 223.

[55]Ibid., p. 223.

tion-influence processes, decision-making processes, the setting or ordering of goals, control processes, and performance goals and training. Thus, presumably all of the human aspects of the organization are covered (hence the comparison to a periodic table in chemistry). The theory is not limited to leadership alone.

Second, the vast majority of the items are "motherhood" items. No one is likely to be against most of the System 4 values, just as no one is against motherhood or for sin. For example, Likert is encouraged that when asked which system they prefer, managers overwhelmingly choose System 4. But to choose System 1 is to recommend, for example, that the company have no confidence and trust in subordinates, while System 4 indicates complete confidence and trust. Nor are the managers likely to prefer subservient and hostile attitudes toward superiors over cooperative attitudes with mutual trust and confidence. In the case of a few of the items, a manager might have some qualms about System 4. He or she might feel, for example, that employees cannot be fully involved in decisions related to their work, for a number of reasons. It might be too costly or time-consuming to inform them fully; or they might not possess the technical training to fully understand the decisions that are made and how they interact with other work areas. The manager might be inclined to say it varies with the task and with what is actually meant by being "involved" in decision making. But when presented with the following four choices regarding desired involvement of employees, he or she has little choice but to select the fourth, perhaps with misgivings: "(1) Not at all. (2) Never involved in decisions; occasionally consulted. (3) Usually are consulted but ordinarily not involved in the decision making. (4) Are involved fully in all decisions related to their work."[56]

Likert himself does not see the items as being "motherhood" items, drawn from a boy-scout creed for organizations. He speaks of the "predominance of System 2 concepts in the available literature on management," though he does not cite any examples.[57] Presumably System 1 is out, and while organizations do not exploit personnel as much as before, they still practice benevolent authoritarianism and thus fall into System 2. He says that the readily available concepts in management theory apply to System 2, but not to System 4. We might take the last five items in his table to see what this would indicate. It shows that the literature on management, if he is correct, would *not* be in favor of: excellent training resources; providing a great deal of management training of the type desired; seeking to achieve extremely high goals; using data gathered for control purposes for self-guidance and coordinated problem solving rather than for punitive purposes; meshing the informal and the formal organizations; having all social forces supporting efforts to achieve organizational goals.[58]

Not only does he say the literature is not in favor of such things, which is simply not true, but he adds that those managers who try to use System 4 techniques have to "keep [as] quiet as possible about it," so low is the faith of management in trust, good communication, high goals, and so forth.[59] Indeed, he reports that managers are not above deliberately destroying System 4 departments in their frustration over

[56]Likert, *Human Organization*, p. 207.

[57]Ibid., p. 109.

[58]Ibid., pp. 209–210.

[59]Ibid., p. 109.

trying to convert them to System 2 departments.[60] Thus Likert decidedly does not feel that all he has done is to name some virtues and vices and allow managers to choose the virtues. Theory itself is predisposed to the vices. Likert is not alone here, by any means; most human relations theorists erect a bureaucratic monster and tilt furiously at it.

Another striking thing about the Likert table is that where these questions have been asked of groups of managers, there is a remarkable degree of consistency among items. The intercorrelations are very high. As Likert points out, if some items are scored System 2, all of them tend to be.[61] It is also the case that where their preferences are asked, the managers all invariably check System 4. (Presumably no one in the various companies where preferences have been asked has read the "available literature on management," which is supposed to favor System 2. Moreover, they have not sought to destroy System 4 departments.) Such consistency might tend to discourage some researchers who attempt to show that their various measures are independent of one another. That is, if leadership, communications, goal setting, decision-making processes, supportive behavior, and so on are separate characteristics of management, then there should be some independence among them. One would expect to find some organizations where communication processes are poor but control processes or the setting and ordering of goals are good. If not, one suspects that only one dimension is being tapped, and there is no point in distinguishing among such factors. The one dimension, for example, might be morale. If things are going well, one is likely to report trust, confidence, decentralized decision making, high goals, participation in goal setting, and so on. If things are going poorly, one backs off from giving System 4 ratings to these items.

However, Likert does not hold this view. Instead, he finds that the very high intercorrelations among the items "and the high split-half reliabilities lead to an important conclusion . . . [i.e., that] every component part of a particular management system fits well with each of the other parts and functions in harmony with them. Each system of management has a basic integrity of its own."[62] For this reason he calls it a "systems approach."

Finally, it is distinctive of his theory (and most human relations theories) that all organizations are considered to be alike.[63] Differences in size, technology, markets, raw materials, goals, and auspices are irrelevant. While much of management theory is moving to a position that there is no single best way to do things, Likert, along with many others, continues to advocate one best way. This is especially surprising because some of the work turned out by Likert's associates at the Institute for Social Research, and cited in *The Human Organization* as evidence for the validity of the theory, runs against this view. Indeed, Likert himself says as much in two chapters of his earlier book, *New Patterns of Management.* In Chapter 6 he distinguishes repetitive work from varied work, and he notes that in the former there is only a slight relationship between attitudes of workers and produc-

[60]Ibid., p. 112.
[61]Ibid., p. 116.
[62]Ibid., p. 123.
[63]Likert, *New Patterns*, p. 241.

tivity, and that "different styles of leadership and management have tended to develop" for the two different kinds of work.[64] The "job-organization" system is generally applied where repetitive work dominates and resembles a bureaucratic model, and the "cooperative-motivation" system applies where varied work predominates. He says that both systems realize high performance and low costs but that both could be better if the "power of each were combined with the other."[65] The problem is that the job-organization system is highly developed in theory and practice and widely accepted, while the cooperative-motivation system "has never been described or stated formally as a management theory."[66] (This is a remarkable statement considering the volume of literature on cooperation and motivation, beginning with Barnard.) Furthermore, the results obtained by the former system are immediately evident, while those of the latter may not be apparent for years because they involve more subtle, though powerful and lasting, changes.

In Chapter 6 of *New Patterns of Management,* Likert indicates his belief that there are advantages to combining the two systems, and he cites the case of a company that had been operating under a cooperative-motivation system but that should move to the job-organization system.[67] In the following chapter, he also admits that there is no one best way to supervise. "Supervisory and leadership practices, effective in some situations, yield unsatisfactory results in others."[68] In this case, however, he does not refer to the difference between repetitive and varied work demands but to differences in the "expectations, values, and interpersonal skills of subordinates." Thus, we have two admitted sources of diversity in organizations or subunits—tasks and member characteristics. If organizations differ, then to claim that System 4 is the best for all organizations either indicates that the scheme has little to do with supervisory style or types of tasks confronted, in which case the "science-based theory" is of little relevance, or it indicates that the scheme can only be applied where work is varied and subordinates are "emotionally mature"[69] and have common expectations, values, and interpersonal skills. If the latter is the case, the theory is highly restrictive.

The Evidence

With these comments in mind, let us turn to the empirical evidence for the superiority of System 4. There is probably no other organizational research unit in the world that has more empirical data on a wide variety of organizations than the one Likert headed—the Institute for Social Research. And, in both above-mentioned books he makes voluminous citations to this literature and acknowledges the help in writing the books provided by the many outstanding members of the

[64]Ibid., pp. 77–78.
[65]Ibid., pp. 82–83.
[66]Ibid., p. 83.
[67]Ibid., p. 85.
[68]Ibid., p. 89.
[69]"Participative organizations require emotionally mature personalities." Ibid., p. 57.

Institute. This is no fly-by-night theory supported by one study or by the work of a few of one's graduate students.

In *The Human Organization,* the evidence offered is of many kinds. Some of it comes from unpublished material and is only reported in sketchy terms. Some of it is in the form of numerous citations to the published works of Institute members. These citations refer to research that does not always support the major tenets of the human relations school (e.g., some of it reports that high morale and high productivity do not necessarily go hand in hand). In addition, these studies were not designed to test the major proposition of System 4 but are generally studies of single work groups or particular leadership techniques. While they may support the human relations viewpoint, they do not support this specific theory that covers all the human aspects of organization. The most important evidence comes from a separate volume that explicitly uses System 4 measurement techniques and concepts in the study of a pajama factory. Likert cites it frequently as substantiating the theory. One other study is reported on in some detail in *The Human Organization* and also constitutes evidence for the theory. We will start with the latter.

Life Insurance Salesmen. The most dramatic and convincing evidence for the effectiveness of System 4 is found in the study of a number of owner-managed sales offices of a large, national life insurance company.[70] The national headquarters designated the top twenty performing units and the bottom twenty—out of a total of about one hundred agencies—to be subjects of this study. Likert compared the two groups on a number of measures, and the scatterplots presented in his book show that the high-performing units clearly had more of the following characteristics than the low-performing units: supportive relationships by the owner-manager, high sales goals set by the manager, high goals set by the salesmen, high peer-group loyalty, positive attitudes toward the manager, group methods of supervision, and high "peer leadership."

Peer leadership meant that the salesmen engaged in leadership among themselves, rather than having leadership come only from the manager or a supervisor. The group methods of supervision involved monthly or bimonthly meetings where each man reported on his past work, successes and failures, techniques that he used, and so on. The other salesmen discussed his work and helped him set goals for himself. They shared ideas and information about "new appeals, new markets, and new strategies of selling."[71] Supportive relationships were indicated by positive answers to such paternalistic questions as the following: How much trust and confidence does your superior have in you? Does he indicate he is confident you can do your job well? Does he try to understand your problems and do something about them? Is he really interested in training you and helping you learn better ways of doing your work? Does he keep you informed and fully share information? Does he value your ideas and seek them and endeavor to use them? Is he friendly and easily approached? Does he refrain from claiming all the credit for himself?[72]

---

[70]Likert, *Human Organization,* pp. 52–77.
[71]Ibid., p. 57.
[72]Ibid., pp. 48–49.

Some questions can be raised about the study. By using only the twenty best performing agencies and the twenty worst performing, the effect of leadership on performance is grossly exaggerated. Even the responses of these two extreme groups overlap on most items. Including the intermediate sixty would presumably weaken the contrast between high- and low-performing groups. In addition, an article by Stanley Seashore and Ephraim Yuchtman dealing with the same agencies reports only ten significant correlations (out of a possible fifty) between several different measures of performance and such things as supportive behavior.[73] An earlier article by Bowers and Seashore finds no correlations between other performance measures and supportive behavior.[74] Thus it is not clear what role the criteria used by Likert to measure performance played in producing his high relationships.[75]

More important, however, is the nature of the sample. Assuming that all the relationships that Likert found were accurate, we still might wonder if the findings could indeed be generalized and used to support the theory. Life insurance salesmen are presumably a somewhat distinctive breed—gregarious, verbal, skilled in friendliness and interpersonal dealings, and accustomed to ferreting out new kinds of appeals and selling strategies. The units studied are small, apparently averaging about twenty-five salesmen and managerial personnel, and do not have complex structures. In some cases there is a supervisor between the manager and the salesmen; in some cases there is none. The salesmen are theoretically in competition with each other for prospects, but rarely would they actually compete for the same prospect. They are paid on a commission basis only, so there is a direct correlation between their effort and their reward, with few organizational factors intervening in this relationship. There is no need for interdependence among salesmen (though the sharing of ideas, etc., will presumably prove beneficial), and there is little competition over scarce organizational resources.

Thus, these are unusual "organizations." The close fit reported by Likert (though not clearly supported by the other reports on the survey) between performance and aspects of System 4 might be due in large part to the enormous importance of high morale, enthusiasm, and techniques of interpersonal relations in this kind of work and the low importance of things that usually make organizational life

[73]Stanley E. Seashore and Ephraim Yuchtman, "Factorial Analysis of Organizational Performance," *Administrative Science Quarterly* 12, no. 3 (December 1967): 377–395.

[74]Bowers and Seashore, "Predicting Organizational Effectiveness."

[75]To confuse things further, Bowers and Seashore refer to the forty agencies as "representative," though they actually are the top and bottom twenty of the one hundred. Other discrepancies in the work of the Institute are puzzling. A strong relationship between accepting *company* goals and productivity, reported by Likert in *New Patterns* (pp. 31–32), turns out to be actually a relationship between accepting *union* goals and productivity when one examines the original study by Seashore that Likert cites. In the original study, there was no significant relationship between accepting company goals and productivity. Some of the graphs in *Patterns* are greatly distorted in favor of the thesis, as a student (Garry Meyers) once pointed out to me (see those on pp. 11 and 20 of *New Patterns of Management*). Recently it was disclosed that the "results" of an Institute study were published in *Personnel* by a member of the consultancy team (Alfred J. Marrow, whom we will meet on p. 107) before the data were even gathered. Neither Likert nor Chris Argyris, the two other members of the team, had anything to do with the misleading article, but the fascinating account of this large effort to reform a bureaucracy reveals the dangers and seductions of the advocate role for social scientists. See the Appendix to Donald P. Warwick, *A Theory of Public Bureaucracy: Politics, Personality, and Organization in the State Department* (Cambridge, Mass.: Harvard University Press, 1975), pp. 219–237.

difficult—group conflicts, divergent group goals, specialization in work groups, competition for scarce resources, daily face-to-face interaction and interdependencies, complex hierarchies, and fixed amounts of remuneration. Likert's statement that the principles illustrated "appear to be applicable to all kinds of undertakings"[76] must be treated with considerable reservation. This is but one more example of the difficulty of generalizing about all organizations.

The problem we have noted with Likert's analysis persists, even after the popularity of "contingency theory" (to be discussed in Chapter 4) has made it quite clear that the type of work done by a unit must be considered when generalizing about principles of management or organization. Johannes Pennings has argued that there were two contending theories, those such as Likert's and a technology-bureaucratic one such as my own.[77] He examined a number of brokerage firms and found that leadership variables of the type that Likert considers played a decisive role, supporting Likert's view of organizations. But the real message of his work is that if you have a number of small independent work groups "selling" to clients as in these brokerage firms—very similar in many respects to the groups of life insurance salesmen—bureaucratic structures and controls are not very appropriate. In the "back offices" of the brokerage firms, where the work is routine and "salesmanship" counts for little—again, similar to the clerical offices of life insurance companies— a bureaucratic model is far more appropriate.

The Weldon Company Test of System 4.   The Harwood Manufacturing Company purchased the Weldon Manufacturing Company in 1962 and undertook to rejuvenate it. Harwood itself was the scene of many of the most famous studies of human relations in the literature[78] and has benefited from the advice, consultation, and wisdom of Kurt Lewin and many members of the Michigan group. The history of the changes in the Weldon Company from the date of purchase is presented in a book by Alfred Marrow, David Bowers, and Stanley Seashore, *Management by Participation: Creating a Climate for Personal and Organizational Development.*[79]

The major points are quite simple and clear: the Weldon Company was incredibly poorly managed and staffed; it lacked proper machinery, layout, and records system; and it had a violent labor history with enormous turnover of personnel. All who supplied chapters to this volume agreed in this assessment, including Harwood's board chairman and Weldon's plant manager. Literally, almost any sensible change in this organization would have improved it. It is worth quoting at length from only one of the several enumerations of company problems, since it indicates some of the

[76]Likert, *Human Organization*, p. 52.

[77]Johannes M. Pennings, "Dimension of Organizational Influence and their Effectiveness Correlates," *Administrative Science Quarterly* 21, no. 4 (December 1976): 688–699; and Johannes M. Pennings and Paul S. Goodman, "Toward a Workable Framework," in Paul S. Goodman et al., *New Perspectives in Organizational Effectiveness* (San Francisco: Jossey-Bass, 1977), pp. 146–184.

[78]L. Coch and J. R. P. French, Jr., "Overcoming Resistance to Change," *Human Relations* 1, no. 4 (1948): 512–532.

[79]Alfred J. Marrow, David G. Bowers, and Stanley E. Seashore, *Management by Participation* (New York: Harper & Row, 1967).

things that can go wrong in organizations. This account is by the Harwood board chairman, Alfred Marrow.

The Weldon Company, at the time of acquisition, was run by two partners; one of them controlled merchandising, and the other manufacturing. We will ignore the manifold problems of the former partner and his sales organization and staff.

The manufacturing division under the other partner-owner had five functional department heads. The plant organization, as in merchandising, was unbalanced, with too few people in management and supervision and too many in control and record-keeping. The imbalance was a result of the manager's effort to control activity through multiple and duplicating records. A large number of clerks were needed, also, because of inventory imbalances, to change shipping dates, suggest substitutions, and answer customer complaints.

Noteworthy gaps in staff and method were evident in the manufacturing division. A single industrial engineer with one assistant attempted to handle all problems of rate study and machine layout. There was no program of research and development. Electronic data processing, although economically available, had not been introduced. There was no personnel department to provide essential records and services.

Within the total enterprise, the merchandising and manufacturing divisions functioned independently rather than as coordinated divisions of a single organization. Coordination was blocked by the clashes of temperament of the two partners and by the absence of any authorized coordination by others. Moreover, each partner employed relatives in key positions. The son of the merchandising partner was employed as sales manager and a son-in-law as comptroller. A nephew of the manufacturing partner was employed as plant manager. Each "side" viewed the other with suspicion.

As a consequence, little communication was maintained between manufacture and sales. Each division became unable to see the other's problems. Manufacturing took little or no account of customer pressures upon the sales department. Sales and designing divisions made little effort to understand the plant complications created by an unrestricted variation of styles and models. Salesmen agreed too readily to sell any type of styling that customers requested without regard to what the plant could produce at a profit. Salesmen, who were generally paid on a commission basis, promised impossibly fast deliveries at mutually conflicting dates. There was little provision for coordination or plant clearance.

Production schedules were set by the sales department. The recurrent conflicts in delivery promises forced them to demand almost daily changes in production priorities and frequently to demand partial deliveries. The effect in the plant was a daily turmoil of priority changes for goods in process and a need to have many kinds of garments in manufacture in small lots at the same time. Costs were raised excessively. Customers were alienated. Late deliveries led the sales people to accuse the manufacturing people of willful negligence and of misinformation; the plant people accused the others of carelessness in imposing impossible schedules. Quarrels and deep antagonisms had extended over a long time, and neither party seemed able to find a way to coordinate sales and production.

The effect of these conditions on the plant supervisory staff was serious. They ignored the increased costs of labor and material due to small runs, rush deliveries, and unbalanced inventories. Production quotas were set arbitrarily, without regard to the frequent disruptions of the work flow. To produce in required quantity, particularly during the seasonal peak, Weldon often had to hire inexperienced employees for short periods and to pay a guaranteed wage for a low output which, for some lines and seasons, doubled and tripled the unit production cost. Supervisors felt justified in meeting the set quota of dozens by every means within reach, and were kept both uninformed and unconcerned in their cost performance.

Work flow fluctuated widely, and workers sometimes went from overtime to layoff in the same work week. Weldon workers came to regard the plant as a place of seasonal or occasional employment. Many would leave as soon as they could find other jobs, while others would be discharged as soon as the seasonal peak was past. Labor turnover thus was high.

In the postwar transition from sellers' to buyers' market, the consequences became drastic. Having retained outdated tools and methods, Weldon forfeited its competitive advantage. Top management tried to counteract mounting losses by cutting expenditures for capital improvement so sharply that by 1962 even spare parts had to be taken from one machine to fix another. Weldon bought little new equipment and made little attempt to keep up with innovations in the tools or methods of manufacture. Their economies thus took a form that exaggerated rather than solved their production cost problems in the long run.

The partners seem to have believed that if they could hold their markets long enough they could find a way to cut costs to a profitable level. They took conventional steps to reduce payroll costs: cutting down on staff, withholding wage increases, calling on their people to make sacrifices, applying strong pressures. Costs did go down, for a time, and sales and production volume was maintained. But morale suffered, and these "economies" also began to add to cost.[80]

It should be noted that the two partners had built up a very good, sizable business; they made the leading quality line in men's pajamas. Nor had it been a tiny organization; in the mid-1950s it had grown rapidly to include five plants employing about 3,500 people. (But there was only one plant with 1,000 workers at the time of the acquisition in 1962.) What the two partners had done so well for a number of years, making the organization "one of the recognized and highly respected leaders in the industry,"[81] was no longer appropriate for a large organization under changed market conditions. The highly centralized, authoritarian methods they had used for so long and with such success were not altered under the new conditions, a situation found with melancholy frequency in industry.

The "change-agents" included a team of consultants, some of them from the Institute for Social Research. They introduced a number of eminently sensible changes. More capital was invested; new machinery was acquired; the layout of the work was changed; lines of communication and degrees of responsibility were clarified; and record keeping, forecasting, and inventory control were introduced or improved. All this was in keeping with traditional management theory. They also instituted T-group sessions, involved management in decision making, reduced the incredible degree of centralization of authority, and treated the workers as human beings. Everything improved. The improvement in output and financial aspects was dramatic; the improvement in human relations and morale was less dramatic, but there was improvement in these areas, too.

[80]Ibid., pp. 12–14.
[81]Ibid., p. 7.

Was this a demonstration of the effectiveness of System 4, as Likert holds? Or was it the result of more prosaic and traditional management techniques, the departure of some key people, and the correction of obvious human relations problems? Bowers and Seashore, with considerable ingenuity and detailed measurement, attempted to assess the reasons for the dramatic increase in productivity. Using the figure of a 30 percent gain in productivity, they conclude as follows: over one third of the gain—11 percentage points—came from the "earnings development program." In this program, an engineer sat down with those employees who were producing at a rate much less than the federal minimum standard in their piecework output and attempted to improve their performance through industrial engineering techniques. Next in order of importance, contributing a 5 percent increase in productivity, was the "weeding out" of low earners. The training of supervisors and staff in interpersonal relations also contributed about 5 percentage points. The group consultation and problem resolution program with the operators contributed about 3 percentage points. The remaining 6 percent came from miscellaneous sources.[82] Thus the showcase of System 4, the group consultation and problem resolution program, accounted for only one-tenth of the 30 percent increase in productivity, and the training in interpersonal relations only one-sixth. The bulk of the change came from classical management theory—even Taylorism—and simply involved training workers and firing those who did not improve. The new machinery, layout, and so forth contributed also to increased productivity, but Bowers and Seashore excluded gains from this source.

Another striking finding was that "dramatic changes in policy, in work arrangements, in interpersonal relationships—and in work performance and pay—were in Weldon accompanied by only modest affective and motivational changes."[83] Thus motivation and morale may have had less to do with output than technical matters such as job design, layout, and new machinery. Bowers and Seashore rather reluctantly concluded that "basic gains in the 'output' of an organization with respect to satisfactions, motivations, and positive feelings often may be harder to achieve than gains in cost performance and work output." These gains in "achieving a more trustful, open, cooperative, and self-determining organizational system" may take place only over a long period of time.[84] Yet, throughout the book, the authors of other chapters insisted that these changes had already taken place.

Bowers and Seashore measured these attitudes in a variety of ways to arrive at their unanticipated conclusion. If, however, they had simply relied on the rating scale that Likert used to measure commitment to System 4, they would have seen a dramatic increase in motivational and affective changes. Managers were asked to rate their organization on forty-two counts—as the company stood prior to the acquisition by Harwood and as it was two years later. The change in all items was dramatic. Apparently, Bowers and Seashore were not willing to use this as a reliable instrument.

[82]Ibid., pp. 181–182.
[83]Ibid., p. 200.
[84]Ibid., p. 201.

Another embarrassment crops up in a chapter by Bowers. Though other chapters contained examples of workers exercising more control over their jobs, participating in decisions, and feeling that control was no longer lodged in a remote headquarters, the measurement of this through the control graph technique (which we will discuss shortly) "shows that the control structure at Weldon did not change much."[85] Either the control graph is a poor instrument—a doubtful conclusion, as we shall see—or large gains in productivity and satisfaction with work and pay can be made without giving groups more influence.

There is indeed some evidence that control remained centralized, though it is given little attention in the book. Bowers and Seashore note: "Some of the demands placed upon Weldon managers by the new owners were, to put it mildly, preemptory and compelling," though they hasten to add that the demands were "always coupled with apparently limitless moral support and practical aid." Similarly, the enforcement of the absence and termination rules among the operators was "uncompromising," though applied only after much encouragement and personal aid.[86] Moreover, while the effect of group sessions on five of the top six members of the merchandising side of the business is described as dramatically successful in one chapter,[87] we learn much later that five of the six had to be replaced.[88] Such prosaic realities of organizational life as preemptory demands, uncompromising application of rules, and removal of top executives do intrude into this enthusiastic book, though they are only parenthetically and apologetically noted.

Finally, Bowers and Seashore make a very interesting and valuable point in their summary. Several people, they say, have argued that an organization is ready for change when it has a history of supportive management, good relations with the union, a fund of mutual trust and good will, and satisfied employees.[89] But, they remark, such a company hardly needs drastic change since it is likely to be flexible and adaptable. The case of Weldon, however, was one of "rescuing the destitute" and required "some coercive steps" by the new management.[90] This is perhaps the main point of the study. If an organization is destitute, almost any sensible effort will make a dramatic difference. Improving human relations is certainly one of the sensible efforts to make, but judging from their own assessment, sensible efforts in the form of classical management techniques had the most effect.[91]

---

[85]Ibid., pp. 213–214.

[86]Ibid., p. 240.

[87]Ibid., pp. 99–101.

[88]Ibid., p. 241.

[89]Ibid., p. 239.

[90]Ibid., p. 240.

[91]A close reading of other studies, old and new, of dramatic changes suggests the important role of quite obvious factors that are not central to human relations theory. I explored this at length in the case of the reputed efficacy of milieu therapy in mental hospitals in "Hospitals: Technology, Structure and Goals," in *The Handbook of Organizations*, ed. James March (Chicago: Rand McNally, 1965), Chapter 22. Bowers and Seashore themselves, in a study of a packaging and printing firm, conclude that participative management theory should be applied within the general framework of classical management theory, and their evidence suggests that some structural changes had to precede changes in interpersonal relations. See their *Changing the Structure and Functioning of an Organization* (Ann Arbor: Institute for Social Research, University of Michigan, 1963). A classic study by Robert Guest can best be

The Control Graph

The last example of the second branch of human relations theory that we shall consider is the work of Arnold Tannenbaum and several associates in the area of the amount of influence, or, as they call it, "control," in organizations. One of the frequent imageries of the 1920s and 1930s in discussion of labor-management relations was the "pie." Commentators held that labor should stop worrying about getting a bigger slice at the expense of management, and management should stop worrying about the size of labor's slice. Instead, they should cooperate to produce a bigger pie. Then both would get a larger slice without worrying about changing the dividing points. We now formulate the issue in more abstruse but exact terms. There are zero-sum gains and variable, or nonzero-sum, gains. If one person gets more, but it is at the expense of another, that is a zero-sum gain. (Subtracting what one gives up from what another gains produces a cipher.) If, however, by combining forces in some way, and by maximizing the use of their resources or their ability to extract resources from the environment, both can get more, that is a nonzero-sum gain. (Adding the two increments produces a total that is more than zero.)

It is a tenet of the human relations school that things are not zero-sum. (Or, to use another popular expression, they are not "win-lose" situations; everyone can win.) This is because better human relations improves efficiency and productivity, creating a larger pie. By allowing subordinates to participate in decision making, more resources are utilized, and all will gain. The first "operationalization" of this idea in organizations (that is, developing ways to measure the variables of interest) was performed by Arnold Tannenbaum and Robert L. Kahn. As elaborated and tested in various types of organizations by Tannenbaum and others, it came to constitute "control graph" theory.[92]

The operationalization is very simple. Respondents in an organization are asked how much "say or influence" various levels of authority have in the organization. The levels might be higher management, plant managers, supervisors, and workers. The responses for each group are averaged, and a graph is constructed. In a union,

---

interpreted in terms of contracting the lines of authority and persistent interference of headquarters in the affairs of an automobile plant that lacked proper facilities, rather than merely as a case of the effect of leadership. See my discussion of this study in Charles Perrow, *Organizational Analysis, A Sociological View* (Belmont, Calif.: Wadsworth, 1970), Chapter 1. The Guest study is Robert Guest, *Organizational Change* (Homewood, Ill.: Irwin, 1962).

In recent years, a number of best-selling books have advocated new ways to revitalize organizations and thus the U.S. economy, sometimes praising Japanese management techniques, corporate cultures, or internal change techniques. These books often have wonderful anecdotes and case materials, and their authors are to be applauded for sensitivity to human relations issues and advocacy of decentralization. I have enjoyed them. But in all cases their data admit of other interpretations, generally what are now conventional structural interpretations about locus of authority, the relation between task and structure (see Chapter 4), and the value of almost any attempted change in a grossly mismanaged division or company. In addition, again as with the human relations classics we have been considering, the reliability of the data and research methods is sometimes questionable and too often simply anecdotal. Nothing much seems to have changed in this popular school of thought since 1979.

[92] The major publications dealing with the theory are included in Arnold S. Tannenbaum, *Control in Organizations* (New York: McGraw-Hill, 1968). A subsequent book reporting on the application of the technique in several nations is Tannenbaum et al., *Hierarchy in Organizations* (San Francisco: Jossey-Bass, 1974).

Figure 1   Hypothetical Control Graph (Industrial Organization)

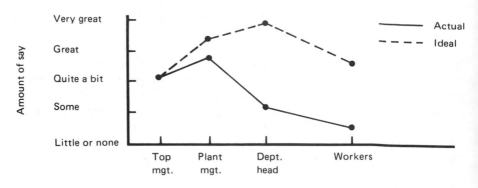

the levels might be president, board, bargaining committee, and members. Thus in some unions the slope of the curve is "positive"—that is, influence goes up as levels of authority go down. The president has the least influence, and the curve rises—with the executive board having more, the bargaining committee still more, and the members the most. (Unfortunately, in one particular case where a positive, or rising, slope was found, the question was ambiguous, asking about influence in *how* decisions are made, rather than, for example, influence over the content of decisions.[93]

In most of the extant studies of business and industrial organizations, the remotest group (e.g., the board of directors; headquarters) is seen as having only a fair amount of influence, but the head of the local unit (e.g., the plant manager) has a great deal, and the various levels under him or her have successively less influence, with the workers having the least. An example is given in Figure 1. In the League of Women Voters, a similar but far less marked pattern was found; the president and the board of directors had similar levels of influence, the membership somewhat less. Thus the measure is sensitive to differences in organizations; those differences make sense, and this increases our confidence in the measure.

More important than the slope of the curve, however, is its *height*, or more precisely, the amount of area under it. This indicates how much influence is perceived by respondents to exist in the total organization. Tannenbaum and his associates found that some organizations have significantly more total influence than others, and the greater the influence, the greater the effectiveness and member satisfaction. The *slope* of the curve is not related to effectiveness and morale. Furthermore, when asked how much influence each of the hierarchical levels should have, respondents almost invariably desire more influence not only for their own level but for all other levels as well. For the respondents it is generally not a zero-sum, win-lose situation.

But is there a relationship between the total amount of influence and organizational effectiveness and member satisfaction, or do effectiveness and satisfaction result in a perception of high influence? Tannenbaum says that the latter may be

[93]Tannenbaum, *Control,* p. 35.

the case "in certain circumstances."[94] The effective organization has more rewards at its disposal, or more "organizational slack" to play with, and thus can allow all members to exercise more discretion, obtain more rewards, and feel that they have more influence. Ephraim Yuchtman examined this problem by correlating influence scores from one date with performance factors obtained one year later.[95] The organizations were the life insurance agencies we encountered previously. He found that high influence in an agency was more likely to be associated with high performance a year later than it was with the performance scores for the same year. Yuchtman concludes as follows: "Thus, although control [influence] may be both a cause and an effect of performance, we feel reasonably confident that in these organizations it is at least a cause."[96]

In an extremely thoughtful summary, Tannenbaum makes the following points that indicate that neither the "traditional bureaucratic" arguments nor the "participative management" arguments have been able to carry the day: organizations with an influential rank-and-file membership can be as effective as those where the workers are relatively uninfluential, in contrast to bureaucratic theory. On the other hand, organizations with influential officers can be as effective as those with less influential officers, in contrast to many contemporary arguments for democratic, participative organizations. Organizations in which *both* the leaders and members are judged high on influence will be more effective than those in which either or both are less influential. This contradicts both the traditional and the participative management schools. Finally, it is more important to maximize the total amount of influence than to try to equalize it to achieve "power equalization." Variations in influence among levels of the hierarchy—unless they are clearly extreme—are quite acceptable. But at the same time, there is no fixed sum of influence as traditional theories tend to assume.[97]

There are some problems with this theory.[98] By and large, however, it is superior to most of the human relations literature. It both recognizes and deals with different types of organizations, and the different findings make sense. It has been carefully tested in a number of organizations. It does not insist that there is one best

[94]Ibid., pp. 58, 74.

[95]Ibid., Chapter 8.

[96]Ibid., p. 127.

[97]Ibid., pp. 309–310.

[98]Among these are: (1) Is "influence" synonymous with control? The question concerns "say or influence"; Tannenbaum and his associates always speak of control. Would different results be obtained if the words "control" or "power" were used in the question? See the discussion of this issue in connection with measuring the reputed power of different functional departments in Charles Perrow, "Departmental Power and Perspectives in Industrial Firms," in *Power in Organizations*, ed. Mayer Zald (Nashville, Tenn.: Vanderbilt University Press, 1970), pp. 59–70. (2) No information is given regarding the standard deviations of responses. Are they highly consistent by level? If not, is the variation associated with morale and satisfaction questions, implying that this is what is really being measured instead of control? (3) In some organizations (auto dealers, Weldon Manufacturing Company) unexpected findings occur that should be more closely examined. (4) In some situations there seems to be a zero-sum effect present. In the delivery stations, the more influence the workers have, the less overall influence there is in the station (ibid., pp. 154–159), and this may also be true of some of the other industrial organizations studied. Unfortunately, in their subsequent study of organizations in several nations, these problems were again neglected (see footnote 92).

way to organize—the relative degree of influence of various groups can legitimately vary, with the slope declining sharply in some organizations but not in others. It generates and uses an *organizational* measure—total control—rather than aggregating morale scores or participation scores. Most important, however, it preserves the best insights of two hostile schools of thought while rejecting the more extreme claims of both.

A POSTSCRIPT

Even as the human relations school, in both its branches, has flourished and dominates organizational theory, so have criticisms of the school burgeoned. In addition to those already cited, Philip Selznick has written a penetrating section in a book on industrial justice in which he argues that there is a difference between fostering hygienic conditions and ability to participate on the one hand, and exercising legitimate self-assertion, which is a *political* resource, on the other.[99] One may treat slaves humanely, and even ask their opinions on matters with which they are more familiar than the master. But to transform their basic dependence and this presumption of their incompetence with regard to their own interests, there must be an institutional order or public process whereby the opportunity and capacity for legitimate self-assertion is guaranteed. Such a political process does not mean conflict and struggle as such but a setting for ordered controversy and accommodation.

A different level of criticisms is provided in two articles by George Strauss.[100] (Strauss knows whereof he speaks, having been identified with the school and having studied under McGregor, whose contribution he acknowledges.) Playing the role of a devil's advocate, he systematically questions such assumptions as harmony, need hierarchy, conflict resolution, and desire for participation that are found in the school.

Our own criticism in this chapter has been different still. We have tried to show that there is only a little empirical support for the human relations school, that extensive efforts to find that support have resulted in increasing limitations and contingencies, and that the grand schemes such as Likert's appear to be methodologically unsound and theoretically biased. Underlying our criticism, however, has been a more basic level of analysis. One cannot explain organizations by explaining the attitudes and behavior of individuals or even small groups within them. We learn a great deal about psychology and social psychology but little about organizations per se in this fashion.

In fact, what we are learning about psychology and social psychology from these

[99]Philip Selznick, *Law, Society, and Industrial Justice* (New York: Russell Sage Foundation, 1969).

[100]George Strauss, "Notes on Power Equalization," in *The Social Science of Organizations*, ed. Harold J. Leavitt (Englewood Cliffs, N.J.: Prentice-Hall, 1963); and Strauss, "Human Relations, 1968 Style," in *Industrial Relations 7*, no. 3 (May 1969): 262–276. Another good criticism is that of Sherman Krupp, *Patterns in Organizational Analysis* (New York: Holt, Rinehart & Winston, 1961). The important review of organizational theories by John Miner, *Theories of Organizational Behavior* (Chicago: Dryden Press, 1982), presents a fairly strong methodological and conceptual critique. Finally, Lawrence Mohr's neglected by challenging work, *Explaining Organizational Behavior: The Limits and Possibilities of Theory and Research* (San Francisco: Jossey-Bass, 1982), raises even more fundamental issues.

studies may be an outmoded psychology and social psychology. People in these fields no longer agree that such things as norms, values, and personality really exist or account for much; these concepts may only give a false sense of order to a world that both the academic and the person in the street desperately want to order. Sociology, too, is having some difficulty swallowing the simple, obvious proposition that attitudes predict behavior. (The proposition that morale predicts productivity is just one specification of this.) Over the years, persistently trying to take the symbolic interaction position of Herbert Blumer seriously, when most were dismissing it as a philosophical canard, Irwin Deutscher has explored the problem of whether what we say predicts what we actually do.[101] The empirical evidence is surprisingly ambiguous. Attitudes often have little relationship to behavior. People who indicate prejudiced attitudes toward a minority group in a survey or interview do not necessarily act as they say in real-life situations, and, of course, those indicating no prejudice will often discriminate in their behavior. The research covers not only attitudes toward minorities but also what we label as basic traits such as neatness, promptness, or honesty.

Following a line parallel with the leadership studies we considered earlier, researchers have tried to specify ever more narrowly the circumstances under which people's attitudes will predict their behavior. The circumstances are surprisingly few in number. The contingencies that must be controlled become enormous, and only in very specific, often trivial, situations can careful research find a sizable correlation between what we say and what we do. For example, the correlation between people's attitudes toward a candidate a few days before an election and the way they actually vote is high; the correlation between party preference and the candidate one selects is also high, but not as high.

Psychologists such as Walter Mischel and Albert Bandura have pushed the matter further, criticizing the notion of personality, and the anthropologist Anthony Wallace has questioned the notion of cultural values.[102] It all has organizational application. Consider two people, A and his subordinate B. A is reputed to have an aggressive personality, B is reputed to be more accommodating—by people who are sympathetic to both. It is quite possible, though, that careful observation, using measures of aggressiveness we could all agree on, would show that B exhibits more aggressive acts than A. But because B is in a subordinate role where aggressive behavior is not considered proper, his aggressive acts are reinterpreted by sympathetic observers as neutral, accommodating, or even "creative." We expect certain kinds of behavior, given the power position of B, so we classify the behavior to fit the expectations and are confident that B does not have an aggressive personality. (Were we unsympathetic to B, we might easily focus only on his aggressive acts which, though more frequent than A's, might represent only a tiny fraction of his behavior.)

A, his boss, is expected to be aggressive. Such behavior gives us confidence that

[101]Irwin Deutscher, *What We Say/What We Do* (Glenview, Ill.: Scott, Foresman, 1973).

[102]Walter Mischel, "Toward a Cognitive Social Learning Reconceptualization of Personality," *Psychological Review* 80, no. 4 (1973): 252–283; Albert Bandura, *Social Learning Theory* (New York: General Learning Press, 1971); and Anthony Wallace, *Culture and Personality*, 2nd ed. (New York: Random House, 1970).

things are well in hand ("what organizations need is dynamic leadership"). He may exhibit far fewer aggressive acts than B, but when he does we nod knowingly and say, "Yes, he is an aggressive fellow." We may even reward him for aggressiveness, reinforcing his occasional aggressive acts and bringing out more of them. Then we are quite confident that he has an aggressive personality.[103] When this splendid quality is mentioned to his parents, they will confirm the diagnosis, saying, "He always knew what he wanted and how to get it." However, in another situation, he might appear quite different, and people could comment on how considerate and accommodating he is, and his parents (recalling items of behavior from the distant past that fitted this description) would say, quite honestly, "Yes, he has always been like that." Indeed, his behavior over the course of a few days or weeks or months probably will fluctuate far beyond what we would predict from our notions of "personality" as a stable set of responses. But because we attend to those things we expect him to do, and overlook the other types of behavior since it would damage the world we have constructed for ourselves and learned to live in, we ignore the fluctuation.

Though the link between the work on attitudes, behavior, and personality and the work on organizations has not been made as yet, we can find leads in the disturbing views of Karl Weick, and James March and Johan Olsen.[104] Weick seems to be suggesting that organizations run backward, so to speak. The thought is not necessarily the father to the deed; in fact, the deed may be father to the thought. Let me illustrate. For no particular reason, or at least none known to me, I may find that I never ordered the textbook that I usually use for next fall's classes. It might be that I simply forgot, or a misunderstanding occurred when I assumed the secretary knew it was a standing order for the fall, or I was out of town that week, or someone had made a disparaging remark about the book a month before that I didn't really recall but that made the act of ordering it mildly distasteful. But now that the deadline has passed, I am forced to explain my behavior. Almost any behavior can find its *post hoc* explanation; we are masters at ordering our worlds in this way. I may decide that the reason I never ordered it was probably that, good as the book is, I would learn more by assigning a number of articles, thus forcing me to read them carefully and integrate them; or that students are now more responsible and hard-working, so we can dispense with the crutch of a text; or that texts have gotten ridiculously expensive; or that I have been assigning too much reading.

During the idle chatter at a party at a colleague's home, I find myself taking one of these positions and arguing it with conviction. Come fall, I act on that conviction (whichever one of the above I might have picked), and indeed, since they are all reasonable arguments and I sincerely believe in the one I thought explained my behavior, it will probably work out well and have a good effect on my teaching. But the explanation was constructed after the behavior; the deed was father to the

---

[103]For excellent organizational examples about sex typing that are consistent with this viewpoint see Rosabeth Kanter, *Men and Women of the Corporation* (New York: Basic Books, 1977). Here power relations are masked under the fictions of norms and personality traits that supposedly "explain" behavior.

[104]James G. March and Johan P. Olsen, *Ambiguity and Choice in Organizations* (Bergen, Norway: Universitetsforlaget, 1976); and Karl Weick, *The Social Psychology of Organizing,* 2nd ed. (Reading, Mass.: Addison-Wesley, 1979).

thought. There is not likely to be any way in which I would casually happen on the "real" reason, which was far more trivial or accidental than my explanation.

Note that the idea that organizations may run backward much of the time is not simply a matter of covering one's tracks, making excuses, lying or fabricating supporting data to justify what we want to do. Nor is it a matter of acting upon faulty information, or confusion created by someone not getting the message. Organizations are full of these events, too. But events of this kind are much more a part of a planned world that we (often mistakenly) believe we can consciously direct or influence to some extent. The difficulty in making organizations work well cannot be overstressed. But in this postscript I am referring to the creation of new thoughts or meanings, to the social construction of a world we sincerely believe was there all along that is stimulated by accidents, random events, misinterpretations, memory failures, and so on. We do not *cover* our tracks; we unwittingly reconstruct the deed because we think that thought must have been behind it. To admit otherwise may be unnerving.

If our thoughts arise from our behavior, then what we take to be statements of organizational or group goals may merely be interpretations of where we have been, not where we intended to go. Statements of goals, by individuals or organizations, serve to give meaning to what is probably a more random, disconnected, accidental, and stumbling process than we have thought. We cannot even state our goals clearly or order them from the most important to the least important in any stable way (a view we shall consider in the next chapter).

These possibilities are unsettling, and at first, second, and even third glance they defy our (carefully crafted) interpretations of our experience. We live with rationalizations for a long time without examining them. But when one starts fresh with a naive view, taking nothing for granted, and looks at social processes in a new way, it is often necessary to begin with the most apparently trivial events. This is perhaps why a school of thought that has explored the "social construction of reality" most carefully—the ethnomethodological school—has generally limited itself to the intensive study of trivial encounters such as greetings exchanged at airports, the opening of phone conversations, and the gambits and expectations used in the employment interview. Perhaps only in the analysis of such encounters can we begin to rid ourselves of our everyday conceptions.

It is quite possible that our social theories in general, and organizational theory in particular, have been altogether too rational. The human relations tradition counters the extreme rationality of scientific management with a romantic rationality, sometimes grounded in Freudian psychology, wherein all sorts of unconscious needs are posited. But what if much of our world exhibits low coherence, accidental interactions and consequences, highly situational (rather than enduring or basic) determinants of behavior, and very specific rather than broad cultural reinforcements and demotivators? For example, what we see as sexual drive may simply be a learning of social scripts about how we should feel and what we should desire, with different scripts for different groups, and with misread and changing scripts in addition.[105]

[105]This theme is explored in John H. Gagnon and William Simon, *Sexual Conduct: The Social Sources of Human Sexuality* (Chicago: Aldine, 1973).

The prospects for such views are really quite startling. In addition to peeling away the myth of rationality we live by, such views might explain why the social sciences are poor predictors of behavior and can find only weak support for their theories. There is less that can be explained than we thought. Not all our theories are directly derived from premises about human behavior, and many of our findings are essentially unexplained correlations. But those theories that are derived from premises about behavior need expensive and painful dismantling; they are overdetermined.106

It is possible that the stabilities we assert are fictitious and that the disorderly universe pictured by novelists such as Thomas Pynchon *(Gravity's Rainbow)* or Joseph Heller *(Catch 22; Something Happened)* are far closer to the mark. (Both authors, incidentally, afford unusual insights into organizational behavior; the first part of *Something Happened,* in particular, is a remarkable description of behavior in a corporation.) On the other hand, there *are* significant regularities in our world, such as the stable distribution of wealth in the United States over the last seventy years; the persistence of class and ethnic divisions; the persistence of discrimination and bigotry in an affluent, highly educated society; the persistence of religious wars, in masked form, even in industrialized, modernized Europe. The bridge between these perverse stabilities and the new view of human behavior remains to be made. It may be an example of what the Marxists consider as a dialectic process or the contradictions of capitalism. But at least we are less confident that explanations for these and other regularities reside in our usual formulations of "personality and social structure" or "human nature." In the next chapter we shall see that a "neo-Weberian" view of organizations has opened the door to the situational, limited-rationality view of human beings.

106The "deconstruction" of the rationalistic edifice of social science and the humanities is a general phenomenon. See Charles Perrow, "Deconstructing Social Science," *New York University Educational Quarterly* 12, no. 2 (Winter 1981): 2–9, and the discussion on page 137 in the next chapter.

4

The Neo-Weberian Model: Decision Making, Conflict, and Technology

DECISION MAKING

The human relations theorists sought to restore individuals with their needs and drives, to a central place in organizational theory, a place denied them by classical management theory and by Weberian bureaucratic theory. While the human relations theorists focused on the individual to an extent that Barnard would not approve, they joined with Barnard by taking for granted what he found necessary to insist on, the moral and cooperative nature of organizations. We have argued that the human relations model is deficient in many respects. It lacks empirical support and conceptual clarity, and it fails to grapple with the realities of authoritarian control in organizations and the true status of the subordinate. But even if our critique is valid, the question still remains: What do we do about individuals in organizations? Do we have to more or less ignore them, as Weber did, because the alternative is to become mired in all their complexities and contingencies? There is, obviously, cooperation in organizations, and it is individuals who cooperate. There are such things as good and bad leadership exercised by individuals and identification with the goals of the organization on the part of individuals. Organizations are something more than the structural categories of the Weberian model —the skeleton of hierarchy, rules, offices, roles, careers, and so on. If we cannot accept the human relations propositions as adequate or plausible, must we ignore individuals?

Herbert Simon and James March have provided, somewhat unwittingly, the muscle and flesh for the Weberian skeleton, giving it more substance, complexity, and believability without reducing organizational theory to propositions about individual behavior. To be more accurate, part of the work of March and Simon does this. Roughly half of their work, as laid out in two extremely important volumes, Simon's *Administrative Behavior*[1] and *Organizations* by March and

---

[1] Herbert A. Simon, *Administrative Behavior*, 2nd ed. (New York: Macmillan, 1957). The first edition was published in 1947; the second edition contains a valuable new introduction. For a thoroughly unsympathetic and even outraged criticism of Simon's administrative theory see Herbert J. Storing, "The Science of Administration: Herbert A. Simon," in *Essays on the Scientific Study of Politics*, H.

Simon,[2] is concerned with the organization as a problem of social psychology. The other half uses a structural perspective; it speaks to *organizational* rather than to *individual* decision making.

"Models of Man"

Two different "models of man" are involved, and a discussion of them will serve to introduce the decision-making view of organizations. When individual decision making is under discussion, people are seen as able to make rational computations and rational decisions once they have decided on their goals. "Two persons, given the same skills, the same objectives and values, the same knowledge and inclination, can rationally decide only upon the same course of action."[3] Goals depend in part on group influences, but these can be mapped out. This is done extensively in chapters 3 and 4 of *Organizations*, involving about 120 propositions with literally dozens of influences impinging on, for example, the decision to stay with or leave the organization. People also internalize the goals of the organization and seek affiliation with groups. They have a number of needs that require satisfaction. Social characteristics—age, sex, status, and the like—influence the decision. Finally, they have aspirations: if these are satisfied, a person's effort is relaxed; if they are not, it is increased.

This portrait of human beings is, if anything, even more complex than the highly contingent human relations models, such as Fiedler's. Yet it is supposed to be the key to understanding organizations. Simon argues, first, that organizations are made up of individuals. "An organization is, after all, a collection of people, and what the organization does is done by people."[4] Therefore, understanding them is "a problem in social psychology."[5] Or, as March and Simon put it more decisively in a later volume, "propositions about organizations are statements about human behavior."[6]

There is another model of the individual in the writings of Simon and March, however. In this second model the complexity of individual wants, desires, and

---

J. Storing, ed. (New York: Holt, Rinehart & Winston, 1962), pp. 63–105. I have reservations about some of Storing's points and miss any attempt to discuss the contributions that Simon has made, but nevertheless, it is an important critique. Probably no theorist would look well after such a detailed, relentless, and searching analysis. Another valuable and critical examination of Simon and organizational theory in general is Sherman Krupp's *Patterns in Organizational Analysis* (New York: Holt, Rinehart & Winston, 1961).

[2]James G. March and Herbert A. Simon, *Organizations* (New York: Wiley, 1958). It will be impossible in this section to separate out the respective contributions of March and Simon when discussing this important book. Since the positions we are concerned with are also at least implicit in Simon's *Administrative Behavior* we will generally speak only of Simon, rather than of March and Simon. March himself will be discussed in the section on conflict.

[3]Simon, *Administrative Behavior*, pp. 13, 39. "Once the system of values which is to govern an administrative choice has been specified, there is one and only one 'best decision'." Ibid., p. 204.

[4]Ibid., p. 110.

[5]Ibid., pp. 1–2.

[6]March and Simon, *Organizations*, p. 26. This, presumably, would rule out of court a proposition such as "the higher the degree of specialization, the higher the centralization."

values and the multitude of the influences on his or her decisions are ignored. Instead, this model makes simplifying assumptions about the individual, so that we can get on with studying the organization rather than the individual. It assumes that the individual is not all that rational and that his or her behavior, within limits, can be deliberately controlled.

In this model humans are only "intendedly rational." They attempt to be rational but their limited capacities and those of the organization prevent anything near complete rationality. For one thing, they do not have complete knowledge of the consequences of their acts. There will be both unanticipated and unintended consequences of action. Second, they either do not have complete knowledge of the alternative courses of action available to them or they cannot afford to attain that knowledge. That is, an individual does not sit down and prepare an exhaustive list of alternatives before making every decision, and even if he or she tried to do so, the list could not be exhaustive. Therefore, people grossly simplify available alternatives and select the first acceptable one. Third, even when the individual has several alternatives, he or she can neither accurately rank them in terms of preferences nor be sure which is the most desirable and which is the least desirable.[7] These limitations on humans conflict sharply with statements by Simon regarding rationality, efficiency, and the "one best decision."

It is important, before we go any further, to note the implications of this view and to distinguish it from Barnard's view of nonrational humans and rational organizations. In Barnard's model, the individual, though nonrational alone, achieves rationality through organizations. Simon's person is intendedly rational, but participation in the organization does not produce a more rational or superior person, nor does it produce an organizationally induced increment of rationality in the individual. Instead, the individual has decisions made "subject to the influences of the organization group in which he participates."[8] This is done, Simon says, through the division of labor, standard practices, the authority system, channels of communication, and training and indoctrination. (He might have noted that these are the building blocks of the Weberian model, but March and Simon dismiss the Weberian model in a couple of paragraphs as too mechanical.[9]) The result is that members are made to "adapt their decisions to the organization's objectives" and they are provided with the information needed to make correct organizational decisions.[10] The organization gains, not the individual. It is organizational rationality that is enhanced through such devices as the division of labor. Simon, in his model of organizational decision making, is concerned with the organization as a tool, or with individuals as tools of the organization.[11] Barnard could not admit to this possibility, because organizations in his view are cooperative systems where the organizational and the individual objective must coincide.

[7]Ibid., p. 138; Simon, *Administrative Behavior*, p. 81.

[8]Simon, *Administrative Behavior*, p. 102. Simon veers more strongly to the view that humans become rational only through organizations in his *Models of Man* (New York: Wiley, 1956).

[9]March and Simon, *Organizations*, pp. 36–37.

[10]Simon, *Administrative Behavior*, p. 79.

[11]"The behavior of individuals is the tool with which organization achieves its purposes." Ibid., p. 108.

For Simon this is not the case; the individual satisfies personal ends (for income, for example) through the organization, but these ends are not necessarily those of the organization.[12]

Given the limits on rationality, what do individuals in fact do when confronted with a choice situation? They construct a simplified model of the real situation. This "definition of the situation," as sociologists call it, is built out of past experience (it includes prejudices and stereotypes) and highly particularized, selective views of present stimuli. Most of the individuals' responses are "routine"; they invoke solutions they have used before. Sometimes they must engage in problem solving. When they do so, they conduct a *limited* search for alternatives along familiar and well-worn paths, selecting the first satisfactory one that comes along. They do not examine all possible alternatives, nor do they keep searching for the optimum one. Rather, they "satisfice," or select the first satisfactory solution. Their very standards for satisfactory solutions are a part of the definition of the situation. These standards go up and down with positive and negative experience. As solutions are easier to find, the standards are raised; as they are harder to find, the standards fall. *The organization can control these standards, and it defines the situation;* only to a limited extent are they up to individuals.[13]

The importance of this assumption about human beings is that it gives to organizational variables (division of labor, communications system, etc.) the predominant control over individual behavior. This control is so extensive that we can neglect individual behavior (supposedly the real stuff of organizational life) in all its multiplicity and variability and deal with group or subunit behavior. It calls for simplifying models of *individual* behavior in order to capture the complexities of *organizational* behavior.

As far as I know, Herbert Storing, in his critical essay on Simon's work, is the only one to note that the organization can manufacture, in its own interests, the ratio of inducements to contributions.[14] But a more serious point about limited, or bounded, rationality has been ignored. Bounded rationality, for Simon and other economists that use the notion (see Chapter 7), is something to be overcome as much as possible through knowledge of cause-effect relationships, better information

[12]In an effort to defend the rational, economic view of human behavior, some critics have pointed out that "satisficing" behavior is really maximizing behavior when one takes into account the costs of search. That is, the person who selects the first acceptable alternative is saying "there may be a better one, but it will not be so much better as to make up for the cost of additional search." March and Simon illustrate their satisficing model with the example of looking for a needle in a haystack—you do not search for the sharpest needle, only one sharp enough to sew with. But the example is not apt; no economist (who is supposed to deal only with completely rational people) would argue that you search for the sharpest needle. The real reason why the Simon formulation is so useful is that the costs of search are usually unknown to individuals. They do not know if there is a sharper needle or how long it would take to find it. Therefore, they cannot take into account the cost of search in many cases. At any rate, Simon does not say that all behavior ignores cost of search, or does not seek maximum solutions, but only says that it is impossible to do so all or most of the time.

[13]This is one of the additional reasons beyond those noted in the chapter on Barnard that the equilibrium model of inducements and contributions, utilized in both *Administrative Behavior* and *Organizations,* is so suspect: the organization sets the terms of the expectations and thus can manufacture the ratio of inducements to contributions in its own interests. This is noted by Storing, *Essays on the Scientific Study of Politics,* p. 106.

[14]Storing, "The Science of Administration: Herbert A. Simon."

and searching techniques, better communication devices, and greater clarity about our goals. Indeed, Simon might be said to have devoted most of his life to the study of intelligence and the possibilities of artificial intelligence to push back the boundaries. Organizations would function better if human rationality were less bounded. But bounded rationality makes possible bureaucratic control as well as domination in general. Because we are *not* superhuman, with full understanding of processes or complete information and precise ordering of our goals, the organization can shape our premises, and ideologies can legitimize domination in society in general. If our rationality were full, no one could put anything over on us or shape our premises. One could dominate only by superior force, and any such domination would be limited to one-to-one relationships, because the many, even if individually weaker, would not permit domination by a few, whom they would outnumber.

With bounded rationality, even a small and temporary advantage in information, resources, or goal clarity can be transformed into a large and stable one. With a small advantage, information is controlled and selectively used; premises alter the unstable goal structure and stabilize it in the interests of the elites; ideologies justify the differences in power. Bounded rationality is, to a small degree, an impediment to organizational effectiveness, but to a larger degree it makes hierarchical structures possible.

Bounded rationality, however, is visited upon the elites as well. Their position is always insecure, for their information, understanding, and goals are never fully rational. This allows for occasional resistance and subtle changes by the controlled. In fact, bounded rationality, by elites or their subjects, creates a great deal of change, for it permits unexpected interactions, new discoveries, serendipities, and new goals and values. Given that we are not superhuman, our very limitations make us human in ways that we should treasure. They create the disorder that brings about change and unanticipated new orders. Bounded rationality is certainly a limitation, and it permits domination, but it also makes domination forever precarious and promotes change. It is hard to treasure a defect that we should continually try to remedy through rational action, but given the human condition, we should recognize it as more than an impediment to the further bureaucratization of social life.

The Model of Organizations

How does the Simon model of organizations work? First we learn that goals are set by the leaders and then broken down into subgoals at each level of the organization. Each lower-order goal becomes a means to a higher-order goal. People do not accept these goals because they necessarily share them or believe in them, in contrast to the cooperative model, but because the organization has mechanisms to ensure that working toward them meets the individual's own personal values. (These personal values, of course, influence the organizational goal to some extent.) In commercial, governmental, and voluntary organizations, the top administrators identify closely with the objectives of the organization;[15] the rest of the organization's members need not. Once established, the goals remain quite stable because of such things as

[15]Simon, *Administrative Behavior*, pp. 120–121.

the high cost of innovative activity, "sunk cost," and "sunk assets." These refer to capital investments that cannot easily be changed (e.g., single-purpose machinery in a plant) and to the know-how or knowledge and the good will. Regardless of "wants, motives, and desires" or the dynamics of decision making in individuals, these nonpersonal aspects stabilize objectives and activities.[16]

Other sources of stability in the organization stem from the routinization of activity through the establishment of programs and standard operating procedures. Changes are introduced only when objectives are clearly not met, and even then the search for new programs follows well-worn paths, minimizing the disruption; the satisficing solution is to select the least disruptive alternatives. Even planning is difficult, for "daily routine drives out planning."[17] To plan—and thus change— routines, resources have to be allocated to units that have as their tasks innovation and planning. Another source of change is the deadlines that provoke crises in which programmed activity must be abandoned. March and Simon devote a chapter to planning and innovation, but it is clear that these are only adaptive responses of an organization, not ends in themselves. Innovation is designed to stabilize the organization and allow routine to be reestablished or to reappear.

The key to the Simon model of organizations is the concept of organizational structure. March and Simon define this as "those aspects of the pattern of behavior in the organization that are relatively stable and that change only slowly."[18] Clinging to their psychological predisposition, they argue that the basic features of the structure "derive from the characteristics of human problem-solving processes and rational human choice."[19] But once we have established that humans do not maximize but only satisfice, attend to only a few things at a time, and tend to factor problems into established and familiar dimensions, the attention to the characteristics of human behavior is not necessary. Because of these limits on human capacities and the complexity of organizational problems, "rational behavior calls for simplified models that capture the main features of a problem without capturing all its complexities."[20]

The simplified model can be described as follows, drawing from the two volumes: it calls for satisficing behavior; sequential and limited search processes that are only mildly innovative; specialization of activities and roles so that attention is directed to "a particular restricted set of values"; "attention-directors that channelize behavior"; rules, programs, and repertoires of action that limit choice in recurring situations and prevent an agonizing process of optimal decision making at each turn; a restricted range of stimuli and situations that narrow perception; training and indoctrination enabling the individual to "make decisions, by himself, as the organization would like him to decide"; and the factoring of goals and tasks into programs that are semi-independent of one another so as to reduce interdependencies. Most

[16]Ibid., pp. 66, 95, 120. Simon treats sunk costs at one point as "mechanisms of behavior-persistence," thus retaining a psychological perspective (p. 95).

[17]March and Simon, *Organizations*, p. 185.

[18]Ibid., p. 170.

[19]Ibid., p. 169.

[20]Ibid.

organizational activity takes most of the conditions as given; "only a few elements of the system are adaptive at any one time."[21]

The view of authority in this model departs from that of Barnard. In March and Simon's view, authority is not bottom-up, emphasizing the power of the subordinate to grant authority to the superior or emphasizing participation as in the human relations school. Instead, the superior has the power or tools to structure the subordinate's environment and perceptions in such a way that he or she sees the proper things and in the proper light. The superior actually appears to give few orders (confirming my own observations in organizations), but rather sets priorities ("we had better take care of this first"; "this is getting out of hand and creating problems, so let's give it more attention until the problems are cleared up") and alters the flow of inputs and stimuli. The image of the order-barking boss is not there, but neither is the image of participative management or of Barnard's soldier deciding whether or not to move forward into battle after receiving the command.

The term "communication" looms large in this model, but it is not the term that is associated with the platitudes regarding clarity of orders or the authoritativeness of the source or even mechanical discussions of "information overload" and "flow charts." Instead, communication strategies center around checkpoints in the channels, the specialization of channels, the widening and deepening of favored channels that may bypass key stations inadvertently, the development of organizational vocabularies that screen out some parts of reality and magnify other parts, and the attention-directing, cue-establishing nature of communication techniques.

For example, let us explore March and Simon's concept of "uncertainty absorption." An organization develops a set of concepts influenced by the technical vocabulary and classification schemes; this permits easy communication. Anything that does not fit into these concepts is not easily communicated. For the organization, "the particular categories and schemes of classification it employs are reified, and become, for members of the organization, attributes of the world rather than mere conventions."[22] This is especially apparent when a body of information must be edited and summarized in order to make it fit into the conceptual scheme—to make it understandable. The inferences from the material rather than the material itself are transmitted. The recipient can disbelieve the "facts" that are transmitted but can rarely check their accuracy unless he or she personally undertakes the summarization and assessment. This gives personnel who are in direct contact with the information considerable discretion and influence. They "absorb" quantities of "uncertainty."

[21]For the quoted passages, see Simon, *Administrative Behavior*, pp. 98–103, and March and Simon, *Organizations*, p. 169. One of the most widely cited sections of *Organizations* concerns the authors' models of the theories of Robert Merton, Philip Selznick, and Alvin Gouldner. I find that these models violate the originals in several respects. But more important, most of the factors that are supposed to be "pathological" processes contributing to the "dysfunctions" supposedly described by Merton, Gouldner, and Selznick reappear in the second part of the book as functional. The pathologies of limited perspectives and subgroup goals and identification turn out to be necessary for the division of labor and provide means of control. Inattention to the complexities of human actors and their wants and needs proves to be necessary. The surveillance and control features of rules and programs are no longer self-defeating, but functional and essential.

[22]March and Simon, *Organizations*, p. 165.

The most significant examples of uncertainty absorption occur at the boundaries of organizations, where information about the environment is obtained. The selective perception, distortions, omissions, and so on that can occur in a marketing unit are numerous, and little can be done to check this tendency, for it is impossible to obtain complete and accurate information. Even the information obtained still leaves much uncertainty because consumer preferences, competitors' actions, disposable income, or the weather may change rapidly. The tendency to tell the boss only what he or she wants to hear, so well noted in the literature, is probably not as important as the tendency to see things only in terms of the concepts reflected in the organization's vocabulary. In this way, we can translate an explanation regarding personal predispositions (the subordinate fears to tell the truth) into an organizational explanation ("truth" is an organizationally established frame of reference, independent of courageous or timid members).

Information sources and uncertainty absorption also have a good deal to do with the amount of consensus in organizations, according to the March and Simon model.[23] Consensus depends in part on the number of sources of information that are utilized and the degree to which uncertainty absorption can be centralized into one unit. If there are few sources of information, or if there is only one processing unit, the possibility that divergent subgroup perspectives will develop is reduced. An industrial organization with only a few customers and a few products would be such an organization, as would a prison or a mental hospital with a steady supply of inmates and patients and little concern about what happens to them after discharge. But if the mental hospital began to develop extensive links with the environment through social workers, public relations personnel, legislative lobbying activities, and contacts with courts and law enforcement agencies—all in an attempt to improve its services and responsiveness to the community—it could expect divergent views to develop regarding the services it should provide, the techniques it should use, and the goals it should pursue. Similarly, an industrial organization with active links to the environment of technological developments, multiple consumer demands, varied suppliers, and personnel sources—all developed to broaden its product base and keep up with changing markets, products, and competitors—could expect internal consensus to decline. This explanation has little to do with the process of choice in individuals, nor, we might add, with the typical explanations of the human relations school. With the decline in consensus, there may well be increased conflict or a decline in the quality of interpersonal relations and organizational goal identification. But poor interpersonal relations and goal identification are not the causes of a decline in consensus or increased conflict; they are the result of multiple·sources of communication and an increase in uncertainty absorption, which in turn reduces the chances for consensus.

One important implication of the March and Simon model is that to change individual behavior you do not have to change individuals, in the sense of altering their personalities or teaching them human relations skills. Instead, you change the premises of their decisions. March and Simon give few examples in their book of concrete problems or instances of organizational behavior, so it is necessary to fabricate one to illustrate this point. (Although the example is fabricated, the idea was suggested in a conversation with James March.) A common problem in organization is how one makes a basic change in the perspectives and values of the organizational leaders. To change the perspectives of the individual leaders themselves, is, we know, very difficult. In large organizations it is often difficult merely to replace them, since those with sufficient experience and knowledge of the organization at the next level are likely to share the very perspectives one wishes to change. Going outside the organization for top management personnel also presents difficulties.

One way, though a slow one, is to change the kinds of experiences that will be had by people who will have access to top management positions. Typically, we might find that the perspectives of top management were shaped by the experiences they had while in the lower echelons of the organization and that these experiences were embedded in conventional career lines. Promotion may have typically been from line rather than staff positions, sales rather than production, home-office experience rather than field or overseas experience, combat-unit assignments rather than political assignments, custodial rather than clinical experience, large rather than small chapters of a voluntary association. We should then start promoting rapidly people who have had deviant rather than conventional career lines. (This is the burden of a perceptive analysis of modern military careers by Morris Janowitz.[24])

There are costs involved in this strategy because, up to the time of the change, those with the most ambition and ability have probably been following conventional career lines, since that has been the quickest way to the top. Therefore, in the short run, some competence must be sacrificed in order to secure altered perspectives. Those with experiences that promote the proper perspective must be rapidly, and quite visibly, promoted, even though they are not the most competent. In time, the ambitious people with high competence and willingness to adopt organizational goals as their own will seek these kinds of assignments. In the long run, both proper values and competence will be found in top management.

Note that this kind of analysis is foreign to the view of leadership held by Barnard and by the human relations school, and it would find no place in Weber's theory of bureaucracy or that of the classical school of management. It is based upon the idea that to shape behavior, you have to shape the premises of decision making —in this case through the use of rewards and sanctions.

Thus, from Simon we learn that it is the premises of decisions that are important, rather than the decision-making capabilities of individuals—once it is established that they are not superhuman. The organization does not control the "process of decision making," as he says they do at several points, but the premises for decision making, as he says only occasionally.[25] These premises are to be found in the "vocabulary" of the organization, the structure of communication, rules and regulations and standard programs, selection criteria for personnel, and so on—in short, in the structural aspects.

[24]Morris Janowitz, *The Professional Soldier* (New York: Free Press, 1960).

[25]Simon, *Administrative Behavior,* pp. xii, 79.

Unobtrusive Control

But March and Simon are not merely "structuralists"; their view of organizations is superior to most sociological views in two respects. First, in the second part of their book, they offer insights that have not often been surpassed in organizational theory. Second, by providing a vocabulary or conceptual scheme for discussing control in organizations without relying on simple-minded views of control, they have enriched analysis. This second point will take some elaboration.

The conventional, structural viewpoint says that rules direct or control behavior. You tell a person what the rule is and that individual follows it or is punished. Or we say that authority is vested in the office, and the commands that issue forth tell people what to do. Coordination is achieved by having one person or group find out what two other groups are doing and direct them to do it in such a way as to make their efforts fit together. Yet the vast proportion of the activity in organizations goes on without personal directives and supervision—and even without written rules —and sometimes in permitted violation of the rules. We tend to deal with this "residue," which constitutes perhaps 80 percent of the behavior, by invoking general concepts such as habit, training, socialization, or routine.

March and Simon, however, fill in a good part of that residue by pointing to mechanisms that do not seem to be activated by directives or rules and by describing what these mechanisms do. Involved are such things as uncertainty absorption, organizational vocabularies, programmed tasks, procedural and substantive programs, standardization of raw materials, frequency of communication channel usage, interdependencies of units and programs. Such mechanisms affect organizational behavior in the following ways: they limit information content and flow, thus controlling the premises available for decisions; they set up expectations so as to highlight some aspects of the situation and play down others; they limit the search for alternatives when problems are confronted, thus ensuring more predictable and consistent solutions; they indicate the threshold levels as to when a danger signal is being emitted (thus reducing the occasions for decision making and promoting satisficing rather than optimizing behavior); they achieve coordination of effort by selecting certain kinds of work techniques and schedules.

Note the extent to which behavior is shaped, or controlled, without reference to conventional items of rules and commands. In most organizational theory, the discussion of such "latent" or unobtrusive means of control of behavior applies primarily to professional roles and their reliance on professional training, standards, and expectations and to informal group pressures. March and Simon make it very clear that the informal group and the characteristics of professionals are not the only sources of unobtrusive control in organizations. Most of us have neglected to locate and describe these unobtrusive controls, either taking them for granted or relying instead on very general concepts, such as the division of labor or socialization, or relatively obtrusive devices, such as rules or job specifications. By moving back from the actual process of decision making to the premises of decision making, March and Simon have begun to fill in a significant gap surrounding organizational behavior. I suspect that their social psychological preoccupation enabled them to do this more easily, but the level of analysis remains a sociological, or structural, one.

Thus March and Simon join the mainstream of the classical theorists, especially Weber, and augment that stream significantly. The problem with humans in organizations is not just that they may go their own, selfish way, and thus need to be kept in line through such devices as hierarchical control, division of labor, job specifications, impartial and impersonal rules and standards, and so on; the problem is also that there are real limits to human rationality, and thus the premises of decisions and the flow of information on which decisions are based must be controlled. As a result, organizations need not only the familiar appurtenances of bureaucracy but also the more subtle and unobtrusive controls of communication channels, organizational vocabulary, and so on. The prospects for spontaneous cooperative activity are dim in this view; what "cooperation" there is, in Barnard's sense, is engineered. The prospects for participative management are also dim; they are reduced to minor innovations within a complex network of established premises for action. The organization is not static, by any means, but change is incremental, partial, hit-or-miss, and channeled in the well-worn grooves of established adaptations.

At this writing, almost thirty years after the appearance of March and Simon's *Organizations*, we can push the notion of what I have labeled as unobtrusive controls a bit further. Think of three types of controls—direct, fully obtrusive ones such as giving orders, direct surveillance, and rules and regulations; bureaucratic ones such as specialization and standardization and hierarchy, which are fairly unobtrusive; and fully unobtrusive ones, namely the control of the cognitive premises underlying action. Direct controls are expensive and reactive. They are often necessary in times of change and crisis, and they always exist, but they do not draw on the accumulated experience, training, or intelligence of the subordinate. Rules are ineffective when situations change frequently, and direct surveillance and orders require continual effort and time on the part of management. Bureaucratic controls, principally specialization and standardization (the matter of hierarchy is too complicated to deal with here), are far more efficient. Because the range of stimuli is greatly reduced by standardization and specializing in one activity, the subordinate has fewer opportunities to make decisions that maximize personal interests rather than the organization's interests. There are also gains in having steeper learning curves, limiting information flow, and so on. But the control of premises, while far more difficult to achieve, is even more effective. Here the subordinate *voluntarily* restricts the range of stimuli that will be attended to ("Those sorts of things are irrelevant," or "What has that got to do with the matter?") and the range of alternatives that would be considered ("It would never occur to me to do that"). Direct sanctions operate in the first type, direct control; remote controls operate in the second—one is simply assigned to a kind of job with more or less standard inputs, methods, and expected outputs; internalized premises for behavior are operating in the third.[26]

Now we can better understand the paradoxical finding referred to in Chap-

---

[26]In "The Bureaucratic Paradox: The Efficient Organization Centralizes in Order to Decentralize," *Organizational Dynamics* (Spring 1977), pp. 2–14, I have suggested that, as industrialization developed, controls evolved from direct to bureaucratic to unobtrusive. A similar but more elaborate scheme can be found in Richard Edwards, *Contested Terrain: The Transformation of the Workplace in the Twentieth Century* (New York, Basic Books, 1979). However, it is important to see that while unobtrusive controls may now be more evident, direct and bureaucratic controls remain in use.

ter 1—the greater the degree of bureaucratization, the greater the delegation of decision making. Because the employee is well controlled, he or she can be trusted to make more of his or her own decisions. In the case of the actual research by the Blau and Aston groups, however, the decisions studied were either-or in nature, could be clearly specified in advance, and had quite visible consequences once they had been made. Such decisions are subject to fairly obtrusive controls. Rules are promulgated in advance, and their violation is apparent; furthermore, they are restricted to quite specialized and standardized matters. Not a great deal is being delegated here, and (unmeasured) controls are firmly in place.

It is in management's interest to delegate as many of these "either-or" decisions as possible, since such delegation reduces the cost to management of giving direct orders. (Otherwise, they may as well be making the analysis and the decision themselves.) Direct surveillance of behavior is reflected by checking outcomes, which is cheaper. Finally, delegation ensures that the decision is made by the person with the most knowledge of the situation.

But in the measurement of centralization of authority the Blau and Aston groups have not included measures of specialization, standardization, or even formal rules, because these are considered parts of structure. Thus delegation has taken place only because another kind of centralization of authority preceded it, an unmeasured kind.

Nor do we measure the more powerful and subtle form of control found in premise setting. (It is, by its very nature, extremely difficult to measure.) We are content to speak of socialization, or culture, or community norms, thus making it both sanitary and somehow independent of the organization. But we could just as well label premise setting as indoctrination, brainwashing, manipulation, or false consciousness.

Premise controls are most important when work is nonroutine (since such work by definition cannot have standardized inputs, throughputs, and outputs and cannot be specialized or governed by rules), and this is one reason scientists and other professionals have such latitude in organizations. Their premises are well set in their training institutions and professional associations. Premise controls are also most important near the top of organizations because managerial work there is less routine, the consequences of decisions are hard to assess immediately, and access to company resources is greatest, providing more opportunities to use company property and power for one's own ends. This is why social class, ethnic origins, and social networks are so important—they make it more likely that certain kinds of premises will exist. Further down the hierarchy, bureaucratic and direct controls increase in importance. But fully unobtrusive premise controls exist at all levels, created and reinforced by schools, the mass media, and cultural institutions in general.

The question that Bendix posed (see Chapter 2)—why are some given the right to command and others the duty to obey in organizations—can only be asked once the premises of the economic order are held in abeyance. This is why it is rarely asked, even by social scientists. For most people it is not a meaningful question; it is just the way things are and presumably have always been. In the United States, workers would have to violate the everyday premises that their organizations and the institutions outside of them constantly reinforce and reproduce if they were to demand, say, that occupants of all managerial positions be subject to direct election by their subordinates and required to run on announced policy platforms (e.g., no speedup, no in-plant pollution or dangerous chemicals, less pay for managers and more for workers). When we measure controls or centralization and decentralization in organizations, we do not include the control of basic premises such as this.

In fact, we do worse. We reinforce these premises in our own work. For example, most effectiveness studies now assume that high morale is an indicator of one aspect of organizational effectiveness. But these morale studies ask how satisfied people are with their jobs, supervisors, career prospects, working conditions, and pay. It goes unnoticed that the definition of morale is in terms of what the company assumes would be good for it. The unstated premise is that high morale means that people find it gratifying to do what the organization wants them to do. So thoroughly grounded is this premise that at first glance it seems absurd to recommend a morale measure that would assume that the happy employee is happy doing what he or she wants, rather than what the company wants. But I would recommend that future morale studies ask such questions as the following:

Is this the kind of organization where you can . . .

Have pleasant chats with others about things that interest you?
Daydream or relax from time to time without being bothered?
Use the organization's facilities for your own personal needs (the telephone, typists, office supplies, machine shop, personnel department, auto maintenance shop, travel facilities, etc.)?
Control the work pace so that if you are depressed or upset you don't have to work too hard?
Hide your mistakes and advertise your successes?
Pick up interesting tidbits about the world by working here, or be more interesting at social gatherings because of what you do here or learn here?
Make use of tediously acquired skills and knowledge so that you have some sense that what you are doing is meaningful and related to your abilities?
Get a friend or relative a job here?
Expect to have a job here as long as you need it?[27]

So thoroughly have researchers adopted the premises of management that it would be heretical to consider the above questions as valid measures of organizational effectiveness. But why not?

CONFLICT

Even the expanded bureaucratic model of March and Simon fails to deal with an obvious and pervasive aspect of organizations—conflict among groups. Of course, theorists and researchers, and certainly members of organizations, are aware that

[27]Charles Perrow, "Three Types of Effectiveness Studies," in Paul S. Goodman, Johannes M. Pennings, and associates, *New Perspectives on Organizational Effectiveness* (San Francisco: Jossey-Bass, 1977), pp. 96–105.

conflicts occur continuously between departments and divisions, and among groups within them. To Barnard, who seldom referred to it, conflict was possibly a melancholy failure of leadership. To Weber, who describes it impatiently and in some detail as it is found in government and political bureaucracies,[28] it sometimes appears to be only a result of human shortcomings such as cowardice, stupidity, and greed. To the classical management theorists it is a failure of adequate control, planning, and execution. For the human relations theorists it is variously a failure of leadership, lack of participative management, or something that is temporarily constructive, because it shows up areas where more work needs to be done. Elimination of conflict is always the goal, even if it is seen as constructive in the short run. For March and Simon, as with the human relations theorists, it is primarily an interpersonal problem, even though the two deal briefly with intergroup conflict. For all, from Weber to Likert, intergroup conflict is a fact of organizational life but not a fact that is built into their models, except as evidence of a failure to utilize the model.

While much conflict in organizations is undoubtedly an interpersonal phenomenon—two people in competition, or with incompatible personalities, or lacking in ability to emphathize with one another—a theory of organizations, rather than one of individual interaction, should be able to accommodate group conflict. Theory should see conflict as an inevitable part of organizational life stemming from organizational characteristics rather than from the characteristics of individuals. Why are sales and production in conflict in all firms—though to greatly varying degrees? Or faculty and the administration in colleges, doctors and nurses and administrators in hospitals, the treatment and custodial staffs in prisons? Why can one generally assume that even within departments there is a good chance of conflict between representatives of different product lines, different treatment technologies (such as social workers and psychiatrists), or different disciplines, such as the social sciences and engineering?

One answer is obvious enough: there is a never-ending struggle for values that are dear to participants—security, power, survival, discretion, and autonomy—and a host of rewards. Because organizations do not consist of people who share the same goals, since the members bring with them all sorts of needs and interests, and because control is far from complete, people will struggle for these kinds of values. To reduce, contain, or use these conflicts is the job of the administrator. The most important conflicts are those that involve groups, since groups can mobilize more resources, extract loyalty, and shape perceptions.

The matter has been little studied beyond anecdotal or descriptive case studies. Some time ago, Philip Selznick pointed out the prevalence and the positive and negative functions of group conflict within organizations.[29] Melville Dalton deals with conflict in a descriptive and rather social psychological, but still valuable, manner in his *Men Who Manage.*[30] The sociological literature on hospitals and

[28]Max Weber, *Economy and Society*, Vol. 3, ed. Guenther Roth and Claus Wittich (New York: Irvington, 1968), 1381–1462.

[29]Philip Selznick, *TVA and the Grass Roots* (Berkeley and Los Angeles: University of California Press, 1949). For a more systematic view, see his *Leadership in Administration* (New York: Harper & Row, 1957).

[30]Melville Dalton, *Men Who Manage* (New York: Wiley, 1959).

prisons has dealt with conflict since it is so obviously a fact of life in these organizations.[31] The general area of labor-management conflict has been well studied, of course, but will not be reviewed here.[32] Recently, some attempts have appeared to conceptualize types of conflicts, where they are likely to occur, and so on.[33] Some researchers in the field emphasize formal groups and rather obvious clashes of interest,[34] and some emphasize a confused, fluid, and "negotiated" order.[35] Others have attempted to build systematic models containing the observed bases of conflict and power.[36] Most of these efforts appear to be consistent with the neo-Weberian model we have described in this chapter.

However, the most interesting speculation on internal conflict in organizations revolves around the question of conflict over goals and, in the process, challenges a number of assumptions about goals in organizations.

The first such challenged assumption is that organizations are oriented toward a specific goal. Almost all definitions of organizations make this assumption. Yet the goals pursued by organizations are multiple, and they are generally in conflict. As Richard Cyert and James March point out in a brilliant discussion that we shall follow closely,[37] those objectives that are agreed on—reforming delinquents, making a satisfactory profit—are highly ambiguous and not "operational." That is, they do not indicate the specific operations or steps that must be taken to achieve them, so there can be many routes to these goals. Further, one is not even sure when they are achieved adequately. Satisfactory profits this year may be at the expense of satisfactory profits three years from now. Thus, to describe the single, specific goal of an organization is to say very little about it. Actual goals are discovered only when the public or official goal is factored into operational goals—those for which specific operations can be discovered.[38] Once this is done, it turns out that several goals are involved, and maximizing one will usually be at the expense of another.

If goals are, in fact, multiple, then another assumption held by some schools of thought (including the bureaucratic and the expanded bureaucratic models) must be abandoned. That is to say, it is not possible for the head of an organization to

[31]Mayer Zald, "Power Balance and Staff Conflict in Correctional Institutions," *Administrative Science Quarterly* 7 (June 1962): 22–49; David Street, Robert Vinter, and Charles Perrow, *Organizations for Treatment* (New York: Free Press, 1966); H. L. Smith, "Two Lines of Authority: The Hospital's Dilemma," in *Patients, Physicians and Illness: Source Book in Behavioral Science and Medicine,* 2nd ed., ed. E. G. Jaco (New York: Free Press, 1972); Charles Perrow, "Hospitals: Technology, Structure, and Goals," in *Handbook of Organizations,* ed. James G. March (Chicago: Rand McNally, 1965), 910–971.

[32]A. Kornhauser, R. Dubin, and A. Ross, *Industrial Conflict* (New York: McGraw-Hill, 1954).

[33]Mayer Zald, ed., *Power in Organizations* (Nashville, Tenn.: Vanderbilt University Press, 1970); entire issue of *Administrative Science Quarterly* 14, no. 4 (December 1969).

[34]Charles Perrow, "Departmental Power and Perspective in Industrial Firms," in Zald, *Power in Organizations,* pp. 59–89.

[35]Rue Bucher, "Social Process and Power in a Medical School," in ibid., pp. 3–48; Fred H. Goldner, "The Division of Labor: Process and Power," in ibid., pp. 97–143.

[36]David Hickson et al., "A Strategic Contingencies Theory of Intra-Organizational Power," *Administrative Science Quarterly* 16, no. 2 (June 1971): 216–229.

[37]Richard M. Cyert and James C. March, *A Behavioral Theory of the Firm* (Englewood Cliffs, N.J.: Prentice-Hall, 1963), chapters 1, 2, 3, 6.

[38]Charles Perrow, "Goals in Complex Organizations," *American Sociological Review* 26, no. 6 (December 1961): 854–865.

fully establish the "preference ordering" of goals. There may be such an ordering, and it may actually reflect the operative goals, but we cannot count on it. Instead, we have to assume that goals should be viewed as emerging from a bargaining process among groups. Furthermore, say Cyert and March, they are subject to a learning process. Aspirations of groups rise depending on the success or failure of group strategies. Therefore we cannot assume that even the leaders of an organization are completely free to rank specific goals in terms of their preference. Organizations are tools in the hands of their leaders, but they are imperfect, not completely controlled, tools, and it is a struggle to maintain control over them. (In his later work, reviewed on page 135, March goes further and views goals as rationalizations of past events, many of which were not intended or anticipated.)

This implies that if we accept the idea of multiple and conflicting goals, which are the result of a continuous bargaining learning process, we must go one step further. Contrary to the theories behind most models of organizations, conflicting goals can be met. Organizations, Cyert and March note, can pursue goals in a sequence; it is not necessary that they all be pursued at once. If pursued in a sequence, growth, for example, may take precedence over profit for a time, and then profit over growth. Both may be pursued and met at the same time, too. The goals of treatment and custody are in some conflict in prisons and mental hospitals, but if the organization is large and complex enough, some units may be providing mostly treatment for their clients, others mostly custody. This is obvious, but it rarely is given much attention, and the problems it raises for characterizing the organization are numerous.[39] More commonly, many goals are not in conflict in the short run; for example, increased market share or sales volume may, but may not, conflict with profit goals.

Pursuing different goals in sequence, or simultaneously, even if they are in short-run conflict, can take place if the environment is "benign"—poses few threats to the organization, has adequate resources, and so on—or if the organization has a lot of "slack." Slack simply means an excess of resources (money, time, personnel, equipment, ideas). When slack is high, several conflicting goals can be pursued if there are sufficient funds. Sociology departments generally resist teaching Marriage and the Family, a very popular service course for nonsociology majors, but as long as they can continue to recruit new assistant professors or instructors in sufficient volume, they can stick a few of them with this task. When departmental growth slows or stops, however, and staffing this course means cutting some "true" sociology courses, the goals conflict. Obvious enough, but the degree of fat in organizations is rarely taken into account in a systematic fashion in research, even in research on goals.

Cyert and March point out that people have a disorganized file drawer of goals

[39]One promising characterization is offered by Karl Weick in "Educational Organizations as Loosely Coupled Systems," *Administrative Science Quarterly* 21, no. 1 (March 1976): 1–19. For a somewhat extreme emphasis upon the largely symbolic character of goals, see John W. Meyer and Brian Rowan, "Institutionalized Organizations: Formal Structure as Myth and Ceremony," *American Journal of Sociology* 83, no. 2 (September 1977): 340–363. For an argument that official goals are generally one of the least important constraints upon behavior, see Charles Perrow, "Demystifying Organizations," in *The Management of Human Services*, ed. Rosemary Sarri and Yeheskel Hasenfeld (New York: Columbia University Press, 1978).

at hand, ready to pull out when situations warrant. There may be more ample resources, or a political payoff is due for joining a coalition of groups to support some other goal, or there may be a trade-off for a defeat in some other area. Goals may thus emerge in a rather fortuitous fashion, as when the organization seems to back into a new line of activity or into an external alliance in a fit of absentmindedness. Goals of a rather low level, but still with consequences for the organization, also emerge as a secondary consequence of a primary function. For example, if employee turnover or increased recruitment is sufficient to warrant enlarging the personnel department, the organization may find itself devoting substantial attention to personnel goals by running training programs, counseling and testing, setting up elaborate retirement counseling schemes, and establishing or revising pension plans. These emerge not because they are necessarily pressing problems for the organization, "but because the submit keeps generating solutions that remind other members of the organization of particular sets of objectives they profess."[40] Solutions are looking for problems, in this case, rather than problems looking for solutions.

In a striking extension of these ideas, James March and his associates have formulated a "garbage can" model of organizations wherein problems are convenient receptacles for people to toss in solutions that happen to interest them, or for interests that are not being met at the time. The can, with its problems, becomes an opportunity or resource. Depending on the number of cans around, the mixes of problems in them, and the amount of time people have, they stay with the particular can or leave it for another. The problem, then, gets detached from those that originally posed it, may develop a life of its own, or get transformed into quite another problem. Solutions no one originally intended or even expected may be generated, or no solutions at all. Some problems simply waste away. In this view the problem or the opportunity is conceptually dislodged from the people in the organization and can be analyzed independently of them. In one striking example, the problem of rewarding a particularly valuable secretary gets mixed up with a stream of quite unrelated and quite unpredictable other problems, interests, and opportunities (and some sheer accidents) and some years later the consequences are the restructuring of a number of university departments. The process is then reinterpreted in a rationalistic account as the inevitable modernization of the university due to forces in the environment, when it was manifestly not that at all. No coherent, stable goal guided the total process, but after the fact a coherent stable goal was presumed to have been present. It would be unsettling to see it otherwise.[41]

By this time, one may wonder if organizational goals can really be so fluid and random, the outgrowth of political bargaining, accident, unintended consequences, and so on. Many are, but the process is not as unstable as this description might indicate. Cyert and March themselves outline some mechanisms that stabilize the

---

[40]Cyert and March, *Behavioral Theory of the Firm*, p. 35.

[41]A short statement of the model appears in Michael D. Cohen, James C. March and Johan P. Olsen, "A Garbage Can Model of Organizational Choice," *Administrative Science Quarterly* 17, no. 1, (March 1972): 1–25. An extended one, with the example given above appearing in Chapter 14 is in James C. March and Johan P. Olsen, *Ambiguity and Choice in Organizations* (Bergen, Norway: Universitetsforlaget, 1976). See the useful reviews of this important but aggravating book in *Contemporary Society* 6, no. 3 (May 1977): 294–298; and *Administrative Science Quarterly* 22, no. 2 (June 1977): 351–361.

goal-setting process considerably. One key one is the budget. Rather than viewing the budget as a rational plan developed by the central authority to maximize the goals of the leader, Cyert and March describe it as "an explicit elaboration of previous commitments."[42] It stabilizes bargainings and expectations for a year or longer. Continual renegotiation of major items is prevented in this fashion, and groups agree to abide, in general, by the rules of the game until they can try to further their own goals in the next budget.

Reference to precedent, usually in the form of rules, standing operating procedures, or informal understandings and traditions, is another stabilizing factor. These precedents "remove from conscious consideration many agreements, decisions, and commitments that might well be subject to renegotiation in an organization without a memory."[43] This is one of the functions of record keeping, files, and people with long seniority. While the organization is, as Anselm Strauss and his associates have stressed, a "negotiated environment,"[44] most of the negotiations have been consummated in the past. Only a few items are under negotiation at any one point in time.

Finally, despite the existence of conflicting groups, changing coalitions, and multiple goals pursued in sequence or simultaneously, it is clear that the vast majority of organizations have interpretable goal structures. The people at the top are in a position to win most of the battles and to shape the nature of the contest that goes on below them. We would be wrong to assume a specific goal with specific means attached to it, and the conflict model of organizations is essential in this respect. But organizations are not such open systems that goals fluctuate continually and rulers never get their way—or at least the issue is in doubt.

Garbage can theory has had an enormous impact in the decade since it has appeared. It greatly illuminates the micro organizational processes of group dynamics, intergroup relations, and the dilemmas of leadership, adding a significant "human" dimension to the static skeleton of more rational and more structural models. For the practicing administrator, I think the garbage can model is extremely valuable, since it makes some kind of sense out of the bewildering shifts, turns, and unexpected outcomes in daily organizational life. It notes that people fight hard to gain access to committees, then rarely attend, because of unstable priorities and limited attention spans. People struggle mightily to formulate rules or plans, then forget all about them as new problems arise and the membership of coalitions shifts. For those doing case studies of organizations it is also indispensable, checking the tendency of social scientists to find reason, cause, and function in all behavior, and emphasizing instead the accidental, temporary, shifting, and fluid nature of all social life. The notion that goals are posited to make sense out of unplanned adaptations and accidental developments, and thus are less plans of action that are rational than rationalizations of unpredictable encounters with diverse and shifting interests, is essential for the case study. A management school I am familiar with shifted in a few years from a unique public-sector orientation that ran contrary to the main-

---

[42]Ibid., p. 33. See also Aaron Wildavsky, *Politics of the Budgetary Process*, 2nd ed. (Boston: Little Brown, 1974).

[43]Cyert and March, *Behavioral Theory of the Firm*, p. 33.

[44]Anselm L. Strauss et al., *Psychiatric Ideologies and Institutions* (New York: Free Press, 1964).

stream in business schools to a conventional private-sector orientation as a result of unplanned adaptations. Defensive about the change when it became apparent to all, the school simply argued that the shift was required to meet the goal of excellence and leadership in the field.

Garbage can theory provides the tools to examine the process and not be taken in by functional explanations. The decision process must be seen as involving a shifting set of actors with unpredictable entrances and exits from the "can" (or the decision mechanism), the often unrelated problems these actors have on their agendas, the solutions of some that are looking for problems they can apply them to, the accidental availability of external candidates that then bring new solutions and problems to the decision process, and finally the necessity of "explaining" the outcomes as rational and intended. The shift from public- to private-sector training will be applauded by all but the students who take the brochures seriously in making their choices, and eventually many of them will reconstruct their reality. But the investigator of the case must "deconstruct" it all. Garbage can theory draws fully on bounded rationality, using incomplete information, lack of knowledge of cause-and-effect relationships, and shifting goals and priorities, but it goes far beyond bounded rationality by conceptualizing dynamic group processes and emphasizing the need to rationalize, to construct something stable out of fluidity that is intolerable for organizations that see themselves as rational.

As such, garbage can theory partakes of a general trend in the social sciences and humanities that is likely to be significant over the next decade or two. This trend can be labeled "deconstructionism." For a couple of centuries we have been "constructing" a world that we view as organized on rational principles, where what happened was intended to happen, where interactions are discrete and quite atomistic, and where progress is continuous. The construction envisions a long age of enlightenment. All this is now being questioned, and we are thus beginning to "deconstruct" this construction.[45] The origins of this viewpoint are many. In philosophy Friedrich Nietzsche challenged the teleology of the "march of progress," and Ludwig Wittgenstein, Alfred Schutz, and many others challenged rationality and explored the notion that what we take for reality is actually only a "social construction of reality" that goes on daily as we try, through our interpersonal exchanges, to seek agreement on what reality is.

In psychology deconstructionism is painfully making its way by questioning our notions of personality, traits, character, and the very idea of human nature itself. (Strong influences, such as operant conditioning, behaviorism, and other physiological theories counter this theory.) In literature and history the work of Foucault, Claude Lévi-Strauss, and the early Sartre attests to the importance of social context and myths and symbols—rather than conventional, unambiguous assumptions of linear development, national character, and "real" events—in explaining cultural productions and social events. In anthropology the interaction of the anthropologist with the subjects is stressed, showing how Western values have been used to interpret the culture under examination, seeing some things, missing others, and

---

[45]Charles Perrow, "Deconstructing Social Science," *New York University Educational Quarterly* 12, no. 2 (Winter 1981): 2–9.

completely distorting still others. Indeed, the subjects, in the process of constructing a social world under these novel conditions, learned to feed the researcher's prejudices and reinterpret their own lives in the process. In social psychology the sudden popularity of "ethnomethodology" (the "methods" people use to interpret one another's actions) deconstructed forever, for some of us, the notions of rationality, functionalism, and an accepted, empirical social reality.

In all of these examples, the atomistic notion that the object of inquiry—whether it is a short burst of speech, a painting, a tribe, a poem, or a novel—could be examined in itself, without reference to ever larger contexts with which it interacts and which it helps to shape, was discredited. The tribe has a history, neighbors, an environment, and certainly a foreigner in its presence disturbing its ways. The "speech act" is encrusted with past speech acts, involves interaction with a receiver, is stimulated by a particular situation, and so on. These structural contexts may seem obvious, but by and large they were either ignored or at best simply asserted, without any investigation into their problematical and largely socially constructed nature.

The deconstructionist movement and garbage can theory have de-emphasized not only rationalism but theories of human nature. Garbage can theory, in particular, avoids the twin rocks of attributing behavior, on the one hand, to impulsive, irrational movtives or such things as greed, selfishness, or power drives, and, on the other hand, to the need to be affiliated, to be loved and respected, to participate, and to realize one's potential. *All of these exist* in the plentitude of human variation and potential, but as primary explanations of complex situations they fail. Embedded in garbage can theory, but unfortunately still not explicated, is the notion of the social construction of reality; it deconstructs not only rational explanations but also personality ones (e.g., greed) and psychodynamic ones (e.g., the need for affiliation). Human nature is as we find it, varying enormously as situations are constructed out of the bureaucratic materials at hand.

Yet the theory remains a primitive digging tool. If it is based, as I claim, on a vision of the human condition, it should be as applicable to an insurance office or steel mill as it has been to exotic "free schools," universities, and powerless, dependent government agencies. Yet no one has tried it on the former. Has the deskilling of work in the insurance offices driven out garbage cans? Does the heat and dust and danger of the steel mill impose a degree of reality that the management school at either Yale or the University of California at Irvine will never experience?[46] We are vaguely told that it may work better in organizations where there are uncertain means and ends, but part of the larger tradition in which I ground garbage can theory suggests that *certainty* over means and ends is a social construction and must be explained itself. Besides, that management classic, *Men Who Manage,* by Melville Dalton, deals with industrial organizations and can be fruitfully read as an example of garbage can theory in supposedly rational, profit-oriented organizations. Larry Hirschorn's account of a highly automated steel-rolling mill even suggests that automation may bring precisely those ambiguities associated previously with low-

[46]James March was dean at the latter, and several sections of *Ambiguity and Choice* fuss over the problem of electing his successor at the school.

technology and nonprofit activities to high-technology, profit-making organizations. The notion of individual productivity is meaningless, since workers simply monitor machines; the work is varied rather than specialized and entails coordination with others; and it involves passive monitoring but high attentiveness and conceptual ability. Under such conditions, where there is ambiguity about tasks, productivity, and measures of ability, the struggles between management and labor are no longer over rights, duties, prerogatives, job classifications, and pay scales—all fairly well-defined items that might succumb to a rational process—but "over the definition of a situation itself, over the meaning of the very conditions that establish the semantic and practical meaning of the terms" that were once the basis of the struggle.[47] Automation has created more ambiguity, perhaps creating more garbage cans.

The coldly logical numeric, scientific field of accounting, largely populated by rationalistic economists, turns out to be such a vast garbage can, full of wonderful examples of the social construction of reality, that a whole journal is devoted to exploring this aspect of accounting (*Accounting, Organizations and Society*, edited by Anthony Hopwood). There are even some attempts to apply garbage can theory to interorganizational relationships. Lee Sproull and associates make a beginning in their study of the National Institute of Education, but this still is largely a case study and not all that indebted to the theory. On the other hand, the rich study by Lee Pressman and Aaron Wildavsky, *Implementation*, is atheoretical as it is written but is an excellent example of an interorganizational garbage can. Another study, which both is indebted to and extends the theory, is Lee Clarke's fascinating examination of how a large network of very diverse, largely otherwise unconnected organizations responded to the highly novel and ambiguous situation of an eighteen-story office building suddenly contaminated from top to bottom by dioxin. In this complex and dramatic interorganizational case study, the social construction of reality was rampant, comic, and tragic.[48]

Thus garbage can theory cannot stop at the gate of the rationalistic business or industrial organization; it must do more to explore its potential within these organizations and tell us more precisely where its limits are. And it must cope with the macro world of interorganizational relationships. Earlier I suggested some mechanisms that provide for goal stability despite the ambiguity of choice and decisions; we need more systematic investigation along these lines. We also need to handle better one of our most fundamental conceptual problems, one rooted in the very way we think and talk about the social world—the relationship between the micro and the macro, between, in this case, the apparent disorder and nonrationality at the group or even the organizational level and the substantial evidence for stability and order at the interorganizational and societal level. Garbage can theory, for all its promise, is a poor digging tool when we stand back and look at the economy or society as a whole. Or, at least, the concepts I use to look at the macro world

[47]Larry Hirschorn, "The Post-Industrial Labor Process," *New Political Science* 7 (Fall 1981): 11–33.

[48]Lee Sproul et al., *Organizing an Anarchy* (Chicago: University of Chicago Press, 1978); Lee Pressman and Aaron Wildavsky, *Implementation* (Berkeley: University of California Press, 1979); Lee Clarke, "Organizing Risk," Ph.D. dissertation, State University of New York at Stony Brook, 1985.

presuppose a number of rather neat boxes (industries, laws, population changes, trade balances, a capitalist class, etc.) rather than a garbage can. I suspect someone will help me out by deconstructing my macro world over the next decade, even as James March and his associates, responding, I think, to broader intellectual currents, have deconstructed the micro world. The practicing executive as well as the organizational researcher are in the debt of March and his colleagues.

TECHNOLOGY

Until now, we have usually treated all complex organizations as being alike. We have done so because most of the theoretical schools have done so. Weber would, of course, admit that organizations are only more or less bureaucratized, since he saw it as an irregular historical process and was avowedly constructing an "ideal type" with his model. Barnard noted some differences among organizations upon commonplace dimensions—business, government, voluntary associations. We noted that the human relations school has moved toward various forms of differentiation—group climate, size, task—in explaining groups, and that Likert acknowledged that things might be different in organizations with routine tasks from things in organizations with varied tasks, but he abandoned the idea in favor of System 4 for all organizations. Finally, March and Simon made a more penetrating stab when they distinguished programmed from nonprogrammed tasks in organizations and briefly examined some consequences of this.[49]

But by and large, organizational theory has not until recently attempted to build into its models any systematic consideration of different types of organizations. The ideas that have been put forth, by Peter Blau and Richard Scott, Alvin Gouldner, Talcott Parsons, and Amitai Etzioni, have not proved very useful.[50] We desire typologies that will order the diversity of organizations in such a way that we can explain differences in structure and/or goals. Organizations of the same type should have similar structures and/or goals. But if the typology is based on either structure or goals, we risk tautologies.

For example, Etzioni bases his typology on the type of power utilized in the organization to gain the compliance of participants, a structural characteristic. This leads him to predict that such organizations as prisons, which use "coercive" power, will have the structural attribute of alienated participant involvement, will exhibit goals of internal order, and will represent a type of organization he calls "coercive." We have not learned much about prisons from this exercise that we did not already know. Prisoners are coerced in coercive organizations by coercive power and do not like it. The economic gain type of organization (e.g., a factory) has economic goals and calculative participant involvement (the members calculate whether the wages are worth it) and uses remunerative power (wages) to gain compliance. Again, we

[49]March and Simon, *Organizations*, pp. 141–148 and *passim*.

[50]Peter Blau and W. Richard Scott, *Formal Organizations* (San Francisco: Chandler, 1962), pp. 42–45; Amitai Etzioni, *A Comparative Analysis of Complex Organizations*, rev. ed. (New York: Free Press, 1975); Talcott Parsons, *Structure and Process in Modern Societies* (New York: Free Press, 1960), pp. 44–47; Alvin Gouldner, *Patterns of Industrial Bureaucracy* (New York: Free Press, 1954).

appear to have only described various aspects of the organization with similar terms. The case is similar with the normative organizations, such as churches—they have the goal of cultural (normative) outputs, members are normatively involved, and normative power is used. Equally as serious as the tautology involved is the neglect of wide ranges of differences within the types. Some churches and schools, for example, are run like factories; some like prisons.

Etzioni's book has the merit of systematically using his typology to explore structural and other properties. But the value of his discussions does not appear to reside in the typology. This is also true of the volume by Blau and Scott, where the typology is quickly abandoned and does not inform the rest of the book. The two authors distinguish organizations on the basis of who benefits from them, and they come up with a familiar typology: voluntary associations (members benefit), welfare agencies (clients benefit), business (owners), and government (the public). Vast differences in structure within each type are ignored. Parsons's scheme is a bit more unusual, since he distinguishes economic organizations, pattern maintenance organizations (e.g., universities, churches), integrative organizations (hospitals, courts, law firms, political parties), and political organizations (the military, government, some aspects of banking). His highly general comments—for example, that the military is the most authoritarian, universities the least, and business in between—hardly enlighten us, and the variations in structure within types are, again, enormous. The typology by Gouldner is a replay of the simple distinction between democratic, authoritarian, and laissez-faire leadership.

This suggests that an adequate typology should be based on organizational characteristics that are conceptually independent of either goals or structure. Size might be one, but it has not proved to have much of an analytical cutting edge, nor has geographic location, age, or physical resources. Organizations have two other characteristics that might provide a basis for a typology: raw materials (things, symbols, or people), which are transformed into outputs through the application of energy; and tasks, or techniques of effecting the transformation. Raw materials vary in a number of ways, such as uniformity and stability. Tasks also vary in a number of ways, including the difficulty of learning them or executing them, their simplicity or complexity, whether they are repetitive or not, and whether they are well structured or ill defined.

One merit of the "technological school," or contingency theory as it has come to be called, is that it provides for some independent leverage in constructing typologies because it focuses on something more or less analytically independent of structure and goals—the tasks or techniques utilized in organizations. ("Technology" is not used here in its commonplace sense of machines or sophisticated devices for achieving high efficiency, as in the term "technologically advanced society," but in its generic sense of the study of techniques or tasks.) Organizations are classified in terms of the kinds of tasks that are performed in them, and this is presumed to affect the structure of the organization (the arrangements of roles for carrying out these tasks) and, to some extent at least, the range of goals that can be achieved. There is no agreement in this rather new school of thought as to how to define technology in any precise way or how to measure it, but the general outlines of a theory are present.

The Basic Argument

In its simplest form, the argument goes like this: when the tasks people perform are well understood, predictable, routine, and repetitive, a bureaucratic structure is the most efficient. Things can be "programmed," to use March and Simon's term. Where tasks are not well understood, generally because the "raw material" that each person works on is poorly understood and possibly reactive, recalcitrant, or self-activating, the tasks are nonroutine. Such units or organizations are difficult to bureaucratize. More discretion must be given to lower-level personnel; more interaction is required among personnel at the same level; there must be more emphasis on experience, "feel," or professionalization. If so, it is difficult to have clear lines of authority, a high degree of division of labor, rules and procedures for everything, exact specification of duties and responsibilities, and so on. There is more craft, or art, or esoteric skills (in the case of professionals) involved.

Organizations, it is assumed, vary considerably in their degree of routinization. One steel mill may be making exotic metals for aerospace purposes; this mill may have high scrap rates because the materials it is working with are poorly understood. Another mill may be turning out galvanized steel for garbage cans with little unpredictability and low scrap rates. One school in a wealthy suburb will try to mold the whole personality; another in the ghetto will try only to maintain order or teach shop. The custodial mental hospital can be routinized; the treatment-oriented one cannot. In all these cases, the advantages of bureaucracy can be realized in the routine situation; the nonroutine organization must pay the considerable price of long periods of personnel training, professional employees, confusion, wasted materials, hit-or-miss efforts, unpredictable outputs, and so on. They charge more.

This is the simplest form of the argument. Actually a number of versions have appeared, stressing different things and constructing more elaborate classification schemes than merely routine and nonroutine.[51] The Woodward scheme proposes

[51] A discussion of the work done in this area up through 1966 can be found in the bibliographic essay at the end of Charles Perrow, "A Framework for Comparative Organizational Analysis," *American Sociological Review* 32, no. 2 (April 1967): 194–208. The same issue of that journal contains a sympathetic review and brief summary of the pioneering work of Joan Woodward; see her *Industrial Organization: Theory and Practice* (Oxford, England: Oxford University Press, 1965). Since that article, an important book by Paul Lawrence and Jay Lorsch, *Organization and Environment* (Cambridge, Mass.: Harvard University Press, 1967), has appeared, which deals with the problem of integrating various technologies within a firm. The general theory has been found useful in explaining some findings in welfare organizations in Jerald Hage and Michael Aiken, "Routine Technology, Social Structure, and Organizational Goals," *Administrative Science Quarterly* 14, no. 3 (September 1969): 366–377; and public health departments in Dennis J. Palumbo, "Power and Role Specificity in Organization Theory," *Public Administration Review* 29, no. 3 (May/June 1969): 237–248; Peggy Overton, Rodney Schneck, and C. B. Hazlett, "An Empirical Study of the Technology of Nursing Subunits," *Administrative Science Quarterly* 22, no. 2 (June 1977): 203–219; Peggy Leatt and Rodney Schneck, "Technology, Size, Environment, and Structure in Nursing Subunits," *Organizational Studies* 3, no. 3 (1982): 221–242. and industry in general in W. A. Rushing, "Hardness of Material as Related to Division of Labor in Manufacturing Industries," *Administrative Science Quarterly* 13, no. 2 (September 1968): 229–245. James Thompson, a pioneer in this area, has elaborated his early scheme in *Organizations in Action* (New York: McGraw-Hill, 1967). Gerald Zeitz finds more satisfaction by personnel in more highly structured roles, supporting the theory, and has a good discussion of the difference between measurements based on group scores and those based on individual scores—a vexing matter that plagues technology-structure research as well as most others. See Gerald Zeitz, "Structural and Individual Determinants of Organization Morale and Satisfaction," *Social Forces* 61, no. 4 (1983): 1088–1108.

three basic models—for unit and small-batch production processes (custom suits, engineering prototypes), for large-batch, mass, and assembly processes (autos, metal industries), and for continuous process industries (oil, chemicals, candy). The present author has proposed a fourfold typology, later expanded to include other "clusters" of technological types[52] based on two independent dimensions, the degree of variability and the degree of uncertainty in search procedures. Other versions will no doubt come along.

Unresolved Problems

There are many problems with this recent development in organizational theory. The foremost has been the measurement (and thus the definition) of technology itself. To be pure, and to keep the concept independent of structure, we should focus on characteristics that are measured independently of human behavior—perhaps the number of items produced per minute, the number of design changes over a period of time, the number of occupational specializations, or the scrap rate. For a number of reasons, this has not proved feasible; organizations vary in these terms independently of what we vaguely mean by technology. Failing here, we should try to focus on actual human behavior—detailed observations of what is actually done. This, too, has thus far been rather unproductive and prohibitively expensive.[53] A "quick and dirty" method is to ask people about the frequency with which they come across problems for which there is no solution ready at hand, and about which no one else is likely to know much. This has the virtue of being an easy method, and it is applicable to all personnel at all levels in all kinds of organizations (and not just the basic work-flow level such as the production line in industry). But it is rather unreliable since people cannot, or choose not to, give "accurate" answers.[54] It also has a more serious limitation: the measure of technol-

---

Measurement and conceptualization problems are examined carefully in Beverly P. Lynch, "An Empirical Assessment of Perrow's Technology Construct," *Administrative Science Quarterly* 19, no. 3 (September 1974): 338–356, as well as in Overton et al., cited above. Some readers have appeared for example, Fremont Kast and James Rosenzweig, *Contingency Views of Organization and Management* (Palo Alto, Calif.: Science Research Associates, 1973). There has been considerable discussion of the issue in connection with the research of the Aston group, mentioned below, but the most serious empirical refutation is found in Lawrence B. Mohr, "Organizational Technology and Organizational Structure," *Administrative Science Quarterly* 16, no. 4 (December 1971): 444–459. Mohr took considerable pains with operationalizing the concept, and while there are problems with the study, it is one of the most careful in the literature, and the most damaging to this viewpoint. It would appear that for many public service organizations there are more important things to do than to maximize the fit between technology and structure in the interests of effective goal achievement. See Perrow, "Demystifying Organizations."

[52]Perrow, "A Framework for Comparative Organizational Analysis"; Charles Perrow, "The Effect of Technological Change on the Structure of Business Firms," in *Industrial Relations: Contemporary Issues*, ed. B. C. Roberts (London: Macmillan, 1968), pp. 205–219; and *Organizational Analysis* (Belmont, Calif.: Wadsworth, 1972), Chapter 3.

[53]For a detailed and sobering discussion of intensive efforts in both these directions, see Joan Woodward, ed., *Industrial Organization: Behavior and Control* (Oxford, England: Oxford University Press, 1970).

[54]I have used this method in a study of industrial corporations; for a very preliminary report on one aspect of organizations, see Perrow, "Departmental Power and Perspective in Industrial Firms," pp. 59–89.

ogy is confused by the effects of structure. For example, the structure of an organization can generate nonroutineness of tasks, as in one firm where tasks *might* have been highly routinized, but the head of the firm did not allow them to be. He deliberately did not use a bureaucratic model (apparently so as to increase his control by requiring that everything come to him for review), and people experienced much uncertainty in what would normally be routine tasks.[55]

There is also disagreement at present as to whether the technological model should be restricted to the basic work-flow process, allowing us to measure it through fairly "pure" indices such as the proportion of single-purpose machines, or whether other aspects of the organization should be included—for example, sales, personnel, accounting, research and development, industrial relations, and so on.[56] These debates will go on for some time.

But the most serious problem with the current state of the technological view is that it reverts to the old dichotomies, putting the new wine into the same old bottles. By clinging to a routine-nonroutine distinction, the technological theories too often place a caricature of Weber in the former and the human relations model in the latter type of organization, and we have a replay of the old social psychological distinction between initiating structure and consideration. What promises to be a way out of these oversimple dichotomies is in danger of becoming trapped by them. Neither the simple bureaucratic model nor the human relations model is adequate, so a theory that tells us which to use is not all that useful. The work of Joan Woodward does not make this mistake; her insights into such diverse areas as types and degrees of conflict, the role of boards of directors, the conditions under which either research and development, production, or marketing will be the critical function in an organization, and the insightful way she uses the distinction between lower and middle management—all these and others suggest the possibility of developing new models as a result of using technology as an independent variable, rather than just trying to find room for old models.[57]

I hope more subtle models of types of organizations will emerge from this effort. The neo-Weberian model we have been discussing, for example, has enough dimensions and room for variations to suggest that there could be more than one variety of routineness. The flavor of improvisation and uncertainty that T. Burns and G. M. Stalker describe for their electronic firms[58] is one kind of nonroutineness

---

Despite problems, the two sets of questions finally used discriminated well among organizations and within organizations.

[55]For a more extensive argument along this important line see John Child, "Organizational Structure, Environment, and Performance: The Role of Strategic Choice," *Sociology* 6, no. 1 (January 1972): 1–22.

[56]David J. Hickson, D. S. Pugh, and Diana C. Pheysey, "Operations Technology and Organizational Structure: An Empirical Reappraisal," *Administrative Science Quarterly* 14, no. 3 (September 1969): 378–397. They restrict the meaning of technology to the work-flow load and, not surprisingly, find that their measure has little to do with other aspects of the organization. Unfortunately this has been cited as evidence that technology has little impact on structure when only a very narrow definition of technology is applied to one part of the organization alone.

[57]One reviewer of Woodward's book complained that she appeared unaware of the U.S. literature on organizations. It may have been her greatest strength; otherwise, she might have just searched for evidence for bureaucracy or cooperation.

[58]T. Burns and G. M. Stalker, *The Management of Innovation* (New York: Barnes & Noble, 1961).

that does not have to piggyback all the tenets of the human relations school. Gouldner's description of the organization of gypsum miners sounds like quite another variant of nonroutineness.[59] We may also be able to find systematic differences among organizations in the extent to which levels of the organizations vary in technology. It is possible for lower-management tasks, for example, to be quite nonroutine while those of middle management are routine; the reverse could also hold. Furthermore, while something like research and development is always likely to be more nonroutine than production, there may be large degrees of difference in some firms and only small degrees in others. As Lawrence and Lorsch point out, the communication problems between units with quite dissimilar technologies (or environment, as they call it) can be substantial,[60] and the organizational structure is likely to reflect this.

We still do not have a good model of political organizations at the higher levels of government. For example, the descriptions of the way that President Franklin D. Roosevelt worked suggest a combination of nonroutine tasks and a traditional form of organization that emphasizes loyalty, assigning several people to the same tasks, spying, and so on.[61] This is a reasonably common style of leadership in administrative units with political tasks, and while it is somewhat illuminating to say that these tasks are nonroutine, and that loyalty rather than efficiency takes precedence where political tasks dominate, we still need a more carefully considered model of such types of administration or types of organizations.

I have not lingered over contingency theory in this book, though it was a major preoccupation for a good part of my career. It is well covered in various publications cited above, and as time goes by it has become well absorbed. The search for major classifying schemes, which I criticized at the start of this section, has abated; simple two-, three-, or fourfold classification schemes are no longer put forth by major theorists. The contrast of hospitals and cement plants no longer excites or stimulates us. I think the technological or task approach has made its point for such clear cases, even though the effect of task on structure is not at all clear in more fine-grained comparisons, such as the public organizations studied by Lawrence Mohr.[62] I believe that the theory is generally sound and should be impressed on the many executives who persist in imposing the same structure on routine production units and nonroutine R&D or sales units. But if we take garbage can theory seriously, along with the interchanges the organization has with the environment (see Chapter 6), and realize that organizations, as tools in the hands of masters, need not be efficient to survive and may be used for more important purposes than the efficient production of goods and services, then we should not expect anything but rather gross fits between task and technology. Where the fit is lacking, we are alerted to a variety of explanations. To pick only three, we might find unintentional mismanagement or, second, the garbage can processes of chance and error. The third is the most important: since

[59]Gouldner, *Patterns of Industrial Bureaucracy*.

[60]Lawrence and Lorsch, *Organization and Environment*.

[61]For a lively summary description of this, see Harold Wilensky, *Organizational Intelligence* (New York: Basic Books, 1969), pp. 50–53.

[62]Lawrence Mohr, "Organizational Technology and Organizational Structure," *Administrative Science Quarterly* 16, no. 4 (1971): 444–459.

organizations are tools and can be used for a wide variety of political and social as well as economic ends, we can expect the willing sacrifice of narrow production efficiencies for other goals. Companies that make cans are generally not run like R&D labs; advertising agencies rarely have the structure of insurance firms. If they do, something really interesting must be going on.

The typology of organizations, of which contingency theory probably provides the most useful model to date, is claiming less interest for another reason. We have become more concerned with the variety of theories about organizations and less concerned about the variety of organizations. In keeping with deconstructionist concerns, we are increasingly nervous in and reflexive about our theorizing, trying to grasp our own social construction of organizations. The fourfold tables now concern theorists, rather than organizational types. There is always a threat of either self-indulgence or retreat from our subject matter in this, but I think we are becoming more aware that theorizing is not a "neutral" activity, but one guided by strong interests and values that need to be explicated.

ANALYZING SYSTEMS

In a recent book and article, I have tried to make use of most of the elements of the neo-Weberian model described in this chapter by attacking a particular problem: How can we understand major failures in systems? I focused on organizations where major failures can have catastrophic consequences. We are all aware of the danger of accidents involving airlines, nuclear power plants, weapons systems, the transport of toxic substances, and the production of genetically engineered plants or microorganisms. Organizational theory ought to be able to say something about safety, rather than just efficiency, in such risky systems. The inquiry, casually begun as a short background paper for the presidential commission investigating the accident at the Three Mile Island nuclear power plant, grew into a major analysis of a number of systems.[63] Some aspects of it are relevant here, for they illustrate the application of the neo-Weberian model to some very real-life and quite urgent problems.

Though the analysis draws on psychology and especially cognitive psychology, as well as garbage can theory, it is relentlessly "structural." There is a strong tendency to blame failures on operator error in almost all accident investigations that I pursued, whether in high-tech systems or low-tech ones such as underground mining. Closer inquiry, however, found these explanations to be retrospective attributions of error that would protect the political position of the organization or industry. Formal accident investigations usually start with an assumption that the operator must have failed, and if this attribution can be made, that is the end of serious inquiry. Finding that faulty designs were responsible would entail enormous shutdown and retrofitting costs; finding that management was responsible would

[63]Charles Perrow, *Normal Accidents: Living with High-Risk Technologies* (New York: Basic Books, 1984), and Charles Perrow, "The Organizational Context of Human Factors Engineering," *Administrative Science Quarterly* 28, no. 4 (1983): 521–541.

threaten those in charge; but finding that operators were responsible preserves the system, with some soporific injunctions about better training. Strong unions, such as the Airline Pilots Union, resist such attributions and have the resources to insist that alternative explanations be sought. But most risky systems have weak unions or none at all.

Garbage can theory highlights the unexpected interactions that can occur in reasonably complex systems. Let me illustrate with some familiar examples that are not confined to risky systems with catastrophic potential: one person's problem unexpectedly finds another person's solution; the composition of a committee accidentally exacerbates the uncertainty that one member feels about her status, causing her to be uncharacteristically withdrawn or unassertive; ambiguity about a budget item or even a typing mistake or verbal error may propel or block a program; rules are suddenly found to interact in a gridlock that creates a Catch-22 situation, and disentangling them affects other delicate balances; departments discover unused funds and start trajectories of development that devour their base, dislodge other departments, or compromise the arrangements that are the basis for their rewards. Sometimes unexpected interactions have positive outcomes; universities and research labs thrive on such unanticipated "synergies." Sometimes, though, they are disastrous for the unit or the organization. If the organization happens to have catastrophic potentials because of toxic or explosive substances, harmful genetic properties, or hostile environments (such as outer space, the air, or under the sea), the possibility of negative synergies, where 2 plus 2 can equal -5 or -5 million, is of great concern.

Many such risky systems exist, and it turns out that all (except genetic engineering, which is just being born) have had catastrophic accidents or near accidents. Investigating a number of these accidents, I found a common pattern. While most accidents in risky systems stemmed from a major failure that could have been prevented, a substantial minority resulted from the unexpected interaction of two or more small failures. That is, nothing is perfect, so we expect everything to be subject to failure at some time, but since we expect the failures, we guard against them with safety devices. What we don't anticipate is that multiple failures will interact so as to defeat, bypass, or disable our safety devices. The unexpected and generally incomprehensible interaction of small failures was found in all the complex systems I studied in any detail, including those with catastrophic potential—nuclear power plants, air-traffic control, air transport, marine transport, chemical plants, nuclear weapons systems and those without space missions, universities and R&D labs, and complex government agencies. The sources of failures were diverse; indeed, an acronym, DEPOSE, was used to summarize the variety of components that could fail (*d*esign, *e*quipment, *p*rocedures, *o*perators, *s*upplies and materials, and *e*nvironment). The resulting accidents were "system accidents," arising from the ability of the system to permit the unexpected interactions of failures. They were, in a sense, "normal accidents" because it is normal (though rare) for such interactions to occur. Indeed, I argued, it is inevitable, since nothing can be perfect; all the DEPOSE components are subject to failure or error.

Can interactive complexity be avoided? Yes, and the history of most technologies, including organizational structure techniques, is the progressive "linearization" of the system, avoiding multiple-use components, proximity of components, common mode connections, unfamiliar or unintended feedback loops, indirect or inferential information sources, and poorly understood processes; the assembly line is the prototypical linear system. But industries and social service agencies that involve "transformation" processes, rather than additive or assembly processes, often must be complexly interactive; there may be no other way to run a catalytic cracking tower, a nuclear plant, or a gene-splicing lab. One reason why the air-traffic control system is as incredibly reliable as it has become over the last twenty years is that complex interactions have been made more linear, but at present there appears to be no way to make nuclear power plants or our nuclear early-warning system less complexly interactive.

Multiple, unexpectedly interacting failures in risky systems still might not be a serious concern if operators could intervene before significant damage occurs. But there is another system characteristic to consider: the degree of coupling present. If coupling is loose, there will be time to devise remedies, other equipment or supplies or personnel can be substituted, parts can be shut down without endangering other parts, and alternative ways of running the system can be utilized until the danger is contained or over. But if the coupling is tight, none of these safeguards is available. Unfortunately, risky systems tend to be tightly coupled as well as complexly interactive. Thus recovery from initial failures, while possible, is difficult in tightly coupled systems. Even if universities were radioactive or explosive, we would not have to worry about them because, while errors are endless and frequently interact, there is a great deal of slack and other forms of loose coupling in universities to prevent the rapid propagation of errors.

Tight coupling is sometimes desirable or even inescapable in systems; we should not make the concept into a replay of the mechanistic-organic distinction. Tightly coupled systems save on energy and materials costs because there is little waste and the most efficient energy source, supplies, and materials are used; their design is simple in that they work in only one way; buffers and redundancies are economical because they are built into the system. Tight coupling promotes rapid decision making, centralized decisions with unreflective responses, strict schedules, rapid changes in product streams where appropriate (as in pharmaceutical and other continuous-processing plants), and immediate response to deviation. Operating efficiency is high. To decouple a continuous-processing plant significantly would raise production costs and could, as in the case of a chemical plant, make it more dangerous, as toxic or explosive materials would be handled several times.

The two dimensions of complexity and coupling are independent of one another; dams are linear, rather than complex, but also tightly coupled, whereas most industrial production is linear but loosely coupled. Both universities and space missions have interactive complexity, but only space missions are tightly coupled. Figure 1 lays out the world according to complexity and coupling. Note that most, though not all, systems with catastrophic potential (dams are an exception) are both complex and tightly coupled.

This is the basis of a serious organizational dilemma: tight coupling requires centralization, but interactive complexity requires decentralization, and it is difficult, perhaps impossible, to have both simultaneously. Figure 2 summarizes the

Figure 1   Interaction/Coupling Chart

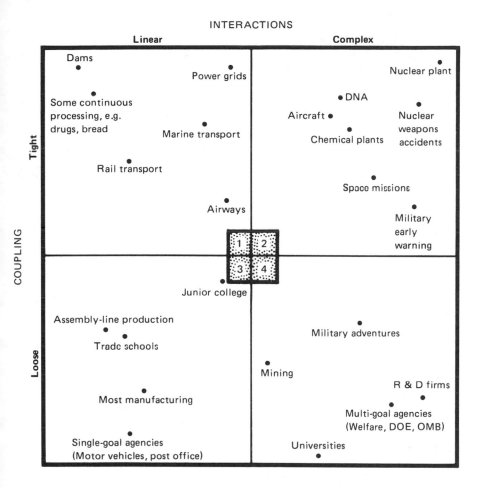

dilemma. In Cell 1, where dams, power grids, and some continuous-processing industries reside, organization needs to be centralized because of the tightly coupled nature of processing, and it can afford to be centralized because in linear systems interactions are expected and visible. But in Cell 4, decentralization is required because of the complex interactions; those persons close to the failures and perturbations of the system need the authority to respond on the basis of their hands-on experience, their ability to penetrate the unexpected interactions of failures if they occur. Fortunately, because such an organization is loosely coupled—and there is thus time to react, a chance to make substitutions, delay activities, and so on—decentralized authority can exist. Cells 1 and 4 therefore require and can afford the authority structures they generally have. No incompatible demands are made on the system.

In Cell 3, where most organizations reside, no constraints dictate either centralization or decentralization. Linearity is compatible with centralization but does not

Figure 2   Centralization/Decentralization of Authority Relevant to Crises

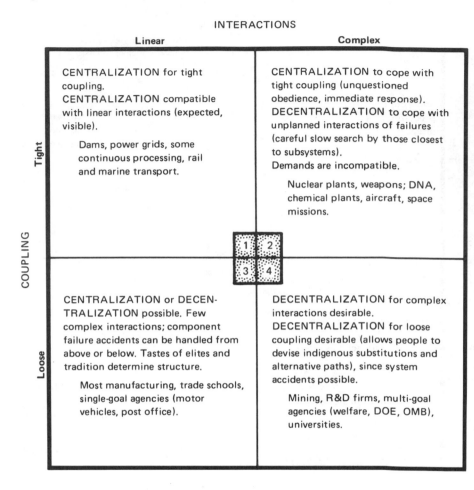

INTERACTIONS

	Linear	Complex
Tight	CENTRALIZATION for tight coupling. CENTRALIZATION compatible with linear interactions (expected, visible). Dams, power grids, some continuous processing, rail and marine transport.	CENTRALIZATION to cope with tight coupling (unquestioned obedience, immediate response). DECENTRALIZATION to cope with unplanned interactions of failures (careful slow search by those closest to subsystems). Demands are incompatible. Nuclear plants, weapons; DNA, chemical plants, aircraft, space missions.
Loose	CENTRALIZATION or DECENTRALIZATION possible. Few complex interactions; component failure accidents can be handled from above or below. Tastes of elites and tradition determine structure. Most manufacturing, trade schools, single-goal agencies (motor vehicles, post office).	DECENTRALIZATION for complex interactions desirable. DECENTRALIZATION for loose coupling desirable (allows people to devise indigenous substitutions and alternative paths), since system accidents possible. Mining, R&D firms, multi-goal agencies (welfare, DOE, OMB), universities.

(COUPLING — Cells: 1, 2, 3, 4)

require it, since failures can be handled from above or below. Loose coupling is compatible with decentralization, but it is not required in this cell because few interactions are unexpected. Unfortunately, most of these organizations opt for centralized structures rather than decentralized ones, on the basis of tradition, the tastes of elites, or (the Marxists say) to instill the proper class values of autonomy for elites and obedience for workers.

Cell 2 presents an unfortunate dilemma. Because of their complexity, organizations in this cell should be decentralized to handle the unexpected interaction of errors. But because of their tight coupling, they should be centralized to ensure immediate response to failures by those who are in a position to understand the problem and choose the correct solution. The dilemma is real; it is difficult to both centralize and decentralize at the same time, and we do not have the wit to design structures that would allow, in an emergency, both local autonomy and centralized control. Since the threat of emergencies is nearly continuous in these systems, centralized emergency-handling structures of authority dominate all others. It is very difficult to balance the on-line experience of the operator devising one plan in an emergency with the system-wide comprehension based on many streams of information; the former is only available to the operator, the latter only to central management. Continual rotation of personnel from bottom to top would spread the skills and the accumulated experience, but such a policy would entail very expensive labor costs and still not guarantee that the operator and central management would agree on the diagnosis and remedy—and an agreement must come within minutes or even seconds. During routine functioning the highly trained personnel would have the problem of staying alert, already a problem with airline pilots on long flights, and one might well wonder if it made sense to have highly educated and intensively trained engineers performing routine maintenance and inspection. (It happens in space missions, but these are short.) Yet they would have to; routine contact with the system is the only way to secure the subtle and indirect sources of information about potential problems. (In France and Japan, nuclear power plant operators are more highly educated and skilled than in U.S. plants, mitigating the problem somewhat. U.S. plants are run by private enterprise, and they make larger profits by using high-school graduates with little experience as operators.)

An organizational or systems viewpoint reveals other things about risk in systems. As I noted, when failures occur, the operators are the first and generally the only ones to be blamed; 60–80 percent of all accidents are officially attributed to operators. Close examination, however, suggests that the figure might be closer to only 30–40 percent, if that. In retrospect, operators might have saved the day if they had zigged instead of zagged, but at the time operators are often faced with contradictory information, unprecedented and mysterious interactions, and the need to follow rigid procedures that are written by the experts and that may be inappropriate in a particular instance. (At Three Mile Island, four trivial failures, three of which had happened several times before without damage, interacted mysteriously. The operators could not know of any of the four hidden failures, so they used procedures designed for a different accident. They were nearly universally blamed for the accident.)

Examination of the design of systems, from a structural point of view, suggests that in general equipment and technology are chosen to require and reinforce centralized authority structures, even where decentralized ones would be more appropriate. Systems are designed to favor elegance rather than ease of maintenance; new, advanced designs and equipment rather than proven ones; compactness rather than ease of access to information and controls; standardized gauges and controls rather than legible and distinctive ones that discriminate among subsystems; centralized information and control rather than many access points to receive discrete information or to activate discrete controls. Training emphasizes subsystem mastery, rather than overall system understanding. As a consequence, we have isolated work stations and specialized tasks, information is not shared, confidence and trust is not built up, and a maintenance worker cannot act like an operator in emergencies. The relationship between operators and equipment is that the operators simply monitor machines, leading to inattentiveness, degradation of skills needed in crises, and overconfidence in hardware. Instead, computers should monitor human performance, allowing operators to do more and keep their attention, skills, and system comprehension alert. But engineers unwittingly make design choices that fit with an idea of centralized structures; top management sends no signals that equipment design should favor a decentralization of power to those who interact with the machines. Human beings are extremely flexible and creative; but most technologies are designed to wither, rather than enhance, these characteristics.[64]

We can move beyond the essentially internal focus of the neo-Weberian model and include the environment to give further insight into the problem of safe systems and the fruitfulness of a structural viewpoint. If we take an industry, rather than particular organizations, as the unit of analysis, we can see the impact of the industry and its ties to society upon the organization and its problems. (Chapter 6 discusses this in more detail.) Some risky systems have evolved to become rather firmly error avoiding; others have evolved just as firmly to remain error inducing. Any organization in an error-avoiding system will differ from one in an error-inducing system, but organizational differences are the consequences, not the causes, of system configurations. Let me illustrate by comparing the error-inducing marine transport system with the error-avoiding airline system.

In the marine transport system a ship a day is lost worldwide. Collisions are a major form of accident, but in most collisions the ships would have passed in the night, or whatever, if one or both had not changed their course in order to bring about the collision (called "noncollision course collisions"). In almost all cases the ships are in visual or radar contact; radar induces collisions because it allows ships to go faster in worse weather or crowded channels, and captains are fined for being late. Sophisticated equipment that approximates that used to great effect in air transport is not required, inoperative, or simply not used. Few international regulations of any consequence exist or are enforced, despite centuries of problems. The U.S. merchant fleet has the oldest ships of any nation, many rusty bottoms more than forty years old, some carrying toxic cargoes, while the recommended ship life is twenty years.

This system has evolved in a context where:

1. Insurers have little incentive to inspect the ships they insure, and shipping firms have little incentive to provide safe vessels and trained crews.
2. Shippers and insurers have a common interest in defining all casualties as the result of operator error, limiting the ability of customers to recover damages under law, but thereby enabling unsafe ships with overworked crews to sail and retarding the development of safety devices and practices.
3. National interests prevent the growth of safety requirements and encourage unsafe practices and equipment for short-term economic gains.
4. In the United States, the weak status and conflicting mandates of the Coast Guard —which provides maritime services, polices, and is trained for combat, all at the same time—makes it vulnerable to the pressure of shippers and insurers.
5. The weak status of the mariners requires them to bear their costs with little opposition.

[64]Perrow, "The Organizational Context," pp. 528, 534–535.

6. Victims of toxic and explosive cargoes are dispersed, unorganized, and almost randomly affected.
7. The organizational structure aboard ship is highly authoritarian.

In contrast, the airline system pays extraordinary attention to safety. Landing, departure, and in-air routines were sufficiently developed within nations so that international cooperation was relatively easy. Accidents are thoroughly investigated because there are several interested parties, and they are well organized (including the high-status pilots' union). The causes of accidents are more easily determined. (Both these conditions result in lower estimates of operator error as the cause of accidents than in the marine environment.) The cargo—humans—is more valuable, and their representatives are organized and have strong interests in safety and causal determinations. Poor operating conditions (e.g., storms, overcrowded facilities) can be avoided with little economic cost. The use of the system is sufficiently elective that lack of safety is penalized (passengers avoiding travel after accidents). Accidents are highly publicized. Crew relations are more cooperative (pilot and co-pilot, rather than captain and first mate, for example), and working conditions are much better.

In principle, the marine system could almost be as safe as the air transport system; indeed, they could share many of the technological advantages that now exist and could have similar organizational structures. The marine system is tending slightly in this direction, but many aspects of the social and economic structure of the industry make any change difficult. No one, I am sure, wants an unsafe system where a ship a day is lost and where the threat of pollution and outright physical destruction is mounting. But except for the fragmented and unorganized customers, everyone involved except the unions—ship designers, shipyards, captains and crews, shipping firms, insurers, marine courts, the U.S. Coast Guard and perhaps similar units in other countries, legislators, and national executives—stands to benefit in a small way from the system as it has developed, and stands to lose more, in the short run, from a reorganization. Even our culture, if I may use that vague concept, resists reforms, as it celebrates the notion of the authoritarian "captain" and his derring-do. Error-inducing and error-avoiding systems, then, are the product of the somewhat fortuitous combination of system elements over time and piecemeal adaptation to problems. An attempt to make the airline system error inducing would be extremely difficult; too many parts of the system would resist. Trying to make the marine transport system error avoiding has proven to be extremely difficult for the same reason: too many parts of the system resist, the accommodations to errors are very stable, and each part of the system sustains the others.[65]

Finally, a systems analysis discloses that the infrastructure of risk analysis and risk assessment that guides the selection and design of risky systems—an infrastructure housed in universities, government agencies, and industry trade groups—reflects its elite origins and values. Experts, largely economists and engineers, help to guide the selection and design of risky systems. We are only beginning to understand their legitimization role. They declare that the public is grossly uninformed and irrational in its fear of risky technologies; the gap between the experts and the public on these policy issues is to be closed by educating the public to agree with the

[65]Perrow, *Normal Accidents*, chapters 5–6.

experts. But the experts have a far narrower view of risk and benefit than the public does, relying on body counts rather than the more social and cultural criteria that the public uses. Poll data indicate the public takes into account such questions as: Do those who bear no risk receive the benefits, while those at risk do not? Is there a catastrophic potential—that is, even if no significant radiation has leaked from a nuclear plant accident, what would happen in a particularly bad accident? Or even though the safety devices have so far worked in the dozens of cases where nuclear weapons were accidentally dropped from aircraft, crushed, or burned, what would happen if the safety devices mysteriously didn't work? Is the technology new and poorly understood? Are the victims related (i.e., killing 50,000 a year on the highways is not as bad as wiping out a whole community of 50,000, because a whole culture is lost in the latter case)? Will future generations be affected?

Careful polling has revealed that these social and cultural aspects of risk enter into the average citizen's evaluation but not those of the experts in the universities, industries, and government regulatory bodies. An organizational analysis of the setting, professional training, and organizational ties of these experts makes their narrow approach understandable. The infrastructure of risky enterprises, which supports, regulates, and legitimizes these enterprises, explains much about the design of the systems and such matters as the attribution of operator error. The policy dilemmas are fairly intractable; we are not about to give up air travel, chemical plants, nuclear weapons, or perhaps even nuclear power plants. I think we should abandon the latter two; they are not essential and incur extensive social costs beyond their catastrophic potential. We can much more carefully regulate genetic engineering and the transport of toxic and explosive cargoes; both are virtually unregulated now. And we can require changes in designs, location, and the scale of the rest, particularly chemical plants, where a disaster of the magnitude of the one at the Union Carbide plant in Bhopal, India, in December 1984 has a quite significant chance of happening in West Virginia and other parts of the developed world. Some aspects of air travel, chemical plants, and even marine shipping will forever remain particularly risky because of interactive complexity and tight coupling, but many aspects can be made more linear and loosely coupled—though at a price that governments and industry will be reluctant to bear.[66]

The problem of safe systems has generally been defined as an engineering one, with some attention by regulatory bodies. I have tried to show that this is a quite incomplete, and often a simply wrong, approach. Using notions from the neo-Weberian model of organizations, such as bounded rationality, system interactions, garbage can processes, degree of coupling of units and processes, the dilemmas of centralization and decentralization, the power of units and the attributions of error and design of equipment that follow, and the support system of experts in the larger society, we can come to a quite different analysis of the problem of safety and design. Organizational analysis will realize its promise, I believe, if it can be shown to illuminate such important public policy questions.[67]

[66]Ibid., Chapter 9.

[67]A striking example of illuminating public policy in the area of accidents is Joseph Gusfield, *The Culture of Public Problems: Drinking-Driving and the Symbolic Order* (Chicago: University of Chicago Press, 1981).

SUMMARY

This chapter has sought to bring the bureaucratic model up-to-date. It does not contradict the description we gave in the first chapter, but it has sought to lay out more systematically some of the aspects of bureaucracy that Weber neglected or assumed. The contribution of the structural half of March and Simon's *Organizations* and parts of Simon's *Administrative Behavior* has not been to understand the organization as a problem in social psychology but as a problem in unobtrusive control through recognizing the importance of shaping the premises of decisions. The Weberian model, with its simple reliance on a few formal properties, gains in both strength and complexity thereby. The contribution of Cyert and March, in their *Behavioral Theory of the Firm*, initially presented in March's article on the organization as a political coalition,[68] was to accommodate the reality of group conflict to the neo-Weberian model. It complicates things further. Although it does not deny the reality of control from the top, it does recognize the difficulty of that control more than Weber was wont to do. The combination of bounded rationality and group interests produces the garbage can theory of organization. We have given it a sympathetic reading; it makes a great deal of sense for both the practicing executive and the theorist. Although it needs specification and development, its application to organizational networks appears to be particularly valuable.

The technological school has argued for the reality and the efficiency of the bureaucratic model by distinguishing it from other models. Organizational structure varies with the type of work done. A fundamental fact about organizations is that they do work; they transform raw materials into acceptable outputs. The characteristics of this work process will tell us more about the structure and function of the organization than the psychological characteristics of the members, their wants, motives, and drives. And it will tell us more than we can learn from the type of output produced (ashtrays, education, rehabilitation of delinquents). It will predict structure. Not completely, and certainly not always. Goals can influence structure, which can then influence the type of technology that will be adapted. An executive may choose to organize nonroutine work as if it were routine, or routine work as if it were nonroutine. In people-changing organizations, he or she may define the way the raw material is to be perceived, and thus select the technology.[69] But in the long run and over a sample of a large number of organizations, these and other sources of variability should wash out. By and large, it is assumed the technology must fit the structure, or the organization will pay a heavy price in terms of efficiency.

Finally, we took a specific problem, system failures, and examined the cognitive, structural, power, and organizational environment aspects with our neo-Weberian model. The focus was on system interactions and control, whether at the level of the operator or elites deciding what kind of risks the rest of us should run. I don't think this analysis could have been done without the theories presented in this chapter, but I would note that at bottom it builds on the Weberian core of bureaucracy.

But in all this, while we have extended and complicated the simple bureaucratic

[68]James G. March, "The Business Firm as a Political Coalition," *Journal of Politics* 24 (1962): 662–678.
[69]Child, "Strategic Choice."

model, we still have not addressed ourselves to the dominant preoccupation of organizational theory in the late 1960s—the environment. With a few exceptions, we have treated the environment as "given" and unproblematical. Furthermore, we have still not given adequate consideration to the possibility that organizations may not be the products of technology and a structure adapted to it, ruled over by a few people who use them as tools. They may be things that take on a life of their own —organic entities or "natural systems" in their own right, going their own way and generating leaders who will follow that way. Here we confront a still more serious challenge to the tool view and the bureaucratic model, with which even a neo-Weberian version cannot easily cope. We turn to it in the next chapter.

5

The Institutional School

ELEMENTS OF THE MODEL

Of all the schools of thought considered in this book, the institutional school is the closest to a truly sociological view of organizations. It combines much of the best, and some of the worst, of sociology as it existed in the 1950s and the 1960s. Its major conceptual framework is that of structural-functionalism, indicating that functions determine the structure of organizations and that structures can be understood by analyzing their functions. A great deal has been written about the structural func tional school,[1] the dominant one in sociology. We will highlight only a few points as they apply to organizational theory. (Though not exclusively derived from the writings of Philip Selznick, the school is best represented by his works; his essay *Leadership in Administration* will be referred to without specific page citations in this section.[2])

Natural and Organic Systems

For institutional analysis, the injunction is to analyze the whole organization. To see it as a whole is to do justice to its "organic" character. Specific processes are, of

[1]N. J. Demerath, III, and Richard A. Peterson, eds., *Systems Change and Conflict* (New York: Free Press, 1967).

[2]Selznick's first two articles present the major preoccupations that the later books revolve about. See "An Approach to a Theory of Bureaucracy," *American Sociological Review* 8 (1943): 47–54; and "Foundations of a Theory of Organizations," *American Sociological Review* 13 (1948): 25–35. This was followed by an impressive case study, *TVA and the Grass Roots* (Berkeley and Los Angeles: University of California Press, 1949; New York: Harper & Row, 1965), that still remains a classic in that tradition. (The newer edition has a valuable preface.) Subsequently, he analyzed the Communist party under the apt title *The Organizational Weapon: A Study of Bolshevik Strategy and Tactics* (New York: McGraw-Hill, 1952). Though the political stance of Chapter 7 of this book is dated today, this volume has not received the recognition it deserves. Organizations are, or can be, weapons. This was followed by a short work, *Leadership in Administration* (New York: Harper & Row, 1957). This rewarding work was written for executives as much as anyone, but it provides a highly literate statement of his major themes and good summaries of his earlier books. A more recent volume, continuing his line of analysis but turning toward the role of law in society, is *Law, Society and Industrial Justice* (New York: Russell Sage Foundation, 1970).

course, analyzed in detail, but it is the nesting of these processes into the whole that gives them meaning. To wrench a process such as leadership or communication free of a specific organization without considering how it is organically linked to the rest of the organization is to drain it of meaning.

The emphasis on whole implies considerable uniqueness about organizations, limiting our ability to focus only on specific processes or to survey a large number of organizations searching, for, say, evidence regarding propositions on hierarchy or control. The implied injunction, then, is to do case studies. This is the forte of the institutional school—the carefully documented and analyzed case study. Comparative analysis is generally restricted to comparisons of case studies.

Because the interchange of structure and function goes on over time, a "natural history" of an organization is needed. We cannot understand current crises or competencies without seeing how they were shaped. The present is rooted in the past; no organization (and no person) is free to act as if the situation were *de novo* and the world a set of discrete opportunities ready to be seized at will. All kinds of structural restraints embedded in the past limit freedom. A "natural history" implies natural forces: organizations as living entities grow in natural ways. The discovery of these forces, as in biology or psychoanalysis, will yield understanding.

Thus, the evolving accommodations and dependencies of an adult-education program to the demands of its clients eventually deny it freedom to control standards.[3] The lack of standards leads to trivial courses on flower arranging and fly tying. They become the mode of survival, not because anyone planned them, but because of the "drift" of the organization responding to enrollment pressures.

The idea of an organic, growing, declining, evolving whole, with a natural history, points up the importance (and danger) of unplanned adaptations and changes. Unplanned aspects of organizations are those that are subject to little administrative control and are often not even noticed until their effects are quite evident, if even then. They are revealed by analyzing how the structure responded to certain processes that were dictated by basic "needs" or functions. Natural forces work their ways quietly, and it is often not until too late that the organization discovers, for example, that its social base in the community—the groups that supply its personnel, receive its services, provide its legitimacy—is "eroded."

A church may be aware that its neighborhood is "deteriorating" and that it must acquire land for larger parking lots so that the congregation can drive from more distant neighborhoods to religious services. But the implications are only slowly grasped because normal activities continue as before. On the one hand, the church does nothing to stem the transition of its neighborhood; on the other hand, it fails to adapt to the new social base by changing its religious services, its pastoral counseling, and its source of funds.

The rise of administrative tasks and coordination of complex specialties leads the hospital to search for a new director among those with training in hospital administration. It does not fully anticipate that this will challenge the authority of the medical staff and perhaps reshape the hospital's goals and "character"—for

---

[3]Burton Clark, *Adult Education in Transition* (Berkeley: University of California Press, 1956).

example, the types of patients it will receive, sources of funds, involvement with other health programs, building programs, and medical specialties.[4]

As corporations grow ever larger and seek security and profits through mergers and expansion, the financial problems become more visible. The route to the top changes: it is less through sales and more often through finance—reached by someone who can master the complexities of funding, mergers, and capital improvements. But then the corporation is likely to lose its ability to search out new markets and make rapid internal adjustments to new technology and markets; it is also less likely to allow waste and inefficiency in the transition periods so as to ensure adaptability. Instead, cost accounting, rationalization, predictability, and the careful husbanding of resources take over. All this was not planned; it was a consequence of changing the line of succession.

The hospital allows rates to rise so that it can finance expensive treatments for a few exotic cases and care for improverished patients and for long-term illnesses. But proprietary hospitals (those that operate for a profit and are usually owned by a group of physicians or a franchising chain) spring up and take the profitable cases, charging less. The profit-making nursing homes skim off the long-term cases that need little care. The voluntary hospital is left with the complex, expensive cases that need expensive stand-by facilities, the charity cases, and the long-term patients who require costly care. The voluntary hospitals did not plan it that way; they were using the routine cases to subsidize the others, and after a time their situation became impossible.[5] These examples reveal the unplanned nature of organizational life and the importance of its natural history.

The Exposé Tradition

The institutional school is of the "exposé" variety. In keeping with a general sociological tradition, it shows that "things are not as they seem." The sociologist, according to this view, looks beneath the obvious surface that preoccupies the other social sciences. He or she looks at the nonpolitical aspects of political behavior, the noneconomic aspects of economic behavior, and so on. The explanation for political behavior is not in the formalities of constitutions and elections, but in the submerged part of the iceberg—ethnic identity, social class, generational experiences, and population changes. The explanation for organizational behavior is not primarily in the formal structure of the organization, the announcements of goals and purposes, the output of goods and services. It lies largely in the myriad subterranean processes of informal groups, conflicts between groups, recruitment policies, dependencies on outside groups and constituencies, the striving for prestige, community values, the local community power structure, and legal institutions.

In the process of uncovering these realities of social systems, an institutional analysis exposes to scrutiny all sorts of deviations from the "obvious." Dalton belongs

---

[4]Charles Perrow, "Goals and Power Structures," in *The Hospital in Modern Society*, ed. Eliot Freidson (New York: Free Press, 1963), pp. 112–146.

[5]For two discussions of these kinds of problems, see Arthur Owens, "Can the Profit Motive Save Our Hospitals?" *Medical Economics* (March 30, 1970): 77–111; and "Power to the Coalitions," *Modern Hospital* (April 1970): 39–40d.

here, with his contrast of the formal and informal chart, as does Gouldner with his description of the interdependencies of the gypsum plant and the local community with its insular values (see Chapter 1). But even more representative than this is the exposure of policy matters. The organization is tangled in a web of relationships that prevent it from fulfilling its real goals, and we can see how it deviates by examining this web. The institutional school is preoccupied with values, and especially the way values are weakened or subverted through organizational processes. Let us look at some examples from the literature.

The Tennessee Valley Authority (TVA), the first (and only) extensive flirtation in recent times with a socialist program in the United States, was established in the late 1930s to produce power, manufacture fertilizer, control flooding, increase the utility of waterways (by building ports and widening channels), and build dams. Aside from these commercial activities, it was also meant to preserve forests and carry out reforestation, help farmers (especially poor ones), and develop recreation areas. Philip Selznick's study of the TVA[6] found that its doctrine of grass-roots involvement and control in the recreation, forestation, and farming programs led to powerful local and national interests achieving control of the agency and subverting these goals. The U.S. Department of Agriculture, the Farm Bureau Federation, the local land-grant colleges and universities, the agricultural extension workers and county agents, and the local political and business leaders "co-opted" the program.[7] They took it over by placing their representatives within the relevant branches of the TVA so as to control policy. As a consequence, all the programs suffered. The poor farmers did not get aid or services, but the better-off ones did; some recreation areas were given over to private business, which destroyed their natural beauty; forests could not be saved from the lumber industry; and so on. By paying this price at the local level, the TVA was able, presumably, to forestall more intense attacks and opposition to the economic program (flood control, power, fertilizer, etc.) at the national level. The organization adjusted to its environment and was changed in the process. Selznick implies that such an accommodation was the only feasible one; it helped save the major programs.

In Sheldon Messinger's analysis of an old-age pressure group formed in the 1930s, the Townsend organization, he shows how the organization managed to stay alive by transforming its political goal of increased support for the aged through a radical economic plan into social goals of fellowship and card playing and fiscal goals of selling vitamins and patent medicines to its members.[8] The unanticipated consequence of fund-raising techniques based on selling items, rather than political programs, was to turn the organization into a social club. The changing social and political scene also, of course, produced a change in goals. In a somewhat similar vein, Joseph Gusfield shows how the Women's Christian Temperance Union (WCTU) had to abandon its attack on drinking per se after prohibition was repealed

[6]Selznick, *TVA and the Grass Roots.*

[7]On the ambiguity of the concept of co-optation, see James L. Price, "Continuity in Social Research: TVA and the Grass Roots," *Pacific Sociological Review* 1, no. 2 (Fall 1958): 63–68.

[8]Sheldon L. Messinger, "Organizational Transformation: A Case Study of Declining Social Movement," *American Sociological Review* 20 (1955): 3–10.

and change to an attack on middle-class mores and life-styles in general, in order to serve the needs of its members.[9] Mayer Zald outlines how the Young Men's Christian Association (YMCA) changed from helping poor migrants from the farm or from abroad, who found the city a fearsome experience, to providing recreation for middle-class suburban youths.[10] The Christian ethics of the early period, designed to sustain the faith of helpless people, gave way to a bland ethic of the American way of life; the practical help and training changed from information and techniques for survival in the urban jungle to physical culture and recreation for youths and adults with leisure time on their hands. In both cases, the organization survived the environmental changes and found a new mission.

Burton Clark's study of a junior college in San Jose, California, shows that because of the low ability of the students, the college in question was actually designed to provide a repeat of the eleventh and twelfth grades of high school and some vocational training.[11] But the students saw success in terms of academic programs that would allow them to transfer, after two years, to a regular four-year college. Neither teachers (who were drawn largely from high schools and local businesses and industry) nor students were equipped to deal with academic programs, so devices were developed to "cool out the mark"—underworld jargon for techniques to convince the victim of a con game that he or she has not been conned, or at least had better not report it. Extensive regulations and counseling devices had to be provided to convince the students that they should take remedial English and sheet metal work. Clark also shows how the remedial and vocational nature of the college was guaranteed by the web of organizations in the community that set up and controlled it.

The Community Chest of Indianapolis, ostensibly rationalizing fundraising activities by minimizing the inconvenience of multiple fund drives and increasing their efficiency, is analyzed as an occupying army by John Seeley and his colleagues.[12] According to this view, it dictated agency goals on the basis of fundraising ability; established fundraising devices that resulted in the working class making heavy contributions to support essentially middle-class agencies (the Y's, Scouts); and used the agency as a testing and training ground for middle-level executives in business.

Charles Perrow shows how the research efforts of a private, voluntary hospital were subverted by the demands of the board of directors and other donors for publicity about the research.[13] As the director of the hospital indicated, the donors gave the money for fancy, elaborate electronic gadgetry in order to see the hospital

---

[9]Joseph R. Gusfield, "Social Structure and Moral Reform: A Study of the Women's Christian Temperance Union," *American Journal of Sociology* 61 (1955): 221–232.

[10]Mayer N. Zald and Robert Ash, "Social Movement Organizations: Growth, Decay and Change," *Social Forces* 44, no. 3 (March 1966): 327–341; Mayer N. Zald and Patricia Denton, "From Evangelism to General Service: The Transformation of the YMCA," *Administrative Science Quarterly* 8, no. 2 (September 1963): 214–234.

[11]Burton R. Clark, *The Open Door College: A Case Study* (New York: McGraw-Hill, 1960).

[12]John R. Seeley, Bulford H. Junker, and R. Wallace Jones, Jr., *Community Chest* (Toronto: University of Toronto Press, 1957).

[13]Charles Perrow, "Organizational Prestige: Some Functions and Dysfunctions," *American Journal of Sociology* 66, no. 4 (January 1961):335–341.

well publicized in national magazines. The researchers, however, resisted such publicity because it was not accurate, would alienate the federal agencies that were providing the bulk of the enormous sums of research money, and would swamp the unit, designed only to do research, with requests for treatment. In another example, the writer shows how the outpatient department of the hospital existed largely as a device for giving evidence of the extensive charity activities of the hospital while it actually suffered from administrative neglect, inadequate staffing, poor quarters and facilities, and a highly selective intake system.[14]

Robert Scott analyzes agencies that seek to rehabilitate the blind.[15] According to Scott, while the vast majority of the blind are aged or are severely handicapped in other ways, the agencies pay little attention to these. Instead, they prefer the "desirable" blind—young people who have some employment prospects—because it is easier to raise money for them. They touch the softhearted and promise economic returns for the hardhearted. However, there are not enough desirable blind to go around, so agencies have to compete with one another to get clients. They then attempt to keep the blind dependent on the agency rather than make them independent, self-supporting members of society—the professed goal.

David Sudnow, in looking at the court procedures in a large metropolitan area on the West Coast, finds that hearing and sentencing procedures for persons accused of crimes resemble a mass-production line.[16] The prosecutor and the defense lawyer (court-appointed) routinely classified defendants on the basis of superficial evidence, convinced the defendants that they should plead guilty to charges less severe than the ones they had been arrested for, and had an understanding with the judge for the routine and expeditious processing of these pleas. Each defendant was passed from defense attorney to defense attorney as he traveled from station to station in the procedure; the truth of the charge was not examined or even considered very relevant. If a defendant objected and wanted to plead not guilty, he was shunted off to a special track where a special group of prosecutors took over the case with vengeance. In this way, the interests of efficiency and routinization were served, though the connection with "justice" was remote. Similar analyses have been made of prisons, reform schools, and, of course, custodial mental hospitals.[17]

In Gary Wamsley's study of the Selective Service System in the mid-1960s, particular attention is paid to the doctrine of decentralization—the grass-roots

[14]Perrow, "Goals and Power Structures."

[15]Robert A. Scott, "The Selection of Clients by Social Welfare Agencies: The Case of the Blind," *Social Problems* 14, no. 3 (Winter 1967): 248–257.

[16]David Sudnow, "Normal Crimes," *Social Problems* 12, no. 3 (Winter 1964): 255–275.

[17]For prisons, see Donald R. Cressey, "Achievement of an Unstated Organizational Goal: An Observation on Prisons," *Pacific Sociological Review* 1 (1958): 43–49; and Gresham M. Sykes, *The Society of Captives: A Study of a Maximum Security Prison* (Princeton, N.J.: Princeton University Press, 1971). For reform schools, see Mayer N. Zald, "The Correctional Institution for Juvenile Offenders: An Analysis of Organizational 'Character'," *Social Problems* 8, no. 1 (Summer 1960): 57–67; and David Street, Robert Vinter, and Charles Perrow, *Organizations for Treatment* (New York: Free Press, 1966). For mental hospitals, see the review of the literature in Charles Perrow, "Hospitals: Technology, Goals, and Structure," in *Handbook of Organizations*, chapter 22, ed. James March (Chicago: Rand McNally, 1965), pp. 910–971. For a basic work, and one of the most perceptive, on the "underlife" of institutions, see Erving Goffman, *Asylums* (New York: Doubleday, 1961).

involvement of little groups of neighbors.[18] This gave enormous legitimacy to an enterprise that had been contested by riots and violence throughout our nation's history. It also buried the decision-making process and its rules in the homely ambience of volunteer citizens doing their best at what was, inevitably, a distasteful job. In reality, Wamsley shows, the system was highly centralized in its basic tenets, giving only trivial leeway (and considerable anxiety and bewilderment in the process) to the local boards. These boards were highly homogeneous—they consisted mainly of older veterans of past wars who glorified their experience, were active Legionnaires, and were overwhelmingly middle class—while the draftees were lower class. Those lower-class individuals who appealed their cases to the board were lectured on the virtues of military life and often went away feeling, as did the board, that military life was best for them after all; middle-class youths found more routine methods of escape.

Philippe Nonet's detailed historical study of the activities of the California Industrial Accident Commission during the first half of this century illustrates the fate of idealism (representing the interests of workers who have been injured on the job) when it has to contend with powerful organizations—the insurance carriers and the employers on the one hand, and the large unions on the other hand.[19] Between the two of them, the unorganized worker became unprotected, and the commission's policy of industrial justice and welfare gave way to narrow legalism and professional self-protection.

These examples suggest some of the "exposé" character of this body of literature. The major message is that the organization has sold out its goals in order to survive or grow. The values that should have been institutionalized have been undermined by organizational processes. The grandfather of this approach was Robert Michels, who formulated the "iron law of oligarchy," which suggested that a few leaders will inevitably dominate even supposedly democratic political organizations and will put their interest in preserving the organization and their leadership of it ahead of the interests of the members.[20]

But exposé of this sort is not a necessary aspect of the institutional school; there is also guarded optimism about the beneficent effects of natural processes. Morris Janowitz, for example, shows how the military in the late 1950s came increasingly under civilian control; increasingly (though not greatly) concerned with economic and political strategies rather than hydrogen wars; increasingly sophisticated and committed to democratic policies and civilian control.[21] The social base from which it recruited officers had been the Southern middle class. Recruitment into the officer corps was now geographically more widespread (thus minimizing the tradition of violence that characterized the South), and more and more officers had technical training in places other than military academies. The routes to the top were now through innovative and novel assignments and activities (foreign advisory posts,

[18]Gary L. Wamsley, *Selective Service and a Changing America* (Columbus, Ohio: Charles E. Merrill, 1969); James W. Davis, Jr., and Kenneth M. Dolbeare, *Little Groups of Neighbors: The Selective Service System* (Chicago: Markham, 1968).

[19]Philippe Nonet, *Administrative Justice. Advocacy and Change in Government Agencies* (New York: Russell Sage Foundation, 1969).

[20]Robert Michels, *Political Parties* (New York: Free Press, 1966), originally published in 1915.

[21]Morris Janowitz, *The Professional Soldier* (New York: Free Press, 1960).

weapons analysis) rather than heroic postures in wartime. Sophisticated political liaison officials were counseling restraint. The complexity of the weapons systems gave power to what might be called, after John Kenneth Galbraith,[22] a military "technostructure" rather than to right-wing generals. Thus, without deliberate planning or even conscious awareness, broad social forces were changing the character of the military establishment. That all these changes need not mean more civilian control or less emphasis on atomic destruction is clear in retrospect. The military built a bridge with powerful industrial and economic interests, intensified the political role of the military abroad, made its domestic surveillance machinery and domestic intervention more effective, deepened its ties with the more conservative elements of Congress, and, with the CIA, exercised considerable power over President Kennedy with regard to the Bay of Pigs invasion and over presidents Kennedy, Johnson, and Nixon with regard to Vietnam and Southeast Asia.[23]

Yet the military are not necessarily more hawkish than civilians. For example, in the 1950s the president of Cornell University advised President Eisenhower that a public relations campaign was needed to persuade people to accept the dangers of nuclear testing and nuclear weapons, and it appears that the Pentagon was more hesitant than President Reagan about having a show of military might in Lebanon (U.S. forces were soon removed, after heavy casualties) and about intervention in Central America. The 1984 invasion of Grenada, judging from the fascinating analysis by sociologist Wendell Bell, was a symbolic political act that had little to do with military realities.[24]

CONTRIBUTIONS

The emphasis on actual organizations with histories and functions in society, and existing in a variety of sectors that we all know of, makes the institutional school's output the most fascinating of any in organizational analysis. After the arid and dense forest of two-variable propositions in the first part of March and Simon,[25] the inventories of hypotheses about leadership,[26] and the axiomatic edifice of Jerald Hage,[27] it is a pleasure to read about a real organization confronting real problems

---

[22]John Kenneth Galbraith, *The New Industrial State*, 2nd ed. (Boston: Houghton Mifflin, 1971).

[23]Several books document these changes. See, for example, Richard Barnet, *The Economy of Death* (New York: Atheneum House, 1969); Seymour Melman, *Pentagon Capitalism: The Political Economy of War* (New York: McGraw-Hill, 1970); and Gabriel Kolko, *The Roots of American Foreign Policy* (Boston: Beacon Press, 1970).

[24]On civilian hawkishness and its contribution to the enormous risk of an accidental nuclear war, see Charles Perrow and David Pearson, "Complexity, Coupling and Nuclear Weapons," Paper presented at Yale University, 1984. On Grenada, see Wendell Bell, "The Use of False Prophecy to Justify Present Action: The Case of the American Invasion of Grenada," Paper presented at Yale University, September 1984.

[25]James G. March and Herbert A. Simon, *Organizations* (New York: Wiley, 1958).

[26]Philip B. Applewhite, *Organizational Behavior* (Englewood Cliffs, N.J.: Prentice-Hall, 1965).

[27]Jerald T. Hage, "An Axiomatic Theory of Organizations," *Administrative Science Quarterly* 10, no. 3 (December 1965): 289–320. See also the comment by Allen Barton and Patricia Ferman, *Administrative Science Quarterly* 11, no. 1 (June 1966), and the reply by Jerald T. Hage in the same issue.

in real time and space. But what does this school contribute to organizational theory beyond a few concepts such as co-optation and precarious goals?

The institutional school's main contribution, I feel, lies in three areas. First, the emphasis on the organization as a whole forces on us a conception of the variety of organizations. Not a hopeless variety such that every organization is unique (which it is, of course, in the ultimate sense, even as every person is unique), but a sense that there are basic characteristics of organizations that must be taken into account, and these can lead, though they have not as yet, to a classification scheme for specific purposes. For example, some organizations are highly dependent on the good will of powerful elites, others have considerable autonomy, and still others exist in a vacuum of autonomy without power. The Community Chest and the San Jose Junior College are dependent; no analysis of leadership style, technology, or Weberian bureaucracy can neglect this. Large business and industrial organizations are largely autonomous, and for that reason leadership processes are presumably different, technology has more leeway, and bureaucratization is essential for efficiency. Prisons, mental hospitals, and many small welfare agencies[28] exist to show that *something* is being done about some problems, but few care just what it is or how effective it is; those who control the organization's resources (legislators, religious boards, etc.) care only that the "something" should not involve scandals and should not cost too much. Here again, the environment for leadership, technology, and structure will be different, and inventories, elegant formal theories,[29] and so on may miss the point. For this nascent emphasis, we can thank the institutional school; it keeps reminding us how widely organizations differ and generates broad bases to classify them. (One such base—the distinction between organizations and institutions—will be discussed shortly.)

Second, the institutional theory points to the real possibility that at least some organizations do take on a life of their own, irrespective of the desires of those presumably in control. All organizations do so to some extent, presumably, but for some this fact is dominant. The matter has not been explored empirically at all, nor has it even been the subject of much speculation (beyond Selznick's distinction between organizations and institutions). But, clearly, important consequences for theory, operationalizations, and the conception of organizations in society will stem from a scholar's disposition to treat organizations as primarily tools, or as primarily things-in-themselves. It makes a difference, for example, if the Department of Defense is seen as a tool of powerful economic elites in our society, protecting their foreign investments, financing their research and development, providing plants and machinery, absorbing surplus productivity, and protecting inefficient organizations such as Lockheed when they are in trouble, or whether it is seen as a gigantic Leviathan, consuming resources to satisfy its own appetite, setting foreign policies

[28]John Maniha and Charles Perrow, "The Reluctant Organization and the Aggressive Environment," *Administrative Science Quarterly* 10, no. 2 (September 1965): 238–257; and Charles Perrow, "Demystifying Organizations" in *The Management of Human Services* eds. Rosemary C. Sarri and Yeheskel Haasenfeld (New York: Columbia University Press, 1978).

[29]Peter Blau, "A Formal Theory of Differentiation in Organizations," *American Sociological Review* 35, no. 2 (April 1970): 201–218.

in its own commanding interest in growth and power, and pursuing a war long after the business elites had wearied of it. The first view is more or less held by Gabriel Kolko in his book *The Roots of American Foreign Policy;* the second is closer to Seymour Melman's view in his book *Pentagon Capitalism: The Political Economy of War.* [30] The fear of the Pentagon is present in both cases, of course, but if one were to try to control this colossus, which is bigger in financial terms than all but a few countries in the world, it would make considerable difference which view was held. The institutional school argues persuasively for the possibility of the latter view, seeing organizations as taking on a life of their own.

The major contribution of the institutional school must surely be the emphasis on the environment. No other model of organizations has taken the environment into account as much. Of course, Weber saw organizational forms as deeply rooted in the social structure, and as part of society, organizations could not help but be so rooted. The progressive rationalization of life, the supremacy of rational-legal authority over traditional authority, was the consequence of capitalism and its bureaucratic organizations, of the state bureaucracy, and of the bureaucratic political, educational, and voluntary associations. [31]

But the institutional school has detailed, for specific organizations and their recent history, the close interaction of organizations and their environments. Some, such as the WCTU or the Townsend organization, are fading daguerreotypes of a bygone age; others, such as the YMCA or the sects analyzed by S. D. Clark, [32] change and flourish with the times. Most are constantly adopting and improvising to keep afloat and to find goals and values that are consistent with their basic dependencies—sources of financial support, legitimacy, personnel, and technologies. No clear "theory" has emerged from this effort, just as no clear theory has emerged to distinguish types of organizations; it may be some time before we have further clarification.

But what kind of theories would emerge? What underlying assumptions would guide them? How would they help us to see how organizations shape our lives and our world, set our priorities, define our sense of what is possible and what is desirable? In this respect, I think, the area of institutional analysis reflects in part what is worst about sociology. It is still tied to the enfeebling assumptions of structural-functional theory and is unlikely to face up squarely to the fact of organizational power in an organizational society. To analyze this school in these terms, we must turn to its most important innovator and persuasive spokesperson, Philip Selznick.

[30]Gabriel Kolko, *Roots of American Foreign Policy* and Seymour Melman, *Pentagon Capitalism,* Melman's empirical evidence is far stronger than Kolko's hasty essay. Melman's position is announced at the outset: the Defense Department's "main characteristics are institutionally specific and therefore substantially independent of its chief of the moment. The effects of its operations are independent of the intention of its architects, and may even have been unforeseen by them." Pp. 1–2.

[31]Another "grand theorist," Joseph Schumpeter, dealt with many of the same themes as Weber, and his *Capitalism, Socialism and Democracy* (New York: Harper & Row, 1950) is still exciting reading today. The most brilliant essay on organizations and environment is Arthur Stinchcombe, "Social Structure and Environment," in *Handbook of Organizations,* pp. 142–193.

[32]S. D. Clark, *The Church and Sect in Canada* (Toronto: University of Toronto Press, 1948), pp. 381–429.

ORGANIZATIONS AND INSTITUTIONS

Basic to Selznick's view of organizations is the distinction between the rational, means-oriented, efficiency-guided process of administration and the value-laden, adaptive, responsive process of institutionalization.[33] Some organizations are merely organizations—rational tools in which there is little personal investment and which can be cast aside without regret. Others become institutionalized. They take on a distinctive character; they become prized in and of themselves, not merely for the goods or services they grind out. People build their lives around them, identify with them, become dependent on them. The process of institutionalization is the process of organic growth, wherein the organization adapts to the strivings of internal groups and the values of the external society. Selznick says that the administrative leader becomes a "statesman" when he or she uses creativity to recognize and guide this process.

The distinction is an attractive one. We can all recognize organizations that have become valued for their own sakes and whose disappearance or even drastic change would have more effect on members and the public than would a mere loss of jobs. Universities are seen in this light when they are under attack; the Marine Corps has such a halo surrounding it; the disappearance of a newspaper is treated in this fashion; even local businesses become prized as familiar, stable resources and depositories of community values. Furthermore, the process of institutionalization is a familiar theme of sociology, and the insights of the structural-functional school are tailored to its analysis. Finally, the image of a mechanical, engineered organization, impersonal and disposable, is an unattractive one.[34]

But the distinction needs to be questioned. Selznick puts forth a more complex view of types of organizations. Besides the distinction between the organization and the institution, he implicitly distinguishes the inflexible, dedicated, unswerving organization, deriving its goals from its participants, from the flexible, adaptive, outward-looking organization—the one impregnated with the values of the community. This is not a repeat of the earlier distinction, for institutions, too, can be inflexible. One of the major tasks of the institutional leader is to weld the members of the organization into a "committed polity," with a high sense of identity, purpose, and commitment. This would seem to imply an inflexible organization, drawing heavily on the internal strivings of its groups and maximizing its "distinctive competencies." On the other hand, the flexible, outward-looking organization need not be responsive to real needs, but only to vagrant pressures. It can be opportunistic,

[33]In original form, it is a contrast of the "economy" of an organization and its institutional aspects. See Selznick, "Foundations of a Theory of Organizations." In *Leadership in Administration* it is a contrast of the degree of institutionalization. Those with less precise goals, for example, are more open to institutionalization (*Leadership*, pp. 5–6, 16.)

[34]The distinction is not merely a product of the middle 1950s, the decade of a search for order and stability after a cataclysmic depression and a horrendous world war. The liberal values it reflects show again in Selznick's *Law, Society and Industrial Justice*, p. 44ff, where the mechanical application is again contrasted with organic and adaptive forms. See also his rejoinder to the criticisms of Sheldon Wolin in Amitai Etzioni, ed., *A Sociological Reader on Complex Organizations* (New York: Holt, Rinehart & Winston, 1969), pp. 149–154.

drifting, and experiencing a failure of leadership and clear purpose. We might chart this elaboration as follows:

	ORGANIZATION	INSTITUTION
Nonflexible, internal source of values	The tool view; a rational, engineered instrument, with technicians directing it	The committed polity, with clear identity and purpose, serving the selfish strivings of its participants
Flexible, external source of values	The drift view; opportunism without goal-directed leadership	Adaptability, responsiveness; impregnated with community values

The tension between the two varieties of institutionalization, commitment and responsiveness, is never resolved and barely admitted.[35]

The matter of commitment to the organization also deserves discussion. Selznick notes in a more recent book that some theorists see dangers in members giving full commitment to the organization, for then the organization subjects them to too much control. As Selznick puts it, they view "the organization as a necessary evil to be approached warily and embraced without ardor."[36] While he recognizes the advantages of limited commitment, he is more concerned that limited commitment often means too little recognition of the rights of participants in organizations—a central theme of his volume. He asks: "Can individual rights in associations be fully protected without some concept of meaningful membership?" Presumably, a wary, limited commitment does not justify protection of one's rights; it resembles the tool view of organizations as limited-purpose rational instruments, while full commitment is the source of protection and is to be found in institutions. One might justly argue, however, that rights need protection independent of the type of organization or commitment. If we can only have rights by which we embrace the values and goals of the organization, these rights may have little meaning.

Selznick takes the matter further still. Explicating a desideratum of the pluralist doctrine—a doctrine that easily justifies the goals of all organizations—he says: "Through significant membership in corporate groups the individual's relation to the larger commonwealth can be extended and enriched."[37] This is true enough—if those groups are in the individual's interests and controlled by him or her. Just as full commitment poses no dangers for those in control, so it enriches their relationship to the larger society. But these advantages are limited to the few at the top. The top management of General Electric (GE), the American Medical Association (AMA), and the University of California no doubt extend and enrich their relationships through these groups, and their commitment can be full. But does the average employee of General Electric extend and enrich his relationship to the larger commonwealth through his job? Does the doctor who favors broader health coverage or better care for those in the ghetto enrich herself through mem-

[35]See, for example, Selznick's *Leadership in Administration*, p. 18.
[36]Selznick, *Law, Society and Industrial Justice*, p. 43.
[37]Ibid., p. 43.

bership in the AMA? She will receive a higher income as a result of the AMA's restrictive trade practices and control of the rate of entry of new doctors, but she will hardly derive an extended relationship to the larger community in the sense that Selznick clearly has in mind—nor will the student at Berkeley (or the assistant professor) protesting war-related research or the 1968 plans to channel students into the physical sciences and professions and out of the humanities and social sciences.[38] A limited commitment, necessary to provide, for the worker, a livelihood, for the doctor, guaranteed access to hospitals and malpractice insurance, and, for the student, certification for employment through the attainment of a college degree, would seem to be sufficient in all cases. Selznick is far more critical of organizations and the way they subvert values than is Barnard, but he comes close to Barnard's view that people finds themselves and their society through organizations.

More serious, however, than the discrepancies between two different types of institutions and the elitist view of commitment is the question of the source of the values to be realized by the organization. For the engineered tool view, that source is presumably the values of the master of the organization. For the opportunistic organization, it is the ebb and flow of opportunities for short-run gain within the organization, where groups vie for power, and outside of it, in the marketplace of ideas and consumer preferences. We may legitimately fear or decry both the engineered and the opportunistic models. But what about the institution?

For both types of institutions, there is nothing to guarantee accountability or responsibility. The committed polity attempts to impose its view on the world; the right-wing Moral Majority and Committee on the Present Danger groups would qualify, as would radical feminists and environmentalists. Granted, perhaps, that these excesses, if they be that, will always be with us, what about the adaptive, responsive institutions that concern Selznick the most?

The Moral Ambiguity of Functionalism

It is here that the moral ambiguity of the functionalist position is most exposed. The Crown-Zellerbach Corporation, with its distinguished leadership (one chairman was an ambassador to Italy; the firm is noted for philanthropic activities in San Francisco, etc.), "adapted" to the community values of Bogalusa, Louisiana, for years, even as the federal government was taking legal action to force the company to integrate its facilities.[39] It was responsive to local community values and strivings —those of the minority white community—with disastrous consequences for the rest of the community—the black and poor majority. U.S. Steel performed a similar rite of institutionalization in Birmingham, Alabama, for years when it ignored job segregation, racial unrest, and injustice until the disruption of production following the riots in the black ghettos, along with some national criticism, forced it to take

[38]According to a document on the "academic master plan" formulated by the university and protested by some student groups.

[39]Vera Rony, "Bogalusa: The Economics of Tragedy," *Dissent* (May/June 1966): 234–242.

slow, hesitant steps to "adapt" to another part of the community.[40] The organization can choose: there is no "community" value; there is only the conflict of group
interests. Selznick's own analysis of the TVA makes this clear. But there his conclusion is *not* that there was effective leadership selecting certain interests to align with
in order to achieve its ends. Instead, he sees a "failure of leadership" and the
melancholy fate of idealism and abstract goals in organizations. His remedy in
Leadership in Administration is equally disturbing: "Creative men are needed
. . . who know how to transform a neutral body of men into a committed polity.
These men are called leaders; their profession is politics."[41] This makes a virtue of
the danger. Creative people did shape the TVA to their own politics. He does not
applaud the results (he says elsewhere that much institutionalization can be pathological), but he does not attribute it to leadership, but to its failure. This suggests
that when we get results we approve of, this is leadership; when we do not, it is a
process of goal displacement.

Michels's insight has thus blinded us all. He showed how people of good will
with liberal values become transformed, through institutional processes that sociologists are so adept at studying, into people who compromise their original goals and
those of the organizations they head in the interests of preserving their own position
as leaders. According to Michels, they do it unwittingly, without conscious malice,
and inevitably. True enough; this does occur. But it is also possible that we cannot
freely assume good will on the part of leaders. What some sociologists like to see
as "goal displacement"[42] may refer only to goals never entertained by the leaders.
The outputs of the organization may be just what they planned.

Consider another example, again from a liberal, concerned sociologist who
wishes to stem some of the evil found in an organizational society. In Harold
Wilensky's lively and informative volume, *Organizational Intelligence,* the grim
array of examples of the abuse of organizational power in all types of organizations
is attributed to the failure of intelligence (information).[43] Wilensky indicates that
if information were of better quality, not distorted by the bureaucratic hierarchy,
if it quickly reached the proper people, and if it were evaluated fearlessly regardless
of career implications and interpersonal dependencies, our organizations would
function much more in keeping with their announced goals—and much more
effectively. In many cases, one can agree; people in organizations do a great many
wrong things and a great many ineffective things, and there are structural sources
of these imperfections. But what is striking is the number of cases where a failure
of intelligence did not seem to be at stake. The information was available; it was

[40]See the description of this case in Clarence C. Walton, *Corporate Social Responsibilities* (Belmont, Calif.: Wadsworth, 1967), pp. 156–172.

[41]Selznick, *Leadership in Administration,* p. 61.

[42]See Chapter 2 of David Sills, *The Volunteers* (New York: Free Press, 1957) for an excellent discussion of goal displacement. For a categorization of goals that would be more meaningful for the kind of analysis I am suggesting here, see Charles Perrow, "Organizational Goals," *International Encyclopedia of the Social Sciences,* rev. ed. vol. 11 (New York: Macmillan, 1968), pp. 305–311.

[43]Harold L. Wilensky, *Organizational Intelligence* (New York: Basic Books, 1969). For a more extensive discussion of the point to be made below see Charles Perrow, "Review of Organizational Intelligence," *Trans-action* 6 (January 1969): 60–62.

simply not in the interests of the leaders to use it. Changing the structure, reducing the levels of hierarchy, eliminating the "pathologies" of bureaucracy would mean little if the goals, perspectives, or prejudices of the elite were not changed. To change these might mean to change the whole structure of society and the goals of all the organizations that support that structure.[44]

Take the case of the military, in particular the Air Force. After World War II an extensive study of the effects of strategic bombing in Germany indicated that its costs, in pilots and equipment, far outweighed its military effects, which were surprisingly slight. Yet in the Korean War, the military bombed North Korea even more heavily than it had bombed Germany. Once again, a study by the Air Force disclosed the poverty of the policy. The message was not heeded. By mid-1970 we had dropped 50 percent more tons of explosives on the relatively tiny, under-developed area of Vietnam than we had used in both the European and Pacific theaters combined during World War II, and had lost thousands of Air Force personnel and planes. This time, in addition to the demonstrated ineffectiveness of this saturation bombing, we were also aware of the disastrous ecological effects of turning large areas of the countryside into a pockmarked landscape where insects and diseases could breed and where the ecological balance could not be maintained. In late 1970 and early 1971 we bombed sections of supply trails in Laos with more intensity than any other area of land had ever been bombed, still without producing the desired effect of interdicting supplies. A ground invasion of the area was necessary.

The problem in all these cases does not appear to be lack of information about the failure of strategic bombing and its high costs. There was plenty of information available, including, but not limited to, two systematic, extensive studies commissioned by the Air Force itself. The problem appears to be that it was in the interests of the Air Force and the military in general to pursue this kind of effort, regardless of its irrelevance to the stated goals of quickly bringing various enemy nations to their knees. No correction of organizational malfunctions would be likely to change these interests. As a matter of fact, according to Melman's analysis, the restructuring of the military in the interests of efficiency that took place under Defense Secretary Robert McNamara—an operation organizational theorists presumably would applaud—led to its enormous growth and power and to the distortion of societal goals of peace and freedom.[45]

---

[44]This poses the dilemma of those who would work within the system and those who would not. Presumably, for Selznick, Wilensky, and most other concerned sociologists, an assumption is made that "good will" is available to be tapped, and if we inform leaders and policy makers, or the students who will have the power in the future, of the way in which they go wrong, they will correct their ways. I have written a book that in part is guided by this assumption and that I consider to be an elaboration and extension of Selznick's *Leadership* book. See Charles Perrow, *Organizational Analysis: A Sociological View* (Belmont, Calif.: Wadsworth, 1970). An alternate view is that the present structure of society allows only minor, remedial adjustments, those that would reduce some of the strains without disturbing the whole. Those who contribute to this effort only preserve the system even as they liberalize parts of it. For a discussion of this more radical view, see Charles Perrow, *The Radical Attack on Business* (New York: Harcourt Brace Jovanovich, 1972). The first book was drafted in early 1968, the second in 1971; in between the two, an "environment" of military occupation of campuses I was on, the continuation of the Vietnam War, and a surge of leftist research "impacted" me.

[45]Melman, *Pentagon Capitalism.*

This is not to say that leaders are all-powerful; there are many constraints on their ability to use the organization freely as a tool. We have considered some of these constraints in previous chapters: the necessity to treat labor as a resource that is more productive if handled well and paid well; tenure provisions for management; limits on arbitrary authority; technological constraints; internal goal conflict; and, most important, cognitive limits on rationality—which entail such things as limited search and lack of innovation. To these we must now add, following the institutional school, more pervasive aspects of tradition and history than the decision-making model envisions: unplanned adaptations, the failure of leaders to have and set clear goals, and internal group strivings. Surely this limits the tool view of organizations; organizations are not simply resources to be utilized at will. But it does not suggest that the leaders of all, or even most, organizations are not in a position to transform a neutral body of members into a polity committed to what the leaders believe to be important, rather than to what the individual members and the plurality of groups in the environment consider important. Organizations are imperfect tools, but the powerful ones appear to do well enough for their masters. Selznick is right; leadership is decisive. My quarrel with him is the implication that leadership is decisive in realizing the goals of the members and the environment, rather than the goals of the leaders.

Trivial Organizations

The work of Wilensky, Selznick, Janowitz, and some others, despite its flaws, has at least paid attention to important organizations in our society. Most of the literature in the institutional school, including my own, has dealt with relatively trivial organizations. There are the freaks, such as the Townsend movement or the WCTU; the accessible welfare institutions such as general hospitals or agencies for the blind; the obvious "social problem" institutions such as mental hospitals, prisons, and reform schools, whose impact on a tiny minority of incarcerated individuals is frightening but trivial compared to the dominant economic institutions of our society. Occasionally, a note of organizational dominance creeps in or is given some sustained analysis, as when the Community Chest is seen as an occupying army, or when the Communist party manipulates voluntary associations, or when a federal narcotics agency is seen as making a menace out of marijuana in the interests of growth and power.[46] But these are exceptions.

There are many reasons for the focus on relatively inconsequential organizations. There are only a small number of researchers doing institutional analysis, as contrasted to the large number involved in the factory studies of the human relations movement. There are problems of access to the powerful, dominant organizations in our society; their sheer size poses one formidable problem. Government and foundation funding plays a key role. The institutions that cope with the deformed products of our society are more visible as social problems than those organizations that contribute to the deformity, and symptoms are safer to treat than causes.

[46]Seeley, Junker, and Jones, *Community Chest;* Selznick, *The Organizational Weapon;* and Donald Dickson, "Bureaucracy and Morality," *Social Problems* 16, no. 2 (Fall 1968): 129–142.

Finally, this focus on trivial, symptomatic organizations is also probably due to a characteristic of the profession as a whole. Sociologists are interested in values, but they have traditionally studied values in cameo settings—the family, small group, small town—or in the organizations that blatantly distort our values, such as prisons or asylums. Academic inquiries do not differ that much from the commercial, nonacademic forms of social inquiry. Television specials will focus on such symptomatic problems of society as racial discrimination, poverty, violence, insanity, and addiction and such isolated groups as migratory workers and Indians. But TV usually ignores the mass media themselves, big business, the military-industrial complex, the propertied elite, the self-serving powerful professional associations. Just so with organizational sociologists. They have neglected, if not avoided, those institutions that create and manipulate our values, despite their preoccupation with values. The corporations that select and package our very view of what is happening—the mass-media institutions such as CBS, the Associated Press, the newspaper chains, the *New York Times*—are almost totally neglected. Their absence until the mid-1970s in the inventory of sociological studies of organizations was conspicuous.

Oddly enough, there is a large body of valuable data on the powerful governmental and economic organizations in our society, including the mass media, but it is scarcely tapped by organizational theorists. I am referring to the massive amount of information to be found in the records of committee hearings of congressional groups and in the reports of governmental regulatory agencies and governmental agencies in general. It is public information. It would not take an agency-funded research grant, extensive field work, or elaborate questionnaires to mine these data.[47]

Organizations and Society

Among the many reasons given above for the failure to go beyond trivial organizations, we should also include the most significant failure of all of organizational theory: the failure to see *society* as adaptive to *organizations*. A view that organizations are protean in their ability to shape society would direct us to the study of the powerful organizations and to the public data gathered by government agencies and congressional committees.

Here, we see the gravest defect of the institutional school in particular, for it has been the one most concerned with the environment. *That school's view of organizations and society fails to connect the two.* Parts of the "environment" are seen as affecting organizations, but the organization is not seen as defining, creating, and shaping its environment. We live in an "organizational society," the institutionalists routinely announce, but the significant environment of organizations is not "society"; they do not realize that the environment is other organizations, and generally other organizations that share the same interests, definitions of reality, and power. Society is adaptive to organizations, to the large, powerful organizations controlled by a few, often overlapping, leaders. To see these organizations as adap-

[47]For an example of using secondary sources with a nontrivial organization to great effect, see Jerry Cates's discussion of the formation of the Social Security Administration: *Insuring Inequality: Administrative Leadership in Social Security, 1935–54* (Ann Arbor, Mich.: University of Michigan Press, 1982).

tive to a turbulent, dynamic, ever-changing environment is to indulge in fantasy. The environment of most powerful organizations is well controlled by them, quite stable, and made up of other organizations with similar interests, or ones they control.[48] Standard Oil and Shell may compete at the intersection of two highways, but they do not compete in the numerous areas where their interests are critical, such as foreign policy, tax laws, import quotas, government funding of research and development, highway expansion, internal combustion engines, pollution restrictions, and so on. Nor do they have a particularly turbulent relationship to other powerful organizations such as the auto companies, the highway construction firms, the Department of Defense, the Department of Transportation, the State Department, the major financial institutions.

Why would the logic of the relationship between organizations and their environment be turned around so persistently? There are technical and conceptual reasons, no doubt. But one important reason is probably the heritage of the functionalist tradition in organizational analysis. A highly oversimplified parable will illustrate, though hardly verify, the point. Imagine an Indian tribe in the Southwest, before the advent of settlers. The tribe lives peacefully and peaceably, bestowing its honors on those who can promise rain, solve disputes, and provide an oral tradition that links the past with the present. A disturbance occurs; a new tribe enters the area and starts to fight our tribe. Over the years of protracted defense and combat, the honors go to those who are most warlike. They become the chiefs and dictate the pattern of culture. They succeed in driving out or subjecting the offending intruders. But now the position of the warriors is threatened; without war there will be no honors for the warrior. So the warriors expand their surveillance of the environment until they come across other tribes, which they challenge and fight. Their power is secured. In time, the once-peaceful group becomes an expanding, subjugating, warlike tribe, seeking ever new territories and spoils to support the military superstructure. The other tribes, perforce, must adapt similarly or be conquered.

By the time the functionalist studies the tribe, its social structure is "functional"; the military should dominate. The environment is hostile, and their lands are challenged. The military is needed to police the areas and to fight off offending and aggressive tribes, which always seem to materialize. Defense is a basic need of all communities; this one is doing a highly effective job at it. Power follows function and is legitimized. The society, like the organization, has adapted. But what has happened, of course, is that those with power made sure that their skills would be the primary requisites for the community. They have shaped the environment, not the other way around. As Joseph Schumpeter noted, speaking of the war machines of ancient times, "Created by the wars that required it, the machine now created the wars it required."[49]

So it may be with organizations in the modern state. Janowitz's predictions about the military, noted early in this chapter, may still bear fruit at some future

[48]I have argued this point in more detail in Charles Perrow, "Is Business Really Changing?" *Organization Dynamics* (Summer 1974): 31–44.

[49]Joseph H. Schumpeter, *Imperialism and Social Classes* (Cleveland: Meridian Books, 1955), p. 25.

time, but right now it seems to matter little that the military was shaped by the changing class structure, new technologies, and ideologies that brought professionals into command. The military has been able, many believe, to create, define, and shape our foreign environment and promote its own goals. It is feared that it is also doing so with our internal environment.

When we look at the matter from this perspective, I think we have additional grounds to question the explanation of goal displacement, natural processes, drift, and so on when we apply our liberal values and the exposé tradition to the study of organizations. The goals of the agencies for the blind may be displaced, but those of the American Medical Association seem very much intact—even though they do change gradually. The large defense contractors are not likely to drift toward refusing to produce weapons; the large banks are not likely to give up their critical role in our economy and our foreign policy. Chase Manhattan is not likely, for example, to pull out of racially segregated South Africa, and it was not drift that put it there. The AMA annually spends millions to stave off national health insurance, but not to attend to health needs of the poor in a country that has a higher infant mortality rate than most other industrialized countries. The contenders for top leadership positions in our large voluntary and economic organizations are those who share the dominant perspectives of the organizations' elites—or they would not be contenders. There are exceptions, of course, but those exceptions stand out for this reason.

It is precisely because the dominant organizations or institutions of our society have *not* experienced goal displacement and have been able to institutionalize on their own terms—to create the environments they desire, shape the existing ones, and define which sections of it they will deal with—that the failure to link organizations such as these with society is so alarming. It is from the muckrakers, journalists, congressional committees, historians, and, occasionally, the economists and political scientists that we learn about the ways in which organizations shape our environment, not, ironically, from the organizational sociologists. The WCTU may drift, but General Motors is making record profits.

In fact, we need not count the WCTU as an exception. A close analysis of those research findings cited at the beginning of this chapter, indicating the exposé character of this school, suggests that for many of the organizations involved the problem was that they *were* tools in the hands of their leaders; that Mr. Townsend found it profitable to shift from political reform to patent medicine; that the Selective Service System was less an agency of Congress than an expression of the conservative political philosophy of its head, General Lewis Hershey, and reflected *his* values and those of the people who appear to have controlled him; that a set of leaders dominated the policies of the WCTU; that the affairs of San Jose State College were firmly in the hands of the leaders of other organizations in the "administrative web" that Clark describes so well; that it is the decisions of the heads of the many agencies for the blind to ignore the old, handicapped, and minority-group members who are also blind. We need not doubt that power was exercised from the top in these organizations, and we may question whether either internal group strivings or a sense of the mission of the organization as a whole was responsible for these policies.

In an earlier chapter, I argued that we have more to fear from organizations than their negative effect on the spontaneity and self-realization of their members; I would now add that we have more to fear from organizations than the displacement of goals we attribute to them. The assumptions we have made about the nature of organizations—whether as cooperative systems or natural systems—have made the task of linking organizations and society in this fashion difficult. A tool view, based on a neo-Weberian view of structure modified by the insights of the institutional school, but not posing the latter's functionalist questions, would serve us better.

SUMMARY

The institutional school has served organizational theory well in several respects. The natural systems view, stressing the organic entity, is analogous to some of the themes of March and Simon. Their notion of organizational vocabularies and the stabilizing force of custom, well-worn communication lines, and so on resembles the institutional view of basic identity, or character, and the "conservative" nature of institutions that resist fortuitous change. The exposé tradition has highlighted the dangers we can expect from even well-meaning organizations in their search for stability and growth and their resistance to character restructuring. It also highlights the "underlife" of the organization, the latent functions and unplanned aspects of complex systems. Above all, the descriptive and historical nature of this school gives us an essential "feel" for how organizations operate, something dramatically absent from the March and Simon volume, for example.

More important than these contributions, however, is what this school presses on us. First, there is the inescapable variety of organizations, a variety that the technological school cannot hope to reflect in its three- or fourfold categorizations. The institutional school has not sought to capture and discipline this variety in a fashion that would serve research and conceptualization as yet, but it provides the leads. (See the development in the next chapter.) Second, institutional theory brings up to those who would use a neo-Weberian model the possibility that organizations do develop an inner logic and direction of their own that is not the result of those who appear to control them. We have challenged this view, but the nagging question remains: When we identify General Hershey or whoever as the "leader," are we merely picking out a person cast up by "the organization" to do its work? I think the evidence is that this is not generally the case, but as yet the question has not been posed with sufficient clarity to even say what evidence is relevant, let alone what kinds of organizations fit which model. But it is a very important question, and the answer may limit the applicability of the neo-Weberian model.

The third contribution is no doubt essential. This school, almost alone among those we have considered, has taken the environment seriously and tried to understand the organization's relationship to it. No neat conceptual schemes have emerged; it is a vastly more complex problem than understanding the internal workings of organizations. But again, I have argued that the school has led us astray. It has seen the organization as adaptive to and dependent on the environment. It has not considered the other possibility, which, for the important organizations in our society, is at least equally possible: that the environment has to adapt to the organization. The major aspect of the environment of organizations is other organizations; the citizen and the "community" fall between the stools.

We outlined some other deficiencies. We questioned the importance of the organizations that this school has been want to study; the question-begging distinction between organizations and institutions, and the school's idea of commitment to the organization; the easy faith that the large and powerful organizations will allow themselves to be infused with liberal values, whereas they may select self-serving ones or, worse still, force their environment to emphasize self-serving values. And we argued that this was an expression of the posture of structural-functionalism that pervades sociology today.

Finally, we examined the more direct challenge to the position that organizations are tools in the hands of masters, and we concluded that it appears that the masters are in substantial command in most organizations, even the weak and trivial (though interesting) ones this school has been most prone to study.

We could have hoped for more, then, from the institutional school. It appears to have been a product of its times—reflecting the disillusionment with radical change in the late 1930s and the 1940s, when the leading spokespersons began their career; and the empty, quiet 1950s, when their students were trained. It is also a product of the guiding perspective of sociology itself since the 1930s—"value free" functionalism, the pluralist doctrine, and the emphasis on norms, values, and culture at the expense of power and the material aspects of existence. New winds, I hope, will stir in this most sociological of all schools of organizational theory, and the tradition of patient inquiry, case studies, historical perspectives, the environment, natural processes, unplanned adaptations, and values will be wedded to a tool view of organizations that gives the devil his full due. Referring to bureaucracy, Selznick once warned against the tendency to gaze at the devil with fascinated eyes, but we should also be warned against the tendency to call for the transformation of people into committed polities in organizations where centralized power and unobtrusive means of manipulation and control are necessities.

It is perhaps ironic that those who appear to understand the devil best—theorists such as Herbert Simon and James March—are the least concerned in their writings with liberal values, goals, and responsiveness, while those most concerned are the least likely to recognize the devil in his consummate disguises. It is more than ironic; it is a melancholy conclusion in a social landscape strewn with the wastes of our organizations.

6

The Environment

If one thinks in terms of waves of theory, the post–World War II period was dominated by human relations theory until the mid-1960s. Contingency theory (the "technological school") was gathering strength and clarity in the early 1960s and hit with solid force in 1967 with three similar formulations by James Thompson, Paul Lawrence and Jay Lorsch, and my own piece.[1] These stimulated a wave of theorizing and research that is now rapidly being absorbed. It has left its mark, as did the human relations tradition, but it has lost its handsome crest of frothy promise. Task, or technology, proves to be an important variable, but not of the overriding importance we first claimed. The new wave-gathering force appears to be the environment.

It was always there in organizational theory, from Weber on. Indeed, the contingency theory of Lawrence and Lorsch was formulated in such a way that the environment set varied tasks for different organizations and units of organizations. Interorganizational relations theory was formulated in the early 1960s.[2] The institutional school, as we have seen, has always emphasized the environment—but not self-consciously so—and did not conceptualize it in any distinct way. The environmental view is trying to do just this—conceptualize it, or tell us how to think about it—and that will be the concern of this chapter.

First, we will start with some work on the recording industry and the pharmaceutical industry, to indicate how an organizational analysis helps us see the issue of bias and cultural control, but even more important, the relationship between organizations and the industry they are in, and between the industry and the rest of society. I will also rejoice in this section that there is now good work on large and powerful organizations, rather than just the trivial ones.

---

[1]James Thompson, *Organizations in Action* (New York: McGraw-Hill, 1967); Paul R. Lawrence and Jay W. Lorsch, *Organization and Environment* (Cambridge, Mass.: Harvard University Press, 1967); and Charles Perrow, "A Framework for Comparative Organizational Analysis," *American Sociological Review* 32, no. 2 (April 1967): 194–208.

[2]Sol Levine and Paul E. White, "Exchange as a Conceptual Framework for the Study of Interorganizational Relationships," *Administrative Science Quarterly* 5 (March 1961): 583–610; Eugene Litwak and Lydia F. Hylton, "Interorganizational Analysis: A Hypothesis on Co-ordinating Agencies," *Administrative Science Quarterly* 6, no. 4 (March 1962): 395–420; and Herman Turk and Myron J. Lefkowitz, "Toward a Theory of Representation Between Groups," *Social Forces* 40 (May 1962): 337–341.

Then we will examine carefully the recent notion of "networks" by seeing what difference it can make if one uses an interorganizational framework rather than an organizational one. It seems quite likely that many of our hard-won conclusions about organizations as such will have to be upset once we look at the network they are involved in. To explore this, I will use a fabricated but realistic extended case study of a network of hospitals and political power.

The notion of networks in particular, and organization-environment relations in general, is still fluid. Competing paradigms appear to be emerging. In the third part of the chapter I will examine one impressive contender—a revitalized population-ecology model—and suggest that our discipline of organizational analysis still goes astray every time it gets a chance. I will try to rein it in at this early stage of development. A more promising evolutionary model proposed by two atypical economists will conclude the chapter.

THE INDUSTRY

A Question of Bias

We will back into the environment gently by first looking at a problem that clearly can have its source in the organization and then examining its source in the environment. This is the problem of bias in the selection of cultural products to be produced. Certain people play the role of creative artist—the reporter, the musician, the film director, the actor—and they come up against the demands of the organization, or even the political or artistic prejudices of the top executives. This is a familiar focus in organizational studies because it examines individual roles. It is similar to studies of the role of the foreman and his cross pressures as he tries to serve the workers under him and the organization over him; or of the scientist supposedly suffering under the lash of company profit objectives when she just wants to do good science; or the departmental manager trying to make his department look good while at the same time subordinating its interests to the interests of the company as a whole.

In the case of the "cultural industry" (vaguely defined here as involving the media as well as literature, art, music, drama, etc.), these role conflicts are reportedly severe, and they always entail issues of bias in the selection of cultural products. Surveys and studies have shown that reporters are more liberal in their views than are the owners of the paper, and thus a subtle censorship is at work because they know that certain kinds of stories will not be selected for publication, and certain kinds of information or observations will not be retained in the story as they write it, so they write what they know will be accepted. The editor does not have to tell them that the publishers want stories reflecting a more conservative view; it becomes apparent. Producers of TV programs often would prefer to handle more controversial and even liberal material but end up following the current bland fads because of the censorship of network owners and sponsors. Musicians are forced to play music that the club owner thinks the patrons like; after hours they play the kind they feel reflects their creative urges. Most movie actors cannot choose their own scripts or directors; directors cannot stop the producers from ordering a change in endings (usually calling for an upbeat one) or editing the film to suit their tastes. Rock groups are told to emphasize certain kinds of sounds or lyrics even if they feel these are mere fads.

These are important problems, but if the inquiry ends with the artist-producer interaction, or stays within the organization, we make the presumption that the system is closed and we may be misled. If we assume the system is open to outside influences, we will look at the conditions under which the owners or producers or whatever operate, generally the conditions of the industry as a whole and its market, and alternative explanations are possible. (Paul Hirsch, in a seminal piece on industrial sociology, advocates such a move from the organization to the industry, giving some examples of the difference it makes.[3])

Can the owners or producers shape the cultural product of the artist against the will of the artist? Of course they can, and it happens regularly. But when is it likely to happen, and how, and why, and how frequently? Is it a characteristic of the kind of individuals who control the organization, or the setting in which the organization operates regardless of the owners or top management?

When a freelance journalist, Seymour Hersh, submitted reports to the *New York Times* and other newspapers on the My Lai massacre in Vietnam at the height of our military involvement, the reports were rejected.[4] It would appear to be a clear case of censorship, since the reports showed the U.S. military in an appalling light, and the reports would have eroded the legitimacy of a long, costly war effort. Such information, even if true, could hardly be welcomed by the media, which are a part of the national power structure and depend on the military and the White House for information and freedom from harassment.

An alternative interpretation, however, is simply that where stories are controversial, the media need strong guarantees regarding the reliability of the reporter and his or her story. Hersh was not, at that time, on the staff of the *Times*, so there was good reason for the *Times* to be cautious.

Both interpretations could be true—it could be politically motivated suppression, or it might be organizational caution. But the second seems to have the edge because after the accounts were accredited (they were not dismissed out of hand), the stories were published. Indeed, the nightly television news was carrying bits and pieces of the U.S. military behavior that suggested such massacres could occur, and the Pentagon was complaining of the "biased" coverage by the television networks. Finally, the *Times* hired Hersh as a staff investigative reporter after his stories were verified. (The popular book *All the President's Men* by Carl Bernstein and Bob Woodward provides interesting examples of the norms the press uses to verify stories, the costs of mistakes, and the drudgery, errors, and lucky breaks associated with this type of media production.[5])

[3]Paul M. Hirsch, "Organizational Analysis and Industrial Sociology: An Instance of Cultural Lag," *The American Sociologist* 10, no. 1 (February 1975): 3–10.

[4]I am following the illustration of Paul Hirsch here: Paul Hirsch, "Occupational, Organizational and Institutional Models in Communication Research," in Paul M. Hirsch, Peter V. Miller, and F. Gerald Kline, *Strategies for Communication Research* (Beverly Hills, Calif.: Sage, 1977).

[5]Carl Bernstein and Bob Woodward, *All the President's Men* (New York: Simon & Schuster, 1974).

This example does not prove that censorship does not occur; it quite obviously does, as do blacklisting, witch hunts, deliberate distortions, and so on. The book *The First Casualty*[6] details the censorship and distortions practiced in recent wars by governments, publishers, and reporters themselves. Indeed, in many socialist countries and in all dictatorships no such thing as a free market for news exists, by design and by explicit policy. But where such a free market is claimed, as it endlessly is in the United States ("All the news that's fit to print" says the *New York Times*), it is worth inquiring whether bias is intended by the masters of these organizations or is the result of organizational and industrial contexts.

The charges of bias, favoritism, suppression of innovation, and so on often occur in the cultural industry for the simple reason that potential suppliers and supplies exist in vast numbers, but very few of them are selected. When this occurs it is very easy to allow ideological bias to enter, and more important, it is easy to believe it enters even if it doesn't. Newsworthy events far outnumber the space available for presenting them; aspiring rock stars or movie stars or authors or painters are legion, while the number who get a hearing is tiny. Among reputable scholarly publishers, about 96 percent of the manuscripts received are rejected; possibly only 10 percent of those received are given any serious attention.[7] Scholarly journals regularly reject 90 percent or more of the papers sent to them. Even after the small percentage of popular music groups are recorded and offered for sale, less than a quarter of the single records produced are ever played on radio stations or video channels (the only marketing mechanism that is effective). The newspaper editor rejects perhaps 90 percent of the stories that come in over the two wire services, Associated Press and United Press International. Film scripts are offered to producers in great numbers, and even after being produced a fair number of films never get distributed. Such massive rejection rates encourage the operation of ideological and cultural biases and invite attributions of biases even when they are not present.

But what are the bases of bias? If the profit motive is dominant, and radical ideas are selling, how many owners and producers are willing to forgo the profits that pushing radical ideas would bring for ideological ends? Some will, of course. But on the other hand, how many of the presumably few left-leaning owners, producers, and sponsors are willing to buck the market trend if radical ideas are not selling and try to introduce controversial ideological material? Very, very few, one suspects. The source of what, from one political or cultural perspective, can be seen as a conservative bias may reside in the financial characteristics of the industry.

For example, television producers cover a fairly wide ideological perspective, but the resulting programming does not reflect it. The selection process operating is fairly subtle. Erik Barnouw notes that television network executives and sponsors do not have to exercise overt censorship.[8] Producers present a variety of programs

[6]Phillip Knightley, *The First Casualty: From the Crimea to Vietnam: The War Correspondent as Hero, Propagandist, and Myth Maker.* (New York: Harcourt Brace Jovanovich, 1976).

[7]Walter W. Powell, *Getting into Print: The Decision Making Process in Scholarly Publishing* (Chicago: University of Chicago Press, 1985); and Lewis A. Coser, Charles Kadushin, and Walter W. Powell, *Books* (New York: Basic Books, 1982).

[8]Erik Barnouw, *The Sponsor: Notes on a Modern Potentate* (New York: Oxford University Press, 1978).

for network executives and sponsors to choose from; the latter indicate by their selection what they think will sell. A program with high ratings may not be continued because the sponsor determines (through the Nielsen rating system) that though it is watched by a large number of people, these people are middle-aged or older and do not spend much money on the consumer products the sponsor is selling. The program is dropped in favor of one that is watched by fewer people, but by people who buy a lot of the sponsor's merchandise. The "creative people" —writers, actors, producers—get the message and offer up programs that seem to draw a segment of the population that is "economically active" with regard to low-priced, mass-produced goods (the young, often the very young). Public television might seem to be free of this, but it isn't. Its government grants cover only a small part of its costs; it must seek the rest from sponsors such as Exxon or Gulf. Thus these corporations have the power to select among the programs offered— or to choose none at all. Producers for public television programs then tailor their offerings in the same way as for commercial television. Exxon is marketing its image, and the market, as the company perceives it, will play a large role in determining the ideological and cultural content. No "censorship" is operating, only unobtrusive controls.

Ideally, for corporations, profits and ideology will work hand in hand. The largest profits will come from producing cultural products whose ideology most supports the private profit system, the class system, sexism, racism, or whatever is in their interests. It is said to be a characteristic of monopolistic capitalism that it is just such a system that can maximize long-range profits for a ruling class through long-range ideological control. But it is not an easy task; unsuspecting things intrude, and the system is very complex and can briefly get out of hand. There may be a flowering of protest songs, novels that challenge the system, cultural heroes who are anti-Establishment, and so on. The history of popular music illustrates the point well. Large profits could be made while the content of the music was safe for the system. But because of some unrelated technological innovations, suppressed tastes were allowed to come to the fore, the companies that dominated the industry lost control of it, and only now are they regaining profitable control and once again apparently trying to shape the cultural product. They are not that concerned about radical lyrics or life-styles; the threat to the system is trivial, and if radical lyrics will sell, they will be sold. But they would presumably prefer the interpersonal focus of The Cars to the social problem lyrics of U2. The following account of this history of an industry draws upon the excellent work of Richard Peterson, David Berger, and Paul Hirsch.[9] Its implication for the study of organizations goes far beyond the question of bias as I shall note at the end of it.

[9]Paul M. Hirsch, *The Structure of the Popular Music Industry* (Ann Arbor: University of Michigan Survey Research Center, 1969); P. M. Hirsch, "Processing Fads and Fashions: An Organization-Set Analysis of Cultural Industry Systems," *American Journal of Sociology* 77, no. 4 (January 1972): 639–659; P. M. Hirsch, "Organizational Effectiveness and the Institutional Environment," *Administrative Science Quarterly* 20, no. 4 (September 1975): 327–344; Richard A. Peterson and David G. Berger, "Entrepreneurship in Organizations: Evidence from the Popular Music Industry," *Administrative Science Quarterly* 16, no. 1 (March 1971): 97–106; and R. A. Peterson and D. G. Berger, "Cycles in Symbol Production: The Case of Popular Music," *American Sociological Review* 40, no. 2 (April 1975): 158–173.

The Popular Music Industry

The Giants Fall.   From the days of Tin Pan Alley (the 1920s) up through the era of swing music (to about 1955), a fortuitous combination of maximizing profits and minimizing system dissent seems to have existed. The music world was dominated by four firms. The domination was achieved by vertical integration: the firms owned the artists through long-term contracts and hired producers who gathered the ancillary talent, produced the record, and packaged the result. The firms also owned the manufacturing facilities and controlled the distribution system. Most hits came out of the musical comedy films and shows, which the giants controlled; they produced the records and distributed them. There were some points of uncertainty; record sales depend on "air time"—repeated playing over radio stations. Not all radio stations were controlled by the giants, so these top firms resorted to bribery ("payola," it was called) to induce disc jockeys to feature their records. (It has been suggested that independents trying to break in used organized crime to threaten stations.) If an independent company (or a big competitor) came up with a hit tune, it was "covered" by the majors—they had their own artists record it, cashing in on the tune's popularity (hence, it was called a "cover record"). The majors also controlled the distribution of the films that featured popular songs, further rationalizing the system. As a result, the four largest firms accounted for 78 percent of the sales of single records from 1948 to 1955; the eight largest for 96 percent.

The system was probably very efficient and economical for the companies. In the period from 1948 to 1955, sales growth was not large, but it was acceptable. Costs were controlled because most people involved were on contracts, and in a rationalized system not much competition existed to drive up the costs of paying artists, producers, and so on. Finally, there seemed to be no doubt that the public was satisfied with Doris Day, Vaughn Monroe, The Ink Spots, and Frank Sinatra, all singing of moon and June. As Peterson and Berger note, two studies both found that "over 80 percent of all songs fit into a conventionalized love cycle where sexual references are allegorical and social problems are unknown."[10] The recording industry at this time reflected the characteristics of most American industry: substantial oligopoly (production concentrated in a few firms), vertical integration, routine production, and little innovativeness except in marginal aspects such as packaging.

Then three changes took place, all of them, ironically, brought about by the industry itself. First, the long-playing record made record production very cheap. The LP actually appeared in 1948, but its impact was slow. Second, with the advent of television, advertising income from radio stations dropped alarmingly (a 38 percent decline from 1948 to 1952), and the majors abandoned network programming on radio and transferred it to TV. This made stations autonomous, and they could be purchased cheaply by local entrepreneurs. Third, the development of the cheap transistor radio resulted in a 30 percent increase in radio set production from 1955 to 1960 and a 27 percent increase in the number of AM radio stations.

The low cost of producing records affected the input side; the low cost of radio broadcasting (cheap stations, many new listeners) affected the output side. The

[10]Peterson and Berger, "Cycles," p. 163.

majors lost control of each to new independent firms that made vertical integration and homogeneous products—the ingredients of success for monopolistic capitalism —impossible for a time.

First, there had to be a profound change in programming for the stations. As Peterson and Berger note, though the idea was simple, it took a full decade to perfect. The audience was gradually no longer defined as a mass audience but as a number of discrete groups with different tastes. Each station picked its particular brand of recorded music and played it all day. But where did all these different tastes come from? Presumably, they were there all the time, but latent; they had never had the chance to develop because the recording and broadcast segments of the industry were controlled by the majors and devoted to the standard fare. The varied tastes were being met on an extremely local level through live performance of jazz, rhythm and blues, country and western, gospel, trade union songs, and urban folk songs. When recorded, which was infrequent, they appeared on small esoteric labels that were sold only locally, were hard to get, and were never played on the radio. (They also broke easily and wore out quickly, as any fan of jazz or gospel, sharpening cactus needles every three plays in the late 1930s and early 1940s, will testify.)

With inexpensive recording and pressing techniques, and disc jockeys hungry for novel sounds that would build up a loyal audience, the boom was on. Between 1955 and 1959 the number of records in the weekly Top 10 increased from 57 per year to 75; the number of cover records dropped to zero; the number of new performers represented each week doubled, and record sales soared. The number of labels and the number of firms tripled. The four firms' concentration ratio from 78 to 44 percent of sales (and to 26.5 percent by 1963). While the sales and profits of the majors continued to climb—they benefited from the freeing of suppressed tastes also—they did not climb nearly as much as those of the industry as a whole, and certainly not like those of the new independent groups. Here was something to worry about, and worry they did. After ignoring the new sounds as fads, they then condemned them. Frank Sinatra, with not only his records but his investments in the industry to protect, called rock-n-roll "phony and false, and sung, written, and played for the most part by cretinous goons."[11] (Ironically, Sinatra was a teenage idol himself earlier and then later linked to Mafia "goons" in a congressional inquiry.)

The Giants Adapt Their Organizations.   Before we examine the way the giants fought their way back to create some degree of profitable order for themselves, let us examine how the industry functioned when vertical integration and a few taste makers no longer dominated. As contingency theory predicts, when faced with a high degree of uncertainty about what would sell and an inability to immediately shape and define the market, firms had to forgo the economies of vertical integration and centralization, and decentralize and contract out for services. Even prior to 1955 there was uncertainty about when tunes or performances would become hits, but since all the tunes and performers were more or less similar, a small stable of both tunes and performers sufficed. The tunes and performers were similar because of the

[11]Ibid., p. 165.

tight control over talent and marketing. After 1955 (an arbitrary year—1954 to 1956 would be more appropriate) tunes and performers multiplied; some of the majors decided to wait out the fad of rhythm and blues records, others were not able to move fast enough to expand their stables; many new performers only lasted a year or so; and hit tunes no longer lasted months, but only weeks.

The response, by both the majors and the new independents (some of whom, like Motown, soon became majors), was to segment the organization and separate the functions. We will consider three functions: producing the master disc or tape (bringing together the performers, songwriters, recording technicians, etc.); manufacturing the records; and promoting and selling them. Manufacturing is the most routine, and it can be separated from the other functions quite easily. If an organization gets a hit record and its own manufacturing division cannot handle the instant demand, it is easy to contract out to independent stamping plants. These plants can survive because several firms will use them, since hits appear more or less regularly. A small production firm need not even invest in manufacturing facilities at all; this reduces the cost of entry into the business.

The promotion and sales division is changed under the new segmented conditions; more uncertainty and spatial dispersion are introduced. Previously, a firm could make a film and also make the records of the songs in the film and sell them in their stores, or records would be promoted over national network shows such as the *Jack Benny Hour* or *Make Believe Ballroom.* Under the new market conditions, the firm must motivate and control many agents around the country who are responsible for pushing the records with disc jockeys and stocking many more independent record stores. This results in a flat organization (many people at the lowest level) with little interdependence among the geographically far-flung promoters and sales representatives. It is "loosely coupled" internally, because there are local hits that are independent of other hits.

The production division is the most "tightly coupled" and absorbs most of the turbulence of the environment, protecting the other divisions as much as possible by being only moderately coupled to sales and promotion, and hardly coupled at all to manufacturing. The production people are expected to create a succession of hit records, so teams of specialists form and re-form around each group of artists and each recording session. Talent scouts scour the clubs, "armed with intuition, empathy, and durable eardrums," as one commentator put it,[12] and the producer does a lot of this work as well. Then there are recording engineers and other studio specialists; background musicians brought in for one record; the artist or group itself; the artists' agent, who is there to protect their interests and promote them; record-jacket designers and writers; and above all the producer, who brings the whole team together. He or she must have a sense of what the particular segment of the public wants, rapport, sincerity, and other interpersonal skills that will bring out the best in the artists and technicians, ideas for packaging, and angles for the promotion division.

Prior to the deconcentration of the industry and market, the producer was on a long-term contract, and his or her decisions were carefully reviewed by upper

[12]Peterson and Berger, "Entrepreneurship," p. 99.

management; indeed, much of the work was comparatively routine because songwriters and artists were under contract and stable relationships were formed. Under the new conditions, though, the producer emerges as the most powerful member of the whole input-throughput-output process. How then does the organization control such a person? First, his or her performance can be exceptionally well monitored; the fate of a record is known within a matter of weeks. If a given producer does not have a succession of hits, his decisions are scrutinized, his latitude is reduced, and his contracts must be countersigned by a vice-president. Second, the organization seeks to minimize the risks entailed in giving one person so much power by increasing the number of entrepreneurial decisions; the firm has many producers turning out many records but needs to invest comparatively little in each one. The market is flooded with records. In 1967 Columbia Records produced an average of one new album a day, and ten new 45 rpm singles each week. The vast majority of these were never played on the air, but some of them were and a few were hits. The profits on a hit are enormous because production costs are so low. The total cost of production, manufacturing, and promotion is often under $50,000; Columbia Records's sales exceed $200,000,000. Thus, a producer can be given a great deal of discretion because of the small investment in each decision. This is quite different from, say, making a pilot film for a TV series. There, top management is involved in each step, and the product is test-marketed. The costs are much greater, so the discretion is less.

Note that the costs of this turbulence are not significantly borne by the record company; they are pushed onto the production phase, where they are absorbed by producers on very short contracts; jittery aspiring artists, most of whom make no money at all for their recording efforts unless they are selected to be played on the air, and whose records have only about a one-in-four chance of bringing them any royalties; the disc jockeys trying to both guess and guide the public tastes; and by those that rent out studios, supply backup musicians, wait for stamping contracts, and so on. Everyone is betting on the big thing, so there are always bettors willing to absorb the costs of turbulence. It is an extreme form of craft production, as described by Arthur Stinchcombe in his seminal article on the environment and organizations.[13]

Thus we have a dramatic example of how organizations adapt to changes in their environments. The notions of contingency theory give analytic power to the work of Hirsch and especially Peterson and Berger, and I have added some of the more recent notions of coupling. But were we to stop here we would have a model of the environment shaping the organization starting about 1955. Before that, the organization more or less controlled the environment. But the organization seeks to control its environment, not to be controlled by it. In the 1970s the majors again managed to shape and control the environment to meet their needs, though they have as yet not been as successful as they were between 1920 and 1955.

The Giants Recover.   After the critical period from about 1956 to 1960, when tastes were unfrozen, competition was intense, and demand soared, consolidation ap-

[13]Arthur L. Stinchcombe, "Bureaucratic and Craft Administration of Production: A Comparative Study," *Administrative Science Quarterly* 4 (September 1959): 168–187.

peared. The number of firms stabilized at about forty. New corporate entries appeared, such as MGM and Warner Brothers, sensing, one supposes, the opportunity that vastly expanding sales indicated. Some independents grew large. The eight-firm concentration ratio also stabilized (though not yet the four-firm ratio). The market became sluggish, however, as the early stars died, were forced into retirement because of legal problems, or in the notable case of Elvis Presley, were drafted by an impinging environment. Near the end of this period the majors decided that the new sounds were not a fad and began to buy up the contracts of established artists and successfully picked and promoted new ones, notably The Beach Boys and Bob Dylan. A new generation (e.g., The Beatles) appeared from 1964 to 1969, and sales again soared.

But now the concentration ratios soared also. From 1962 to 1973 the four-firm ratio went from 25 to 51 percent; the eight-firm ratio from 46 to 81 percent, almost back to the pre-1955 levels. The number of different firms having hits declined from forty-six to only sixteen. Six of the eight giants were diversified conglomerates, some of which led in the earlier period; one was a new independent, the other a product of mergers.

How did they do it? The major companies asserted "increasing central control over the creative process"[14] through deliberate creation and extensive promotion of new groups, long-range contracts for groups, and reduced autonomy for producers. In addition, legal and illegal promotion costs (drug payola to disc jockeys, for example) rose in the competitive race and now exceeded the resources of small independents. Finally, the majors "have also moved to regain a controlling position in record distribution by buying chains of retail stores."[15] The diversity is still greater than it had been in the past, and may remain high, but it is ominous that the majors have all the segments covered. As an executive said, "Columbia Records will have a major entry into whatever new area is broached by the vagaries of public tastes." But for a concentrated industry, the "vagaries of public tastes" are not economical; it is preferable to stabilize and consolidate them. This would be possible through further control over the creative process and marketing.

It appears to be happening. In 1983, instead of eight firms controlling 81 percent of sales, as in 1973, six firms account for 85 percent of sales—a concentration ratio exceeding that of the pre-1955 days. In addition, according to a news report, payola is back again as the concentration ratio in the industry rises. As record sales declined in the early 1980s, the large companies stopped using internal promoters to push records and instead hired independent promotional agencies. The laws against payola, following scandals in the 1960s and again in 1974, make it awkward for the majors to engage in bribery directly; hiring outside groups would make these groups, rather than the majors, liable if violations were discovered.[16] Payola, to be successful, requires a format that controls tastes; an open market in music would find

[14]Peterson and Berger, "Cycles," p. 170.

[15]Ibid., p. 170.

[16]The advantages of loose coupling are many. Firms generating toxic wastes similarly benefit from hiring other firms to dispose of them; when it is done illegally, the large corporation generating the waste can claim innocence.

too much variety to make it successful. In keeping with increasing concentration in the industry, the format is the rise of stations broadcasting only the Top 40 hits. (If this all you hear, it is all you can purchase.) The station programmers are vulnerable to bribes of cash, drugs, automobiles, and real estate from the promoters. The independent promoters collectively received $50–$60,000,000 in 1983 from the record companies, including about $10,000,000 from the largest record manufacturing company, CBS.[17] Thus the majors have not only fought back but won more than they lost in the heyday of unmanipulated consumer demand.

Some Conclusions. We started our history of the popular music industry with the question of bias. Do industrial elites exercise bias in selecting what we see or hear, or do they merely respond to public tastes? In this instance, the formats for popular music before 1955 primarily served the economic interests of the majors—a variety of tastes would have meant loss of some economic control and loss of efficient production. Any concern with tastes per se was probably quite secondary. If homogeneity is once again established, it will still probably be for economic reasons, not because punk rock or disco (or whatever is in vogue as you are reading this book) is ideologically preferred by the majors. But even though ideological biases probably played a trivial role in this case, public tastes did not necessarily play the major role. Some public tastes were probably suppressed for a long time, and, of course, tastes can be manufactured as well through repetition and availability of a limited range of products. Economic considerations appear to have been foremost, and an industry analysis makes this clear.

This example of an industry in a changing environment allows us to sort out a number of additional observations that are more important for organizational analysis:

- Organizations do "adjust" to environmental changes, such as technological developments and product substitution (TV for radio), but the drive is to control and manipulate the environment.
- The turbulence can be created by the organizations' own efforts to rationalize and introduce new innovations (TV, LP records, transistor radios, and now, videos, compact discs, and portable cassettes). As the cartoon character Pogo might say: "We have met the environment and he is us."
- New technological developments do not determine cultural outcomes. For example, mass markets and cultural homogeneity are not due to the invention of the radio or records or TV; all three are compatible with diversified, segmented markets that reflect diverse cultural styles and interests. But the way new technologies are used by powerful firms can create "massification."[18]
- The most salient environment for the majors is other majors; despite competition among them, they collectively evolve strategies to eliminate or absorb threatening independents.
- The public is poorly served in the process. If we have to hope for the accidental conjunction of three major technological changes (LP records, TV, and transistor radios) to have a diversity of tastes served, we are in deep trouble.

[17]Robert Lindsey, "Payola's Return to Records Reported," *New York Times,* March 6, 1985, p. A14.
[18]Hirsch, "Organizational Effectiveness."

- Many consumer-goods industries are highly concentrated, and innovations on standard goods are marginal or cosmetic, not offering a diversity of substantial choices. (As with junk foods, such as salted snacks, sugared cereals, and nitrates in meats, some innovations are not even improvements, but poisons.)
- The costs of turbulence and change, when they occur, are "externalized" to dependent parts of the industry and thus are borne by artists, producers, and other creative people, or satellite firms that provide standby facilities. The majors did not show any decline in profits during the turbulence; the costs could be passed on (just as the costs of a fiasco such as the Ford Motor Company's Edsel did not cause a drop in Ford's dividends, the cost having been borne by workers through a drop in employment).

The Pharmaceutical Industry

Hirsch[19] points out that had the record industry been as successful as the pharmaceutical industry in securing state (that is, federal government) entitlements of various sorts, it could have protected itself much better and not have been subject to strong competition from new companies. The popular music industry tried; it lobbied for legislation that would have given a firm an exclusive license for recording and promoting a new song. The industry argued that it was entitled to a royalty any time a record was played, but it was unsuccessful. Radio stations, naturally, fought this attempt, since they had an essentially free product to use on the air.

In contrast, the pharmaceutical industry was strikingly successful. The two industries were quite similar in organizational terms, Hirsch notes. Both had mechanized and simple production technologies. Both used external "gatekeepers" (physicians and disc jockeys) to introduce and advertise their product. Profits overwhelmingly came from the sale of new products. Both were dependent on technological inventions and had grown much faster than the average industry since 1945. The big threat to the major pharmaceutical companies was the manufacture of drugs under generic names by small competitiors. So they formed a trade association that within eight years got legislation in thirty-eight states prohibiting the substitution of chemically equivalent drugs that were to be sold at about one quarter the price of the brand-name drug. In this way, captive markets could be preserved and the costs of entry into the industry became very high. They were not subject to the kind of competition that the majors in the record industry were after 1955.

Next, the major firms brought pressure on the U.S. Patent Office to change its interpretation of the law that no "naturally occurring" substances could be patented—in particular, antibiotics. The prices of antibiotics had fallen drastically in the 1940s and early 1950s as new firms started to produce them. In 1955 penicillin, for example, cost only 6 percent of what it had cost in 1945. The firms were successful, and they patented everything in sight (in 8 years, 6,107 new prescription drugs and 2,000 variations on antibiotics). Unpatented antibiotics yielded a profit of about 20 percent; patented ones, a profit of 75 percent or more.

Finally, the major drug companies bought off one of the major gatekeepers, the

American Medical Association. The AMA had strict requirements regarding advertising drugs in its twelve journals in the 1940s, including one that required advertising by generic name, rather than brand name, except for the original producer. It published an annual handbook on drugs for physicians. With pressure and the lure of high advertising revenues, all this changed. The manufacturers now wrote the book advising doctors on drugs, and the AMA book was discontinued; any drug could be listed by brand name; and the AMA's Council on Drugs was replaced by a committee with more lenient standards. Between 1953 and 1960 AMA income from advertising tripled. (Hirsch documents an unusual degree of job mobility between the AMA and the pharmaceutical trade association, and AMA lobbying support for the industry when it battled the weak FDA.) The record companies used payola as an equivalent device, but of course it was an illegal tactic, while those of the pharmaceutical industry were legal.

Thus, to our list of observations about the environment we could add the following: the power of the state to regulate and disburse entitlements is probably the single most important means of controlling an environment. This is notwithstanding the fact that the state can also block attempts to control environments, as with antitrust laws, limits on deceptive advertising, protection of unions and regulations on pensions, workers' compensation, and so on. It is to the role of the state in capitalist societies that much of the exciting work on organizational environments is turning. A major debate at present is whether the state is primarily a "tool" of the capitalist class, an umpire reconciling the diverse interests and conflicts of the capitalist class in order to preserve its hegemony, or an independent entity with organizational needs of its own, thus serving as a broker between the capitalist class and other classes, and meeting its own needs for growth and power in the process.[20] The logic of this book would tentatively suggest the latter, since it views organizations (including government agencies) as resources for many groups, but it is an area we are not prepared to explore here.

The Nontrivial Organization.   Fortunately, the new interest in the environment comes at a time when there is also a new interest in organizations other than hospitals and social agencies, or the efficiency of factories or groups of salespeople. The modern world is also made up of banks, investment houses, pharmaceutical companies, brokerage firms, television networks, newspapers, record companies, not to mention conglomerates and multinational firms. All of them are now receiving attention as organizations, rather than as incidental settings to test theories of internal structure or process, and much of the attention involves the interactions of these organizations in industries and networks. Indeed, Immanuel Wallerstein has challenged us with a stimulating treatise on the emergence of world capitalism; his work deliberately eschews a national focus in favor of an international one, an analysis parallel in some respects to what we shall offer when we discuss networks in the second part of this chapter. The individual unit, nation, or organization must be understood in terms of the network in which it

[20]See the thoughtful article by John Mollenkopf, "Theories of the State and Power Structure Research," *The Insurgent Sociologist* 5, no. 3 (Spring 1975): 245–264.

exists.[21] Interlocking directorates among the 500 largest industrials and the largest banks and retail firms are being studied in explicit network terms.[22] Journalists of high quality are aiding us.

Robert Caro has analyzed the career of Robert Moses, the czar of city building, in a massive work of great sociological interest.[23] Two other journalists (or investigative reporters as they are now called), Jack Newfield and Paul DuBrul, explore the interdependencies of major financial institutions, industry, and political corruption that brought about the mid-1970s financial crisis in New York City in a stunning work that sheds a glaring light on the paucity of most organizational and interorganizational analysis.[24] Graham Allison of Harvard uses an implicit organizational set model to analyze the frightening Cuban missile crisis of 1962, in one of the few scholarly books that asks the question: "What difference does it make if one use a rational organizational model, a bureaucratic power one, or a political actor one?"[25] The notion of analyzing an industry rather than one or two organizations within it —commonplace with economists but virtually absent from the organizational literature—is strongly urged by Paul Hirsch in a seminal piece,[26] and we have followed up on it in our examination of popular music and the drug industry. Mayer Zald has raised the crucial question of how society seeks to control organizations.[27] Amitai Etzioni adopts an organizational framework in much of his discussion of what might lead to a just and active society,[28] as does Michel Crozier in his criticism of contemporary France.[29]

Clearly, the large, powerful organizations of our society are now under scrutiny

[21]Immanuel Wallerstein, *The Modern World-System: Capitalist Agriculture and the Origins of the European World Economy in the Sixteenth Century* (New York: Academic Press, 1974).

[22]Peter Mariolis, "Interlocking Directorates and Control of Corporations," *Social Science Quarterly* 56 (December 1975): 425–439; Thomas Koenig, Robert Gogel, and John Sonquist, "Theories of the Significance of Corporate Interlocking Directorates," *American Journal of Economics and Sociology* 38 (1978): 173–183; "Interlocking Directorates as a Social Network," *American Journal of Economics and Sociology* 40 (1981): 37–50; Koenig and Sonquist, "Studying Interrelations Between Corporations Through Interlocking Directorates," in *Power and Hierarchical Control, ed.* Tom Burns and William Buckley (New York: Sage 1977); Beth Mintz, Peter Freitag, Carol Hendricks, and Michael Schwartz, "Problems of Proof in Elite Research," *Social Problems* 23, no. 3 (February 1976): 314–324; Peter J. Freitag, "The Cabinet and Big Business," *Social Problems* 23 (December 1975): 137–152; Beth Mintz, "The President's Cabinet, 1897–1972," *Insurgent Sociologist* 5: (Spring 1975): 131–148; Peter Mariolis, "Bank and Financial Control Among Large U.S. Corporations," Ph.D. Dissertation, SUNY at Stony Brook, 1978; Mark Mizruchi, *The American Corporate Network: 1904–1974* (Beverly Hills, Calif.: Sage, 1982); and Davita Glassberg and Michael Schwartz, "Ownership and Control of Corporations," *Annual Review of Sociology* 9 (1983): 311–332. The best summary of all this work is Beth Mintz and Michael Schwartz, *Bank Hegemony* (Chicago: University of Chicago Press, 1985.

[23]Robert Caro, *The Power Broker: Robert Moses and the Fall of New York* (New York: Random House, 1975).

[24]Jack Newfield and Paul DuBrul, *The Abuse of Power: The Permanent Government and the Fall of New York* (New York: Viking, 1977).

[25]Graham T. Allison, *Essence of Decision: Explaining the Cuban Missile Crises* (Boston: Little, Brown, 1971).

[26]Paul Hirsch, "Organizational Analysis and Industrial Sociology."

[27]Mayer N. Zald, "On the Social Control of Industries," *Social Forces* 57 (September 1978): 79–102.

[28]Amitai Etzioni, *The Active Society* (New York: Free Press, 1968).

[29]Michel Crozier, *The Stalled Society* (New York: Penguin Books, 1974).

by at least a few analysts (aided by journalists of high quality), and they are being considered in network or environmental terms. The field is alive and well.

THE NETWORK

Initially the environment was anything "out there" of interest to the researcher. Progressively we have begun to catalog things that we should look for "out there." The first step was the analysis of two or three interacting organizations, initially labeled interorganizational analysis, with the emphasis on the effect of the other organizations on the "focal" organization—the one we were primarily interested in. Then the idea of a set of organizations came into the literature, with some implicit criteria for what organizations should be considered in the set.[30] From there we went to the idea of networks of organizations, focusing on the properties of the networks rather than any one organization in it. (The work we have just considered, on industries, is not explicitly a network analysis, since it doesn't deal with the interaction of specific organizations. It is a specification of a part of the environment.) While still primitive, and possibly distorted by heavy borrowing from the biological sciences, the concept of networks is the most exciting development in this new preoccupation with the environment. We shall deal with it in several ways in this part of the chapter.

Think of conceptualizing the environment as a nested-box problem; inside each box is a smaller box whose dimensions are constrained by the larger box. Each box is independent to some extent of the large boxes (and the smaller ones within it) and can be analyzed as such. But it is also quite dependent on the shape of those within and without it. Extended to social organization in general, we get the familiar hierarchy of forms, with the familiar problems of infinite regress and infinite progression. The group is made up of individuals, but the individuals are made up of organs, the organs of cells, the cells of atoms—that is the regress. But the group may exist in a department, the department in a division, the division in an organization, the organization in an industry, the industry in a region, the region in a nation, and so on up to the universe—infinite progression.

Galaxies and molecules aside, we do not know where to either begin or stop. Can you analyze the division without analyzing the organization it exists in or the departments within the division? Worse yet, we are a part of this hierarchy, so our thinking about it is conditioned by our presence within it. The general rule that most social scientists follow is that whatever "level" is selected as the unit of analysis— say, the group—we had better make at least a cursory examination of the levels above it (department) and below it (individuals). Here is where our basic assumptions or, to put it less favorably, our stereotypes come into play. We may think of ourselves as reasonably open-minded about the nature of groups and as trying to discover this nature, but if we see individuals as basically rational, materialistic beings, that will

[30]William M. Evan, "The Organization-Set: Toward a Theory of Interorganizational Relations," in *Approaches to Organizational Design*, ed. J. D. Thompson (Pittsburgh: University of Pittsburgh Press, 1966), pp. 175–191.

Table 1 Basic Issues for All Levels

Is the system goal-directed, or does its direction merely emerge as the product of multiple interests and uses?

Is rationality, intended rationality, or nonrationality emphasized in analysis?

Rationality aside, how much emphasis is placed on random, nonpurposive, and accidental behavior?

Is change seen as orderly or disorderly, continuous or discontinuous, progressive, cyclical, or random?

Is the unit seen as independent or dependent on levels above and below it?

Is the basic form of interaction of units cooperation, conflict, or superficial contact and adjustment?

Are the subunits of the level tightly or loosely coupled?

Is behavior governed by cultural norms and values or by economic and self-regarding ones?

Are norms and values stable or fluctuating with the situation, or are there even such things as norms and values?

Is behavior a function of conditioning, learning, sentiments, norms, or traditions?

foreclose much inquiry. Similarly, if we believe that groups within departments are striving to be efficient (rather than striving to maximize comforts or not particularly striving for anything), that also will shape our inquiry. We would not think of looking for some things and would amplify others. Some of the most bitter disputes about organizational analysis turn upon basic preconceptions, especially those concerning human nature. These preconceptions can foreclose open inquiry.[31]

Moving from organizational to interorganizational analysis to sets and then to networks does not signify any particular progress on this problem. Conflicting views of basic social processes or human nature are mainly carried over to the extended hierarchy. For example, do networks develop or only change; is change generally orderly or disorderly; are network ties rational or nonrational? But at least we are now in a better position to conceptualize levels above that of the organization and to uncover and expose for inquiry some assumptions about basic social processes. Perhaps the greatest return will come from flexibility on these issues. For example, recent work in cognitive processes, discussed at the end of Chapter 2, has led me to emphasize accident, random choice, and poorly ordered preferences much more than I did in the past, but without assuming that most of life is like that. This should enable me to recognize these processes when they do occur but not bend every occurrence to either fit them or exclude them.

Levels of Analysis

In Table 1, I list some basic issues that must be dealt with, no matter what the level of analysis is. To some extent these may be empirical problems, to be solved by

[31]This is the force of Chris Argyris's denunciation of Peter Blau, James Thompson, myself, and others in his *The Applicability of Organizational Sociology* (New York: Cambridge University Press, 1974).

Figure 1   The Great Chain of Being

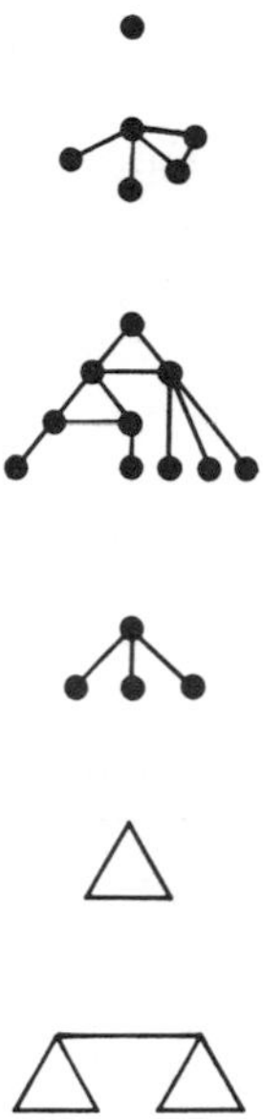

	Levels	Some topics
•	INDIVIDUAL	
	GROUP	
	DEPARTMENT	
	DIVISION	
	ORGANIZATION	
	INTERORGANIZATION	Competition; cooperation; contacts; exchanges; dominance
	ORGANIZATIONAL SET	Set size; boundary personnel; heterogeneity; stability

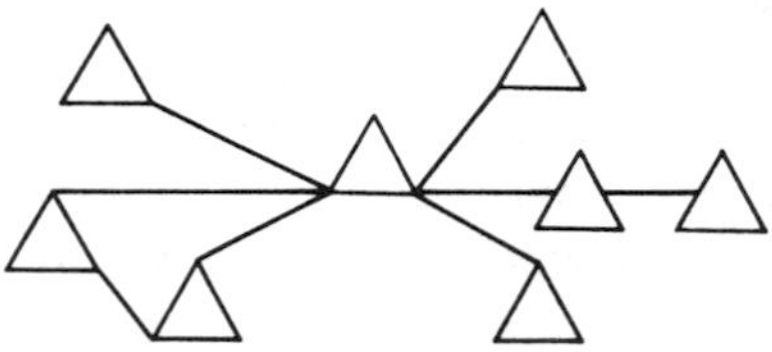

looking at actual data and behavior. Change may be orderly for some systems but disorderly for other systems, for example, and research might determine that. Or some organizations (or small groups or world capitalism) might be seen as basically goal-directed entities controlled by a dominant group or person; whereas other organizations or some parts of world capitalism may be seen as collections of resources that all kinds of groups, rather than a controlling elite, try to latch on to and use for their own ends.

However, I believe that we are rarely as open as that; we are not prepared to invoke cultural, other-regarding norms in some cases and economic, self-regarding ones in others. Instead we tend to favor the data that suggest one or the other. We lean toward the data and problems that would suggest that change is orderly (or disorderly), or we tend to ask the kind of questions that would "prove" that organiza-

Figure 1 (continued)

Levels	Some topics
NETWORKS See Figure 2	Tight or loose coupling; strength of ties; regulatory functions; scope and diversity of organizations in network; network persistence; power centers
INDUSTRY	Norms; internal controls; concentration and monopoly; growth and decline; modern; traditional
REGION	Regional dependencies; expanding and declining regions; federal policies; specialization
NATIONAL (U.S.)	Conglomerates; interlocking directorates; role of government (the "state") in capitalism
WORLD	Multinationals; dominant and dependent countries; extractive or manufacturing economies; world capitalism versus socialist sectors

tions are more or less rational instruments or that they are congeries of utilizable resources. Over time, analysts tend toward one or the other positions on this list, or only slowly change their way of seeing things. You might read the "Basic Issues" list now (p 193) to try to see to what extent you would lean toward one or the other of the alternatives.

Figure 1 (pp. 194–195) lays out the familiar hierarchy of social actors, from the individual to the world system, but we have now inserted the recently conceptualized levels of interorganizational analysis and networks. I indicate some of the major topics of the more general and unfamiliar levels and how we represent some of the levels in diagrams.

Figure 2 presents an example of what a network diagram might look like, with the length of the lines indicating closeness of the organizations. It is a very simple

Figure 2   Imaginary City Health Network

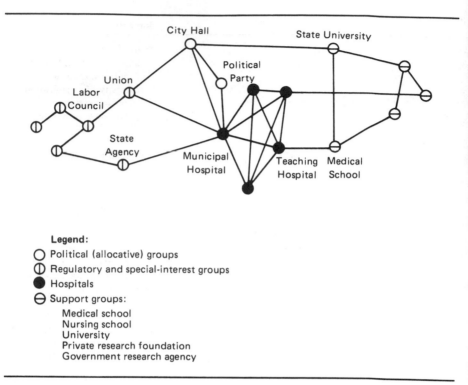

Legend:
○ Political (allocative) groups
⊕ Regulatory and special-interest groups
● Hospitals
⊖ Support groups:
   Medical school
   Nursing school
   University
   Private research foundation
   Government research agency

conception, since it does not indicate the kind of information, resources, dependencies, influences, and so on that move through the channels, nor their direction, and it leaves out the whole funding complex of governmental subsidies, tax breaks, and "third party" fund sources such as insurance companies and medicine. Yet, simple as it is, it has some revealing characteristics.

A Simple Network

Let us assume that Figure 2 deals with part of a health system. The five hospitals (solid dots) would be said to be *tightly coupled;* a "disturbance" or change in any one of them would quickly have ramifications for all the others. Each is linked to the others directly; there are eight links, the maximum number possible. The five organizations on the right (support groups), however, are only *loosely coupled;* they all deal with training or research, but they are not very interdependent. The six organizations on the left can hardly be said to be coupled at all; only two of the six have more than one tie to this network (though they may be tightly coupled to other networks not considered here). These are, let us say, regulatory and special-interest groups.

An action by an organization in this group (i.e., the auditors in a state agency) that affects the municipal hospital run by the city will have consequences for all the organizations in the hospital cluster. It may be the only way for the state auditors to influence the standards and practices of the private and voluntary hospitals, since only in some areas can they control these directly. The results of a state requirement that patients be offered drugs by their generic name rather than by their brand name, to reduce costs to patients and cut profits to dominant drug companies, could set up a chain of interactive influences in all the hospitals and might spill over into other billing practices. This is what we mean by a tightly coupled network; change is fast, and the interactive effects may be unpredictable.[32]

The effect of this change on the large medical school in the area would be considerably "dampened," however, since it is linked only to the voluntary hospital that is the main teaching hospital for the medical school. The medical school is not likely to respond to state agency directives that affect primarily the municipal hospital, though some effects will be felt. Nor are the other organizations on the right-hand side likely to be affected. They are linked to one another and to the medical school, but not closely.

City Hall has the farthest reach of any of the organizations, even though it is not closely tied (in terms of distance of line) to any but the dominant political party. It can reach into the supportive network on the right, the regulatory and interest group network on the left, and the hospital network both directly and through the political party. No other organization has this degree of reach and centrality. The number of ties it has to the health system (all groups except the political party and City Hall itself) is small—only three. The municipal hospital has six. But City Hall can reach farther. Once we know something about the six ties of the hospital, the diagram suggests that the municipal hospital is at the center of the network only by reason of its dependence and its use by other organizations; its centrality does not necessarily mean dominancne.

Though the medical school and the teaching hospital are crucial for the support cluster and the hospital cluster, since they provide the sole important link between the two, they are isolated from the political, the regulatory, and the special-interest organizations. (The diagram is oversimplified in this and in other ways; a self-respecting medical school would not have to go through the state university to reach City Hall, since medicine is too powerful for that in most cities. A more complex diagram would note a more complex relationship.)

None of the organizations on the left are depicted as particularly important, even though they include the hospital council, the labor council, a union to which some municipal hospital employees belong, the welfare department, state regulatory agencies, and perhaps the Community Chest. The labor council has four links, but they don't go anywhere in this network.

The diagram does not suggest that an organization on the edge of the network can only reach, say, City Hall on health matters by literally going through one or two or three other organizations. Of course, direct ties exist and are used for routine and symbolic purposes. What are depicted here, though, are ties that indicate strong

[32]Karl Weick, "Educational Organizations as Loosely Coupled Systems," *Administrative Science Quarterly* 21 (March 1976): 1–19.

influence or power, and the direction may go both ways. For example, if the state university wished to improve the quality of care in the municipal hospital, it might have little clout if it went directly and preached to officials there. However, if it activated City Hall and the dominant political party (which probably allocates positions in the hospital on the basis of patronage), it could exert leverage. Furthermore, if it encouraged the medical school, which is nominally a part of the university but really quite separate, to put pressure on the teaching hospital, which in turn relieves a fair bit of the overcrowding in the municipal hospital by taking away the valuable clinical cases for teaching purposes, a good deal might be done. It is unlikely that the university would care in the normal run of things. But suppose its own internal network of interdependencies—student interests, faculty members connected with the social sciences, and some liberal associations—made it important to take a posture of public service and drain off some student discontent with a special sequence of field courses with social and political content. It could be done.

There are a number of points to be made about this exercise in simple network analysis. First, even though all organizations may be quite aware of each other, and do routine business with each other on occasion, everything does not affect everything else. The number of possible ties in this (simple) network is immense, but most of them would mean little. The popular research techniques of watching mail flows, counting telephone contacts, or giving checklists to executives could be very misleading. Parts of the network are buffered from changes in other parts because there is no powerful link. Some powerful links are not all that obvious (the political ones, in this case). A weak tie may provide a strong link, paradoxically, in network analysis, though there is no good illustration in my example.[33] Some "central" organizations, in this case the municipal hospital, may be central only as a resource for other groups but otherwise may be quite dependent. The hospital supplies jobs for the party and City Hall; provides teaching cases for the teaching hospital and thus the medical school; relieves the private, voluntary hospital from having to care for poor and undesirable patients; supplies members for the union; and gives state agencies leverage with the other hospitals. It is a very useful organization, quite apart from its manifest functions of caring for the poor.

Second, the analysis suggests different degrees of density in different parts of the network. While everything is not tied to everything else, one part of the network is highly interactive, another one only somewhat so, and the third—the regulatory and special-interest groups—hardly interactive at all. Of course, the investigator chooses how to measure the degree of interaction between any two organizations, so it is she who constructs the network to show the density of various parts. This takes more than a count of phone calls or logging of mail; it takes political judgment and detailed case histories. But network analysis allows that kind of information and judgment to be utilized, laid out, and subjected to criticism from others.

Third, the emphasis, the unit of analysis, is the network itself, not the particular organizations in it. Our conceptual vocabulary is not yet developed enough to label this network in any revealing way (moderately complex, multidensity, triadic, or

[33]Mark Granovetter, "The Strength of Weak Ties," *American Journal of Sociology* 78 (May 1973): 1360–1380.

whatever), but it has properties of its own that would distinguish it from other networks. Even if our interest is primarily in one organization, the next level up—network—is crucial, as I indicated in my remarks about Figure 1. The state agency becomes more understandable as an organization in itself if we know that it is cut off from the patronage system, loosely tied to organized labor, loosely tied to most hospitals and tightly tied to the municipal hospital, and cut off from all support groups. In another city or state, a similar agency might be tightly linked to the dominant political party and the patronage system, to the medical school and other support groups including the university; thus its power might be considerable. We can best understand a particular organization if we understand the network it has to play in.

Furthermore, we could use network analysis to examine changes over time. The federal government has become more active in health politics, it supplies more and more of the funds for construction, equipment, and patient costs, so it can require health organizations to do things in order to keep receiving funding. Thus, over time, it can increase the density of parts of the network, perhaps by adding organizations such as "health maintenance organizations," and decrease the importance of other organizations (perhaps organized labor or the local medical society). Charting networks over time would show such shifts.

Network analysis is obviously not limited to health organizations. An industry such as steel might also be analyzed in these terms. To convert our rudimentary diagram, consider the center cluster as the primary producers, the right-hand cluster as the industrial customers, with the medical school being a major auto manufacturer whose actions will affect the appliance industry and others in the cluster. City Hall, the central one despite its apparent isolation, is analogous to the central banks, and the left-hand cluster the supportive infrastructure and government. Laumann and Pappi[34] have attempted such an analysis in a small German town and an industrial city in the Midwest using techniques that allow the graphic representation of social distance. The technique is complicated and still somewhat controversial, and as yet, the findings are not much different from what conventional analysis might predict with much less effort. Still, it is a pioneering effort and organizational theorists should consider it seriously.[35]

Another recent development involves "blockmodeling" techniques developed by Harrison White and Scott Boorman.[36] The notion here is that actual ties between organizations are not necessary for them to be in a similar position in a

[34]Edward O. Laumann and Franz U. Pappi, "New Directions in the Study of Community Elites," *American Sociological Review* 38, no. 2 (April 1973): 212–230; E. O. Laumann, Lois M. Verbrugge, and F. U. Pappi, "A Casual Modelling Approach to the Study of a Community Elite's Influence Structure," *American Sociological Review* 39, no. 2 (April 1974): 162–174; and E. O. Laumann, *Networks of Collective Action* (New York: Academic Press, 1976).

[35]A scheme that inspired my illustration, and is more useful for organizational analysis than Laumann's, is presented by Howard Aldrich and David Whetten, "Organization Sets, Action Sets, and Networks: Making the Most of Simplicity," in *Handbook of Organizational Designs*, vol. 1, ed. Paul Nystrom and William Starbuck (New York: Oxford University Press, 1981), pp. 385–408.

[36]The most accessible introduction to applying this technique to organizations is Paul DiMaggio, "Structural Analysis of Organizational Fields," in *Annual Review of Research on Organizations*, vol. 8, ed. Barry Staw and L. L. Cummings (Greenwich, Conn.: JAI Press, forthcoming).

network—a position called "structural equivalency." Two state agencies may have only the most trivial interaction, but since both have important interactions with City Hall and the university, only trivial ones with health agencies, and perhaps strong dependency relationships with the labor council, they are in equivalent positions in the structure even though they themselves don't interact. In a large data set, "structures" can be discerned that are not visible through ordinary analysis and may be quite nonintuitive.

A Health System Analyzed

To illustrate the development of increasingly sophisticated views of the environment over time, I will again use an example from the health field and review the fictional history of research on "Westwood Hospital." While fictional, it draws on the experiences of researchers, illustrates how far we have come, and demonstrates the importance of network analysis. Let us say Westwood is a private voluntary hospital in Regional City serving largely a middle- and upper-class clientele. A study made in the early 1960s would have focused on the internal structure and leadership, with some vague reference to the environment. In the late 1960s it would have been an interorganizational study, focusing on Westwood, but now examining the major organizations it had contact with. This shift from an organizational to interorganizational framework would have considerable impact. For example, in the early 1960s, one might have made an intensive analysis of the characteristics of key medical officers—the chief of staff, chief of surgery, and so on. The administrator of the hospital and the president of the board of trustees would have commented on the kind of person they desired, and the matter would be fully "explained"—they selected the best women and men. But in the late 1960s it would be noted that Westwood was a teaching hospital for the major medical school in the area, State University Medical School. This meant that medical school professors and students used the patients in Westwood as teaching material. The school would have a major interest in who was chief of staff or chief of surgery at the hospital. It could easily turn out that appointments to such key offices were really dictated by the dean of State University Medical School, and the judgments of the trustees and the administrator counted for little. After the fact, the latter would justify the selection on the basis of vague qualities (such as leadership, outstanding skill as an internist, ability to cooperate effectively with the medical school), but they actually would have had little choice.

A second example: the administrator of the hospital may have wanted to cut back on the outpatient department because it cost so much and attracted too many poor patients. But these patients were useful teaching cases, so the medical school dean would have discussed the matter with a trustee of Westwood one day at the country club, and no cut would be made. Interviewed by an organizational researcher in 1962 as to why the outpatient department was maintained, the administrator probably would have said "public service" to the researcher, but "the power structure" to himself. Interviewed by a researcher in 1968, who had taken the trouble to conduct some interviews at the medical school first (thus using an interorganizational framework), the question could have been phrased: "How important is it to the trustees to keep the affiliation with the medical school—for example, is this why you have such a large outpatient department?" The answer would have been: "Of course, that tie means a lot to them, and while the department gives me problems, it also helps the hospital to have all those interns and residents around doing the work the private physicians are too busy to do." A public service is provided, but now it appears that this was a side benefit, not the major purpose. The difference is substantial. A rational, official goal perspective is replaced by a political perspective that sees the organization as having multiple functions, one of which may be, but not necessarily to any great extent, public service.

By 1973 there could have been a further shift in conceptualization. A researcher might not even have Westwood in mind as the focal point of her research. In the course of trying to understand how the medical "system" works in Regional City, she would interview executives at the four major hospitals, the medical society, the medical school, a few rehabilitation agencies, the Community Chest, and the hospital council. The questions would probably be simple ones—how much contact does each have with the others; who initiates the contact; what is the principal business transacted (e.g., sharing resources, sending or receiving patients, providing information, coordinating development plans, etc.)? Unfortunately, we would probably not be privy to the insight that Westwood and the medical school have a symbiotic relationship, wherein each feeds on the other, and that this keeps the tradition of free or low-cost care to the poor alive. Counting contacts will not disclose that. But nevertheless the researcher would find that Presbyterian Hospital is at the center of the system, of which Westwood is a part, directing information and requests to the other hospitals and sitting on more community boards than any other. She would be able to note that Westwood seeks information from Presbyterian before acting and presents requests for expansion or a larger slice of the Community Chest budget to committees whose chairpersons are closely tied to Presbyterian.

Now Westwood again looks different. It is a fairly dependent part of the whole. What the 1962 researcher saw as a major battle between the medical staff, administrator, and the trustees concerning the form of expansion could now be seen as a very narrow issue, the terms of which were set by Presbyterian and, say, the medical school. Westwood could decide to do either A or B, but it was not allowed to consider D, E, F, and G, any one of which might have been much better and perhaps avoided the internal conflict that the choice of either A or B created.

By the 1980s, another researcher might be able to put Westwood into a still larger context. For example, she might find that the medical system in Regional City is made up of clusters of highly interactive organizations and interests, but the clusters themselves are only loosely connected to each other, such that major federal policies have strong effects upon some clusters but weak ones upon others, and that federal policies in turn are shaped by national interests that are formed out of numerous cities such as Regional City. (The rising involvement of the government makes an interorganizational or network viewpoint more necessary now, but it would have been just as appropriate in the 1950s and, of course, has always been appropriate for modern business and industry.)

To be more specific about the link between federal policies and local networks, suppose we find that Westwood is about to expand greatly with highly specialized facilities and expensive new wings, using a mixture of federal, state, and city tax dollars, Community Chest funds, and private donations. This is a sign, one might have thought, of a healthy expanding organization, drawing resources from its environment and providing services in return. There is a dynamic administrator at the head, and his relations with the trustees and the medical staff are excellent.

A network analysis might reason differently. Suppose we simplify things greatly and say there are two aspects of government aid to medical care. One system is concerned with medical research, innovative techniques, and upgrading of hospital standards. The other is concerned with the distribution of medical services—matters such as excess beds in some areas, excess operating equipment that is rarely used, and the access of the poor to medical care. Each system has its own network of public and private organizations, but the two systems are only loosely joined to each other; there are different agencies, different politicians, and different commercial groups in each cluster. (The two clusters share a basic set of beliefs about health matters, however. Neither would advocate socialized medicine, for example.)

The first system is a tightly coupled network. There are many points of interaction where information, advice, help, and resources are shared and traded. It includes the powerful medical-equipment industry and the medical-supply industry (two of the most profitable industries on record for over two decades, along with the pharmaceutical industry). These actively promote research, innovation, new equipment, and more beds in more hospitals. It also includes the organized medical profession, the heads of the large metropolitan medical centers where most of the research is done and the highest-quality care is provided, and the insurance industry. One indicator of a tightly coupled network is the extent that people can move freely among the organizations. Though it has not as yet been documented, there are strong suggestions[37] that people move freely among: (1) government health agencies; (2) the American Medical Association; (3) the equipment, supply, and drug companies; (4) the leading medical centers; and (5) the major insurance firms such as Blue Cross or Prudential.

Let us say a "disturbance" occurs in this sector. A Congressman wants to show that he supports something that is noncontroversial, so he selects health research as an issue, builds a powerful committee, and gets bills through that literally flood the agencies with money. In a tightly coupled network the effect is immediately felt. Regional City political leaders belong to the Congressman's party; they have additional links to members of the network through prep schools, elite vacation spots, memberships in private clubs, and so on. They are making plans even before the new government programs are announced. One is to upgrade hospital standards by providing funds for expensive new equipment and services (all rarely used).

Presbyterian Hospital is the natural candidate to receive this largess, but it is already glutted with expensive gadgets, and it lacks space for expansion. The blacks in the adjoining area have protested expansion plans. The matter will be taken care of in time, for the banks in Regional City have been persuaded to "red line" the

[37]Barbara and John Ehrenreich, *The American Health Empire: Power, Profits, Politics* (New York: Vintage Books, 1971).

area (refuse to lend money to those in poor areas who want to improve their properties or put up new buildings); the police are withdrawing and concentrating in the adjacent middle-class area. Soon it can be declared a disaster area, and the hospital will acquire condemned land for new buildings, parking, housing for nurses, and so on. But that will take time. So Westwood Hospital becomes the logical choice to receive the funds. But there are problems. The medical school wants more control over appointments to its staff, and middle-income people want easier access to beds. Both of these can be accommodated with some effort. But some segments of the local power structure insist that lower-income people in Westwood's area should continue to have access to it. It is a middle-class hospital but admits a sizable proportion of lower-class people too, largely but not exclusively for teaching purposes.

Meanwhile, in another part of the federal bureaucracy, there are other developments. This "distribution" system is less tightly coupled than the "resource" system described above, so things move slowly, and the pressure groups around this part of the Federal bureaucracy have only partially shared interests. There are liberal politicians, liberal groups such as the National Council of Churches and the NAACP, liberal foundations, and, in uneasy alliance, some consumer-oriented health groups ranging from moderate to radical. The general concern is for more equitable access to health facilities for low-income people and the very poor. But there is also a concern with the extraordinary growth in cost of the health system and attendant wastage.

In particular, Regional City is declared as an overbedded city—an excess of beds per population—by a key federal agency. The consequences could be severe; Westwood might not expand, and some hospitals with low standards could be closed. Liberal groups nationally and in Regional City are fighting to prevent the closing of poorly financed, poorly run, poorly cleaned, poorly staffed, overcrowded old hospitals in the declining inner city, because the poor cannot get into the better outlying hospitals in the areas. Enough beds have been built in the suburbs to produce an overbedded situation, but there is overcrowding in the central city. In Regional City the target of the federal agency is Good Samaritan Hospital—a firetrap with largely foreign-trained physicians, a high turnover of nurses and technicians, chronic shortage of sheets and bandages, beds in the halls, ancient operating equipment, and largely uninteresting teaching cases. In Regional City a link is finally found between the two systems—the resource-expanding system and the beleaguered distribution system—and an accommodation is worked out. The administrator of Presbyterian Hospital and the administrator of Good Samaritan Hospital have a little chat after an inconclusive meeting of the Regional City Coordinating Council for Medical Care. Until now, they have never conversed, because they move in two very different systems; until now, the Coordinating Council had rarely done much, and this was the first time the chief administrator of Presbyterian had not sent an assistant but came himself.

The accommodation involves a number of informal agreements. First, Good Samaritan will be allowed to conduct a fundraising drive that will be independent of the Community Chest campaign. This is an unusual event and normally the Chest would have prevented it, but the head of the Chest is also a key trustee of

Presbyterian and a judge belonging to the dominant political party. Presbyterian and Westwood will both give the drive full support and ask their large donors to contribute part of their annual tax-saving contributions to Good Samaritan. Second, the city will be persuaded to condemn some property next to Good Samaritan, evict the low-income tenants from two stable apartment houses, and let the hospital take the buildings over for expansion. Third, federal antipoverty funds, channeled through the state and the city, will be used to finance the expansion of Good Samaritan, as long as the liberals will not protest the use of antipoverty funds to help Westwood Hospital expand as well.

Finally, the city ambulance service, which has traditionally been run from Good Samaritan because of its central location, and staffed by them, will be taken over by Westwood. Why? Because this service allocates emergency cases to the major hospitals and can be designed to ship the interesting cases to Presbyterian and Westwood—for teaching purposes and to justify the new exotic facilities—and the uninteresting ones to other hospitals and, in particular, the poor and the disruptive ones to Good Samaritan. Many emergency patients designate the hospital they wish to go to, but the ambulance crews have some latitude, and they will be attentive to their new superiors. The switch is justified on the grounds that Good Samaritan loses money on the ambulance service since the city reimbursement rates are so low. This is true, but hospital operating costs in an era of prepayment for the nonpoor are of little concern to middle-class hospitals, so Westwood won't suffer.

The results of the compromise are extensive. Poverty money that had been tied up by political controversy and charges of mismanagement and corruption can now be allocated to both the poor and the rich hospitals. Neither of the good hospitals will be flooded with undesirable patients but will receive a sufficient stream of good teaching cases, increase occupancy somewhat, and justify expansion of beds and facilities. The poor hospital will receive resources and some relief from its crushing burden of poor patients. There is even vague talk of a geriatric hospital that could be attached to Good Samaritan to segregate the dying poor. (Westwood and Presbyterian have the bed space to handle the dying nonpoor.) Both the resource and the distribution systems are satisfied, since there will be federal money for more facilities and yet a poor hospital slated for closing will be revived. The overbedding problem is intensified, unfortunately, but it is primarily a bed-distribution problem and there is no easy solution for that (as with the problem of the maldistribution of physicians).

At the proper time, if the systems were well managed and well coordinated in just this one instance, it would be convenient to have the local spokesperson for the poor clamor for an expansion and improvement of the only hospital the poor can be assured of getting into, whereupon the conservative mayor would show his responsiveness and leadership by announcing plans for the expansion of Good Samaritan. Meanwhile, Westwood officials would call a press conference and discuss the new challenges of medical technology and how they plan to meet them. Most trustees of Westwood, not privy to our network analysis, would be thrilled by the leadership their hospital is showing.

A naive researcher operating out of an organizational analysis framework, or even an organization set one, would not be likely to even connect the two events —the expansion of Westwood and Good Samaritan. She could cite the latter case as an example of the creative use of antipoverty funds, the responsiveness of local officials given the new-found power of the blacks, and the generosity of large donors. If she were studying Westwood, she might discuss how an organization adjusts to the turbulent environment of technological change, or how dynamic, farsighted leadership makes a difference for organizations, or how an organization's "problems" can be solved if administrators, trustees, and medical leaders sit down and plan and work together. All of these are possible; such things do happen. But in this case, none of them did in fact occur. Westwood was a rather dependent part of a system in which it had nonobvious links to both Presbyterian and Good Samaritan; it was allowed to act, and it was given a script; the script reflected a struggle at the federal level; and the best and the worst hospitals in the city made the actual compromise that created Westwood's script.

The analysis just presented bears a stronger resemblance to sophisticated muck-raking journalism than it does to conventional organizational analysis.[38] This is not surprising. Our preoccupation, as the previous chapters of this book demonstrate, has been with the organization. Political reporters are concerned with how organizations can be used in political and social struggle. They cast a larger net; doing so changes the picture.

To summarize this lesson: only a network analysis, and one that reaches up into the national system, can properly describe what happened to one of the organizations. Dynamics at the organizational level or at the set level would be seriously misinterpreted without this larger understanding. It was particularly important to know how tightly or loosely connected the systems were, the dependencies of the organizations, the circumstances in which very weak links (the Coordinating Council) could prove to be crucial, and the rationalizations and justifications that masked the actual process. When we can perform actual analysis such as this one we will have moved organizational analysis a very long way from its present status.

The Network and the Background

But even the fictitious example of Westwood Hospital still carries the trace of conceptual baggage that should be closely examined. I described two general positions in the national context of health care—an expansionary one with emphasis on new technologies, research, and high standards of care (for elite hospitals), and a distributive one concerned with the poor, the application of present knowledge to

[38]The example of the ambulance firm in this account was inspired by Murray Milner's excellent *Unequal Care: A Case Study of Interorganizational Relations in Health Care* (New York: Columbia University Press, 1980), and by a series of news articles in the *New York Times* in early 1978 dealing with "patient snatching" by the city ambulance system. For two other excellent medical studies that verge on a network analysis, see Robert Alford, *Health Care Politics* (Chicago: University of Chicago Press, 1977); and Kenneth McNeil and Edmond Minihan, "Regulation of Medical Devices and Organizational Behavior in Hospitals," *Administrative Science Quarterly* 22, no. 3 (September 1977): 475–490. The health field has probably moved the farthest in an interorganizational direction; indeed, the topic originated there. But the specific organization-environment studies have not been particularly imaginative. Though not concerned with interorganizational matters per se, the best insights still come from the several outstanding works of David Mechanic and Eliot Friedson.

the segregated sectors of society lacking in decent care, and the maldistribution of beds and physicians. What is not revealed is the extent to which the two systems share the same values, and the extent to which both would reject socialized medicine, a massive reduction in emphasis on new technologies and research, and a massive increase in preventive facilities, public health measures, and occupational and environmental standards. Outside of the truly radical literature on health care, there is a common "ground" against which we see the "figure."[39] A network analysis presents a figure, which is largely visible because of the background which it is set off from; dissolve that background and the figure is no longer so visible. The nature of the background highlights the figure and thus suggests what we should examine. It should be the task of the sociologist to examine the background as well.

Only one substantial piece of research has moved in this direction. It is not all that new—the research was conducted from 1968 to 1970 and published in 1974. But none of the several new extensive network studies that I know of since makes any attempt to consider the ground as well as the figure. In most of our work on networks, our conceptual and ideological baggage, developed in the context of solving managerial problems within organizations, has merely been put on a new train and opened up again at a new destination without having been enriched or changed by the journey. Network analysis should permit us to challenge our previous understandings, and this one piece of research makes a tentative step in that direction. The book in question is Roland Warren, Steven Rose, and Ann Bergunder's *The Structure of Urban Reform.*[40]

Warren and his associates examined the operation of the Model Cities program, part of the Great Society program of President Lyndon Johnson, which was designed to introduce new community action agencies into urban areas, to stimulate coordination among all agencies concerned with social problems, and to promote innovative responses to these problems. The problems had been documented extensively since the early 1960s when the civil rights movement, the peace movement, and the student movement heightened public awareness of poverty, decay, discrimination, and helplessness in a rich and bountiful society. One part of the analysis was that existing social agencies were too entrenched in traditional ways of doing things; in addition, their actions were not coordinated, even though the problems demanded coordinated attack; and, finally, there were unattended problems and areas of life that would need new agencies. The Model Cities program was designed to rectify the situation.

The prevailing conception at the time (and continuing today in most quarters) was that attempts to deal with poverty and decay were chaotic because of the hundreds of organizations, each going its own way, refusing to cooperate, fighting one another for money, areas of influence, and even clients. Executives were so distracted by the chaos and interactions that they had little time to plan or direct their own agencies. Model Cities programs were introduced to produce cooperation and coordination through centralized planning and through large chunks of new money.

[39]This point and the analogy were suggested by John Meyer.

[40]Roland Warren, Stephen Rose, and Ann Bergunder, *The Structure of Urban Reform* (Lexington, Mass.: Lexington Books, 1974).

Warren had been thinking and writing about community agencies for a long time, and he was gradually beginning to question these very plausible conceptions of how the agencies interacted. He and his associates conducted a fairly intensive study of six key agencies in each of nine representative cities during the stormy years 1968–1970. Rather than assuming what the situation was and then looking for new solutions, they asked:

1. How much actual interaction was there between the agencies in this supposedly dense network of interactive relations? Very little, it turned out to the surprise of most of us. Agencies mostly went their own way.
2. Well, what about the contest over "domains" and competition for funds? Very little actually occurred; where it did, it was not because an organization saw an opportunity and moved aggressively to occupy the "niche" of another, but because one occasionally bumped into another without looking and had to sort the problem out.
3. What, then, about the lack of coordination? Little was needed; there was an overall consensus as to who should do what, a division of labor or of sectors, and new formal coordination mechanisms did not increase the efficiency of the agencies. As others have pointed out, coordination has costs associated with it, as well as presumed benefits, and there may be substantial gains with redundant, uncoordinated activity and substantial costs with coordination that eliminates backup facilities.[41]
4. But with new coordinating agencies and new funds, was there not an increase in innovative attacks on problems? If there was, it was exceedingly small, since the agencies averaged only five to six minor innovations and one moderate innovation per year; there were virtually no major ones (defined as involving a shift from emphasizing individual deviance or deficiency as the cause of urban problems to an emphasis on the dysfunctions of the institutional structure such as lack of jobs, discrimination, exploitation, and so on). They note that others who have reviewed the history of the Model Cities program have come to similar conclusions regarding the lack of innovation.[42]

What, then, can we make of it all? Rather than a picture of a disorganized, crowded interorganizational field with great competition for scarce funds and other resources, the research teams came away from their two years of continuous field observations in nine cities with evidence of a high degree of organization, with stable patterned relationships that had little contest or conflict, very little contact or interdependence, and almost no change. Why? Because the agencies shared a common "institutionalized thought structure."[43] This is the "ground" that, once seen, altered the nature of the network or "figure" that would be set off. Warren and his associates stress the similarity of this thought structure not only within each of the cities but among the cities, even though they differed widely in other ways. The thought structure holds that American society, though hardly perfect, is essen-

[41]Martin Landau, "Redundancy, Rationality, and the Problem of Duplication and Overlap," *Public Administration Review* 29, no. 4 (July/August 1969). Robert Morris and Ilana Hirsch-Lescohier, "Service Integration: To What Problems Is It the Presumed Solution?" in *The Management of Human Services,* ed. Rosemary C. Sarri and Yeheskel Hasenfeld (New York: Columbia University Press, 1978).
[42]Warren, Rose, and Bergunder, *The Structure of Urban Reform,* p. 90.
[43]Ibid., pp. 19–25.

tially sound in its institutional composition. Problems are transitory, the result of temporary malfunctions, or reside in the character of individuals. Furthermore, "any group of people who share the same interests and concerns can organize and bring their interests to the attention of appropriate governmental bodies,"[44] and if they don't, it's their own fault. (This is the sociological doctrine of "pluralism," which has come under increasing attack in the last fifteen years.) Furthermore, if problems still remain, a constant process of organizational reform and comprehensive planning and coordination will rectify them if people are tolerant and patient.

Guided by such assumptions, there is little need for interaction, let alone conflict among the agencies. When a new agency comes in, there is some disturbance but plenty of room to accommodate the newcomer and its money. Agencies agree on the nature of the clients, the basic soundness of the system, and the ameliorative steps that should be taken. When more radical philosophies are occasionally espoused, they are quickly made to conform to the institutionalized thought structure.

Warren, Rose, and Bergunder explicitly do not argue that lazy administrators or greedy politicians or callous, indifferent agencies lay behind the ineffectiveness of the programs. (This would be the emphasis of both run-of-the-mill muckrakers and of those liberals who persist in using a strictly organizational perspective, focusing on leadership.) The interorganizational field was not even deliberately structured to protect the interests of the individual agencies; given the institutionalized thought structure, their interests were bound to be protected. To them, the problems were temporary, or they resided in the deficient character of those with the problems. It is customary in some quarters, the authors say, to criticize the agencies for promoting their own needs rather than those of the poor, yet given the prevailing assumptions about the problem and the structure of relationships among agencies that is consistent with their view of the problem, agency needs are bound to take precedence. If one agency steps out of line, it is necessary to force it back into line or the whole web of understandings and relationships will be disrupted.[45] Finally, the web is neither as dense nor as complex as we generally think; there is surprisingly little interaction, conflict, or need for accommodation. As they repeatedly insist, focusing on one organization, or a pair of organizations, would be quite misleading; only when the network is examined is the single organization placed in the proper perspective.

THE POPULATION-ECOLOGY MODEL

The human ecology, population-ecology, or the sociological formulation of natural selection theory has been around for several decades in sociology, but only in the last few years has it found its niche in organizational theory.[46] It has lodged there,

---

[44]Ibid., p. 21.

[45]Ibid., p. 34.

[46]The first and most influential statement of the ecological view of organizations was Michael T. Hannan and John Freeman, "The Population Ecology of Organizations," *American Journal of Sociology* 82, no. 5 (March 1977): 929–966. See also Michael Micklin and Harvey Choldin, eds., *Sociological Human Ecology: Contemporary Issues and Applications* (Boulder, Colo.: Westview Press, 1984), especially the

I think, because once we began to consider the environment seriously, we were tempted to think of the environment as a more or less unanalyzed thing that could *act.* The language of this school of thought is decisively anthropomorphic: environments act, organizations respond; environments select some organizations for extinction and allow others to survive. This is the meaning of natural selection—it is "in nature" or "natural" for some organizations to be "selected out" or "negatively selected" (killed) and others to be "selected in" or "positively selected" by the environment.

There must be natural laws behind this, the theorists reason, that will explain the types of organizations we have. Indeed, such laws are being discovered for the survival of types of fish in lakes or fruit flies in a laboratory or prehistoric tribes faced with the onset of an ice age. They have been used to explain the succession of racial or ethnic groups in areas of Chicago. Why not explain populations of organizations in the same way? Organizations can be said to exist in an ecological setting, just as the pond is an ecological setting for fish. Independent of any of the individuals in these organizations or individuals directing them, they may be subject to laws governing the competition for resources; they may have the ability to adapt to changes in the pond, to retain adaptive forms or programs within them; and to grow complex as the pond grows complex. Principles formulated for general systems theory are adapted, such as the law of requisite variety: organization structure should be only as complex as the complexity existing in the environment. To be less complex reduces adaptability; to be more complex signifies waste.

This raises an old problem that has dogged sociology: because groups and society resemble the natural world in many respects, we tend to interpret things as being "in nature" or natural, or, in our favorite formulation, as "functional." Sociology is a liberal profession, so it is not inclined to extend the mantle of natural to all things; differences in income or on scores on standardized tests between blacks and whites are not considered natural; they are developed by people through a process of discrimination. But in less touchy areas, we are inclined to say that if a pattern of behavior exists, or if it has existed for a long time, it must serve some societal purpose or have a function; it is the task of the sociologist to discern that function. On the other hand, there have always been critics of this approach who see the social world as a human construction, indeed, as largely made by an identifiable minority of men and women. Patterns of behavior can have functions, not for "society" but for specific individuals or parts of society such as classes. The pattern of behavior may be quite dysfunctional for other parts, generally for the weaker, dependent, conquered, or enslaved parts. Slavery was certainly a functional pattern of behavior for landowners in the South, but not for the slaves. Thus the critic of the functionalist position is likely to insist on identifying specific groups and avoiding abstractions such as "society" or "man." Similarly, in my criticism of the ecological view of organizations I will insist on identifying specific aspects of the environment

---

focus on the structure of organizations rather than on the population of organizations in one essay of that volume: John D. Kasarda and Charles E. Bidwell, "A Human Ecological Theory of Organizational Structuring," pp. 183–236.

and asking whose interests are served. The natural selection approach, by speaking only of the environment, neglects these considerations.

Often attached to the functionalist and the ecological perspective is an evolutionary one. Those patterns of activity that serve a group or society best will be reinforced and maintained, those that don't will disappear, and the end result is the evolution of a form of activity that provides the best service. Society evolves in the direction of more efficient ways of meeting needs, even though an occasional way may provoke unwanted consequences that society must then cope with. Sometimes it is added that society evolves toward creating ever-higher needs, such as self-fulfillment for individuals rather than just survival. These views have ancient roots in social thought. In recent generations, partly in response to the Social Darwinism we encountered in Chapter 2, they were in some disfavor. But, "conservative" Darwinism was replaced by a "reform" Darwinism; the latter sees progress as under human control rather than the result of survival of the fittest. This progress is not absolute but relative to our evolving intentions.[47] Even this view had its problems, so today, those who look for evolutionary patterns are quick to disclaim any imputation of value in their scheme. What is new is not necessarily better; one can have evolution without "teleology" (the notion that there is some ideal toward which all things strive). But it is hard to avoid the association of ecological adaptation in human societies with the notion of evolution toward higher forms, explored better fits, more efficiency, and so on. Talcott Parsons, who has explored evolutionary ideas, has recently been criticized on these grounds,[48] and in the scant organizational material in this framework I find the same problem.

The ecological model identifies three stages in a process of social change.[49] First is the occurrence of *variations* in behavior. They may be intended or unintended; it doesn't matter. In organizations, a production crew might gradually vary its techniques, or a shortage of gasoline might lead to a variation in truck-delivery practices. Second, natural *selection* occurs as some variations are eliminated because they are undesirable and others are reinforced because they work. The criterion of effectiveness is simple survival. Third, there is a *retention* mechanism that allows those "positively selected variations" to be retained or reproduced. Since nothing ever stands still, either for those in the organization or for its environment, over the long run positively selected variations that become stable activities will be subject to further variation. The new delivery system may be "selected out" as still another system gets positively selected and built into the structure or behavior of the organization. In the grander scheme of things, the development of a bureaucratic model of organizations was a result of variations in practices, with the firms that tried bureaucracy being successful, thus positively selected. (We shall explore our example of this in Chapter 8.) Meanwhile, the environment changes for some firms,

[47]Mathew Zachariah, "The Impact of Darwin's Theory of Evolution on Theories of Society," *Social Studies* 62, no. 2 (February 1971): 69–76.

[48]See the excellent discussion of evolutionary theory in Mark Granovetter, "The Idea of 'Advancement' in Theories of Social Evolution," *American Journal of Sociology* 88 (1979): 489–515.

[49]Donald Campbell, "Variation and Selection Retention in Socio-Cultural Evolution," *General Systems* 16 (1969): 69–85. Walter Buckley, *Sociology and Modern Systems Theory* (Englewood Cliffs, N.J.: Prentice-Hall, 1967); and Amos Hawley, *Human Ecology: A Theory of Community Structure* (New York: Ronald Press, 1950).

debureaucratization takes place in those dealing with nonroutine tasks, and new decentralized firms appear. This evolution differentiates organizations into types and creates new variations and selection and retention processes.

Let us examine variation first. As with the ecologists and biologists, natural selection theorists in organizations are fond of citing the huge number of organizations in any society and the rapid rate of change—births, deaths, takeovers. In 1957, for example, 398,000 new businesses were created in the United States, about the same number were transferred to new owners, and almost as many failed outright.[50] This generates a great deal of variation, allowing selection and retention, and leading to better fits with the environment. If only fifty firms were created, fifty transferred, and forty-eight died, there would be less chance for the proper "niche" to be found in the environment—the "environment" would have less to select from when it selected positively or negatively.

But the vast majority of the business firms in the United States are extremely tiny. Sixty-eight percent of them had sales of under $25,000; 2 percent of them accounted for 76 percent of the sales. The figures in assets are even more striking: 61 percent of all corporate assets were controlled by one-tenth of one percent of firms in 1972.[51] So the great variation provided by many different units is a variation among trivial organizations that are, in addition, operating at the sufferance of the few large ones. This suggests the model is not appropriate for giant organizations.

But the theorists note that the large organizations also experience variation, selection, and retention *within* them. Here there is a change from the natural model. In contrast to natural organisms, such as fish or amoebas, artificial ones have the capacity to change extensively through structural alteration, thus avoiding extinc-

[50]Howard E. Aldrich, *Organizations and Environments*(Englewood Cliffs, N.J.: Prentice-Hall, 1979).

[51]Ibid., p. 42. Aldrich is in the curious position of being very aware of the concentration of power, and on pages 111–112 he even admits that this stand restricts the applicablity of a population-ecology perspective. Even so, in the first part of the book he makes grand assertions for this model. A later article with William McKelvey (see below) reveals other cracks in the perspective. The perspective clearly needs some settling in.

Mark Granovetter, no fan of the population-ecology model, indirectly supports the importance of small size in the world of organizations in "Small Is Bountiful: Labor Markets and Establishment Size," *American Sociological Review* 49 (June 1984): 323–334. He does so only with "establishments," which include branches of plants, banks and fast-food or dry-cleaning chains. The article might best be retitled "Small Is Trivial, Large Is Powerful," since organizational size is more important than establishment size if a small number of organizations control the capital, labor, and production policies of their many establishments. Establishment size is still large in the manufacturing sector. Seventy-five percent of manufacturing employees, for example, work in establishments with more than 100 employees. I suspect that a fair proportion of the remaining 25 percent work in branch plants, rather than in small businesses. In the trade and service sectors, establishment size is quite small, but I expect most of these are not independent businesses but branch operations. The 1 percent of service organizations that have more than one establishment employ more than 37 percent of all employees in service. Thus there are some very big firms, and there are also large firms with only one establishment. Only 2 percent of retail firms have more than one establishment, but these employ 51.6 percent of all retail employees. And only 5.4 percent of manufacturing firms have more than one establishment, and these employ 76 percent of all manufacturing employees. Thus a small minority of organizations are either very large establishments in themselves or control, through branches, an additional 37 to 76 percent of employees, depending on sector. The size of an establishment has an important social psychological effect in the workplace, but personnel policies, capital investment policies, plant closing and location policies, and labor-substitution technologies are also key variables. Certainly births and deaths of small establishments are decisions that the headquarters of multiestablishment firms make. Small organizations, whether independent or dependent establishments, are trivial organizations.

tion. When fish learned to walk, if that is what they did, it took place over hundreds of centuries; when J. P. Morgan learned to buy up several steel plants and form U. S. Steel Corporation in order to dominate the market, he did it in a matter of years. The evolution of a divisionalized structure at General Motors took decades, but that is a mere mite in terms of natural evolution. The structure was adapted by those industries where it was appropriate, but not by others, illustrating the variability in environments. Organic evolution, then, entails the survival or extinction of entire units; social evolution includes this—all those failing small businesses—but also the structural change of units. (Whether this addition violates the theories borrowed from biology and ecology is not clear. Some population-ecology theorists, such as Aldrich and William McKelvey, admit the structural change of units. Hannan and Freeman have clung to a unit-survival or extinction model by and large.)

But, one can argue, the merger process at the end of the nineteenth century when Morgan formed U. S. Steel and the centralization of power that Alfred Sloan of General Motors effected in the 1930s were not necessarily adaptations to a changing environment. These executives *created* a new environment, and other organizations (and communities, families, and individuals) had to do the adapting. In fact, Gabriel Kolko[52] demonstrates that the mergers of the nineteenth century were quite uneconomical for the first ten or so years and were brought about largely for stock manipulation. *Someone* benefited, of course, or they would not have gone to all that trouble, but it was not society, the communities, or even the industry. Given the new form, ways were found to make it work, but that is quite contrary to the model's logic. Much the same analysis could be made of Sloan's structural changes; society had to adapt to the consequences of them.[53] Karl Weick has been the most forceful advocate of the view that organizations create, or "enact" their environments deliberately, rather than passively await the judgment of the environment to select them into or out of it. He notes that "managers construct, rearrange, single out, and demolish many 'objective' features of their surroundings" as they literally define and create their own constraints in an "enactment-selection-retention" view.[54]

"Why are there so many kinds of animals?" asks a famous essay in ecology. "Why are there so many kinds of organizations?" echo Hannan and Freeman.[55] But this question highlights the difference; in most areas of economic power—railroads, auto manufacturing, oil production and marketing, steel production—there are very few organizations, and they are of the same kind. There are three major U.S. auto manufacturers, and while organizational theorists could pore over the differences among them, in species terms they are very similar. In the social world, then, a different kind of logic seems to be operating. There is not much variation among units; a few giant organizations dominate the many small ones; the giant ones rarely

[52]Gabriel Kolko, *Triumph of Conservatism* (New York: Free Press, 1977).

[53]Charles Perrow, "Is Business Really Changing?" *Organizational Dynamics* (Summer 1974): 31–44; Emma Rothschild, *Paradise Lost: The Decline of the Auto-Industrial Age* (New York: Random House, 1973).

[54]Karl Weick, *The Social Psychology of Organizing*, 2nd ed. (Reading, Mass.: Addison-Wesley, 1979), p. 164.

[55]Hannan and Freeman, "The Population Ecology of Organizations," p. 939.

die (there is little negative selection); and in the public sector, efficiency and adaptation are not effective criteria—we simply do not let public schools and garbage collectors go out of business. If there is little variation and little negative selection, then, what is the value of the theory?

One has the same problems when dealing with internal variation and selection. Here, the organization is the environment for the groups within it. Now, of course, there is change within organizations. For example, some people are fired, groups are disbanded, practices are changed, new technologies are introduced. I have been negatively selected myself on occasion and have selected out others; most of us will have our turns. Which statement was the more illuminating for steelworkers to make when they were laid off in massive numbers starting in 1977: "I was fired today by the environment" or "In its shortsighted concern with profits the major steel companies in the United States refused to modernize their plants and take cognizance of worldwide overproduction of steel during several years of stagnation of the world economy, so they had the workers and the single-industry communities bear the cost of their mismanagement, dramatizing the cost in the media. This brought pressure on the federal government to institute a variety of 'welfare' programs for the industry that will further subsidize inefficient management and plants through tax breaks and import restrictions. This solution makes the workers more tractable and displaces the burden of ineffective management to the taxpayers in general"?

The second statement sees the "environment" in terms of specific groups and interests, political and economic power, choices and decisions that are made by people and could have easily been different. The first statement—"I was fired today by the environment"—suggests that vague natural forces were working in that direction. It is almost as if God does the negative and positive selecting.

Or take the law of requisite variety—organizations will be as complex as their environment. In some cases, it makes some sense; as corporations grew, the unions had to grow in complexity, differentiating and specializing to cope with their antagonists (though they are far less differentiated and specialized than the corporations they deal with). In other cases, it makes more sense to see organizations as creating their environment and displacing the costs of operation onto the environment. The differentiation and specialization of industrial tasks that took place at the end of the nineteenth century, we have argued, were means of labor control and wage reduction. There was no "environment" out there with a complexity that had to be matched. The policies changed the environment, which had to react with social legislation, industrial conflict, and community disruption, but the reaction was not in terms of law of requisite variety.

Thus the new model of organization-environment relations in the strict natural selection form of Hannan and Freeman, Glenn Carroll,[56] and others tends to be a mystifying one, removing much of the power, conflict, disruption, and social-class variables from the analysis of social processes. It neglects the fact that our world is made in large part by particular men and women with particular interests. Instead, it searches for ecological laws that transcend the hubbub that sociology should attend to. It will have a promising future, I fear, because it is allied with the

[56]Glenn R. Carroll, "Organizational Ecology," *Annual Review of Sociology* 10 (1984): 71–93.

prestigious natural sciences,[57] is amenable to the statistical tools we have developed and the emphasis on large surveys, and is, in a curious way, comforting.

The evolutionary model is itself evolving from the pure birth-and-death model of natural selection, and I think that relaxing some of the unrealistic assumptions of the pure model and "contaminating" it with much more social, rather than biological, dynamics will make its insights more productive. The work of Hannan and Freeman forces us to look at populations of organizations, to consider the conditions under which organizations are likely to be born and die at significant rates and those under which this is not likely to happen, to examine the conditions under which "generalist," multipurpose, or multigoal organizations will have advantages and those under which specialist are more likely to survive, and to assess more accurately when strategic decision making by leaders will make a difference and when it will not. These are important variables. There is no agreement about their effect, but the three variations on the pure model that I will briefly review indicate the direction in which research might move to evaluate these effects.

William McKelvey and Howard Aldrich are card-carrying evolutionists, but recent work by them pays more attention to the internal competencies of organizations, trying to specify the adaptations that permit survival; they also forward a notion that makes niches less of a passive, "out there" environment of systems, and more of an enacted one. McKelvey attempts to specify the "competence elements" of organizations—such as knowledge and skills embedded in the personnel, and records and routines of the organization that increase its survival. This is close to Philip Selznick's concept of "distinctive competencies," but its more specific nature makes it more available for comparative analysis. It goes far beyond a simple distinction of generalists and specialists. It acknowledges that chance is linked to internal organizational processes; it does not merely represent uninvestigated variations from which the environment selects. More important, McKelvey and Aldrich try to include the role of government policies that change the environment in which organizations operate, thus bringing in power, at least through the back door. They note, for example, that the airline industry, until deregulation, could pass on the costs of high wages and slack management to customers, a significant inefficiency at the system level. Power is implicit in the discussion of specific industries, as when large firms in the electronics industry create markets for small firms and can dominate them.

McKelvey and Aldrich further specify how competencies become retained, as through manuals and informal training that passes skills on to younger people when the older leave—hardly a novel notion, but one that is needed to make firms more dynamic and changing, since the pure birth-and-death model treats competencies

---

[57]Rather it is allied with a superficial reading of these sciences; for example, the basic tenet that a turbulent environment favors complex structures, taken almost for granted by this school and echoed in contingency theory, is not a basic tenet of ecology and biology. Under turbulent conditions *simple* structures may survive best; only if there are rather unique and strong selection pressures (such as might be found in human communities where symbols and power play such dominant roles) is the correlation between stability and complexity likely to appear. See the brief note on this in Granovetter, "Idea of Advancement" and his reference to the work of Robert May, *Stability and Complexity in Model Ecosystems* (Princeton, N.J.: Princeton University Press, 1973). See also Stephen Gould, "A Threat to Darwinism," *Natural History* 89, no. 4 (1975): 9.

as the results of a nearly random process. Significantly, they note that there is little struggle for existence in regulated industries, educational institutions, hospitals, government agencies, or the military. Organizations, they argue, have more ability to adapt than organisms, altering niches and their own ability to be steered. The contrast of organizations and organisms is essential if we are to pursue population-ecology models.

These writers provide a role for strategy and structural changes. Uncertainty is the key variable here. In industries where certainty is high (presumably highly concentrated ones), managers can ensure survival through strategic choices and structural changes. But where considerable uncertainty exists, internal selection guided by leaders will have less of an impact than will the classical variables of variation, retention, and struggle. (McKelvey and Aldrich could have noted that highly concentrated industries and large government bureaucracies, capable of exercising strategic choice, are also capable of shaping the environment of the firms where uncertainty prevails and where the classical variation, selection, and retention model is supposed to operate.) Finally, they stress, as Richard Nelson and Sidney Winter have done before them (see below), the very important point that "sometimes resources are so generous that no selection takes place."[58]

This enlarged view might meet some of the objections that Graham Astley and Andrew Van de Ven make in a survey of current organizational theory. In one section of their essay, they raise the extremely important point that a population need not be defined "as a simple aggregation of organizations governed by external economic forces," as in industrial economics and population ecology. Instead, following *human* ecologists such as Amos Hawley, much cited but rarely used, a population is an integrated system with functional interdependencies, some members drawing resources directly from the environment, others indirectly through other members. Members develop symbiotic relationships that ensure the continued existence of the interorganizational network as a whole and thus are protected from the ravages of the environment. Competition (and thus births and deaths) among members is muted by the overriding need to share resources and protect the collectivity. Social and political, rather than economic, forces are emphasized. Drawing on Hawley, Astley and Van de Ven say, "While some degree of power is held by all units, this power varies inversely with the number of steps that a unit is removed from direct environmental contact, with the result that power relationships between organizations grow ever more elaborate as interorganizational networks attain greater closure." This comes close to Kenneth Benson's notion of "political economy," they add, since political negotiations regulate the flow of economic resources through the network. This enlarged view of a population, emphasizing network properties rather than isolated organizations in a population, is consistent with network analysis, industry as a context of organizations, and the notion of "sectors" that we will encounter at the end of the next chapter. It brings many sociological variables back into analysis. A subsequent article by Astley develops these themes

---

[58]Bill McKelvey and Howard Aldrich, "Populations, Natural Selection, and Applied Organizational Science," *Administrative Science Quarterly* 28 (March 1983): 115; and Bill McKelvey's massive *Organizational Systematics* (Berkeley: University of California Press, 1982).

and also highlights the role of radical, discontinuous changes that occur with the wholesale extinction of old populations and their replacement by new ones. Selection pressures are temporarily suspended, and random processes come to play a key role.[59]

The final evolutionary model we shall consider in this chapter comes from Richard Nelson and Sidney Winter's book *An Evolutionary Theory of Economic Change.*[60] This work extends the notion of competencies and power found in the McKelvey-Aldrich model, is consistent with the human ecology view of Hawley and Astley and Van de Ven, and is quite sociological. (Nelson and Winter are economists, and one main thrust of their book is a devastating critique of the theory of firms and industries as found in neoclassical economics.)

Nelson and Winter's model is a loose, commodious evolutionary model that emphasizes many processes familiar to sociologists, such as incremental change and gradual adaptation; limited rationality in the area of cause-effect relations, goals, information, and internal cohesion; and a healthy skepticism regarding efficiency and equilibria. In keeping with more advanced network theorizing, Nelson and Winter point out that environments are not necessarily external; pricing policies of the firms bring the environment in. Economists today are mathematical modelers; mathematics is the language of the field. So Nelson and Winter construct a mathematical model for an industry, employing some of those variables that most economists ignore, and demonstrate that it does better than the models currently in use.

Nelson and Winter restrict their theory to organizations that are large and complex, provide goods and services on a repetitive basis, and have at least some criteria for efficient operation. The natural selection model has no such restrictions, so we should recognize the limitations of Nelson and Winter's notions of routine and survivability that we shall discuss. But their model does have the merit of dealing with nontrivial organizations in our economy. Chapter 5 in their book discusses the key matter of routines in organizations; I will focus on this, since it illustrates an evolutionary model in practice, and not incidentally it is the best discussion of routines in organization that exists in the literature. Routines severely limit the neoclassical view of "optimal choice from a sharply defined set of capabilities" *(96)* and also demonstrate an internal survival mechanism that contrasts with the natural selection view of the economic environment as accounting for all births and deaths. Internal routines, copied from other organizations in many cases, will dampen the effects of environmental perturbations over time.[61] I will summarize

[59]W. Graham Astley and Andrew H. Van de Ven, "Central Perspectives and Debates in Organizational Theory," *Administrative Science Quarterly* 28 (1983): 245–273; quotes are from pp. 258, 260. See Amos Hawley, *Human Ecology: A Theory of Community Structure* (New York: Ronald Press, 1950), and "Human Ecology," in *The International Encyclopedia of the Social Sciences*, vol. 4, ed. David L. Sills (New York: Crowell-Collier and Macmillan, 1968), pp. 328–337; Kenneth Benson, "The Interorganizational Network as a Political Economy," *Administrative Science Quarterly* 20 (1975): 229–249; and W. Graham Astley, "The Two Ecologies: Population and Community Perspectives on Organizational Change," *Administrative Science Quarterly* (June 1985): 224–241.

[60]Richard Nelson and Sidney Winter, *An Evolutionary Theory of Economic Change* (Boston: Belknap Press, 1982). Page numbers in parentheses in the text refer to this book.

[61]More technically, the comparative profitability of routines determines which routines will predominate over time. Profitability, in turn, depends on the characteristics of the market prices that confront the

some of the key propositions of this chapter to illustrate the fruitful interaction of economics and traditional organizational analysis.

"Organizations *remember* by *doing.*" *(99)* They keep records and write manuals, but memory involves more than this. Organizations detail aspects of routines such as signals from machine wear or incomplete pieces of work that trigger action, coordination aids that evolve without clear intention, modifications of equipment, and the evolution of informal structures and work environments. There are also routines, seldom needed, for meeting changing circumstances. Knowledge itself is a product of routines; it must be exercised or used, they add, to be available and routines do this. There is little room for optimal choices of sharply defined alternatives or other features of rationality in this view.

Nelson and Winter recognize internal politics: "Routine operation involves a comprehensive truce in intraorganizational conflict. There is a truce between the supervisor and those supervised at every level in the organizational hierarchy: the usual amount of work gets done, reprimands and compliments are delivered with the usual frequency, and no demands are presented for major modifications in the terms of the relationship." *(110)* Vested interests are a key in this model. Members seek to assure that their interests are recognized and preserved. "The result may be that the routines of the organization as a whole are confined to extremely narrow channels by the dikes of vested interests." Fear of breaking the truce keeps organizations on the "path of relatively inflexible routine." *(111)* Preserving routines is work. Routines are not the sign of stasis or inefficiency but are targets, sought after but never fully reached. Management tries to keep routines under control, to keep them from changing too much; management's job is to deal with disruptions to routines and re-establish them. *(112)* Control of routine is not limited to production but extends to purchasing supplies and to socializing new members when the carriers of the routine leave. Inputs must be selected, modified, monitored, and, if all else fails, adapted to fit the routine. *(114)* Copying the routines and technologies of other organizations is not effortless, as orthodox theory suggests, but hard, thus providing barriers to entry and limiting competition. The existing organization has the advantage in evolutionary terms for replicating its effective units and thus expanding; other organizations lack the routines.*(119)*

"Routines are the skills of an organization." *(124)* (Nelson and Winter emphasize tacit knowledge and lack of conscious awareness, using the work of Michael Polanyi to good effect.[62] See also page 154 of their own book.) If top management intervenes at lower levels, it is because of trouble with the routines. Centralized control is not really possible, so there are problems and pathologies unless there are routines. Organizations are poor at improvising; they must emphasize routines, but

---

firms with similar routines. And the price vector depends on the routines of all the individual firms existing at a time, a dependence discussed in market theory. No theory of long-run evolutionary change, therefore, can logically take the environment of a collection of firms as exogenous. Thus the notion of profitability contributes less to the understanding of the long-run pattern of changes than a first glance might indicate. Ibid., pp. 160–161.

[62]Michael Polanyi, *Personal Knowledge: Towards a Post-Critical Philosophy* (New York: Harper Torchbooks, 1962), and *The Tacit Dimension* (Garden City, N.Y.: Anchor, 1967).

these bind them in a net of negotiated practices that is difficult to alter. *(125)* Nevertheless, there is innovation, and this is what Nelson and Winter are most interested in. Routines provide the occasion, paradoxically, for innovations. Without routines one cannot detect the trouble that falls outside of the routine. Deviations from routines lead to the examination of inputs, the market, existing routines, and so on, which may lead to innovation. *(129)* Unfortunately, Nelson and Winter do not really tell us what are *not* routines, and thus everything that is useful is in danger of being defined as a routine. But nevertheless their list, only selectively summarized here, is indispensable for understanding routines, one of the key defining characteristics of bureaucracy. (They focus on incremental, internal change to produce innovativeness, something they value without question. I would emphasize such things as collusion, market power, power over the government, and the social costs of innovation much more than they have done in such a discussion.)

EPILOGUE

The environment is alive and well and blessed with attention by some of the finest organizational theorists around. In fact, we have hardly finished with it in this book; it figures significantly in the next two chapters as well. I think the rather narrow beginning of this area of study, perhaps stimulated by quantitative analysis techniques that needed a topic, is being overwhelmed by more sociological concerns. In fact, a recent article by the sociological parents of this school, Hannan and Freeman, bring institutional factors into the natural selection model, weakening some of the original assumptions but extending the application.[63] As noted above, their work has led to a focus on populations of organizations and survival tactics that can be joined with more traditional concerns such as strategic choice and even power. As we venture forth into the environment, we can make use of the concepts of population-ecology models, and certainly the evolutionary ones, as I will try to demonstrate in Chapter 8. There is exciting work being done on the link between organizations and locations that could be linked with the evolutionary approach.[64] The concepts of all three schools reviewed in the last section—natural selection, human ecology, and evolutionary theory—should have selective application to the extensive work done on corporate director networks and the dynamics of classwide rationality, once the disabling assumptions of biology are removed from an intensely social system that has power at its center.[65]

[63]Michael Hannan and John Freeman, "Structural Inertia and Organizational Change," *American Sociological Review* 49, no. 2 (1984): 149–164.

[64]Roger Friedland and Donald Palmer, "Park Place and Main Street: Business and Urban Power Structure," *Annual Review of Sociology* 10 (1984): 393–416.

[65]Davita Glassberg and Michael Schwartz, "Ownership and Control of Corporations," *Annual Review of Sociology* 9 (1983): 311–332; and Beth Mintz and Michael Schwartz, *Bank Hegemony* (Chicago: University of Chicago Press, 1985). See also Michael Useem, "Classwide Rationality in the Politics of Managers and Directors of Large Corporations in the United States and Great Britain," *Administrative Science Quarterly* 27 (1982): 199–226, and *The Inner Circle: Large Corporations and the Rise of Business Political Activity in the U.S. and the U.K.* (New York: Oxford University Press, 1984).

7

Economic Theories of Organization

Theories simplify. By now you may have concluded that the various theories we have laid out are rather complicated, but compared to life itself, they are simplifying mechanisms. They allow the theorist to zero in on one aspect of a phenomenon and see how far he or she can take it. Rational bureaucratic theory disregards those aspects that the other theories count as central, and the favor is returned by human relations theory, "garbage can" theory, and the others we have considered.

Fortunately, over time theorists are forced to include bits and pieces of alternative theories, compromising simplicity and limiting generality, and in this way we seem to make progress. For example, rational bureaucratic theory must admit that rationality is an elusive goal and seek explanations for the widespread failure to rationalize everything. Garbage can theory cannot totally ignore bureaucratic structures or rational behavior, so it tends to limit its own application to nonprofit organizations and to perverse examples of bureaucratic structure (thus admitting the existence of bureaucratic structures). Human relations theories come to incorporate structural differences based on technology in a tentative way, and thus the theories' universal application is qualified. But a simplifying insight remains at the core of each: rational division of labor and hierarchical control in the case of rational bureaucratic theory; limited rationality and happenstance in garbage can theory; or the importance of humans with feelings and values in the human relations theories.

But we shall consider one last set of theories that simplify the world of organizations in yet another way. These are economic models based on individuals, rather than organizations, and on competitive self-interest among individuals. Not all economic models are this restrictive, even though individual self-interest is the hallmark of economic theory. The evolutionary model of the firm that we considered in Chapter 6 included cooperation, emergent group interests, and various goals, such as security and predictability, that are the products of self-interest only in the tautological sense that behavior is motivated and thus intended. The venerable but small field of industrial organization assumes profit maximization, but of the firm, and even this assumption is conditioned by great uncertainty and "satisficing." Like evolutionary theory, it gives prominence to many variables that organizational theorists are concerned with, such as market power, oligopoly, and administered pricing.

But these theories have been around for some time and, unlike the two we shall consider here, do not claim to supplant the supposedly defective field of organizational theory. My remarks in this chapter, then, are limited to the new economic models based on individual competitive self-interest: _agency theory_ and _transaction-costs economics_.

The basis for these theories is as old as economics itself, but its application to organizations is new, dating back only a decade or so. (Crucial elements of the theories were prefigured by Chester Barnard with his inducements-contribution calculus, and especially by the first half of James March and Herbert Simon's _Organizations_, where rational individuals calculate their self-interest in deciding whether or not to join the organization and then whether to work or shirk.) In the past decade these two economic theories of organization have had a great deal of success. Numerous conferences have been organized around both; programmatic pieces are appearing in sociological journals; the number of appreciative citations to economic models is rising in mainstream organizational journals such as _Administrative Science Quarterly;_ and economists make bold claims to revolutionizing the primitive field of organizational analysis. As with all theories, we can learn something from agency theory and transaction-costs economics, since they emphasize something the others hide. But as with all theories, they also distort; in fact, I will argue that their distortions outweigh the value of what they highlight. Most important, as with all theories, there two models implicitly contain a set of values with political implications—an ideology by which true believers see the world. In the case of agency theory the ideology is both blatant and conservative; in transaction-costs economics it is somewhat less so.

First, some background on the new discovery of organizations by economists is in order. With some exceptions, such as the industrial organization literature, economists have not felt a need to pay much attention to the organizations that drive the economy, producing its goods and services, or even those regulating it and adjudicating its disputes. "Neoclassical" economic theory simplifies social life to the point of treating organizations as if each were only a single person, an entrepreneur. The organization and all its members comprise only "the shadow of one man," who gathers resources, produces goods and services, and sells them at a profit. The theorists know better, of course, but neoclassical economics works at a level of abstraction where the entrepreneur can stand for the firm. Just as the human relations theorists ignore the biological complexity of the individual and classical management theorists ignore the individual personalities and interpersonal interactions of members, so neoclassical economists ignore the complexities of the organization when they deal with the economy, though in all these cases something is lost by ignoring such complexities.

Economists deal with markets—that is, buying and selling; with resource allocations such as land, labor, and capital (e.g., capital should flow to the firm that can make the highest return on it); and with the equilibrium of perfect competition (e.g., large profits by a few organizations will attract other organizations until the profits are evenly spread and no larger than in other sectors of the economy, producing an equilibrium until new products, technologies, marketing techniques, etc. disturb it). Variations among individual firms, imperfections in the market (such as market power that restricts entry of potential competitors), the secrecy and deception that limit information about profits or economic opportunities or technologies—all these are known to exist but are ignored just as the variations in cognitive ability or energy level are in other theories of organizations that we have considered. Any discipline is free to choose the level of abstraction—cell, human, group, organization, society, world—that it wants to work at and ignore the complexities of those below and above it.[1]

But does neoclassical economics work? Well, not too well. The conservative economist and Nobel laureate Milton Friedman[2] thinks that neoclassical economic theories are correct but that, since the United States does not follow them, they have not been tested properly. But others find that since the assumptions of classical economics, such as perfectly competitive markets, often do not apply, more realistic theories are needed. They seek to qualify the neoclassical assumptions of costless information, a thoroughly decentralized economy, unlimited rationality on the part of the entrepreneur, costless transactions with other entrepreneurs, superhuman ability to perform calculations and see into the future, and the concern only with profit maximization. Those reworking classical theory have not tried to destroy it but to give better explanations of how it works, more in line with practical realities.

The economist Joseph Schumpeter in 1950 said, yes, there is monopoly rather than perfect competition, but a monopolist will survive only if he behaves as if his monopoly was about to be broken by competitive forces, so he must continually devise new technologies and products to provide temporary monopoly profits on specific products.[3] There has grown up a whole literature on oligopolistic competition—competition among a handful of, say, oil firms that account for most of the production and thus can collectively control a whole market—generally arguing that such competition can be made to fit the neoclassical theory. It is also admitted that entrepreneurs have strategies, producing a literature on corporate strategy and industry structure. They do not just throw goods at the market and prosper or fail. In some cases the strategies are analyzed through "game theory," which operates on many of the same assumptions as economic theory (it was invented by economists) but looks at the payoffs of different strategies such as cooperation, going it alone, cheating, bargaining, and so on.

Uncertainty has become a major topic in this literature—uncertainty about the market demand, the ability to produce a new product, the true costs of producing it, the role of government regulation, and the reaction of competitors. The general field of the economics of information has undergone two decades of explosive development. Some problems, ignored by classical economics and analyzed by information theorists are: What is the best form of "search" when information is limited and there is uncertainty—in other words, real-world conditions and not those of neoclassical economic theory? What are the "equilibrium properties" of such uncertain conditions (i.e., how do differences in resources and efficiencies get evened out

[1]Herbert Simon, "The Architecture of Complexity," *Proceedings of the American Philosophical Society* 106 (1962):467–482.

[2]Milton Friedman, *Essays in Positive Economics* (Chicago: University of Chicago Press, 1953).

[3]Joseph Schumpeter, *Capitalism, Socialism and Democracy* (New York: Harper & Row, 1950)

and produce stable situations under uncertainty)? These have been "modeled" in complex equations by economists, but rarely do the models use empirical data. Likewise, the problem of sharing risks has been modeled without data, as have the problems of what constitutes rational expectations about the future and how individuals or firms "signal" their distinctive competencies so that others may make use of them. Terry Moe, a political scientist reviewing the field, asserts that "the economics of information is perhaps the fastest growing and most exciting area of microeconomic theory."[4]

Thus, reaching into the lower levels of abstraction (the "micro" level of individual firms and decision makers in them, rather than the "macro" level of markets and economies), the economists are correcting for the weaknesses of neoclassical theory. They are not, in a fundamental sense, challenging its basic assumptions, which diverge greatly from those of sociological literature on organizations. Some basic assumptions they remain committed to, with occasional exceptions, are: a focus on the individual (rather than the group, structure, culture, etc.) as the "unit of analysis" (that which analysis starts with); a view of the individual as a rational being maximizing a single utility (generally a trade-off between money and leisure) rather than as a sentient one with conflicting goals, vague values, and personal ties to others; a view that the firm is committed to efficiency in the narrow sense of that which maximizes owner profits, rather than the broader sense of employee and community welfare, including employment stability and conserving natural resources; and a belief that all transactions and economic behavior are governed by equilibria—that things will even out eventually such that maximum efficiency in the production of profits rules. Finally, economists believe that high profits for owners are sufficient evidence of efficiency and that efficiency benefits society because resources are not wasted. This last assumption is generally left implicit, but it is a powerful one, since it allows the theories that explain economic behavior to serve also as normative prescriptions for society.

Although all theories simplify, their most extreme simplifications must be at the levels above and below the one at which they choose to work; at the level at which they do their work, they must be rich and complex. The simplification of self-interest may not be disabling at the level of the economy or industry (though I still think it is, since it is such an incomplete attribution of human motivation), but when it is brought down to the level of the firm, it is unwarranted. At the level of the firm it is appropriate only to simplify the dynamics of the economy or industry as a whole. Worse still, the simplification that might have been tolerated at the higher level of the industry or economy is utilized at the firm level, with expansive claims to generality. When economists in the two traditions we will consider venture into the foreign world of organizations, their simplifications protect them from the complexities of the organizational world that the resident organizational theorists must cope with, and these simplifications allow them to generalize without restraint. But they focus on something the organizational theorist does not—cheating, on your boss, partner, or customer. This, according to economists, is the reason for bureauc-

---

[4]Terry Moe, "The New Economics of Organization," *American Journal of Political Science* 28, no. 4 (November 1984): 739–777; the quote is on 741.

racy in the first place, and they are astonished that we organizational theorists give it so little consideration. For spotlighting this fact, we may thank agency theory and transaction-costs economics, though the point can be interpreted in more structural terms quite different from those the economists use.

If you plunge into organizations from the upper world of grand and arid abstractions, the logic of the argument is quite simple. There are only "markets" —people exchanging goods and services freely, seeking the lowest price if buying and the highest if selling—and anyone can make a contract with anyone else. If I have a skill as a secretary, I go to the marketplace and sell my services to Yale University, which needs it, and I then buy a chicken. In the same way, another person might sell her chickens and buy feed from a third individual. Economic activity is a series of contracts. Some are very short in duration (called "spot" contracts), as when you purchase a candy bar; some are long, as when you hire yourself out as a worker. Every person in a large firm has a contract with at least one other party; for instance, the chief executive officer has contracts with his or her subordinates and with the members of the board of directors. The firm is little more than a bundle of bilateral agreements, free to be broken by any party and freely entered on, just as the purchase of the candy bar. I am oversimplifying, of course, but the exceptions to this view are treated as just that—exceptions or qualifications that complicate the analysis.

What advantage could there be in reducing the complex, baffling things that we have been considering in this book to such simple abstractions as contracts, when we know that so much else, such as trust, norms, traditions, and accommodation, exists? The economists' emphasis forces us to examine the conditions under which contractual relations will dominate and when they will not. Both the appearance of trust and the violation of trust require explanation. We need not accept the economists' view that all interaction is contractual, but we need to specify when it is and when it is not. A parallel exists in our daily life; we tend to take for granted social norms that emphasize trust and reciprocity, and most behavior reflects these norms. Only when these expectations are violated do we cry "But that was not the understanding" or "After all I have done for him . . ." or "She never pulls her fair share of the load" or "It is his job to do that." When we say these things, we are invoking contracts, even if only implicit ones, and this is the heart of economic thinking.

Economists see life as an endless series of contracts and analyze organizations as such. This forces other social scientists to specify either the situations in which we must resort to contracts because other forms of interaction no longer guide behavior or the situations where other forms make contracts unnecessary. Organizational analysts have not met the challenge well; we mutter something about poor leadership, poor monitoring of the reward structure, particularism, or favoritism to explain such violations of norms. But for economists working in our field, contracts are all that matter in organizations, and the expectation that they will be violated when possible is not an occasional dilemma but the root problem of organizations. Contracts and their violation are the basis for agency theory and play a key role in transaction-costs economics. We will start with agency theory because it is the far more radical simplification of organizational behavior. Transaction-costs economics is more complex, more sociological, and not incidentally, less politically conservative, even though it builds upon the same economic theories as agency theory.

AGENCY THEORY

Principals, Agents, and Moral Hazard

Agency theory, unlike transaction-costs analysis, does not have a clear problem to which it offers a solution. It appears to reflect a concern with applying the most stark assumptions of economics—maximizing utilities, where net utilities are rewards (money) minus effort—to explain contracts and thus organizations. If such a minimalist assumption can cut through all the concepts, studies, and volumes of theory that organizational analysts have piled up, it will, as some of its proponents claim, "revolutionize" organizational theory. Its ambitions are large, but the theory is hardly subject to empirical test since it rarely tries to explain actual events or make predictions. (In contrast, transaction-costs economics tries to explain the shift from markets with many organizations to "hierarchies" or industries dominated by a few very large firms.) But agency theory raises some fundamental problems about organizations that conventional theory does not explicitly address, and, curiously enough, it can alert us all to the extent to which, when pushed to the wall, we invoke agency theory's assumptions and lose our way in analysis. For these reasons the theory deserves a close analysis and critique. Now that it has entered the field of organizational analysis, it will be with us for a long time.

In its simplest form, agency theory assumes that social life is a series of contracts. Conventionally, one member, the "buyer" of the goods or services, is designated the "principal," and the other, who provides the goods or services is the "agent"—hence the term "agency theory." The principal-agent relationship is governed by a contract specifying what the agent should do and what the principal must do in return (e.g., pay for the goods in a certain time, pay a wage and benefits, give specified notice of termination of the relationship, etc.). But the principal-agent relationship is fraught with the problems of cheating, limited information, and bounded rationality in general. The relationship has been explored in two distinct literatures: mathematical formulations with a limited number of variables and no data, and more complex models with some attempt to use data. The mathematical formulations of "pure" agency theory are strictly logical in their formulation and make heroic, and therefore unreasonable, assumptions. Only three factors appear to be considered in these models: the preferences of the parties, the nature of the uncertainty (what situations give rise to more or less uncertainty), and the information available (how the principal knows about the behavior of the agent). We will generally ignore these mathematical formulations and proofs and concentrate on a model that is somewhat more realistic and certainly more complex.[5]

This more elaborate model says that for many tasks there is an advantage in

[5]See Michael C. Jensen, "Organization Theory and Methodology," *The Accounting Review* 8, no. 2 (April 1983): 319–337, for a review of the differences and for citations.

cooperative effort, or teamwork. But it is often impossible to establish contracts with each member to determine his or her "marginal product," or particular contribution to the effort. If four men lift something onto a truck, how can we tell if they all worked equally hard? (The example is trivial, but the problem is not. You have probably been on a committee where you suspected that some slacked and others, generally including yourself, did more than their share.) In order to distribute the rewards from this task fairly, the relative contributions of each member must be determined. The solution, incredibly enough, is capitalism! Here is how two leading agency theorists, Armen Alchian and Harold Demsetz, say it happens.[6]

Origins of Capitalism. The members of the group performing the cooperative task cannot trust one another to give honest reports of effort, so they hire someone to determine the input of each and thus to determine the rewards due each member. This new person's salary comes out of the profit; the return to each worker is reduced a bit in order to pay her. But to be effective, she must have the authority to replace shirkers or incompetent workers and to settle any disputes about relative efforts. And to be sufficiently motivated to do an accurate monitoring job, she should be able to do more than get a salary; she should get any profits left over after the others have gotten returns equal to their estimated contributions. Her profits are called "residual profits"; their returns are said to equal their estimated "marginal products." Why the monitor needs the residual profits any more than the others is not explained. One could argue that the work of the monitor is less strenuous, risky, and more pleasant than lifting freight onto trucks. The incentive to do a good monitoring job should be higher because of the comparative ease of the task, so she does not need higher returns than the workers. Monitors could be salaried, and workers could divide up, according to the monitor's judgments of contributions, the profits of the enterprise. (In fact, one of the very few forms of worker ownership and self-management that is widespread in our society does something similar: doctors and lawyers form partnerships, divide the profits, and hire office personnel and accountants to monitor and perform other tasks. There is a curious literature in economics on why workers do not hire capitalists, rather than the other way around, but considering it would take us far afield.)

If the monitor did not get a residual profit, the argument goes, she could shirk herself and make more than the workers, without actually doing the necessary monitoring. The excess profits (Marx called them "surplus value") constitute the inducement to work hard at monitoring. But since she also has the power to hire and fire, she really is almost a capitalist (but technically only an entrepreneur, unless she invests her own money). In a loose sense she owns the firm, hiring and firing and determining rates of pay and pocketing the excess. She does not even have to invest any money; economists put monetary values on "good will" and "reputation"

[6]Armen A. Alchian and Harold Demsetz, "Production, Information Cost, and Economic Organization," *American Economic Review* (1972): 777–795. See also Eugene F. Fama, "Agency Problems and the Theory of the Firm," *Journal of Political Economy* 88 (1980): 288–305. Eugene Fama and Michael Jensen, "Separation of Ownership and Control," *Journal of Law and Economics* 26 (June 1983): 301–325, and Michael Jensen and William Meckling, "Theory of the Firm: Managerial Behavior, Agency Costs, and Ownership Structure," *Journal of Financial Economics* 3 (October 1976): 305–360.

(and these go into asset statements when a firm is sold), and she will be the repository of these, and thus the "owner" or capitalist.

We can extend the fable. If the monitor pays the workers too little, the team can go elsewhere and find another monitor (losing good will, however); there are no poor or dependent workers unable to risk unemployment in these models—all have the resources to move anywhere, and no costs of breaking family, friendship, or community ties are sufficiently high to be considered. According to the model, if other would-be entrepreneurs note that the firm makes a great deal of profit, then another group will form a team to load trucks for less and take away the business from the monitor.

If the monitor decides that it would be profitable to buy a fork-lift truck, increase production, and expand the business, she will borrow money from people who have excess money to invest. The investors will get together and, the level of trust being as low as it is in these models, select some of their members to make sure she uses their money to make the greatest return to them as stockholders. The monitor is now the agent of new principals; she is a chief executive officer, or CEO. The new monitors constitute the board of directors, watching over their investments and those of other stockholders. In fact, they are elected to the board, in the only instance of democratic procedures in capitalist firms (in this case, one dollar one vote rather than one person one vote). Now we have a full-fledged capitalist firm with a board of directors, a CEO, workers, and capital equipment. It all started because the four people loading trucks feared that some of them would not do their own share of the work.

Some Problems.   Elegant as this explanation for capitalism and hierarchy is, it has numerous flaws, according to some economists (and, of course, it has nothing to do with the way the vast majority of firms were actually formed). Critics of the account argue that there are other alternatives to a single monitor with profit-claiming status; that the solution proposed by Alchian and Demsetz is not the optimal one; and that the techniques of monitoring and of determining remuneration, the effects of types of monitoring on workers' motivation, and the direct costs of monitoring are ignored and will greatly affect the efficient solution to the problem. In fact, rotating the monitor, sharing the monitoring, paying a wage, and so on all have advantages.[7] Louis Putterman, a mildly skeptical commentator, questions the reluctance of Alchian and Demsetz to call the "contract" an authority relationship. (An authority relationship is more complex than a contractual one; it is harder to withdraw from, and a broader range of activities than those that can be specified in a contract are affected.) No authority relationship exists, say Alchian and Demsetz, because the worker can quit just as easily as the boss. (These economists apparently assume the labor market for workers is as good as that for economists.) They grant the monitor (now a capitalist) "profit claimancy" and allow the monitor to hire and fire in order to "discipline team members and reduce shirking." But Putterman notes that the

[7]See the discussion in Moe, "The New Economics of Organization," and in Louis Putterman, "On Some Recent Explanations of Why Capital Hires Labor," *Economic Inquiry* 33 (April 1984): 171–187; On the last point, see James A. Mirrlees, "The Optimal Structure of Incentives and Authority within an Organization," *The Bell Journal of Economics* 7 (Spring 1976): 105–131.

boss can dismiss any or all of the workers, while they cannot dismiss her, so the relationship is not the symmetrical one of contracts but an asymmetrical one.[8] The problem of power keeps recurring in the new economics; it cannot be ignored or relations assumed to be symmetrical, any more than Chester Barnard could claim the army was a democracy.

Another serious problem exists with this model. Not only does it assume costless exit from the firm and entry to another position as noted, but it almost exclusively emphasizes shirking by subordinates (agents) as the only form of egoistic, self-interested behavior that must be guarded against. The possibility that the capitalist (principal) might lie to the workers about profit levels or threats of lost business, falsify the records of their outputs, endanger agents' health, all to extract more profit, or simply shirk her responsibilities is ignored or swept aside by mentioning that a firm will protect its reputation. But the need for a firm to protect its reputation as an employer by not exploiting workers is hardly pressing. A firm's reputation will generally be unknown to most job seekers, and if known, will have an effect only if the labor market is very tight, there is an opening in a high-reputation firm, and the reputation is accurate. The reputation that is the mode in the industry, of course, could reflect highly exploitative practices; a variation in reputation says nothing about its absolute values.

The response might be that if a firm's reputation is below average, the workers can go elsewhere, but what if "elsewhere" also exploits? If the assumptions of economists about free markets and equilibrium make any sense, an equilibrium level of exploitation would be reached and there would be no point in going elsewhere. (It would be established just at that point where further exploitation would so weaken effort, or so threaten revolution, that the marginal return of a lower wage, unsafe conditions, or more intensive monitoring would be less than the cost of lower productivity or revolution.) If these standard assumptions of a competitive equilibrium do not hold and the level of exploitation varies, then workers still face the problems of finding less exploitative places and getting a job in one, incurring the costs of moving, and so on. Exploitation of employees would appear to be a problem at least as great as, and probably far greater than, shirking by employees, given the self-interest assumed to drive the model and the obviously superior resources of the monitor, entrepreneur, CEO, or capitalist. Yet the problem of exploitation, or even shirking, by the principal is rarely considered by agency theorists.

It is possible that this is a defect of the analysts, and not of the theory itself.

[8]See Putterman, "On Some Recent Explanations . . . ," p. 175; and Oliver Williamson, *Markets and Hierarchy: Analysis and Antitrust Implications* (New York: Free Press, 1975), pp. 67–70. Economist Greg Dow, commenting on a draft of this chapter, makes a more basic point: "There is a genuine problem for Alchian and Demsetz here. If the labor market is really perfectly competitive, no worker suffers a 'punishment' from being fired since identical contractual terms are immediately available at other firms. Hence, it is unclear why the boss needs authority to hire people, or what this accomplishes. Moreover, since workers can leave any time, no worker can be paid less than the expected payoff elsewhere, and no punishments via docked wages will work either. In reality, some likelihood of unemployment is needed to make such threats effective." It is clear that economists, as well as capitalists, need unemployment to make their system work, but the notion of a freely competitive market in equilibrium would seem to exclude any possibility of unemployment. Dow points to the fairy land that economists inhabit. See, for example, C. Shapiro and J. J. Stiglitz, "Equilibrium Unemployment as a Worker Discipline Device," *American Economic Review* 74 (June 1984): 433–444.

That is, would things be fine if the theorists considered contract violations by the principals as often as the agents? It would help, but it would probably hopelessly complicate the model because it would highlight the superior resources of the principal in organizational settings, drawing attention to this asymmetry in the contract. (Agency theorists are more likely to consider violations by both sides when they examine contracts between firms, rather than within firms.) It would force the issue that these are authority rather than contractual relationships; and it would raise the issue that monitoring is primarily available to the principal and difficult and, except for unions, not a part of the contract for agents. Thus, it is quite possibly not just an oversight in applying the theory but a means of disguising some essential facts about organizations.

In addition, the possibility of organized action by workers, who presumably fear exploitation from management more than shirking by fellow workers, is rarely considered, though it is a prominent feature of industrial societies. Where unions are considered by agency theorists, they are not seen as responses to management abuses, but as an instance of "risk sharing" by workers, much as firms might engage in a joint venture or insurance companies in co-insurance.

Finally, would it help if the emphasis were not on shirking but on other violations of the contract by the agents? Subordinates presumably try to get away with a great deal. To extend the range of violations considered in the theory would greatly complicate the analysis (actually an advantage, since the matter is complicated), and it would also force consideration of an extension of violations by the principal as well as the agent. For example, agents might violate the contract by "whistle blowing," or going public about illegal practices encouraged by principals; or by protesting unsafe working conditions, racism, or sexism. Agents may be informally punished by refusing to grant them overtime work. The contract will probably not specify equal pay for equal work; any attempt to redress this by agents would then be a violation of the contract. By bringing in a host of issues such as these, all prominent in industrial relations, the one-sided nature of the contract would be highlighted; shirking by agents would decline in significance, and possible exploitation by principals would increase.

Adverse Selection and Moral Hazard. Two other concepts utilized by agency-theory economists in analyzing organizations will be reviewed before we examine the possible utility of all this for organizational analysis. They have been called "the essence of organizational analysis," but this is open to question. The first is called "adverse selection." Applicants for a job represent themselves as highly qualified, but the information the employer has to go on is crude—past experience, references, education, and so on. The applicants do have a good idea of their "true type," however. ("Type," in this literature, includes training and skills, along with such qualities as honesty and industriousness.) The employer offers a salary to the applicants. Those who feel they are worth more turn down the position and seek employment elsewhere; these the employer would have liked to hire (but would not offer enough to attract them, it should be noted). Those who know that their "true type" is worth less than the salary will accept. The poor employer ends up with many of the less qualified and few of the highly qualified; he or she cannot discriminate among the applicants because they all say their type is appropriate to the salary, and the employer loses the best. The salary could be raised to get the best, but the mediocre would still be among those willing to accept the job. Finer judgment could be used in reviewing applicants, but this entails costs and will not completely overcome the problem of misrepresentation by the applicants; besides, the employer is probably already screening as finely as company resources permit. The end result is less than optimal recruitment—because of the self-interested, guileful behavior of agents.

A related problem, called "moral hazard," occurs after selection. Like adverse selection, where the problem is that applicants know their "type" and employers do not, the "moral hazard" problem also stems from "informational asymmetry"— parties having unequal information. The employer cannot be sure the employee is not shirking on the job, generally seen in this literature as substituting leisure for work.[9]

A typical problem occurs with this logic. A person may have knowledge of her "type" (skills, training, honesty, etc.) as it existed in the context of her previous job, but she cannot know what is required in the new job and thus does not know whether she will be particularly competent or not. Worse yet, she may have been misled about working conditions (safety, pressure, adequate equipment, fairness of supervision, advancement possibilities, etc.) and will find it difficult and costly to seek a better job. Agency theory sees only bilateral contracts, but it curiously tends to neglect the bilateral nature of contracts when constructing its models and equations; it sees principals as at the mercy of agents, who supposedly know their true type, but it ignores the agents at the mercy of the principals, who know their type but do not reveal it to the agents. The principals, too, have a type that can be misrepresented or changed; this is one reason why labor contracts are initiated by unions, not employers. The contract is a means of making the employers' type explicit and binding. Agency theory appears to be ideologically incapable of keeping an eye on both sides of the contract.

Theories Compared.   In an admiring and very clear review of economic theories of organizations, Terry Moe says of adverse selection and moral hazard: "These, of course, are the essence of organizational analysis, whether the substance has to do with decentralization, division of labor, formal rules, structure, communication, or ownership vs. control: all are reflections of efforts to control the productive efforts of organization members."[10] He is correct that agency theorists see it this way, but wrong with regard to the field of organizational analysis. Because we have a society of bureaucratic organizations, the problems of adverse selection and moral hazard

---

[9]The term "moral hazard" stems from the literature on insurance. A firm with insurance need not make reasonable efforts to avoid losses because the insurance company will pay, and the insurance company does not have the information about the level of effort the insured firm has made to prevent losses. If you have insurance, you may not pay much attention to, say, fire safety, because you are covered and the probabilities of a fire are quite low. But the insurance company wants you to practice safety because if many clients are lax, it will earn less money due to the claims they must pay out. If fires are very expensive but rare, insurance firms have a difficult time rating clients' willingness to follow safe practices. See the useful discussion in Moe, "The New Economics of Organization."

[10]Ibid., p. 755.

(i.e., of competitive self-interest in maximizing individual utilities) are relatively trivial ones compared to others. To see this we will rate organizational theories on their tendency to recognize the asymmetry of power and resources in the organization. Agency theory comes close to zero; the model of a cluster of contracts or principal-agent exchanges, if not actually designed to hide asymmetries of power and resources, certainly gives it little recognition. Human relations theory does better; at maximum it recognizes the *responsibility* of masters with power and resources to use them wisely and humanely; at minimum it recognizes the cost of not doing so in terms of alienation and withdrawal of effort by subordinates, and it argues that masters will get more returns through humane treatment and involving subordinates in decisions. This is a theoretical advance over agency theory because it begins to recognize that behavior is structurally conditioned; there is a germ of structure even in Likert's System 4 model.

Bureaucratic theory does even better. It openly accepts power differences as an inherent element of organized society and allows us to see how power operates through structural devices such as specialization, formalization, centralization, and hierarchy. It makes no assumptions that organizations are basically cooperative systems in which the ruled share the goals (and profit or output) of the rulers or masters, as the human relations model implicitly does. But neither does it assume that the ruled are in an endless competition among themselves and with the rulers to maximize the utility of rewards minus effort. Instead, it assumes that while shirking and misrepresentation of one's type will be problems in organizations, employment status is evidence that employees have accepted the necessity of the unequal power relations and can do little to maximize their utilities at the expense of employers. Bureaucracy assumes that there is a wage-dependent population and that the control of employers over employees is legitimate; shirking and the like under these conditions will be only minor problems. The major problems are establishing routines, changing them when needed (innovation), and coordinating the work of employees. Given legitimized inequalities of power, employee utilities are not likely to be achieved by shirking or misrepresentation of one's type; utilities will reflect those values the human relations school would rightly emphasize: safe work, interesting work, opportunity to use and develop skills, some autonomy, influence in decisions that affect not only working conditions but the efficiency of the organization. At the end of Chapter 1, I added several they have neglected, including job security; none reflect shirking or misrepresentation.

The neo-Weberian model treats inequalities of power more seriously than the simple Weberian model. According to the neo-Weberians, power is contested within the organization. Groups legitimately vie for it, as in the contests between sales and production. They also seek to use the organization for their own ends, quite possibly at the expense of the goals of the masters. These ends are rarely shirking or misrepresentation of type. Instead, they are group uses that shape the goals of the organization, increase employment security, preserve routines, increase esteem and prestige, and increase access to relatively minor preferments and comforts. The analysis of these dynamics makes minimal reference to self-interest; indeed, because of the bounded rationality this model assumes, one's interests are problematical at best. Furthermore, the role of premise setting and unobtrusive controls in general overrides the possibility of the simple determination of self-interest.[11]

Structure and Moral Hazards.   The adverse-selection and moral-hazard problems analyzed by agency theorists are based on strong assumptions about human nature. In contrast, a structural approach would examine the context that elicits behavior, and it would recognize considerable plasticity in behavior, in part because of bounded rationality. Let me give just two examples dealing with adverse selection and moral hazard. For most organizations there is considerable slack with regard to selection: the very best applicant from the pool is not needed; one who is just good enough will do. Since neither the applicant nor the employer can be very sure about each other's type or qualification, both depend heavily on subsequent events to effect a minimally desirable match. The training of the employee and the type of supervision and other working conditions will have much more to do with performance than will lack of information as to the employee's real type. Organizations recognize that the costs of optimal selection are high and the techniques uncertain, so positions are designed to fit the average person. Adverse selection and the subsequent moral-hazard problem, then, are fairly trivial problems for the organization.

To take another example, the nature of the task will influence selection and moral-hazard problems, as well as promotion policies. For such workers as entertainers or people selling luxury items, it is important to find outstanding performers quickly, reward and keep them; the rest do no harm to the organization, and turnover can be rapid. But for other positions, the benefits of exemplary performance to the organization are minimal; what is needed is predictable performance, as in assembly-line jobs and continuous-processing industries or with airline pilots. Here, an employee can't speed up even if he tried; if he did he would disturb the station sending him the material and the one receiving it. Error is costly in these organizations, so they are designed to avoid mistakes. This means that adequate performance is very easy to achieve. Organizations will promote people only after long periods.[12] These structural considerations will override the problems of determining true types and avoiding moral hazards, and they account for different evaluation and promotion policies. The first, where outstanding performance is rewarded, will encourage selfish behavior; the second, where error-free behavior is required, will encourage behavior that takes the consequences for others into account.

Self-Regarding Versus Other-Regarding Behavior in Organizations

Why, then, bother with agency theory? First, because it is growing in popularity; organizational theory will have to live with it over the next two decades at least, I suspect. Grand claims for it go uncontested. Michael Jensen, for example, proclaims a "revolution in the science of organizations" based on agency theory. "The science

[11]In the language of Greg Dow, "Preferences are endogenous and a well structured firm will minimize egoism [personal communication]." That is, preferences are generated within the organization, rather than brought to it, and the organization's social structure can create preferences that are not egoistic.

[12]David Jacobs, "Toward a Theory of Mobility and Behavior in Organizations," *American Journal of Sociology* 87, no. 3 (1981): 684–707.

of organizations is still in its infancy, but the foundation for a powerful theory of organizations is being put into place" through agency theory. Political scientist Terry Moe says the principal-agent literature "represents a major advance beyond the usual sociological methods of organizational analysis."[13] Such claims invite close examination. As we shall see at the end of this chapter, thoughtful, influential sociologists such as Harrison White and Arthur Stinchcombe are giving it serious attention.

Second, it is worth examining because it does point to a problem in organizations that is insufficiently addressed: the occasion for self-interested behavior rather than other-regarding behavior. Economic theories of organizations pose this problem in stark, utilitarian terms, permitting us to deal with it in a straightforward manner and forbidding us to ignore it. The self-interested behavior that lies behind agency theory is not the "essence of organizations," as Moe says, and organizational theory has been correct in dealing primarily with structural problems; but self-interest is still a problem worthy of investigation if it is posed as a variable, rather than a fixed property. I think that we pay insufficient *explicit* attention to the conditions under which self-interested behavior, especially with guile, occurs, when behavior with neutral effects on others occurs, and when other-regarding behavior occurs. It is implicit in our discussions of working conditions, morale, incentives, and so on, but agency theory forces us to frame it far more carefully.

The principal assumption of agency theory is that people maximize individual utilities, defined as reward (generally monetary) minus effort. I would now like to treat this assumption as a variable: Under what conditions will people in organizations maximize their own utilities regardless of the consequences for others, and when will they forgo an increase in utility or even suffer a loss because of the consequences for others? It turns out to be both a very important and very difficult question, and only a sketch of an answer can be given here.

The conditions favoring unselfish behavior have been addressed and debated for centuries, and one continual problem is that of tautology. In the very long run all behavior can be regarded as self-regarding, even risking one's life to save a drowning person, because all behavior is motivated, and thus the "self" must have wanted to do it; this becomes a large tautology, incapable of disproof. I do not want to identify other-regarding behavior with altruism, but with something far more prosaic in its impact, akin to "common decency" and "mutual respect." (If one prefers to regard all behavior as self-interested, then let my distinction stand for degrees of self-interested behavior.[14]

Thus, we should consider only short-run consequences where some immediate

---

[13]Jensen, "Organizational Theory and Methodology," p. 324; Moe, "The New Economics of Organization," p. 757.

[14]If this distinction is unacceptable, Paul DiMaggio, in a valuable personal communication, suggests the distinction might better be between high-trust systems, with reciprocity and a collective orientation, versus competitive, self-regarding, individualistic systems. The tautology of motivated behavior being self-interested is mitigated here; a collective versus an individualistic strategy is posed instead. Organizations can be designed to encourage cooperative strategies or individualistic ones, somewhat along the lines of the contrast that Joyce Rothschild-Whitt makes in her discussion of collectivist organizations, or if that seems unrealistic for the reader, the weaker proposals of Rosabeth Kanter. See Joyce Rothschild-Whitt, "The Collectivist Organization: An Alternative to Rational Bureaucratic Models," *American Sociological Review* 44 (1979): 509–527; and Rosabeth Kanter, *The Change Masters: Innovation for Productivity in American Corporations* (New York: Simon & Schuster, 1983).

self-interest such as status, power, or income appears to be sacrificed in order either not to harm another or to actually help another. If no gain or no loss for one's self is occasioned by an action that helps or at least does not hurt another, it will be called neutral—for example, passing on to another a bit of praise for a third person that you heard ("I hear that Szymanski did a first-rate job on that"). Other-regarding behavior entails some loss to one's self. For example, the praise passed on reflects poorly on your own behavior, though it may strengthen the group to which you belong ("I hear Szymanski really pulled my chestnuts out of the fire on that one. We will look okay after all"). Self-regarding behavior entails some loss to another and may in addition weaken the group (failing to report the praise because it might detract from your own worth). What are the *organizational* conditions for self-regarding behavior?

Conditions favoring self-regarding behavior. In the world of organizations, competitive self-regarding behavior appears to be favored by such conditions as the following:

- *Continuing interactions are minimized:* This occurs in a highly fluid ("unimpacted") labor market where job seekers are not constrained by family or other personal ties to friends and the community when they seek work locations; when there is "spot" contracting in a labor market—as in migrant labor, temporary help, high-turnover/fast-food franchise—that maximizes free movement of labor; when the emphasis is on individual promotions or individual, rather than group, job rotations; or when loyalty to the firm rather than to more proximate groups such as your own department and the groups it interacts with is rewarded.
- *Storage of rewards and surpluses by individuals is encouraged:* Such a situation arises when the tax structure favors individual rather than group rewards; organizational hierarchy promotes it; steep salary structures reinforce it; and a stable class system (minimal redistribution of wealth) provides the context for it.
- *The measurement of individual effort or contribution is encouraged:* This is done through personnel evaluations, promotions, piece rates, and celebration of leadership. It is a continuing legacy of nineteenth-century individualism, celebrating individual rather than cooperative effort.
- *Interdependent effort through design of work flow and equipment is minimized:* Work flow and equipment can minimize cooperative effort and responsibility by breaking up tasks and favoring assembly lines; precise contractual relationships promote this, as do the presumption that shirking is potentially rampant and the installation of surveillance systems to thwart such shirking.
- *A preference for leadership stability and generalized authority dominates:* Leaders are held to be all-competent and are expected to play a leadership role continuously; this is possibly a legacy of individualism and private ownership rights. The alternative is to alternate leadership tasks according to the skills of the individuals, thus avoiding stable patterns of dependency in subordinates and self-fullfilling assumptions of expertise in leaders.
- *Tall hierarchies are favored.* These are based on unequal rewards and notions that coordination must be achieved by giving orders.[15]

[15]In Chapter 1 we saw that tall hierarchies could entail delegation of authority and could be associated with more productive technologies. To achieve these and avoid structures favoring self-interested behavior requires more matrix-type structures (dual leadership for the mixing of functional groups, such as sales and production, and product groups, such as rayons and polyesters), differentiation through profit centers, and very possibly just smaller organizations and more of them.

It is possible to design organizations that minimize at least some of these characteristics. Some small, innovative high-technology firms appear to, and Rosabeth Kanter argues that large ones can as well. Japanese firms appear to minimize several of these characteristics, and cooperatives go even further.[16] Moderate-sized capitalist firms and even those with routine technologies could certainly embrace these principles. Creating such organizations depends on the nature of other organizations that one interacts with. An organization that exploits employees and consumers would be more profitable for the owner and, through competition, could force out more other-regarding structures. It may be true, as human relations theory argues, that the exploitative organization is less efficient because it produces alienation and may even have some reputation problems, making it difficult to attract adequate employees if they are in short supply. As reviewed in Chapter 3, the evidence for this is quite mixed; exploitation of workers probably pays off for routine technologies and under some industrial market conditions. But even if this were not true, the firm that exploits workers, consumers, and/or communities has an advantage that more than compensates for any motivational or reputational costs: it externalizes social costs that the nonexploitative firms internalize. Because of the self-regarding posture of its top management, which will force the same attitudes on the rest of the personnel, it is more likely to save money by polluting the environment, cutting costs on safety, allowing hazardous working conditions, extracting long hours from managers (a social cost to them and their families), selling goods with defects that are hard to attribute to the firm and that may take years to become apparent, cooperating with organized crime to cut wages or dispose of contaminated wastes, and so on. While a positive correlation between profitability and externalizing social costs cannot be demonstrated, there is little anecdotal evidence to suggest it is negative.

In addition, society might make it difficult to sustain other-regarding structures. Banks may require permanent leadership before they will invest in an organization, for example; they are reluctant to make loans to worker cooperatives. Walter Powell notes that public television stations can secure corporate sponsorship more easily if they bureaucratize along conventional lines, even if their technology favors a more fluid structure. I have noted that engineers favor equipment designs that minimize interdependent work and group responsibility, thus reproducing a hierarchical structure that favors individual, rather than group, accountability.[17]

This assumes that there is no innate tendency to either self- or other-regarding behavior in people; either can be evoked depending on the structure. Agency theorists examine the structures favored by capitalism and bureaucracy and find much self-regarding behavior; they then assume that this is human nature. They neglect the enormous amount of neutral and other-regarding behavior that exists (and must, for organizations even to function) and the structures that might increase

---

[16]Kanter, *The Change Masters;* Rothschild-Witt, "The Collectivist Organization."

[17] Walter Powell, *Getting into Print: The Decision Making Process in Scholarly Publishing* (Chicago: University of Chicago Press, 1985); and Charles Perrow, "The Organizational Context of Human Factors Engineering," *Administrative Science Quarterly* 28, no. 4 (1983): 521–541.

it. What they take for granted should be taken as a problem: why have we encouraged so much self-regarding behavior?

Agency Theory: A Dangerous Explanation

Finally, agency theory should be carefully examined because it may be dangerous. Theories shape our world; they encourage us to see it a certain way, and then we exclude other visions that could direct our actions. Managers preoccupied with cheating will forget coordination and the extent to which the context they create for behavior can evoke either cheating or cooperation. Scholars using agency theory to examine organizations will do the same and easily find evidence that can be interpreted to fit their model. This model gives scant attention to the cooperative aspects of social life and ignores how exploitation is structurally encouraged by the asymmetric distribution of power in bureaucracies. By paying explicit, but critical, attention to it, we will not ignore self-interested behavior, nor will we assume that it is the essence of organizations.

The most insidious danger of agency theory is that all of us apply it in our daily life when we shouldn't, and we should be aware of this. For instance, we all downplay the degree of luck actually at work when we get an above- or below-average subordinate; instead, we take the credit for selecting the good subordinate and blame the subordinate if he or she turns out to be bad. Greater awareness will remind us to invoke bounded rationality and structurally generated conflicts rather than attributing opportunistic self-interest to those who disappoint or frustrate us. Personnel staffs try to hide or downplay the imperfections of the hiring process, attributing flaws to the employees rather than to the process of matching suitable jobs and applicants. This is understandable; if they admit the limited effectiveness of their craft, they may have fewer opportunities to practice it. Yet agency theory is being applied in the case of the agent who is blamed for poor performance when a recognition of the difficulty of assessment by the principal would be more accurate. Managers are wont to blame problems on subordinates' lack of qualifications or self-interest; any evidence of even trivial cheating or shirking justifies their attribution of blame. Yet it is likely that poor management or a faulty structure is a better explanation.

In short, we are all agency theorists far more than we think! Stated abstractly, the theory sounds heartless, simplistic, and even pointless, as it assumes that organized social life is nothing more than a series of contracts between people with the resources to pick or choose the contracts they like. But if we reflect on our daily justifications for our actions, we can see that we use agency theory daily to appropriate the gains, and overlook the losses, that attend our efforts. The theory allows those of us fortunate enough to supervise to play the seductive role of long-suffering principals victimized by the duplicity of ne'er-do-well subordinates, after the fashion of the Social Darwinists such as Elbert Hubbert in *A Message to Garcia*, discussed in Chapter 2. If we are aware of how ready we are to make this judgment, we will be more alert to the role of structures and contexts, and guard against both inefficient and unjust ones. By examining agency theory critically, we highlight the extent to which behavior is evoked by situations, thus calling for changes in situations rather than personnel; how the selection process will always be imperfect but the victim, the hired person, is not necessarily to blame; and how organizational positions must be designed to cope with wide variations in "type." Agency theory is an easy out for all these problems.

TRANSACTION-COSTS ECONOMICS

Another contribution of economics to organizational analysis that we shall deal with (a third, evolutionary perspective, was covered in Chapter 6) is transaction-costs economics, or TCE. In the early decades of this century, John R. Commons pointed to the importance of transactions in the economy, and in the 1930s Ronald Coase narrowed the term and again asserted its importance. But it was not picked up and developed until Oliver Williamson almost singlehandedly made it into an important force in the 1970s. He is TCE's most forceful spokesperson and continues to develop the theory today. It represents an advance in complexity over agency theory, since it places more emphasis on bounded rationality and acknowledges more of conventional organizational theory. It claims to be a new paradigm that will explain better than all other organizational theories the change in this century from many small organizations (a market) to a few giant ones (a hierarchy).[18] The claim has been taken seriously by sociologists and economists. At least one book has been devoted to an appreciation of Williamson's work, the organizational journals are devoting space to it, and William Ouchi of *Theory Z* fame is an enthusiastic convert.[19] New "paradigms" are not that frequent in organizational analysis, so the rapid growth of this one deserves some scrutiny. As with agency theory, we will find that TCE poses important problems that conventional theory has dealt with inadequately and thus enriches the field. But like agency theory, with which it has much in common, its selectivity—the simplification inherent in all theory—hides a great deal, and that which is hidden has political and ideological implications, though they are less conservative than those of agency theory.

Transaction-costs economics is an efficiency argument for the present state of affairs, as most mainstream economic theories are. It argues that the appearance of giant organizations in some industries represents the most efficient way to produce goods for an industrial society. Distortions are acknowledged, and the government is advised to get out of this or that, but in general capitalism and the free market produce the most efficient economic system, even as the market is supplanted by hierarchies. Williamson is explicit regarding efficiency, by which he means the efficiency of organizational forms, not the efficiency of specific practices, machines, sales techniques, or transportation devices, though the efficiently run organization

---

[18]Oliver Williamson, "Organizational Innovation: The Transaction-Costs Approach," in *Entrepreneurship,* ed. J. Ronen (Lexington, Mass.: Heath, 1983), pp. 101–134. The basic work by Williamson is his *Markets and Hierarchies: Analysis and Antitrust Implications* (New York: Free Press, 1975). A new volume under preparation by Williamson incorporates more organizational and sociological variables and attacks a wide range of problems from the markets-and-hierarchies viewpoint.

[19]Arthur Francis, Jeremy Turk, and Paul Willman, eds., *Power, Efficiency, and Institutions* (London: Heinemann, 1983). William Ouchi, "Markets, Bureaucracies, and Clans," *Administrative Science Quarterly* 25 (March 1980): 129–141.

will seek out these other operating efficiencies. Discussing the shift from many organizations to a few large ones over the century, he says, "I argue that efficiency is the main and only systematic factor responsible for the organizational changes that have occurred."[20]

There are four components in his theory: uncertainty, small-numbers bargaining, bounded rationality, and opportunism. Bounded rationality and opportunism are ever-present but will only give rise to large firms where there is uncertainty and small-numbers bargaining.

"Uncertainty" refers to changes in the environment that the owner cannot foresee or control. It provides the dynamic element that makes a market unstable.

"Small-numbers bargaining" means that once a long-term contract has been signed, with suppliers, workers, or customers, the normal market situation is disturbed. The parties to the contract have privileged positions because they have more experience with and more specialized resources to serve each other than those in the market that sought but did not get the contract. For example, if you find that your supplier's quality is slipping, you may be reluctant to break the contract and find another because you are set up to deal with that supplier; you have made an investment in routines and experience with that firm's supplies, procedures, and idiosyncrasies, and that investment will be lost. Or, within the firm, after employees have worked for you for a while, they gain experience and skills; if they threaten to quit or strike, you cannot simply hire others who will immediately be as productive. The term "small-numbers bargaining" indicates that rather than many firms or workers being available to meet your needs, only a small number are—perhaps only one in the case of a sole-source supplier. If there is also uncertainty in the market, small-numbers bargaining can be a problem.

A related concept is "asset specificity." If, by working for a firm at a specialized job, I develop certain skills that job seekers outside the organization don't have, I have specific assets, and this gives me some bargaining power. The employer has to think twice about firing me or about refusing my demand for a raise. While I think this concept is useful, the bilateral nature of exchange renders it opaque: since these assets are specific to this firm, it gives my boss some power, too—my specific skills will give me no bargaining advantage with another potential employer, because my skills are specific to this one organization. This is rarely acknowledged by Williamson. A similar bilateral relationship occurs between supplier and customer, which Williamson does acknowledge.

"Bounded rationality" creates a problem because of "opportunism." Imperfect information about suppliers or workers allows these people to behave opportunistically. (It also allows the boss or buyer to do the same to them, of course, but Williamson is no more likely to consider this possibility than agency theorists are; even William Ouchi neglects it.[21]) The supplier will claim that she is having labor

[20]Williamson, "Organizational Innovation," p. 125.

[21]Ouchi, "Markets, Bureaucracies, and Clans." See also Victor P. Goldberg, "Bridges Over Contested Terrain: Exploring the Radical Account of the Employment Relationship," *Journal of Economic Behavior and Organization* 1 (1980): 249–274. Goldberg does the same thing but tries to give the radical economists a fair hearing.

problems, raw-material problems, or whatever, and can't deliver on time. The buyer has no way to investigate this, and since another supplier cannot suddenly expand to meet his need, and since it is expensive to guard against such problems by having large inventories, he is at her mercy.

From the point of view of the supplier, the "favor" can be returned: the buyer might say that the sales of his firm have fallen off unexpectedly and he therefore needs only 60 percent of the supplies he intended to buy that quarter. The supplier, who has already produced most of them, has a contract with the customer and might want to say, "That's your problem; your sales are off because of your high prices or low quality, which have already provided you with excess profits; you should cut your prices or improve your quality. I shouldn't have to lose sales and thus profits because you want me to bear the risks of your high prices or low quality, or even slack demand." But as a supplier, she has no reliable information about the buyer's profits on this item, about any unusual quality problems he has, about the efficiency of his operation, or even about the firm's demand. If the supplier is only one of four for these items, she might even think that the buyer was getting a cut-rate deal from a competitor and thus buying less from her. She cannot simply sell her goods to other customers; they all have longstanding relationships with their suppliers. Invoking the penalty terms of the contract would be expensive and would alienate the customer. So she has to take the loss.

Thus a change in the market (or a bargain from another supplier)—that is, uncertainty—combined with small-numbers bargaining, the lack of information, and the possibility of opportunism all combine to create what is called a "market failure." No longer is there the ideal market of neoclassical economic theory: a large number of suppliers and producers bargaining daily such that the lowest possible prices will be established and changes in demand will be immediately felt and adjusted for, and where opportunists are punished by not finding people to trade with the next day. Instead we find uncertainty, small numbers, bounded rationality and opportunism—that is, a failure to achieve the classical market.

Well, that's serious. (It is also the rule in our economy; the markets of neoclassical theory are few in number and small in impact.) What is to be done about it? Williamson and capitalists have a solution: integrate forward or backward. That is, you can buy out the person you sell to (or set up your own organization in competition with your customer), called "integrating forward"; or you can buy out your supplier (or build your own source of supply), called "integrating backward." (The term that covers both is "vertical integration." Another concept, "horizontal integration" involves buying out a competitor, clearly a move that has little to do with transaction costs and much to do with market power.) If the supplier is part of your firm, you can control her. That eliminates the leverage she had as one of a handful of suppliers that you had to depend on. She won't dare lie about labor problems or raw-material problems because you can check the books (controlling opportunism). And you will not have to write all those contracts with her, trying to specify complex future contingencies, and have your people checking to see that all the promises are fulfilled. This way you reduce the costs of transacting business (hence the term "transaction-costs economics"). There will be other economies, such as economies of scale (saving money by buying in bulk). Your personnel department can probably take over personnel work by adding only a few people, because of economies of scale, so many of the supplier's personnel people can be fired. Your added employees may get you a cheaper health insurance rate. And so on. But such economies are likely to be small, and Williamson does not stress them.

Transaction costs, then, primarily concern writing and monitoring long-term contracts that are complex because of all the contingencies introduced by uncertainties and by the disposition, in what he calls "human nature as we know it," to lie, cheat, and steal. For Williamson, minimizing transaction costs is the key to efficiency, and his model explains concentration of production in large firms better than several competing theories, including Marxist and other power theories, historian Alfred Chandler's theory of coordination and throughput speed, technological arguments, and those that deal with the strategic use of finance.[22]

The development of large firms, so evident in twentieth-century economic history, does not occur in all areas, however, and Williamson's ability to explain why markets will persist in some areas while they disappear in others would indicate the power of his theory. The question has often been asked: Why, if giant firms are more efficient, do we not have just one giant firm? Here the potential payoff of TCE becomes apparent.

Markets, Williamson argues, will continue to exist if spot contracts will do the job efficiently. The market for supplies is cleared each day, so to speak, if transactions are one-shot and no long-term contacts need to be written. The firm that wishes to buy some furniture asks for bids and selects the lowest, just as a person shops for a TV set. There is no opportunity to cheat on long-term delivery contracts, no "first-mover advantages" (where the first firm to get the contract has an inside track on all future contracts because of small-numbers bargaining). Markets can also survive if there is little uncertainty in price, volume, production costs, labor relations, and the like, even if the market is not a spot one. Standard supplies (toilet paper, business forms, batteries, picks, and shovels) are available from many sources, have clear prices, and their quality is readily judged. Markets will also survive if the costs of entry (starting up a production facility) are low; entrepreneurs will see that existing producers are making a lot of money, so they will enter the market and thus bring the price down because of competition. The cost of entry will be more likely to be low if the technology is well known. Predictable high-volume demand also reduces uncertainty and favors market transactions instead of vertical integration.

Thus hierarchy replaces markets when there are long-term contracts in an uncertain environment and the barriers to entry are reasonably high, because the costs of opportunism are reduced by substituting an authority relationship ("You now work for me") for a contractual one. (Williamson's major departure from agency theory is his admission of authority relations; they replace contractual disputes with "fiat." Agency theorists deny authority relations and insist there are only contracts, even in firms.)

[22]Williamson, "Organization Innovation," p. 125.

The Value of the Theory

Transaction-costs theory has been both praised and severely criticized. Leaving the criticisms aside for a moment, what does this theory do for us? For the average organizational theorist, it introduces a number of variables that we unfortunately otherwise neglect. The notion of small-numbers bargaining is implicit in some of our work, but making it explicit makes it more valuable and will lead to more development of the idea and the closely associated concept of asset specificity. We are wont to invoke vague terms such as tradition or trust when we encounter long-term relationships between firms and suppliers, firms and customers, or even a supervisor and workers. A good part of that tradition or trust may lie in the bilateral dependence of each of the parties. The supplier and customer each depend on the other because of asset specificity. The assets of the supplier are highly specific in order to meet the specific demands of the customer, and the customer's products are made more specific or inflexible because of the specificity of the supplier's components.[23]

A similar argument can be made regarding the tasks the supervisor wants done and the skills the workers have developed. Asset specificity, in a sense, demands the continuity that we call "tradition" and produces the repeated interactions that we call "trust." Locating the sources of tradition and trust in an economic relationship does not remove the social and cultural content of these transactions. One reason trust may appear in bilateral exchanges is that the parties get to know crucial noneconomic information about each other and their interdependence. Political, ethical, and cultural values are exchanged and modified. The economic relationship becomes "embedded" (as Granovetter terms it, in his important essays on economics and sociology)[24] in social and cultural exchanges, and the strictly economic and strictly self-interested nature of the exchange is modified.

The bilateral relationship may not be equal, we should note. Generally, the larger or more powerful member has the greater leverage. For example, if the buyer is larger than the supplier, its purchasing power allows it to find another source of supply, and probably more readily than the supplier can attract another customer. Similarly, the employer would prefer to retain the experienced employee but can replace him or her, while the employee will have more trouble finding another employer, unless an unusual skill or an unusual labor market is involved. But any analysis of the concepts of trust and tradition had best be aware of Williamson's discussion of small-numbers bargaining and asset specificity.

Nor have organizational theorists paid much attention to the characteristics of market transactions. The ability to distinguish spot from long-term contracts, many bargainers from only a few, degrees of substitutability of goods or services, and stability and instability of demand, technologies, and so on may not appear to be

---

[23]Note, though, that using this concept, with its clear bilateral implications, reduces any differences in efficiency between markets and hierarchies, because relationships in both will tend toward an equilibrium. Since hierarchies have replaced some markets, Williamson must explain the disappearance of bilaterality, and the trust it implies, on other than efficiency grounds.

[24]Mark Granovetter, "Economic Actions and Social Structure," *American Journal of Sociology,* November 1985; and "Labor Mobility, Internal Markets, and Job Matching: A Comparison of the Sociological and Economic Approaches," unpublished manuscript, Department of Sociology, State University of New York at Stony Brook, n.d.

a significant contribution. In one form or another these ideas are used by many theorists. But Williamson links them together, makes them explicit, and demands that issues of market concentration, monopoly power, the growth of huge organizations, and the like be addressed with these considerations in mind. In particular, formalizing the argument about transactions allows us to focus on the important question of why hierarchies replace markets. (As we shall see, Williamson's discussion has prompted us to note that, actually, many markets have strong hierarchical components, and many hierarchies behave like markets. This has opened up interesting inquiries into evolving forms of interdependencies under advanced capitalism.)

Furthermore, since Williamson's concepts can be applied to both relationships among and relationships within organizations, we derive a fruitful link between the nature of markets (interorganizational relationships) and the nature of firms (intraorganizational relationships). By allowing us to make the link, Williamson also brings into organizational analysis a field that it has neglected—industrial economics, which deals with the characteristics of industries (concentration, size, rates of change, characteristics of customers, and so on)—though the literature has left the firms themselves as empty shells. Williamson provides us with some of the most relevant aspects of industrial economics, packaged for organizational theory.

Finally, Williamson turns the problem of "why so many big firms?" into "why big firms (hierarchies) in some areas and not in others?" This is a more interesting and more tractable problem.[25] Marxists have an answer of a sort for the first question: the disappearance of small firms and the growth of big ones is the product of the dynamics of capitalism—a ceaseless search for ever more profits, wherein the big fish gobble up the small. But they have no answer for the second question: When will markets (small firms) persist, despite the existence of powerful organizations nearby that seek ever more profits? These are questions that an organizational theory that has finally met the environment should be preoccupied with; we deal with it at the margins of our work, but we have not directly confronted it. Williamson has.

The Criticisms

While we may appreciate Williamson's development of useful concepts such as asset specificity, his attention to transaction costs, and the questions he has raised about the shift from markets to hierarchy, we do not have to embrace his theory. The principal criticisms, as much as Williamson's work itself, have enriched the field. An extended example will illustrate some major criticisms one can make of TCE, and then we will review the criticisms of other scholars.

Consider a firm called Engines, Inc. It has about 1,000 employees, it produces engines for air-conditioning systems, and it buys out a firm, Radiators, Inc., with 300 employees, that supplies radiators for these engines. Engines, reflecting its new acquisition, renames itself the ACE Company (for Air-Conditioning Equipment). TCE would have us believe that the costs of long-term contracts between Engines

---

[25]The historian Alfred DuPont Chandler also raises the issue in this form and treats it as the main question a historian of business organizations should answer. See Alfred D. Chandler, *The Visible Hand: The Managerial Revolution in American Business* (Cambridge, Mass.: Harvard University Press, 1977).

and Radiators were too high, so Engines bought Radiators—in 1980, let us say. ACE now controls all the people who were owners and employees of Radiators and can reduce opportunism on the part of these people and save on lawyers who write contracts and accountants that monitor them. But is there really a saving?

Prior to 1980, there were two sets of transaction costs: the costs of writing and monitoring the contracts between Radiators and Engines, and the costs that each of the firms incurred in dealing with other parts of its environment. The second set of costs is not reduced. When Engines buys Radiators out, it must continue to deal with the problems that Radiators had to deal with—for example, buying metal and other supplies and dealing with the government, with labor, the community, and so on. As we shall see, these costs may actually rise because the form of transactions will change somewhat under the new ownership. The transaction costs associated with the Radiators-Engines relationship will certainly change, but I believe that they are actually likely to rise, rather than fall, as far as ACE is concerned.

If the market for air-conditioning equipment declines, ACE cannot simply tell its supplier of radiators that it is canceling its order (with due notice, or even a penalty) or cutting the size of a new one, thus making the supplier suffer all or most of the loss. ACE itself has to absorb the loss of business (fixed capital lying idle, layoffs with unemployment insurance costs, excess managerial staff, and loss of profit-generating activity). The sum total of transaction costs remain; their location is different. (One problem with TCE is that the definition of a transaction cost is altogether too flexible to test the theory convincingly, but shutting down facilities and laying off experienced employees seem to qualify as transaction costs.)

Now suppose the opposite happened, and the demand for air-conditioning equipment soars. ACE's radiator division can build new facilities to expand its production no faster than Radiators could have (though it might get capital a bit faster if ACE has some lying around); there is no saving here. In fact, there might be a loss. Radiators might have added facilities to meet the new demand, calculating that if the rise in demand by Engines turned out to be temporary, it still might be able to sell any excess radiators to other engine companies. But ACE might find it awkward to become a supplier to its own competitors (though this happens regularly in a few industries, such as electronics), and the competitors would probably prefer to buy from suppliers they can control rather than from a competitor. Thus ACE is less likely to risk an expansion of facilities. Some flexibility is lost in the acquisition.

Well, what about opportunism? Ms. Radoe, once the head of Radiators is now the general manager of the radiator division of ACE. According to TCE, she can now be watched much more carefully (ACE has the information on her behavior), and any disputes between her and, say, the chief operating officer, Mr. Enginee (the former head of Engines, who now oversees the radiator and engines divisions) can be settled "by fiat"—that is, by a direct order. Before, there were transactions costs —contract writing, bargaining, legal actions, and so on. Now, if Mr. Enginee needs support for disciplining Ms. Radoe, he can turn to the chief executive officer of ACE, Mr. Banke. Mr. Banke was an officer of the bank that provided the loan for buying up the radiator company. As a condition of that loan, he was made CEO of the company. (He need not know anything about air conditioning, but he must know about transaction costs, according to TCE, because these efficiencies count the most. He does, as a finance expert and banker.)

But what is Ms. Radoe likely to be doing in her new position? Here we will use the assumptions about opportunism and competitive self-interest that Williamson shares with agency theory. We will assume that the firm is structured, as most are, to encourage competitive self-interest. When Ms. Radoe headed Radiators, she worked extremely hard because she owned the company and received the profits from it. There was no motiviation to shirk on her part. But at ACE she gets a salary (and perhaps a bonus), rather than direct profits. She has less incentive to work hard and more to shirk, or even steal. Reflecting the incentives problem, ACE may develop an elaborate bonus plan based in part on the performance of Ms. Radoe's division and in part on the performance of the firm as a whole, as other companies have done. (Such plans have led to fierce controversy over internal pricing decisions within firms—a substantial transaction cost.) Is the radiator division being charged more than its share of the overhead, and are its internal profits thus being set lower than they would be if it were independent? Robert Eccles details the extensive transactions costs and political problems of internal pricing schemes, necessary once the market no longer exists. He concludes from extensive research that firms perceive the costs of *internal* transactions to be higher than external ones, and he does not find TCE useful in understanding the transfer pricing problem.[26]

No doubt, given the emphasis on opportunism in TCE, Ms. Radoe will also be required to monitor it in her subordinates, just as she did when she owned the firm. But she has less incentive to do so; their shirking or stealing will have a trivial effect on her income, though it should not become so gross as to invite an inspection from Mr. Enginee or Mr. Banke. If there is a bonus plan, she will take up her superior's time by arguing about internal pricing, as Eccles documents.

Furthermore, Mr. Enginee, who used to watch her intermittently and from a distance when she was his supplier, now has to watch her continually, as her superior. Her radiator division draws on the resources of ACE and affects its accounting, personnel practices, and so on. Another set of transaction costs has increased. If Ms. Radoe allowed rampant opportunism on the part of her employees when she headed Radiators, it was of no concern to Mr. Enginee. It just meant she got less out of her staff and thus lower profits. But the price to Mr. Enginee was not affected, so he did not need to bother about it. He was only concerned with the contract, not her whole firm. Now he is held accountable for the whole division; if performance slackens, the profits to ACE are reduced.[27]

One can imagine Mr. Enginee going home one night to tell Mrs. Enginee,

[26]Robert G. Eccles, "Control with Fairness in Transfer Pricing," *Harvard Business Review* (November–December 1983): 149–161; "Transfer Pricing as a Problem of Agency," unpublished manuscript, Harvard Business School, February 1984; and *The Transfer Pricing Problem: A Theory for Practice* (Lexington, Mass.: Lexington Books, 1985).

[27]Setting the radiator division up as a "profit center" within the firm is of little help. Contracts must still be written. If it is made maximally independent, with no more interactions than when it supplied radiators to Engines, it may as well have remained a separate firm since there are no transaction-cost savings—with one very important difference: when it was a separate firm, ACE would not have "appropriated its profit stream," as economists put it. That is, the profits now go to ACE, not to Ms. Radoe. We will later count this as possibly the primary motive for acquisitions.

"What a mistake. I read Oliver Williamson and it looked as if Engines, Inc., was ripe for savings on transactions costs. You know, he is the one that called Perrow's theory 'bankrupt' in that book where Perrow criticized Williamson.[28] Well, we had this small-numbers bargaining situation with big Ms. Radoe, and long-term contracts, uncertainty about product demand, and all the rest, including opportunism on her part—she claimed those leaky radiators were the result of poor handling by us and threatened to sue us if we refused to pay. So I decided to buy her out. She was working 80 hours a week and she didn't like her reputation for driving her employees, so she was willing to come to work for us.

"But I had to let Mr. Banke come in as CEO in order to get capital for the buyout. Williamson never mentioned that there are large costs in acquiring even small firms. It was profitable, so we could raise the money, and it should increase our profits—Mr. Banke and the stockholders will get them, not Ms. Radoe. But it saddled us with 300 employees and all kinds of commitments at a time when sales were falling. We are losing money, not her." (Or "Now that sales are booming, we're the ones who have to pay for the increase in overtime and other special production costs; before, she would have had to take less profit on each item because of the contract, at no cost to us." [*TCE neglects to consider all transaction costs. Flexibility in response to changes is reduced.*]

"Furthermore," he continues, turning up his custom-built air-conditioner as he gets more heated, "I have had a hell of a time getting their accounting and information-management system to link up with ours. Theirs was fine for their product and volume, but ours doesn't work well for them. But we have to have an integrated financial statement by law, and the bankers demand certain kinds of reports, personnel practices needed to standardize, and so on. So I had to hire more accountants, and Ms. Radoe complains that she can't watch performances and budgets as closely now." [*Internal coordinating costs rise when different operations must be combined. Accounting and surveillance systems must be standardized while variable, tailor-made systems would be more effective; there are costs to decentralizing large, complex systems that do not appear in smaller, simpler ones.*]

"And there's more. In 1979, before we bought Radiator, I used to call up two or three other radiator firms and find out what they were charging for various models, and she knew it, so she kept her prices in line. Now I don't have a good idea of the costs of our radiators because of internal pricing problems. The accountants say the radiator division is a "profit center," but it has to contribute to the firm's overhead and advertising costs, some personnel costs, a lot of staff running back and forth to her city, and we just don't know if the prices they charge us for radiators are fair or not. It would cost us a lot to find out if they are fair." [*Internal pricing and internal cost systems are unreliable and expensive; the market provides comparatively cheap and reliable information.*]

"When Radoe had labor trouble before the merger, we just invoked the contract and it cost her plenty to fight that union, but it was her money (and her temper). We gave a little, of course, because we couldn't hang a good supplier and

[28]Oliver Williamson and William Ouchi, "A Rejoinder," in *Perspectives on Organization Design and Behavior*, Andrew Van de Ven and William Joyce, eds. (New York: Wiley Interscience, 1981), p. 390.

buying elsewhere was expensive. But all in all it cost us only about 10 percent in profits for the quarter. But now we have to bear the total cost. Our industrial relations manager doesn't know that union. The union is mad because of the strike years ago. It's very hard to put a price on the quality of labor relations when you buy a firm. Those agency theorists call it reputation and think that it can be priced like radiators, but it's hard to verify and easy for a firm to exaggerate with a bit of strategic public relations, classy accounting, and mimicry of leading firms in the field. The people at Radiators misled us, and I think we should have paid less because of the labor problem. Any settlement they get will rev up our other union. And while Radoe was willing to do battle with the union and take the losses when she headed the firm, now I don't really think she sees the urgency of the labor problem as much as when she owned Radiators." [*Costs of acquisitions are poorly estimated and subject to opportunism. Reputation is subject to "isomorphic pressures."*[29]—*that is, firms come to look alike by imitating superficial attributes of leading firms. Unexpected interactions are increased in large systems.*]

"We are still having problems with leaky radiators and the squabbling and charges between the radiator division and the engine division is worse than before the acquisition, because personality clashes now make it more difficult. Not only are there problems with getting information about who is really responsible in the market (Williamson calls the problem 'information impactedness'), but it can be worse in your own firm, especially when you try to do two different things, such as making engines *and* radiators; the two processes and the organizations and the personnel are just different." [*Information (and control) within the firm is subject to political and personality problems that may make it more expensive and less reliable than in the market. Coordination of diverse activities within a firm is expensive; such coordination is not needed in the market.*]

"I would like to sell the division, but the transaction cost of selling it, after all those of buying it (which Williamson never mentioned), would just be too great. I agree with Perrow. You should integrate forward or backward only when it means you can get more market control or get your hands on a very profitable piece of property and keep those profits for yourself." Mrs. Enginee's only comment was, "Dear, you read too many books."

As lighthearted as this vignette may sound, it contains some important points. As Williamson himself notes in one chapter of his book on TCE, there are transaction costs within the firm as well as between firms, and his examples suggest that some are higher in hierarchies than in markets.[30] We should also note that markets can be efficient in establishing prices, whereas firms find "internal pricing" (the allocation of costs to various units) difficult and highly politicized. The incentive structure is also artificial and politicized in hierarchies as compared to markets.

[29]Paul J. DiMaggio and Walter W. Powell, "The Iron Cage Revisited: Institutional Isomorphism and Collective Rationality in Organizational Fields," *American Sociological Review* 48 (1983); 147–160.

[30]Williamson, *Markets and Hierarchies*, Chapter 7. In a new work in progress, he emphasizes this even more. Since transaction costs have not been operationalized, making measurement possible, the fundamental issue of whether they are higher between firms or higher within them will probably never be settled. See my comments on this issue in "Markets, Hierarchies and Hegemony: A Critique of Chandler and Williamson," in *Perspectives on Organization Design and Behavior*, pp. 371–386.

Settling disputes by fiat is difficult because of the very things Williamson has made us aware of—asset specificity and small-numbers bargaining *within* the firm. Not all transaction costs are counted in Williamson's argument. Uncertainty affects internalized units as severely as it affects independent firms in the market; fluctuation in demand and supply, labor problems, problems with competitors, and so on do not disappear, and their resolution may be more difficult in a large firm. Opportunism, to the extent that it is a problem, will accompany the acquired firm, because it is a hierarchy itself, and will persist within the acquiring firm. Costs that could be externalized and risks that could be borne by the independent firm must be internalized by the acquiring firm, and the acquiring firm may have less flexibility in dealing with these problems because of long-term commitments and the power of groups with specific assets within the firm. Finally, while my account at several points favors markets over hierarchy, it does not assume a neoclassically perfect market. These rarely exist. Markets tend to be concentrated, rigged, protected, and inefficient. However, I would give two cheers for markets, and only one for hierarchies, if only because of the power of giant firms to shape our premises to their own ends. But in any case the TCE argument is markets versus hierarchies, so the comparison has to be in those terms.

Lying behind my fiction is a more general point that goes beyond the critique of TCE: there is an advantage to decoupled units in a system, and a disadvantage to tight coupling. For instance, Radiators, Inc., devised accounting and information-management systems that were tailored to its specific operations; integrating it with the systems that were good for Engines, Inc., entailed changes that made the new system less efficient. The labor relations of Radiators may have been bad from some points of view, but they were not entangled with those of Engines. In the combined firm, any settlement for the radiator division has an impact on the engine division. Engines was buffered from changes in demand by Radiators, which absorbed some of the shock; ACE has to absorb all the shock.

Furthermore, Engines had people who knew how to deal with large suppliers and thus could act quickly if demand rose; ACE lost some of that expertise, raising its transaction costs. When demand was down, Radiators suffered, but at least it could look for other customers, lowering its price (and profits). But as a division of ACE, it has more trouble selling radiators to ACE's competitors. As a division, it probably can't trim its overhead during slack times as well as it could as an independent firm; some of the overhead costs assigned to it in ACE are "lumpy"—that is, not divisible; overhead is a difficult thing to cut in large firms during retrenchment because of structural problems; it affects all divisions regardless of their individual needs.

Finally, it is possible (though hardly inevitable) that Radiators could more easily change its production methods and incorporate new technologies than the division within ACE. As an independent firm, it could do what it wanted with production as long as it met the quality standards of the customer, Engines, Inc. As a division, it interacts with the rest of the organization at many points, and changes may be resisted at some of those points by people who see disadvantages in such alterations. (Were ACE to provide significant research and development services for the division, this might change, but some evidence suggests that smaller firms are the more innovative.)

These are arguments for loosely linked components of a system where there are likely to be uncertainties or shocks from the environment or from within. Tightly coupled systems have advantages, certainly; resources can often be used more efficiently, there is less redundancy and waste, and the processes are faster. But these advantages appear only if there is little uncertainty in the system—few exogenous shocks (those coming from without the system), few endogenous shocks (those coming from within), plenty of time to recover form shocks, and many different paths to recovery. Most industries do not have these luxuries, and thus loose coupling is likely to be a more efficient system property than tight coupling. Loose coupling is associated with a large number of small units engaged in straightforward bilateral exchanges.[31]

CAUSES OF HIERARCHY

Efficiency, as realized by the reduction of transaction costs, is thus an uncertain accompaniment of vertical integration, and some flexibility and buffering may be lost in the process. Clearly, in a comparison of two firms in the same industry with the same market power, political ties, and so on, the more efficient will prosper and survive, and lower transaction costs will make some unknown contribution to efficiency. But comparing firms with efficient and inefficient internal operations is not the issue; it is the grounds for vertical and horizontal integration in parts of the economy that must be explained. That explanation will not be in terms of efficiency. Even if our large firms grew without acquisitions—that is, grew internally by creating units that extended backward or forward integration—their success need not be attributable to more efficient production, distribution, and product development. It could be due to increased profit margins stemming from eliminating competitors, raising prices, receiving direct and indirect government subsidies, benefiting from special tax laws, and so on. Nor is there any evidence that firms generally acquire inefficient firms and make them efficient; the evidence, which we shall review later, is that firms acquire profitable firms (and then watch the profitability of the acquisition decline). While profitability does not mean efficiency, the lack of profitability is at least some argument for inefficiency. Thus we should look elsewhere for an explanation of the appearance of large firms and the decline of markets in some sectors.

The historical evidence on the growth of large firms is striking and attests to various forms of market power and government support that have little to do with organizational efficiency. The major industries of the United States—oil and chemicals, iron and steel, automobiles, electrical goods, food processing, railroads, and now electronics and television—are as concentrated as they are not because the leading firms saved on transaction costs or were efficient in other ways, but because they could control the market, labor, and government and were backed by powerful

[31]Charles Perrow, *Normal Accidents: Living with High Risk Technologies* (New York: Basic Books, 1984), Chapters 3, 9.

financial interests.[32] The control of the market and government by firms in even the most concentrated industries was certainly not absolute; competitors, labor, and sectors of local and national governments still give them considerable trouble. But if one can reduce the number of competitors and generate demand, maintain a tractable labor force, and secure aid or cooperation—or at least not provoke resistance—from the government, one can grow large at the expense of small competitors, suppliers, and customers. (In a moment I will explain where such concentration is not likely to appear.)

The reasons for big firms are quite diverse; one reason may be savings on transaction costs and other sources of organizational efficiency, but possibly it is of only modest importance, rather than of primary importance, as Williamson asserts. Only a sketch of an answer to the question can be given here. A firm requires various "factors of production" such as land, labor, capital, supplies, technologies, and outlets. Advantages in any of these areas by one firm will lead to the firm's growth relative to its competitors. Growth also requires at least tolerance on the part of the government, though state enabling factors (antiunion legislation, limits on liabilities, tax policies, tariffs, etc.) and state resources (contracts, loans, access to minerals on public property, etc.) will be beneficial to growth as well. Many of these government policies and resources will favor a whole industry, allowing it to prosper and grow, thus providing an incentive for some in the industry to take over other firms. (There is little incentive to absorb enterprises in a low-profit or low-growth industry; while the purchase price will reflect the stock market's evaluation of the industry and the firm, to the extent that future growth possibilities are good and greater market control over pricing and competitive products is possible, firms will reap advantages from attractive industries regardless of the existing stock price. Some governmental policies, such as a particular tax ruling, may be specific to individual firms.

Next, for the firm to grow there must be market growth, through the discovery or creation of new markets or the expansion of existing ones. Since a firm's growth will be challenged by the growth of other firms, assuming the market is not infinite, the firm must keep competitors out entirely or, failing that, limit or reduce the number of competitors. Thus, aside from efficiency, a number of devices can be used to gain market growth and reduce competition. The discussion of the popular music industry in Chapter 6 nicely illustrates the point. Under oligopolistic conditions, transaction costs for the majors were high, not low, as the majors maintained stables of recording stars, controlled outlets, and had producers and manufacturing units on their payrolls. When intense competition set in and numerous small firms entered the market, as entry costs dropped, the transaction costs were probably greatly reduced: companies contracted out to producers, stars, and manufacturers and let these parties bear the risks. But this also meant that the small firms could reap the profits when they were lucky, so the big firms got control of the market again, reappropriating the profits by controlling competition.

Another example of an attempt to eliminate competition in growing markets

---

[32]For a survey of industries and their history of aggressive market control by industrial economists—a breed apart from and ignored by the "new institutional economists"—see F. M. Scherer, *Industrial Market Structure and Economic Performance*, 2nd ed. (Chicago: Rand McNally, 1980), especially Chapter 6.

was Andrew Carnegie's effort. At the end of the nineteenth century, his iron and steel company grew phenomenally (and later became the basis of U.S. Steel). An associate of Carnegie, James Howard Bridges, addressed the issue of transaction costs. Carnegie was a fanatic on cost cutting in production areas and developed sophisticated bookkeeping devices to keep his transaction and production costs low. However, Bridges stated that "it was other considerations than increased efficiency and economy that promoted the first and perfect combination of the Carnegie properties"—that is, the growth of his empire. There was no plan to the acquisitions, Bridges said flatly. Instead, as he detailed, Carnegie coveted the high profits of other corporations; maneuvered to get rid of an officer; and even eliminated a competitor by getting the railroad pool to cut it out of deals to provide cheap freight, enabling him to buy the competitor at distress prices. (At the time, Carnegie, paying dividends of 40 percent, was not suffering a profit squeeze.) He found the profits of the ore companies to be very large, so he moved in and, through a combination of financial power and threats, acquired a good bit of the Mesabi Range in Minnesota; and when the ore boat companies would not reduce their prices, he set up his own. His company was immensely rich and powerful. He did not have to worry about transaction costs, and they did not motivate his actions.[33]

Because of the factors of production, it is unwise to consider strategies of market growth and competition only in terms of the firm; other organizations in the environment are crucial. Perhaps of most importance is the source of investment capital—a competitive but still concentrated system of banks, insurance companies, investment houses, and venture capital firms. Holding liquid (readily available) assets, they can provide the means for one firm to buy out competitors (with no efficiency gain), to finance price wars that force out competition, to buy up and destroy competitive goods or services (as the DuPont and General Motors interests were able to destroy much of urban mass transit in the United States in order to increase the demand for cars and force the construction, through taxes, of roadways for them to drive on[34]), or to relocate to a low-wage area. Banks, insurance companies, and investment firms can make legal or illegal donations to politicians and political parties here and abroad in order to influence government actions that will tend to increase concentration in industries and reduce competition. They are not particularly concerned with the efficiency of a loan applicant, but with the opportunities the applicant's industry provides and the applicant's ability to exploit opportunities in that area.

Firms, generally with resources from the financial community, may also use the patent system and other legal and illegal devices, to gain control of new technologies and in some cases to restrict the development of these innovations in order to increase market control and thus the size of their own organizations. (Charges of suppressing innovations are common but hard to prove. Industrial espionage is widespread and acknowledged, however.) Firms may conspire with suppliers or

---

[33]J. H. Bridges, *The Inside History of the Carnegie Steel Company* (New York: Aldine Press, 1903), pp. 135, 168, *passim*. See other examples in Perrow, "Markets, Hierarchies and Hegemony," pp. 371–386, 403–404.

[34]Glen Yago, *The Decline of Transit: Urban Transportation in German and U.S. Cities, 1900–1970* (New York: Cambridge University Press, 1984).

customers to undercut competitors and drive them out with illegal rebates, espionage, and defamation; concentrated industries benefit all concerned—suppliers, producers, and distributors. Of course, fraud and force can be used to gain market control or other advantages, and our industrial history right up to the present is replete with examples. Some of our largest firms actively used fraud and force in their early history, quite possibly contributing significantly to their present dominance. The age of the "robber barons" coincided with the great vertical and horizontal concentrations of industrial power.

As a few firms eliminate the rest of the competition and integrate vertically, many opportunities for exercising power appear. Prices and thus profits can be increased. With larger and fewer firms, the cost of entry for potential competitors rises, despite the attraction of large profits; new firms must start large. Market domination also slows the rate of innovation, limiting expensive changes and prolonging the returns on expensive capital investments. Fewer producers also lead to more coordinated lobbying activity regarding tariff protection, subsidized research, investment tax credits, and so on; more concentrated economic power with regard to labor; more plant-location incentives from local government; and local tax abatements. These are a few of the benefits of size in our economy. Thus, even if the acquired facility is not highly profitable in itself, it may add to the power and thus the profits of the acquiring firm.

Why, then, do we not have a few large firms dominating each industry? Why is steel concentrated, while furniture is not? Traditionally, factors such as size of capital investment, transportation costs, perishability of goods, and so forth have explained the differences in concentration rates (equivalent to the degree of hierarchy; technically hierarchy is a feature of organizational forms, not of industries, but if a decent-sized industry has, say, more than 50 percent of its capacity in the hands of four firms, those firms will be very large and in almost all cases hierarchical.) I would like to look at these factors in a somewhat different light and argue that markets persist where large profits are not available and, in some cases, where government policy prevents concentration.

Until recently, when financial considerations prompted the growth of conglomerates—firms that bring together unrelated businesses, such as W. R. Grace and ITT—most profit-seeking acquisitions were in closely related fields, such as suppliers, competitors or distributors. The acquiring firm simply had more information about these types of firms and had experience with the product. Economies of scale and benefits may result from smoother coordination of the enlarged input-through-put-output cycle achieved by acquisitions of closely related firms, but I believe these were secondary motives. Firms with resources will attempt to buy firms that are making good profits; transaction-costs savings or economies of scale are of little importance if the profits to be gained are small. The purchase price will reflect the profitability of the firm, of course; profitable firms will have high stock values and cost more. But future profits are to be realized by the market power and political power that come with increased size; neither unprofitable firms nor unprofitable industries favor the realization of such power.

Of course, the firm targeted for acquisition must have sufficient amounts of profits (regardless of the rate of profits) to offset the costs of purchase and integration. A very large firm will not usually be interested in a tiny one, no matter how profitable, though it does happen. A moderate-sized firm, however, may well be interested. Note that the increased profits of the acquiring firm do not mean that the acquisition is more profitably run or that transaction costs have been saved, but only that its profits have been appropriated—that is, assumed by the acquiring firm. (This is important in judging efficiency questions; increased profits or rates of profit after acquisition do not necessarily mean more efficiency; they can mean less competitive pricing, tax advantages, and so on.)

In addition to market control and profitability considerations, financial manipulation plays a role in mergers. In some cases, for example, the profit rate of acquired subsidiaries will actually decline after the merger, but capital accumulation by investors and officers, rather than a profit for the firm, is then the goal. This occurred when U.S. Steel was formed by the purchase of many steel companies. Much money was made through issues of watered stock (exaggerated share values), making the acquisitions very profitable for the investors, even though operating efficiencies declined. The decline was offset by the new combine's enormous market power. Today, stock manipulation, appropriation of cash flows (milking the profitable acquisition without reinvestment), buying footholds in new markets, and so on figure prominently in merger and acquisition strategies—so prominently that it has become a national scandal. Lower transaction costs presumably play no role in these manipulations; indeed, transaction costs are greatly increased, but fortunes are made anyway.[35]

Though it is somewhat less apparent today because of the weakness of unions, control of labor has also been a motivation for acquisitions, resulting in increased profits, though not increased production efficiency. Acquiring facilities in low-wage areas, acquiring nonunion facilities in order to attack the unions in the existing facilities, and absorbing a sufficient proportion of the local work force to be able to control local wage rates are some of the tactics corporations use.

But markets still remain for small or moderate-size firms. Many highly profitable small firms are not targets for acquisition; they can exist in small or localized markets. For example, the market for specialized luxury goods is small, and the market for ethnic goods or foods is generally localized. Some items have small markets because they are unique or idiosyncratic. We speak of such markets as

[35]While it is not conclusive, the evidence about the performance of acquired units should indicate skepticism regarding the efficiency of acquisition policies. David Birch followed 6,400 firms that were acquired during 1972–1974 and compared their growth rates before and after acquisition with the 1.3 million firms that were not acquired. He found that, in Rothschild-Whitt's summary, "conglomerates tend to acquire fast-growing, profitable, well-managed businesses, contrary to the theory that they seek out poorly-managed, inefficient firms"—that is, conglomerates do not acquire those that might have, among other things, high transaction costs. However, growth is not speeded up after the acquisition; in fact, "Firms that remain independent grow faster than acquired firms." A congressional study found that firms that were acquired subsequently had lower rates of job creation, productivity, and innovation. See David Birch, "The Job Creation Process" (Cambridge, Mass.: MIT Program on Neighborhood Regional Change, 1979); and Committee on Small Business, U.S. House Representatives, "Conglomerate Mergers —Their Effects on Small Business and Local Communities" (Washington, D.C.: U.S. Government Printing Office, House Document No. 96–343, October 2, 1980). Both are discussed in Joyce Rothschild-Whitt, "Worker Ownership: Collective Response to an Elite-Generated Crisis," *Research in Social Movements, Conflict and Change* 6 (Greenwich, Conn.: JAI Press, in press), a sobering, informative review of worker-ownership developments.

"niches"—small corners in the economy where a few producers can make a lot of money but where demand is fairly inelastic (it won't grow much because it is so specialized) so there is no possibility for increasing market control or expanding the market. The large firm has no interest in such firms; though the rate of profit in some niches is large, the absolute amount of profit can be small; additionally, this amount must be great enough to offset the substantial costs of integrating small, diverse businesses into a large firm. Acquisitions involve transaction costs and organizational redesign costs, as illustrated in the ACE case.

Industries need not be forever unprofitable or confined to niches. In the nineteenth century the modest profits of the hundreds of small flour mills made them an unlikely target for acquisitions, because they sold to middlemen and grocers who dumped the flour into one bin labeled "flour." But by promoting branded flour through advertising ("as pure as the drifted snow"), market control was achieved, a few large milling companies soon dominated the industry, and they still do.[36] Much the same thing has happened with restaurants serving limited, quickly prepared meals. Small restaurants—mom-and-pop operations requiring long hours for low profits—have always existed. As the demand for quick meals outside the home increased, heavily advertised chains moved in and took over the market. By combining the advantages of centralized control with nominal local ownership, they have been able to reap the advantages of low-paid local labor with high worker turnover and of nominal (franchise) owners who work the long hours that mom and pop once did. Centralized buying, heavy advertising, and rigid procedures have no doubt contributed to the profitability of these chains, so in this one case we might say that profits may stem from efficiencies, including centralized control of transaction costs.

The creation of large, market-dominating firms also requires the acquiescence of the federal government. Large firms flourish in the defense industry because the government favors them for reasons of military strategy. In fact, such firms are occasionally bailed out by handsome government contracts because letting these companies go under would remove resources the government feels we need. One does not start up a giant aircraft and missile firm easily or quickly. Here, "efficiency" is of secondary importance.[37] Similarly, in banking, while state banking laws have restricted the centralization of banking in the United States, a change in laws could produce a movement toward hierarchy that would not be caused by transaction-cost efficiencies but rather by market control and the acquisition of profitable properties.

A final concern, in this case, leading to the absence of hierarchy, is a recognition that some degree of loose coupling is efficient. This appears to be the reason why the three big U.S. automobile companies control, but do not own, their distributors.[38] The retail dealers sign long-term contracts that govern the number and type of cars they are allowed to receive (important for a hot item), the cars they must receive (important for disposing of the "dogs"), how much of the cost of failures

[36]Charles Perrow, "Markets, Hierarchies and Hegemony."

[37]Seymour Melman, *Pentagon Capitalism: The Political Economy of War* (New York: McGraw-Hill, 1970).

[38]Kenneth McNeil and Richard Miller, "The Profitability of Consumer Practices Warranty Policies in the Auto Industry," *Administrative Science Quarterly* 25 (1980): 407–426; J. Patrick Wright, *On a Clear Day You Can See General Motors* (New York: Avon Books, 1979); and Harvey Farberman, "Criminogenic Market Structures: The Auto Industry," *Sociological Quarterly* 16 (1975): 438–457.

they must bear under the warranty, how much they can charge for repairs in some cases, how much advertising they must do, and so on. The dealers have discretion only on trade-in prices, preparation prices, or other deals that make the final selling price somewhat flexible. Otherwise, they are quite constrained; indeed, the manufacturer may unilaterally and without warning raise the wholesale price to dealers without posting a higher retail price, thus cutting the dealers' rate of profit. The argument is sometimes made that car dealers represent flexible adaptations to local markets and thus are more efficient than if owned and controlled outright by the manufacturers. This does not appear to be the case; they cannot order just the makes and volume they wish, the prices can be changed, warranty work is tightly regulated by the manufacturer's complex contracts, advertising is regulated, and so on. The dealers can be flexible and adaptive in their used-car line only.

As a result, the dealers must absorb the market declines (they have to cut their profit to get rid of the quota of cars they must buy), even though they cannot fully participate in market rises (they cannot get all the fast-selling models they want). Cost of entry is not large for them, but as small businesspeople they do invest their own capital and thus tend to make little or no profit in poor times. A few dealerships do very well indeed, but most do not. Yet there are always small businesspeople willing to take the risk. Thus the manufacturers are buffered from fluctuations in the market for cars and from the yearly gamble on model changes and new models. Since the overall profitability of dealerships is only modest and subject to much uncertainty, it is not worthwhile for the manufacturers to integrate forward into a business over which they already have considerable control.

Our many dealerships really constitute a "controlled market," with many small firms rather than either a hierarchy or a true market. Most franchises, as in the fast-food industry, are devices to spread risks and buffer the headquarters from uncertainties. Given the limited entrepreneurship opportunities that our economy offers for people who lack wealth or unique skills, there are always many who are willing to work very hard for low and risky returns. Though controlled somewhat, these people still have more autonomy than employees of large corporations do.

Thus we would expect to find small firms persisting in areas of the economy that show low overall industry profitability (unless the industry can be restructured to promote branded products or other forms of market control); where there are idiosyncratic factors despite high profits (local markets, niches); where the market cannot grow despite profitability (inelastic demand); or where government restrictions obtain. Finally, hierarchies are probably self-limiting; at some point, which varies according to technologies, capital requirements, the shape of the market, and so on, firms probably lose control over some of their subsidiaries, and complex internal interactions, and they lose the ability to respond to external shocks. The subsidiaries are sold off, or their efficiency declines to the point where they lose money despite substantial market control and other advantages of size, and someone else moves in. Some minimal efficiency *is* necessary, of course, but transaction costs rarely play a significant role.

This brief sketch of some of the forces contributing to hierarchy and economic concentration in our society stands in marked contrast to economic motives for efficiency in the face of opportunism and transaction costs. It is neither original nor novel, but it suggests the range of structural variables that are neglected by economic interpretations of organizational behavior.[39]

BEYOND MARKETS AND HIERARCHY

Evidence is accumulating that the economist's contrast of markets and hierarchy may be misleading; perhaps only a small part of our economy, and even less of other economies, would support the contrast. We certainly have large firms, but they may be so large as to operate like markets, and markets appear to be so organized as to make the notion of independent price givers and takers questionable. These "markets" may be governed by forces that most economists would not recognize as plausible.

A striking piece by Ronald Dore, a British sociologist familiar with Japanese history and industry, argues that Japanese industry is more efficient, overall, because the contracting involves a significant degree of good will, give-and-take, long-term planning, and in general, an avoidance of opportunism. The classical market that economists posit is efficient only in allocating goods (if that). Citing the work of renegade economist Harvey Liebenstein for support, Dore argues that a number of other efficiencies are more important, and they are realized by trust, noncompetitive relationships, and mutual assistance in time of need. These other efficiencies include rapid spread of innovation; shared information on changing market situations and consumer choices; aggressive search for new uses of labor and capital if old markets decline; flexibility in task assignments; and the disaggregation of industry when desirable (for example, the move from hierarchy to small firms in Japan's textile industry). Finally, Dore questions whether this is necessarily a product of Japanese culture; much more cut-throat, self-interested practices prevailed in Japan during the 1920s and again immediately after World War II. He also finds evidence for good will and suspension of self-interest in the United States and Britain, especially in industries or firms noted for their emphasis on quality rather than quantity. There is a mine of research projects in this attractive essay. [40]

[39]There are other criticisms of Williamson's work and of the related work of Alfred Chandler. Williamson explored the early history of capitalism, arguing that hierarchies proved to be more efficient than cooperatives and inside contracting, but the economic historian S. R. H. Jones has written a devastating critique of Williamson's evidence and interpretation. Similarly, Richard Du Boff, a historian, and Edward Herman, an economist, have reviewed Chandler's work very critically, presenting evidence that the emergence of several of the hierarchies Chandler described had much more to do with market power than with coordinating efficiencies (and I have made a similar criticism with more modest evidence). In a volume devoted to Williamson's work, Arthur Francis has offered a perceptive essay on the issue of efficiency versus market power. See S. R. H. Jones, "The Organization of Work: A Historical Dimension," *Journal of Economic Behavior and Organization* 3, nos. 2–3 (1982): 117–137, replying to Oliver Williamson, "The Organization of Work: A Comparative Institutional Assessment," *Journal of Economic Behavior and Organization* 1 (1980): 5–38 (with a further exchange in vol. 4, 57–68). See also Richard B. Du Boff and Edward S. Herman, "Alfred Chandler's New Business History: A Review," *Politics and Society* 10, no. 1 (1980): 87–110; Perrow, "Markets, Hierarchies and Hegemony"; and Arthur Francis, "Markets and Hierarchies: Efficiency or Domination?" in *Power, Efficiency and Institutions*, Arthur Francis, Jeremy Turk, and Paul Willman, eds. (London: Heineman, 1983), pp. 105–116.

[40]Ronald Dore, "Goodwill and the Spirit of Market Capitalism," *British Journal of Sociology* 34 (December 1983): 459–482. Harvey Liebenstein, *Beyond Economic Man: A New Foundation for Microeconomics* (Cambridge, Mass.: Harvard University Press, 1976).

As organizational analysis steadily moves toward the macro field of industries and the economy as a whole, it should look to cultural variables such as trust and orientation toward the collectivity to explain the dynamics of modern capitalism. As it does, it will question not only the importance of efficiency motives and contractual costs, but the very notion of a continuum from markets to hierarchy. Increasingly, macro organizational perspectives see the attempts to organize—to coordinate and control—as a mixture of contracts and hierarchies, and I would question even the utility of these analytic terms. The line of inquiry that sees a mixture of market and hierarchy is quite new, and new terms may have to be invented to grasp it, but it is exciting. Let me sketch the problem.

The economist's emphasis on rationality, or even bounded rationality, neglects the complexity of markets and hierarchies in the following respects: the problem of organization, including the organization of organizations, is one of both coordination and control; self-interest and opportunism, or the rational calculation of short-run gains, are important, but are not the most important parts of the problem. Hierarchies do not provide control by fiat, or authoritarian order giving, but through bargaining, much as market contracts do. There are strong elements of markets within hierarchies. On the other hand, markets have strong elements of hierarchy within them. The distinction between markets and hierarchies is greatly overdrawn. The continuum from market to hierarchy is less like a ruler than a football, with a vanishingly small pure type at each end, and a swollen middle that mixes the two (as Sidney Winter once put it in a seminar). Organizational theory—in its move from the single organization, to dyads, to a focal organization interacting with several others, to an organization having relations with a vague environment, and then to network analysis—is now recognizing the dense ties that unite buyer and seller, organization and government and trade groups, and even distant organizations through interlocking boards, advisory committees, and political groups. The "society of organizations" is a dense and ever-changing network of reciprocating competition and cooperation; very little of organizational life remains at the two ends of the "football."

Oddly enough, Williamson's fascinating empirical case study of a cable TV franchise illustrates the middle of the football (and many sociological variables such as power).[41] The city of Oakland put out bids for a cable TV network service. After getting the contract, the low bidder then acquired asset specificity by installing part of the service; it then sold out to a larger firm that had been one of the bidders, and the new firm then demanded and received very favorable new contract terms. Williamson's account makes it clear that there was hardly a market to begin with, that what little there was soon disappeared, and that the city, as principal, lost control to the agent, the cable TV franchiser, transforming a nominal market relationship into a hierarchical one. The transaction costs for both were very high, but Williamson does not recommend hierarchy, wherein the city would buy out the cable TV firm or establish its own; that would be tantamount to recommending socialism. The net result was that the city and its taxpayers lost, and the private firm

[41]Oliver Williamson, "Franchise Bidding for Natural Monopolies—in General and with Respect to CATV," *Bell Journal of Economics* 7, no. 1 (Spring 1976): 73–104.

won. Opportunism with guile was there in large quantities, but from a larger perspective it would be better to simply call the situation capitalism.

Arthur Stinchcombe considers several companies such as defense contractors, large civil engineering firms, and franchise networks, and he notes how their relations with their customers tend to be hierarchically organized, even though these would seem to be examples of markets.[42] For example, the Department of Defense is very intimate with the contractors and places inspectors and accountants in their firms, much as a large corporation puts inspectors and accountants into each of its divisions. The same kind of thing occurs outside the defense area. Chevrolet, in its relations with its suppliers, treats them almost as profit centers and risk bearers and controls much of what they do. On the other hand, hierarchies develop profit centers and divisions that bargain with each other and the main office in a marketlike arrangement, encountering the large costs of simulating a market with "shadow prices" and numerous accounting practices. Harrison White goes even further in a very suggestive paper that also argues, in effect, that the principal-agent model is misleading. He describes organizational relationships as reflexive ones that oscillate, dissolve, and revive, making it difficult and arbitrary to designate who is agent and who is principal. Ranging from the Roman Empire to high-technology industries, his paper is an effective though not very explicit criticism of TCE.[43]

Such interdependencies among organizations are troublesome, subject to corrupting influences, inefficient, and mysterious, both to those involved in them and to social scientists looking at them. But they are essential, because of the complexity of information problems, incentives, controls, coordination, innovation, and change. The interdependencies are subject to contextual influences such as long-term relationships, storage of surpluses, calculation of group efforts, and all the variables I cited earlier as determinants of the extent of self-interested versus other-regarding behavior. To single out a concept such as markets versus hierarchies, and to assume self-interest as the motive, is to sweep aside reality and a host of fascinating, productive problems. Neither TCE literature nor agency-theory literature rises to the occasion.

Sociologists and other organizational theorists have hardly begun to rise to the occasion either, but they are positioned to do so because they embrace a more systemwide viewpoint, with attendant developments in network theory, evolutionary models, and attention to the environment in general, as celebrated in Chapter 6. Their work is not disabled by assumptions of rational or primarily self-interested

[42]Arthur Stinchcombe, "Contracts as Hierarchical Documents," *Work Report* 65 (Bergen, Norway: Institute of Industrial Economics, 1984).

[43]Harrison White, "Agency as Control," unpublished paper, Harvard University, 1983; and Robert G. Eccles and Harrison White, "Firm and Market Interfaces of Profit Center Control," unpublished paper, Harvard University, February 1984. See also, for an industry study, W. Graham Astley and Charles J. Fombrun, "Technological Innovation and Industrial Structure: The Case of Telecommunications," in *Advances in Strategic Management*, vol. 1 (Greenwich, Conn.: JAI Press, 1983), pp. 205–229. For an interesting discussion of industrial markets in Sweden, developing the notion of heterogeneous markets (in contrast to the homogeneous ones found in neoclassical economic theory) and of "nets" (those parts of the industrial "network" where strong complementarity pervails), see Ingemund Hagg and Jan Johanson, *Firms in Networks—New Perspectives on Competitive Power* (Stockholm, Sweden: Business and Social Research Institute, September 1983).

behavior. Rather, they study the contexts that call out rational, nonrational, self-regarding, and other-regarding behavior. This broader inquiry is, in part, occasioned by the challenge that economists have presented by their foray into the world of organizations. This challenge evokes the menace of the novel and film *The Invasion of the Body Snatchers*, in which aliens occupy human forms, but all that we value about human behavior—spontaneity, unpredictability, selflessness, plurality of values, reciprocal influence, and resentment of domination—has disappeared.

8

Power in Organizational Analysis: Illustrations, Summary, and Conclusions

A SUMMARY MODEL OF A POWER VIEW

As we have learned, theories simplify, and this last chapter will be no exception. In it I will try to do the following: first, I will lay out the basic assumptions that should guide organizational analysis. This constitutes a brief summary of the theory that has survived the critiques I have made in the book. Second, I will indicate how some of the extended examples and discussions in the book reflect the role that power plays in these basic assumptions. We could end there, but I will review two additional theoretical thrusts—the role of myths and symbols, and that of historical evolutionary accounts. Both are new, and both grow out of the theories discussed in Chapters 5 and 6. I treat them separately here in order to illustrate how a power view would modify their emphasis and enrich them. I should note that I am not proposing a theory of organizations; technically, theories are quite specific things with assumptions, propositions, and "operationalizations." This discussion is closer to the idea of orienting assumptions, or basic perspectives. Its key notions are that organizations are tools and that power makes them go; power should be neither as neglected nor as implicit as it has been.[1]

Power

There are many definitions of power. We encountered an attractive one in the work of Arnold Tannenbaum at the end of Chapter 3—a non–zero-sum view in which the amount of power generated within an organization could vary from low to high. An organization that allows its employees autonomy and a broad scope for action will have larger resources to draw on than one that doesn't. An organization that

---

[1]The emphasis on power here is certainly not novel, though it is far from widespread. It is, I hope, consistent with such widely different books as Stewart Clegg and David Dunkerley's attempt to relate organizations to society, and Jeffrey Pfeffer's more internally oriented essay on power in organizations, and with much more in between. See Stewart Clegg and David Dunkerley, *Organizations, Class and Control* (London: Routledge & Kegan Paul, 1980); and Jeffrey Pfeffer, *Power in Organizations* (Marshfield, Mass.: Pitman, 1981). See also the equally valuable book by Jeffrey Pfeffer and Gerald Salanzick, *The External Control of Organizations* (New York: Harper & Row, 1978).

convinces its employees that their goals are compatible with those of the leaders will generate more capacity for action and in this sense more power. While a non–zero-sum view is important and useful, I would argue that this constitutes a subcategory of power, a variable that comes into play only after a more basic, zero-sum definition is applied. Most resources in organizations and society can be expanded; much effort is wasted in unproductive conflict and even shirking, which often requires effort. Organizational theory should attend to this problem. But there is a larger one: the distribution of risks and benefits among all. Here the power of some is at the expense of others. Organizations facilitate the generation of zero-sum power.

Consider a system as generating valued outputs (goods, services, profits, wages, interesting work, social status, or whatever) based on its resources (capital, equipment, employees, markets, legitimacy, and so on). In my scheme, power is the ability of persons or groups to extract for themselves valued outputs from a system in which other persons or groups either seek the same outputs for themselves or would prefer to expend their effort toward other outputs. Power is exercised to alter the initial distribution of outputs, to establish an unequal distribution, or to change the outputs. We could put it in terms of goals: there is a struggle over either the content of the output or the distribution of it. This is a "power over" rather than a "power with" view; it deals with the type of pie and the division of the pie, not its size. The question of the size of the pie, increasing the output no matter who gets it, is an important one, but it cannot operate independently of the distribution issue and the content issue, which are prior and thus the more important concerns.

It is true that power "gets things done," but what must be done and what is done with the output is more important than power as "empowerment" or capacity. In more concrete terms, a tight labor market gives job seekers the power to extract higher wages or better working conditions. A cohesive group generates the resources to increase the output of a product line the members produce, thus increasing their ability to extract the outputs of job security, wages, and working conditions over those of groups producing a different product line. A regulatory agency, using laws and enforcement agencies, may have the power to lower a company's emission of pollutants and thus make the air cleaner for all and command more job security and employment benefits for agency members. The company may find, as is commonly the case, that the investment it must make in antipollution devices actually lowers its long-run costs, but it did not know this initially and viewed the lowered emissions as contrary to its economic interests. These are all examples of zero-sum power. We would have a non–zero-sum gain, with a bigger pie, were the regulatory agency able to convince the company that it was (1) in the company's own economic interests to install the equipment, since the output of profits that it controls would rise; (2) in the public's interest, since health would improve; and (3) in the agency's interest since it would lower enforcement costs and improve the agency's goal-achievement record. This is an important issue, but note how it is framed by the prior issue of zero-sum power; the company and the agency must be convinced that each will not lose.

Power, as used here, is zero-sum, relational (over someone), exercised both inside and outside the organization, and concerns an output of organized activity that is valued and an output that is produced only at some cost.

Descriptive Propositions

The argument of this book may be summarized for the most part by three major propositions:

1. Basically, an organization is a tool that masters use to generate valued outputs that they can then appropriate. The most essential theory to explicate this is bureaucratic theory, as outlined in Chapter 1. This theory emphasizes hierarchy, specialization, formalization, and standardization. Nothing is as important as the master's ability to imperatively specify and coordinate the work of employees. The formal structure of the organization is the single most important key to its functioning, no matter how much it may be violated in practice; the violations themselves reflect the constraints of the formal structure. Imperative coordination is achieved primarily through direct controls (orders, associated with hierarchy) and bureaucratic controls (standardization, specialization, and formalization). Bureaucratic theory, based on the work of Max Weber and subsequently elaborated by others, is the single most essential element of a theory of organizations.

   It is not possible to discuss imperative coordination without emphasizing power as we have defined it. A bureaucratic theory takes as given an unequal distribution of resources in the initial state and thereafter. Power maintains the inequality.

2. The first and most major *qualification* of the bureaucratic model is, as discussed in Chapter 4, bounded rationality: shifting and unclear preferences, limited information, and limited knowledge of cause-and-effect relations. It has consequences for both the master and the employees.

   2a. For the master, bounded rationality means that the ambiguities about cause and effect and personal preferences that reside in the employees permit the master to use unobtrusive controls and premise setting. Were employees fully informed and completely rational, they would be unlikely to allow the surplus from their labor to be retained by the master. (The matter of public organizations would require a more complicated formulation.)

   2b. Bounded rationality makes the employees susceptible to unobtrusive controls, but since the master is also subject to bounded rationality, there is a limit on the effectiveness of his or her control—and thus a source of power for the employees. They have leverage to realize some of their own ends, even when these conflict with those of the master. Employees are not passive, even if they are not formally or informally organized to resist authority; they can contest authority and, to a minor degree, shape the premises of superiors and, to a still more minor degree, affect organizational goals.

   2c. Bounded rationality ensures considerable change in the behavior of the organization as a whole, though largely as a result of the unintended consequences of purposeful actions. Some of the change is undesired by all; some is innovative and beneficial to at least some groups. Bounded rationality is not the only, or even the most important, source of change, since there will be changes in the environment and in the goals of the masters. But some change is due to unexpected events that are inevitable because of bounded rationality. The more the analysis is concerned with small groups or parts of the organization, the more change and fluidity will be apparent; the more the analysis is concerned with organizations or an industry over time, the less important is this (or any) source of change, because some internal changes dampen the effect of others and because external constraints are powerful for all organizations.

3. Given bureaucracy with bounded rationality, the next most important qualification is group usage, as distinct from individual usage of the organization by masters and employees. Group usages are internal and external.

   3a. Internal formal groups, such as departments or work groups, seek to use the organization for such ends as promotion of ideological positions or public policies, protection of groups and expansion of group power, control of working conditions—including degree of effort, safety, interpersonal interactions, and job security—and satisfaction of personal goals. Internal informal groups do the same, but the membership cuts across that of formal groups and tends to offset the centrifugal effects of multiple group strivings by binding groups together, sometimes in unexpected ways. Group usage both responds to bounded rationality and overcomes it; it may facilitate imperative coordination, as Barnard saw —"oiling the mechanism," so to speak—but more likely it interferes with imperative coordination. Owners and managers are forever trying to convince both formal and informal groups of workers that employee ends should support those of their superiors. Groups mobilize resources to change, control, or use the multiplicity of outputs of organizations, and this can never be of indifference to the masters.

   3b. External formal and informal interest groups seek to use the organization and its power to affect public policy and values, to appropriate the organization's surplus, to support other organizations or groups, to sell it goods and services, to control its impact on the environment (e.g., plant location, wage rates, pollution policies, civil rights practices, tax payments, and so on). A variety of mechanisms exist to enable others to use the formal organization. Generally these are formal organizations themselves, such as voluntary associations, clubs, business associations and trade groups, consumer groups, schools and colleges, unions, political parties, government bureaus, and organized crime.

   The master or masters of the organization are the chief focal point for external groups, but the boundaries of organizations are very permeable, allowing access at any level, sometimes linking an internal group with an external one. A scientific association, for example, may influence the behavior of scientists in the organization; national unions clearly penetrate through the local affiliate; most managers have professional associations that seek to influence them and that they influence in turn. The influence mechanisms range from ideology to corruption; they reflect the inability of the master to exercise full control, and the contest for power goes on not only within the organization but among groups that seek to use it.

The lack of full control is due to bounded rationality, and also to the dependence of the organization on external resources and clients or consumers. Since the organization must ceaselessly make exchanges with the environment, groups in the environment have access to it and seek to use it.

Levels of Analysis

So far our perspective has been limited to explicating a single organization. Once exchange with the environment is considered, analysis can focus on the interaction of organizations rather than on the interactions of groups inside and outside the organization. In view of the importance of the environment to organizational theory in the last decade, the scope of interactions between organizations should be roughly specified. The nature of power will shift as one moves up to higher levels of analysis that take in broader interactions. The higher the level, the more controls that are unobtrusive and premise-setting are used. We saw in Chapter 6 how radically different the explanation of the organizational behavior of a hospital became when the focal concern shifted from the organization to the networks in which it existed. Here, we shall identify the levels of networks, the state, and the cultural system. Each has substantial impact on any organization, and each conditions the struggle for power.

1. Depending on the problem at hand, the interaction of organizations can be conceptualized as (a) a network of actual *direct* exchanges by organizations (and interest groups, which will be treated as organizations here), which is the most limited concept; (b) an organizational field, which includes *indirect* interactions with other organizations—that is, those that occur through an intermediary organization; (c) an industry, in the case of economic organizations, which includes unorganized consumers, suppliers, competitors, trade associations, and regulatory agencies, where the contacts may be direct, indirect, or symbolic (such as through laws), or through "structural equivalences" (see page 199); (d) or finally a sector, which includes all of the above but also political phenomena, culture, symbols, and myths. Delineating a sector, when so much is included in one, is difficult, but the term is more restricted than "society" or "region" and broader than "industry," since two industries may be shaped by the same cultural and political forces while a third is shaped by different ones. Some sectors, such as the health-care sector, will be quite large and include components as diverse as polluting industries and unemployment policies. The recreational sector would be comparatively small. A sector analysis (discussed below) forces us to consider political and cultural factors.

2. At a still more general level, the state itself is a part of the interactions of organizations and conditions the form of interaction of all organizations.

Major changes in resource flows, development of technologies, interactions with foreign governments, regulatory and tax policies, redistributional income policies, and the like flow from local and national state policies, and sectors and the organizations within them seek to control or influence state actions.

3. Beyond even this grand level is the cultural system of symbols, values, and cause-and-effect beliefs that are society-wide and common to all sectors. The cultural system is greatly conditioned by bounded rationality; indeed, our limited rationality gives rise to the cultural system of symbols, values, and beliefs about causation. This is a major option-setting context of interest groups, organizations, and sectors. Some examples of this pervasive cultural system are: acceptance of employee status by 85 percent of the working population; acceptance of giant corporations and (more recently) giant government, and acceptance of rapid technological change and the view that problems will succumb to "technological fixes."

Another example is the decline over two centuries of group and community referents for justifying actions and the rise of the individual as the measure of good. This shift has been gradual, and some outrage about excessive individualism still surfaces. In the 1984 presidential election, the Republican campaign theme "Aren't you better off now?" was criticized because its referent was the well-off individual, which seemed to ignore the poverty of voiceless groups, the decay of cities, and heightened international tensions. But the notion of collective freedoms and collective responsibilities is on the decline. (It is ironic that individual rather than community welfare is now a major value when great collectivities, in the form of organizations, have come to dominate our lives; it may even be an uncomprehending reaction to the absorption of the family, neighborhood, and independent groups by the large organizations.) Finally, there is the cultural reluctance, given our view of individual liberty, to assess/ the externalities, or social costs, of organized activities.

All of these cultural aspects are challenged at times; acceptance may be grudging and initially under duress, as in the case of the gradual acceptance of wage dependency in the nineteenth century. Changes are generally gradual but may involve sharp breaks, as in the sexual revolution of the 1960s and 1970s.

This perspective on organizations has been used in much of this book. It may help to recall some of the specific cases and arguments we have introduced. In Chapter 5 on the institutional school, I insisted that while "drift" occurs, as the result of incompetent leadership, the assumption of good will with incompetence on the part of leaders may not be correct in most cases. Our perspective indicates that we should always examine the possibility that organizational masters prefer unofficial goals over official ones and may even make sure that official goals are not achieved. We should then search for extraorganizational interests that are served by what appears to be, from a leadership perspective, drift or goal displacement. This may not be a problem that can be corrected by making organizational practices more efficient; it may be an intentional outcome. By examining the setting in which the organization functions, including the values available in the sector, we may find explanations for an apparent lack of leadership or of "proper" organizational practices.

In Chapter 6 on the environment, the changing market conditions in the popular music industry were interpreted in terms of a confluence of sector and industry changes that the majors could not control. Changes in technology produced changes in entry costs for the industry, and this tapped suppressed cultural demands in the sector as a whole. The response was decentralization and uncertainty, but the power of the major firms gradually reasserted itself to control the industry again and even to shape cultural tastes to some extent. Here we had considerable bounded rationality as well as new groups, with their own interests, that could emerge for a time. Organizational efficiency had little to do with the dynamics; market power and financial resources did. In Hirsch's comparison between pharmaceuticals and record companies, the level of access to state power appeared to explain the different rates of profitability and stability of the two industries. The reinterpretation of Westwood Hospital's expansion involves power at all levels, including leadership of the various hospitals, the network of interacting hospitals, the health industry, and the sector, which included state activity. At each ascending level we found more powerful explanations for the expansion program and the form it took. Indeed, a focus on only one of the hospitals would very likely have produced incorrect interpretations.

We criticized Barnard and the human relations school because they neglected power as a variable. Barnard was willing to use power under the guise of rational and correct analysis in describing the food relief program, but he denied its existence when discussing the cooperative nature of organizations. The human relations school, by assuming a natural convergence of goals among participants, saw inefficient organizational practices as the main problem organizations faced. We suggested that goals were not shared, and while it was certainly better to treat employees with respect than not, there might still be quite legitimate grounds for conflict between managers and the managed, that the question of the uses (goals) of the organization was completely neglected, and that for some technologies an authoritarian, bureaucratic structure appeared to produce more outputs for the masters and less for the workers.

The human relations school is at least concerned with problems of supervision and a few other aspects of working conditions; the economic theories of organizations reviewed in Chapter 7 gave it scant attention. Again, the issue of unacknowledged power differentials appeared to undermine the analysis of the economists. The work of this school generally assumed that managers and owners are at the mercy of opportunistic workers, whereas it would appear that the superior resources of the former encourages exploitation of the latter. Efficiency was said to account for the appearance of giant corporations, whereas our analysis suggested that it was irrelevant and that market power and government aid or tolerance, given certain structural conditions, were much more plausible arguments.

Even the bounded rationality formulation of March and Simon in Chapter 4 on the neo-Weberian model had its limits. It inadequately considered the question of how the power of masters is enhanced by their capacity to set premises, because of the bounded rationality of subordinates, and limited, though to a lesser extent, by their own bounded rationality. The analysis of accidents that concluded that chapter involved the low power of operators, resulting in inappropriate attributions of error; the power of organizational elites to create technologies that will support a hierarchical, bureaucratic structure where such a structure is not necessary; and the power of elites in society to define risks and benefits in such a way that others bear the risks while the elites reap the benefits—an example, in addition, of the role of myths and symbols, when we move to a cultural level of analysis, in interpreting what is happening in an industry or organization.

All of these are grand claims for the importance of a power analysis, but let me note that they are not inconsistent with more mainstream concepts of bureaucracy, contingency theory, resource dependence, and some concepts of the evolutionary and the economic interpretations of organizations. All of these schools had things to teach us and concepts and theories to add; not all their notions need to be rejected. But almost all of them miss, some narrowly and some widely, the notion of power. Organizations generate power; it is the inescapable accompaniment of the production of goods and services; it comes in many forms from many sources; it is contested; and it is certainly used.

ORGANIZATIONS AS MYTHS AND SYMBOLS

As yet one more example of a body of theory that needs to be recast in terms of a power theory, consider the quite new and popular one of organizations as symbols and myths, sometimes referred to as a cultural interpretation. Its roots lie in the institutional school, one of the oldest in our field and considered in Chapter 5. It stresses values and symbols and is firmly in the "exposé" tradition of that school. In this section I will examine the application of the myths and symbols to public schools, arguing that a cultural approach is necessary, but it must be informed by an awareness of political and organizational power. After a critical examination of the role of schools in society, I will indicate some of the promising leads that the theory of organizational myths and symbols has given us.

In the early 1970s a group of researchers from the School of Education and the Department of Sociology at Stanford University carried out a large survey of superintendents, principals, and teachers in San Francisco school districts. The initial reports indicated something was amiss in these organizations. Reforms were announced with enthusiasm, and then they evaporated. Rules and requirements filled the cabinets, but teachers taught as they pleased, and neither principals nor superintendents took much notice. State and federal money was flowing in, and elaborate reports suggested compliance with the conditions set by government, but little seemed to change in the classroom. Studies of child teacher interactions indicated that children and teachers were unaffected by what teachers and students in the next classroom did, by what the principal said or did, by the school district, by the sources of outside funds, or by the teacher-training institutions. Rationalistic theories of organizations were clearly inappropriate in this setting; the bureaucratic controls were simply not working, and no one seemed to notice or care. Rationalistic theories would never predict such loose coupling in a hierarchical system, but existing notions of informal organization, open systems, the environment, human relations models, and so on were also irrelevant.

Later in the decade John Meyer and Brian Rowan addressed the puzzle by arguing that the real function of education is to sort and certify people; imparting skills and knowledge is not really that important.[2] But since our cultural values insist that skills and knowledge *are* important, these must be affirmed, regardless of the reality. So the classroom activities are sequestered from the view of principals, districts, and government at all levels, and the appearance of educational outcome is measured by meaningless statistics on the number of students processed, the qualifications of teachers, the curriculum, and the number of programs for the disadvantaged. Nothing really measures what students have learned. The public is reassured, the social class system is stabilized, the teaching profession is protected, the cost is low, and a minimally sufficient degree of socialization and knowledge is produced. Meyer and Rowan call the reassurance a "rationalizing myth" and see the function of the schools as largely symbolic.

Meyer and Rowan's article is one of the most powerfully argued organizational history pieces in the sociological literature, despite its brevity. Yet there are problems with it. First, while school personnel are seen to benefit from the failure to measure outputs and thus bring about improvements, it is not clear that the self-interest of school personnel, or of anyone else, is the source of the problem. No adequate explanation for the state of affairs appears; it is almost as if myths and symbols are given causal efficacy, as if they constitute some force that creates the situation. I will try to show that a power view of organizations can provide some explanation for the discrepancy between goals and actualities in the school system. The second problem is that when parts of the public and the government, both at local and federal levels, attempt to change the behavior of the schools, Meyer, in later work, uses his cultural interpretation to dismiss the attempt as a myth-creating enterprise itself. Rational action, it appears, cannot exist; all is myth. But a power view would reject this. Finally, the symbolic view neglects the irrelevance of much education, given today's economic and social class systems; the discrepancy between goals and reality might be seen as primarily protecting the economic and political system, and only incidentally protecting the school personnel.

How can we explain the gap between the symbols and the reality of education? Assuming, for the moment, that the schools actually teach very little, or that even if they do teach something it has no relationship to credentialing students, what would create and sustain this condition? In the nineteenth century schools taught people to read, "Americanized" foreign immigrants, and prepared children for the discipline of the factory. The schools were quite successful at this, and despite struggles over culture and religion in the classroom, the public supported them for good reasons. But even if the schools had performed very poorly in terms of making students literate, acculturated, and socialized into a society of organizations, there were powerful groups that came to depend on the schools, regardless of their official success. The public schools offered, and still do offer, employment for educated women with few other career opportunities; employment for minorities and other upwardly mobile groups (much public-sector activity presents job opportunities for

[2]John W. Meyer and Brian Rowan, "The Structure of Educational Organizations," in Marshall W. Meyer and associates, *Environments and Organizations* (San Francisco: Jossey-Bass, 1978), pp. 78–109; the essay has been reprinted in John W. Meyer and W. Richard Scott, with the assistance of Brian Rowan and Terrence E. Deal, *Organizational Environments: Ritual and Rationality* (Beverly Hills, Calif.: Sage, 1983).

these groups); opportunities for colleges to establish training programs and recruit students; and work for the construction industry. Schools are steady consumers of supplies of all sorts, from bathroom tissue to books; they provide space for public functions and recreational groups, and they are also babysitters for working mothers. But most important of all, as the twentieth century matured, schools delayed entry into the labor market for 12- to 17-year-olds, who had always worked since time immemorial. Our economy could not have absorbed these millions of adolescents, and the massive idleness of the unemployed youth would have created grave social problems. Thus, irrespective of the school system's performance, a number of groups found that institution useful.

But so far this "group usage" view tells us only that outputs other than education made the schools viable. This is important, for it explains lack of protest in terms other than myths and symbols. But why was there not, in addition, an insistence on real education, instead of on mere certification? I would suggest that the answer is that the kind of output that Meyer and Rowan think would match the reality with the goals is increasingly irrelevant. In the schools that they studied in the 1970s, there were fewer and fewer academic goals that were relevant for students, in terms of employment or even citizenship. The real "myth" is not that schools educated, but that education was at all still relevant for many urban youths. This myth is deliberately created by groups who need an "operator error" explanation, so to speak—one that blames the victims of an evolving economy or, in this case, the schools and especially their students. *The economy does not need many skilled people, and it has an excess of unskilled job seekers;* and perhaps conservative economic and political elites find the polity can function increasingly well without informed citizens. The schools are left to the usages of those who have no particular concern with their quality. These are rash claims, and I cannot do justice to them in this book. I can sketch an organizational power interpretation, however, that is consistent with them.

But first let me review an extension of Meyer and Rowan's historical article. It appears in an important book on organizations and environments by John Meyer, W. Richard Scott, and various co-authors.[3] In this book Meyer and Scott (primarily the former) discuss attempts to reform the schools in the 1960s and 1970s and treat these attempts as myths themselves. The actual record appears to be quite different. I will first explain how I see these events; then I will examine their interpretation.

Since the 1960s there has been considerable protest by insurgent groups about the treatment of minorities, the handicapped, and the poor in the nation's school systems. Until 1981 when its role began to decline, the federal government was pressured to act with the carrot of federal funds and the stick of performance reporting. Social-action groups such as the civil rights movement and federal agencies concerned with the War on Poverty demonstrated that public schools were discriminating against the poor, the minorities, females, and the handicapped, or at least the needs of these groups were not being met. Here, at last, was some attention to the discrepancy between classroom activity and professed goals. Federal money was allocated to fund special programs that would correct discrimination and improve education. Indeed, the research of the Stanford University group that highlighted the discrepancy was a part of this movement. As the Stanford group and

[3] Meyer and Scott, *Organizational Environments.*

many others discovered, the schools made few changes; in fact, they often diverted the money to servicing the already advantaged. The government got tougher and established more and more requirements, paperwork, auditors, and so on—what we usually call bureaucracy. (Much of it was inefficient and fumbling, as many attempts to change the behavior of entrenched organizations will be.) The schools rebelled, called for local autonomy (but still expected federal funds; though they didn't want dollars for special programs for the disadvantaged), and told horror stories about the federal bureaucracy. Many local interests outside the schools preferred to discriminate against the disadvantaged and supported the schools' revolt. Frustrated and defeated, the federal government turned to largely unrestricted and unmonitored block grants; concern about the disadvantaged had declined during the Nixon years (and seems to have evaporated entirely under the Reagan administration), and the local schools were either strong enough to resist performance monitoring or were too amorphous to control.

This is an organizational usage-and-power interpretation. Meyer and Scott present a quite different one. They treat the pressure exerted by community groups and the federal government to improve the lot of poor, black, and handicapped students with ill-concealed disdain. Mere myths, they assert, explain the growing rules accompanying the federal government grants, such as the myth of rationality; the problem of insufficient compliance with these regulations is not mentioned. That the poor might be helped by more resources directed at them, rather than channeled off to the advantaged, is also treated as a myth, since schools don't teach but only accredit. There are some distressing examples of blaming the victims and of cynicism about the reformers' motives. There are sour complaints about lack of standards in schools but pity for the teacher commanded to spend more time working with the poor. The traditions and identities of local groups are treated as absurd, and the term "hillbilly school board" is used. But when the reformers do likewise and charge that local boards are recalcitrant and opposed to reforms, Meyer does not accept the charge as legitimate and treats it as merely a way of legitimizing the unwarranted intrusion of the reformers. Reformers are scorned; they are the "disorder-discovering interest groups" that are concerned with the poor or the pregnant, and they opportunistically "quickly adapt to the language of equality," manipulating a supine Congress that "almost at random emits equalization programs for ever more groups." Meyer has scorn for all those "new types of handicapped pupils (some undiscovered as of a decade or two ago)." What are we to make of this phrase: "the treatment of putatively unequal groups of students (e.g. minorities, the poor, female students, and the handicapped)"? Is there any serious doubt that these groups are not equal with the rich, whites, males, and the healthy?[4]

Thus does an unrestrained myths-and-symbols view gloss over unpleasant realities, group interests, and power. It can be the unwitting carrier of a conservative laissez faire analysis that ignores basic inequalities in our society. The ultimate cynicism about organizations is to say that those who are damaged by them are merely creating legitimizing myths by their protest. The important problem is not the documentation of myths and symbols that substitute for education, though that

[4]Ibid., pp. 220, 211, 209, 218, 255, 244, 225, 236.

is a beginning, but how a society can tolerate functional illiteracy in one-third of its adult population (16 percent of whites, 44 percent of blacks, and 56 percent of Hispanic peoples, according to a book by Jonathan Kozol[5]). The role of symbols is crucial, but we should search for powerful interests behind the distortions that the symbols hide. As Chapter 6 on the environment argued, the results we get may not be due to organizational failures but organizational successes.

Symbols in particular and culture in general are not politically neutral; they can be created and propagated by political and economic elites. In a society of organizations, a theory of organizations is needed to appreciate this fully. This brings us to my assertion that schools may be the scapegoats of political and economic policies; we may have less use for them as imparters of skills and training for citizenship than we had in the past and more use for them as storage centers, delaying the impact of idleness and defeat for 20 percent of their graduates. The myth in this case is the "crisis in the schools," proclaimed in the 1980s by presidential commissions and policy groups that represent both conservative and middle-of-the-road political interests. Illiteracy is mentioned, but the emphasis is on the failure of the schools to prepare students for our high-technology future; students are not taking enough math and science, these critics complain. The Japanese and the Russians are far ahead of us in math and science, and Japan may win the economic contest and Russia the military race. But the emphasis on failing schools may simply disguise a failing economic system that cannot use an abundance of skilled young people. We cannot even absorb literate job seekers, let alone place well-educated ones in jobs that would use their skills. Perhaps 25–35 percent of recent college graduates are overqualified for their jobs, and the percentage is increasing, since 25 percent of the young entering the labor force have four years of college. (They are overwhelmingly white and not of the lower class.) In the booming 1960s, 75 percent of college graduates seeking employment found professional or managerial jobs. But in 1980 only 60 percent did. Education is now only weakly related to productivity; as years spent in school have lengthened over the last several decades, productivity has declined. Perhaps the quality of education is not as high as it once was, and perhaps more emphasis on basic skills and science and mathematics would help. But it seems far more likely that the movement to service industries, where few skills are required and productivity is hard to increase, weakens the correlation of education and productivity.

Similarly, there is only a weak relation between what is learned, measured by test scores, and what is earned. A recent study of high-school graduates compared those testing in the 97th percentile with those in the 50th percentile; the high-testing group earned only 10–20 cents an hour more than the low-testing group. Perhaps the skills of the high scorers are not utilized by their employers; perhaps the employers do not need them. (Recall that routine is the touchstone of bureaucracy and service jobs are the source of labor-force increases.) Vocational education rose by 33 percent between 1972 and 1979, while the appropriate job opportunities rose by only 15 percent. For example, two-year vocational education degrees rose by 690 percent, while jobs in those areas increased by only 12 percent. We are not

[5]Jonathan Kozol, *Illiterate America* (New York: Anchor, 1985).

exporting high technology or even skilled jobs to other countries, as might be expected if we lacked skilled labor here. Instead, we are exporting the lowest-skilled jobs; those for which we have an abundance of manpower.

The prevailing assumption is that our labor-force skills must be upgraded to fill the high-technology positions. But high-tech industries *reduce* skill requirements and demand only minuscule numbers of highly skilled personnel. For example, while jobs for computer programers will expand by 150,000 between 1978 and 1990, we will need 1,300,000 more janitors, nurse's aides, and orderlies; there will be nine unskilled jobs in these categories alone for every computer programmer. The biggest single growth category is a high-technology one—data-processing machine mechanics—but it will expand by only 100,000, while kitchen helpers and fast-food employees will expand by eight times as much. If you are thinking of a career in the expanding high-technology sector, you may be encouraged to know that of the five fastest-growing occupations in the economy as a whole in relative terms (that is, the percentage increase, rather than the absolute number), four are indeed in this area: data-processing machine mechanics, computer systems analysis, computer operation, and office-machine servicing. (Paralegal services are the fifth.) Between 1978 and 1990, 518,000 of these high-growth positions will become available. But if you miss one of these you may instead end up in one of the five occupations where the *absolute* growth is largest—2,934,000 instead of 518,000: janitors, nurse's aides and orderlies, sales clerks, cashiers, and waiters and waitresses. An eighth-grade education will suffice for most of these; only two require much literacy.[6]

Our society is creating a permanent underclass of people who may never have any need for the skills they learn in the eleventh and twelfth grades, if they last that long, and whose functional illiteracy is hardly a handicap in a life on the welfare rolls or in the world of crime. This underclass could comprise 20 percent of the popula-

[6]These summaries, ironically, are from a Stanford University institute, the Institute for Research on Educational Finance and Governance, *Policy Notes,* 4, no. 3 (Summer 1983), pp. 1–7. For a technical article with references to the research, see Russell W. Rumberger, "The Changing Skill Requirements of Jobs in the U.S. Economy," *Industrial and Labor Relations Review* 34 (1981): 578–590, and his *Overeducation in the U.S. Labor Market* (New York: Praeger, 1981). There is also a substantial literature on training and on certification. See, for example, Ivar Berg, *Education and Jobs: The Great Training Robbery* (New York: Praeger, 1970); and Randall Collins, *The Credential Society: A Historical Sociology of Education and Stratification.* (New York: Academic Press, 1979).

Harold Wilensky and Anne Lawrence are among those who disagree with this picture of employment prospects, arguing that the first jobs of well-educated high-school graduates and of college graduates are bound to be below their qualifications because they are entry-level jobs, but the studies reported consider this. Employers, they say, choose entry-level employees who have the skills to move up the job ladder, so education eventually pays off. But there are no job ladders for janitors, nurse's aides, orderlies, or most fast-food workers—the positions in which most jobs are becoming available. Wilensky and Lawrence argue that education inculcates discipline, and this is true, but reform schools might be more relevant for future food handlers than secondary schools that emphasize math and science. Finally, these authors argue, without evidence, that education promotes the fast learning needed in high-technology industries. This is probably true, but not much fast learning of new tasks is required for cashiers or sales clerks. Many also point to the wild diversity in the quality of education, especially the low quality of inner-city schools. Just so. If teenage unemployment is greater than 50 percent in our inner cities, it might help to explain, better than a failure of the schools, the high dropout rate in those areas and the classroom discipline problems that make any learning even harder. See Harold L. Wilensky and Anne T. Lawrence, "Job Assignment in Modern Societies: A Re-Examination of the Ascription-Achievement Hypothesis," in *Societal Growth: Processes and Implications,* Amos H. Hawley, ed., (New York: Free Press, 1979), pp. 202–248.

tion if no major structural changes are made in the next few decades.[7] The voting rate of this group is very low, so members are not a political threat. Increasingly, the census takers cannot even find them. The schools cannot hold them, and upgrading the schools will not help them. Employment will not increase if everyone gets a meaningful high-school diploma. We do not compete with other nations in service sectors of the economy, so better education for the masses will not help us in international competition. Better education should produce a more informed citizenry, ready for "lifetime learning," but if I were an elite concerned with my income, class position, and the opportunities for my offspring, I would think twice about a more informed citizenry in an economy that survives on defense and service jobs with an increasingly polarized income distribution and a growing permanent underclass. The political scene of the mid-1980s suggests that reassurance, not information, is the key to political success.

Thus the symbolic nature of schooling is overstated. There is a large element of myth and ritual in it, and Meyer and Rowan's historical account is brilliant. But that account may be appropriate only to the past, when literacy, Americanization, and socialization into a permanent wage status may have been all that the schools really needed to do. In the 1970s and 1980s, though, the cultural approach to organizations requires that powerful interests outside of organizations, including the state, must be taken into account. The view I sketched at the beginning of this chapter would ensure this larger perspective.[8]

The cultural approach of John Meyer and his associates is given to excesses, I have argued, if it does not consider power. But a cultural approach is still essential. I noted earlier how important it is to recognize the cultural level of symbols, values, and cause-and-effect relationships. Meyer and Scott in fact lay out in their book the beginnings of a very useful scheme that classifies organizations in terms of their emphasis on technical versus institutional evaluations of effectiveness. Technical organizations, such as manufacturing firms, are judged by their outputs; they monitor production and protect their technical core from the environment. Institutionalized organizations, such as schools, are judged by their forms rather than their output; they do little monitoring of production, and they protect their forms or structures from the environment, since these are the main sources of their legitimacy. Technical organizations use structures to make their work efficient, but institutionalized organizations use structures to indicate conformity to social and cultural expectations. The actual work processes can be decoupled from the structure. Meyer and Scott also develop the notion of "sectors," which discriminates on the basis of the mix of technical and institutional criteria and includes institutional factors (laws, government relations, public visibility, and prestige), support organizations, and legitimating organizations. Medical care, for example, is a sector that combines organizations with both technical and institutional criteria, as does bank-

---

[7]William Julius Wilson, "The Urban Underclass, Social Dislocation, and Public Policy," in *American Minorities and Civil Rights: Where Now and Where Headed,* ed. Leslie Dunbar (New York: Pantheon, 1984).

[8]The Meyer and Rowan article we have been discussing was followed by a much more famous but quite misleading piece by them, "Institutionalized Organizations: Formal Structure as Myth and Ceremony," *American Journal of Sociology* 83 (1977): 440–463. Here virtually all organized activity is seen as myth creating; it is an unfortunate example of overextension of an important insight.

ing. Neither technical nor institutional criteria are particularly relevant for evaluating the personal service sector. Schools are low on technical but high on institutional criteria. This is a realistically complex way to subdivide the world of organizations, and I believe it deserves much development. If power relations are explicitly recognized, a sectoral analysis of education—one that recognizes the low impact of technology on structure and the importance of structure for legitimizing the system —should be very valuable.[9]

The cultural approach has also been used to good effect, with appropriate attention to other factors, by Paul DiMaggio and Walter W. Powell. They explore the institutional pressures that make organizations within the same field resemble one another, independent of any efficiency reasons. These pressures include the power of dominant organizations and the state to coerce conformity in structure and practices, consistent with a power model; the drive to imitate seemingly successful organizations to try to achieve similar success or merely to look acceptable, consistent with a cultural model; and the role of professionals and their networks in demanding and producing similarities in background and orientation, a structural and power interpretation. DiMaggio and Powell avoid the extreme of saying that structural reorganizations, such as divisionalization, are always imitative or merely signals of modernity, but they give examples that appear to make signaling the main motive, and efficiency can suffer as a result. Their viewpoint alerts us to processes that are easily neglected, but it does not insist that these imitative, coercive, and professional power processes are the only ones. At least implicitly the bureaucratic core identified at the beginning of this chapter remains intact.[10]

AN EVOLUTIONARY THEORY OF BUREAUCRACY

Our last illustration of the importance of a qualified power model of organizations concerns evolutionary and population-ecology theories, which we discussed in Chapter 6. There I argued that social systems can avoid the life cycle of natural systems,

---

[9]The sectoral analysis undercuts many of the book's other excesses—for example, the tendency to treat hospitals as only institutionalized, with effective medical treatment being seen as "less important" than ritual procedures (Meyer and Scott, *Organizational Environments*, p. 39). (In Chapter 6 of that book, hospitals are recognized as both technical and institutional.) Unfortunately, at many places the analysis resembles those of schools that I have criticized strongly; it treats serious problems such as worker safety, pollution, and discrimination against women and minorities in the workplace as myths. Attention to power in society and careful consideration of the mix of technical and institutional criteria would avoid these excesses.

[10]Paul J. DiMaggio and Walter W. Powell, "The Iron Cage Revisited: Institutional Isomorphism and Collective Rationality in Organizational Fields," *American Sociological Review* 48 (1983): 147–160. Support for the cultural model of Meyer and Scott and DiMaggio and Powell also comes from a surprising source—the highly rationalistic field of accounting. There has been a recent surge in what was once called "behavioral accounting" (that is, look at what is done, not what is theorized). The lively British journal *Accounting, Organizations, and Society*, edited by Anthony Hopwood, explores a variety of myths of accounting, its highly political character, the great discrepancy between theories of accounting and actual practices, and the way accounting practices can prevent an organization from, for example, conceptualizing market changes and responding to them. Mainstream professors of accounting are now paying some attention. See the important articles by Carnegie-Mellon and Harvard professor Robert J. Kaplan, "Accounting Lag: The Obsolescence of Cost Accounting Systems," unpublished manuscript, Harvard University, March 1984, and "The Evolution of Management Accounting," *The Accounting Review* 49 (1984): 390–418.

since many very large businesses and industrial organizations have survived for several decades, and many public organizations, such as public schools, are not allowed to die, though they may be merged. I also called for attention to the power to create environments and thus control the conditions for survival. Since their appearance in the mid-1970s, population-ecology theories of organizations have become more sociological and, indeed, increasingly resemble traditional organizational theories as they factor in institutional variables and recognize the insights of the older school of human ecology. The work that we will examine now, by John Langton, is especially promising, since it deals with the origins of bureaucracy. It even includes a discussion of such neo-Marxist concerns as deskilling and the exploitation of labor. Thus power is not ignored. But power plays an extremely weak explanatory role; the central dynamics are still variation, selection, and retention. Furthermore, Langton's account illustrates only a faint attention to the last set of variables in the qualified power model outlined at the beginning of this chapter: the larger system in which the organization is embedded. It is for this reason I have chosen the model to conclude this chapter and book.

John Langton's article on the Wedgwood pottery firm in eighteenth-century England is a very good piece in several respects. It covers a long time period, as an evolutionary, population-ecology study should, but rarely can do because of data limitations. It deals with a historically important industry that significantly shaped the development of bureaucracy in England, rather than with a population of relatively trivial organizations over a decade or two. It acknowledges some power issues. And it is quite learned in the best sense of the word.[11]

Langton's account begins with the general rise in the British standard of living in the eighteenth century. This rise brought about an increase in tea and coffee drinking, which created a demand for inexpensive, good-quality earthenware pots and cups that the existing potteries could not fill. One potter, Josiah Wedgwood, after much experimentation, produced an inexpensive but good product, "Queen's Ware." He then sought high-volume production to meet the demand, and this required better roads for safe shipment, a canal adjacent to the new factory for moving raw materials, and a labor force that could be made to work for long hours under intense discipline for low wages.

Wedgwood and other potters pressured Parliament to build the turnpike, and then Wedgwood pressured Parliament to build the canal. He acquired a site on it when he was sure it would be built. The work force, Langton notes, was produced by the enclosure movement, in which the nobility began to use their land for raising sheep instead of for agriculture, forcing the tenants who had farmed these lands for generations to look for other means of support. However, this work force needed disciplining, since, according to contemporary accounts accepted by Langton, it was accustomed to bouts of idleness, drinking, games, and gambling. Discipline was provided by the local preacher John Wesley, who offered the workers the alternatives

---

[11]John Langton, "The Ecological Theory of Bureaucracy: The Case of Josiah Wedgwood and the British Pottery Industry," *Administrative Science Quarterly* 29 (1984): 330–354. Page references in parentheses in the text refer to this work. My own source for British history in this period is largely Francis Hearn, *Domination, Legitimation, and Resistance: The Incorporation of the Nineteenth-Century English Working Class* (Westport, Conn.: Greenwood Press, 1978).

of eternal damnation or subordination to authorities. Discipline was also provided by adopting the techniques of an industrialist Wedgwood knew—a rudimentary form of bureaucracy involving task specialization, formalization of authority, standardization, and hierarchy. The result, after much experimentation and development, was high-volume production and extremely large profits for Wedgwood. Potters who did not follow his example failed; others survived, but none on the scale of Wedgwood. The example illustrates a behavioral evolutionary account of the development of bureaucracy.

All these steps bear closer examination before we conclude that Wedgwood was an example of variation (discovering how to make Queen's Ware), selection by the "environment" as the best fit, and retention of the innovations. An alternative explanation is that the state favored such institutions as large factories producing luxury goods for private profit and that it provided the resources, including the labor. When Wedgwood started his first small operation in 1759, the state still reflected the interests of the landed nobility; it was not until the early nineteenth century that the growing merchant and new capitalist classes gained control. But in the period of Wedgwood's growth, the new commercial interests achieved many victories in Parliament and in the courts. These triumphs helped Wedgwood and bureaucracy quite directly.

Going back to the beginning of Langton's account, it can be equally well argued that consumption of nonnutritious coffee and tea was an upper-class affectation that spread to the middle classes and served no survival function for society. Expenditures of physical and social resources on more elegant pots and cups might be seen to be inefficient in a society with pressing health and social problems. (Langton does not assert that good pottery and tea drinking were necessary for the survival of society, of course, but because of the character of some evolutionary thought it is worth making this point in passing.) While the turnpike and canal that Wedgwood pressed for no doubt served important trade functions for necessities as well as luxury goods, they were provided by the public, and their capital costs were not fully reflected in the price of goods that traveled on them (i.e., the state did not recover its costs in building them by charging merchants for their use). One or a few pottery firms, then, extracted public resources not available to others. Presumably no inquiry was made as to whether Wedgwood (and any other potters that benefited) was more deserving of the particular location of these facilities than, say, many agricultural areas producing necessities.

Certainly the enclosure movement, which provided the labor supply, was resisted by those who were dispossessed and by social critics, was sanctioned by the state, and bestowed large economic benefits on the large landholders. They no longer had to honor traditional norms or the actual laws that bound communities together. Langton describes the movement in functional and positive terms as making "labor more mobile and more free to move about" *(341)*, but the peasants did not see it that way at all. Many were forced either to work unaccustomed hours for low wages in factories or to starve. (Indeed, there is some evidence that during a recession Wedgwood prevented his idled workers from seeking other employment, even though he was not paying them; he curtailed even this freedom.) The negative description of the work force as brutal, ignorant, drunken, and given to idleness, a view prominent among the upper classes at the time, is not questioned by Langton, but should be. There was a great emphasis on sports and games (brutal by our standards, but traditional for the working class), fairs, wakes, family time, rest, and leisure. All were eliminated with Wedgwood's ten-hour day, six days a week, with perhaps two holidays a year. Langton goes further in siding with the employers over the employees. Referring to Wedgwood's work force he says: "Certainly they felt no *ethical* obligation to work in diligent, conscientious, and regular fashion." *(342, italics added)* Since they were poorly paid, had lost much of their leisure, and were producing very large profits for Wedgwood, one wonders why Langton assumes the ethical obligation was the workers', and not Wedgwood's. It may even be that excessive drinking appeared with dispossession, desperation, long hours, and unwholesome work and was thus a dysfunctional consequence of the dislocations accompanying industrialization.

Preacher Wesley's influence appeared to be to demand long hours of work under intense discipline, under threat of damnation and hellfire. It is possible that the success of Wesley and Wedgwood depended on the disruptions of the enclosure movement and the increasingly repressive tactics of the central government as it tried to put down unrest. Most important, the greatly increased hours and hard work did not swell the wages of the workers, as they would have under subsistence farming and even tenancy, but only the profits of the owner. This was a relatively new phenomenon, since in most other forms of livelihood until then (such as farming and skilled trades), the returns from harder work and longer hours primarily benefited the worker. Langton acknowledges that the workers produced unprecedented profits for Wedgwood, but he neglects to add that they did so even as they gave up their traditional form of work, pace, and hours, as well as much of their social and recreational lives.

Thus, in this examination of the key factors in the "evolution of bureaucracy" and enterprise success, we find state power and considerable dysfunctions for a large segment of society rather than efficient adaptation to a vague "environment." Langton notes some of the dysfunctions for the workers, but he explains their acquiescence to the system by appealing to the concept in behavioral psychology of "reinforcements," provided by Preacher Wesley with fear of hellfire and by employer Wedgwood with fear of unemployment. I would prefer to call these "reinforcements" threats, symbolic and real, and add that they were buttressed by state power that was putting down rebellions all over England by the end of the eighteenth century. Langton also makes no critical analysis of the consequences for the families of the workers, their communities and culture, and above all, how bureaucracy shaped their future options by legitimating wage dependence. The new "environment" Wedgwood was presumably merely adapting to was novel and repugnant to much of the population. Wedgwood was not trying to get an efficient fit with this environment; he was forcefully helping to create it.

That this evolutionary explanation rests on unexamined assumptions about the environment and the neglect of social costs can also be seen by imagining, to use evolutionary language, an alternative history. We should not assume a "historical necessity"; constructing what historians call a counterfactual inquiry will indicate outcomes that were possible but did not happen. Let us assume first, in order to get the story going, that no effective outcry was heard as the upper and then the middle classes began to engage in the nonnutritious and quite idle practice of drinking tea and coffee in large volume. No Methodist preacher was there to assail this waste of social resources or this personal indulgence, and no Langton to remind them of their "ethical obligation." However, we will assume that the state did determine that the enclosure movement was an unreasonable violation of the peasants' traditional rights and the nobility's traditional obligations, and that such a movement could easily create a dependent, vagrant population with poor health and radical proclivities, all in the name of private profits. Pretend that the state concluded that the costs of almshouses, relief for the poor, health problems, family disruption, and a loss of cherished independence for those dispossessed would be too great for society as a whole to bear. Thus converting commons to sheep runs would be possible only if those dispossessed of their traditional rights and livelihood were given sums of capital to enable them to move and take up new trades. (Manufacturing at this time required very modest capital investment; barriers to entry consisted largely of government favors such as those Wedgwood probably received.) Just as, in Langton's account, the state permitted land to be taken from peasants, in our example it now permitted peasants to be reimbursed. (Actually, this assumption is not so ridiculous. For a time, Parliament levied a small tax on those landowners who drove off their farmers; it was to help with the growing expenses of local almshouses and charities. It was a beginning, but both landholders and the new bourgeoisie fought it.)

The wool industry would not reap the immense profits that it actually did, but it could grow at a modest rate as long as the expected profits were distributed fairly to those who bore the burden of enabling it to grow. Scattered about the land would be peasants with the means to start, say, potteries. They would be the beneficiaries of what Langton calls "a particular reinforcer (reward, resource)." There is no reason to limit state reinforcers to large, established capitalists. With so many well-capitalized potteries, evolutionary theory would predict a very good chance that some firms would eventually invent something like Queen's Ware. Indeed, it might have appeared earlier under such conditions.

This salutary distribution of the wealth to be made from the wool trade would foster the growth of numerous trades. Let us say that Wedgwood were such a peasant, starting a pottery. Petitioning the state for a turnpike and canal, the state would say: "Users of specialized, indivisible goods, such as a canal by the property you have bought, will be required to pay a part of the capital costs as well as user fees. If what you produce is not deemed a necessity, and is not in sufficient demand to command a price that includes reimbursement for capital and upkeep, it probably should not be sheltered by a free grant. Pottery need not be shipped great distances; it is inefficient to build roads for it, unless the cost is reflected in the price of your Queen's Ware. Furthermore, we wish to encourage decentralized industry, in the interests not only of more equitable distribution of wealth, but of the variety that fosters innovation and selection. You also may have speculated on the land near the canal you wish; speculation is dysfunctional for social evolution. Valuable information, such as our likely favorable action on your petition to have us build you a canal, should be available to all, for otherwise it restricts variation and natural selection, leads to speculation, and promotes great extremes of wealth. If the canal is nevertheless built, for reasons other than your pottery, you shall contribute to its cost in accord with your speculative benefit."

Let us say the transportation system does evolve, and the demand for pots and cups is so great that even with the costs internalized, Wedgwood's firm threatens to expand to over 200 employees. Now the state would interfere with evolution, from one point of view, but merely be a part of evolution from another, by declaring that in the interest of preventing riots, revolts, poverty, child labor, mendicancy, and ill health (and perhaps alcoholism or even coffee drinking), no member of the firm, including the owner, shall make more than four times as much as the most poorly paid worker. (In Wedgwood's case, the poorest would be the 25 percent of the work force that were children, mostly girls, whose low wages surely contributed much to the "efficiency" of his bureaucracy and its fit with the environment.) Such an action would not be unusual, in Wedgwood's time the state regularly used its power to affect wages, generally to prevent their rise. By 1795 it was passing acts that imposed fines equivalent to six months wages on any two people who met to conspire to raise their wages, and fines on those who lent these people money to defend themselves against the charges. The state could just as well control the ratio of returns to effort by setting a maximum spread of wages and income. It had already upheld the enclosures, punished those who met together to seek increased wages, eliminated employer responsibility for industrial accidents (through the fellow-servant rule), and so on. Increasingly the state was protecting Wedgwood at every turn, so it could now, in our imaginary history, protect workers. Whether this fits evolutionary theory or not is an open question; but evolutionary theory generally ignores state power.

The consequences would perhaps be less tea and coffee drinking, since pots would be expensive and there would be fewer idle rich, and more games and sports; more leisure time for all; more innovation and entrepreneurship because of the decentralization of resources; more effective use of resources (Wedgwood died very very rich, presumably having loaned his money to rich industrialists while alive, making him and them even richer); shorter working hours; no child labor; fewer accidents (there would be incentives to make work safe, because the workers could choose to avoid unsafe establishments); a religious emphasis on love and community instead of hellfire and damnation; and so on.

All this would be very functional for society. Its impact on the social sciences would have been profound, for many social scientists believe that what exists was somehow inevitable, rather than assuming that history is full of branching points, only one of which we actually took, while others were quite possible and often favored by some groups. Max Weber, writing a century after our imaginary history of industrialization took place, would have proclaimed that the communitarianiza tion of the world was inevitable, rather than proclaiming the inevitability of bureaucratization; Michels would have formulated the iron law of equality, not the iron law of oligarchy; the evolutionists would still see the survival of the fittest, but the idle rich would now be the unfit and the small entrepreneur and the worker the fit, a view that Adam Smith actually held. And Langton would not have written about how bureaucracy evolved through a natural process of selection "by virtue of its more effective competition for resources" *(336)* or how bureaucratic elements "help an organization achieve a better fit with its environment, allowing it to compete more effectively with other organizational forms for vital resources." *(337)* Instead, he might have written of the "ecological theory of small, nonbureaucratic, decentralized organizations." He might also have written not of the behaviorism of modern psychology, emphasizing rewards and punishments from superiors who set our premises, but of the "behaviorism" of the Man from Galilee and his radical social doctrine.

The moral? Beware of the functionalism that assumes that a pattern is, in Langton's words, "historically expected, given certain initial conditions" *(351)* if those conditions assume that efficient production for society is the driving force. Consider, at least, that the "certain initial conditions" might have been the distribution of power among interest groups and the state. Assuming a slightly different set of these interests, a quite different pattern would be "historically expected" under evolutionary theory. If so, the theory that the pattern is "historically expected" is less important than is determining the interests and powers that set the pattern. Langton writes as if the "highly adaptive set of traits" Wedgwood evolved were solving a problem for the system; more accurately, they were creating problems for most system members. Beware of unspecified "environments." The bland concept may mask powerful interests that consciously do the selecting. Even if there were any "natural process of evolution" for social systems, economic and state power can deflect it. Beware of "efficiency" arguments that do not ask, "Efficient for whom, and at what costs to others?" Ask instead about "externalities," the social costs of organized activities that are not included in the price and are borne by those who benefit very indirectly, if at all, from the activity.

Then join me in the difficult task of rewriting the history of bureaucracy with an expanded vision of the environment and externalities. I believe that a power theory of organizations—starting with the solid rock of bureaucracy, modified by bounded rationality and considerations of internal and external group interests, extended to networks and sectors that include the state, and closely attentive to externalities (the costs borne by the weaker members of society)—will show the way. It will be an organizational analysis all the way, because it is through organizations (at least since the time of Josiah Wedgwood) that classes are constituted and reproduced, stratification systems created and stabilized (and changed in some cases), political processes tamed and guided, and culture itself shaped and molded.

Bibliography

Alchian, Armen A. and Demsetz, Harold. "Production, Information Cause, and Economic Organization." *American Economic Review* 62 (1972): 777–795.

Aldrich, Howard. *Organizations and Environments.* Englewood Cliffs, N.J.: Prentice-Hall, 1979.

———. "Technology and Organizational Structure: A Reexamination of the Findings of the Aston Group." *Administrative Science Quarterly* 17, no. 1 (March 1972): 26–43.

——— and Whetten, David. "Organization Sets, Actions Sets and Networks: Making the Most of Simplicity." In *Handbook of Organizational Designs,* vol. 1, edited by Paul Nystrom and William Starbuck. New York: Oxford University Press, 1981, pp. 385–408.

Alford, Robert. *Health Care Politics.* Chicago: University of Chicago Press, 1977.

Allison, Graham T. *Essence of Decision: Explaining the Cuban Missile Crisis.* Boston: Little, Brown, 1971.

Applewhite, Philip B. *Organizational Behavior.* Englewood Cliffs, N.J.: Prentice-Hall, 1965.

Argyle, Michael. "The Relay Assembly Test Room in Retrospect." *Occupational Psychology* 27 (1953): 98–103.

Argyris, Chris. *The Applicability of Organizational Sociology.* New York: Cambridge University Press, 1974.

———. *Interpersonal Competence and Organizational Effectiveness.* Homewood, Ill.: Dorsey Press, 1962.

Astley, W. Graham. "The Two Ecologies: Population and Community Perspectives on Organizational Evolution." *Administrative Science Quarterly* 30, no. 2 (1985): 224–241.

——— and Fombrun, Charles J. "Technological Innovation and Industrial Structure: The Case of Telecommuncations." In *Advances in Strategic Management,* vol. 1. Greenwich, Conn.: JAI Press, 1983, pp. 205–229.

Astley, W. Graham and Van de Ven, Andrew H. "Central Perspectives and Debates in Organizational Theory." *Administrative Science Quarterly* 28 (1983): 245–273.

Axelrod, Robert. *The Evolution of Cooperation.* New York: Basic Books, 1984.

Bandura, Albert. *Social Learning Theory.* New York: General Learning Press, 1971.

Baritz, Loren. *The Servants of Power.* Westport, Conn.: Greenwood Press, 1974.

Barnard, Chester. *The Functions of the Executive.* Cambridge, Mass.: Harvard University Press, 1968.

————. *Organization and Management.* Cambridge, Mass.: Harvard University Press, 1948.

Barnet, Richard. *Economy of Death.* New York: Atheneum, 1969.

Barnouw, Erik. *The Sponsor: Notes on a Modern Potentate.* New York: Oxford University Press, 1978.

Barton, Allen and Ferman, Patricia. "Comments on Hage's 'An Axiomatic Theory of Organizations.'" *Administrative Science Quarterly* 11, no. 1 (June 1966): 134–141.

Becker, Howard S., ed. *The Other Side: Perspectives on Deviance.* New York: Free Press, 1964.

————. *Outsiders: Studies in the Sociology of Deviance.* New York: Free Press, 1963, pp. 147–163.

Bell, Gerald. "Determinants of Span of Control." *American Journal of Sociology* 73, no. 1 (July 1967): 90–101.

Bell, Wendel. "The Use of False Prophecy to Justify Present Action: The Case of the American Invasion of Grenada." Paper, Yale University, September 1984.

Bendix, Reinhard. "Bureaucracy." *International Encyclopedia of the Social Sciences.* New York: Free Press, 1977.

————. *Work and Authority in Industry.* New York: John Wiley & Sons, 1956.

Ben-Porath, Yoram. "The F Connection: Families, Friends, and Firms and the Organization of Exchange." *Population and Development Review* 6, no. 1 (March 1980): 1–30.

Benson, Kenneth. "The Interorganizational Network as a Political Economy." *Administrative Science Quarterly* 20 (1975): 229–249.

Berg, Ivar. *Education and Jobs: The Great Training Robbery.* New York: Praeger, 1970.

Birch, David. "The Job Creation Process." Cambridge, Mass.: MIT Program on Neighborhood Regional Change, 1979.

Blau, Peter M. *The Dynamics of Bureaucracy,* 2nd rev. ed. Chicago: University of Chicago Press, 1973.

————. "A Formal Theory of Differentiation in Organizations." *American Sociological Review* 35, no. 2 (April 1970): 201–218.

————. "The Hierarchy of Authority in Organizations." *American Journal of Sociology* 73 (January 1968): 453–457.

———— and Scott, W. Richard. *Formal Organizations.* San Francisco: Chandler, 1962.

Bowers, David G. and Seashore, Stanley E. "Predicting Organizational Effectiveness with a Four-Factor Theory of Leadership." *Administrative Science Quarterly* 11, no. 2 (September 1966): 238–263.

Bramel, Dana and Friend, Ronald. "Hawthorne, the Myth of the Docile Worker, and Class Bias in Psychology." *American Psychologist* 36 (1981): 867–878.

Braverman, Harry. *Labor and Monopoly Capital.* New York: Monthly Review Press, 1975.

Brayfield, Arthur H. and Crockett, Walter H. "Employee Attitudes and Employee Performance." *Psychological Bulletin* 52, no. 5 (1955): 396–424.

Bridges, J. H. *The Inside History of the Carnegie Steel Company.* New York: Aldine Press, 1903.

Brown, Wilfred. *Exploration in Management.* New York: John Wiley & Sons, 1960.

Bucher, Rue. "Social Process and Power in a Medical School." In *Power in Organizations,* edited by Mayer Zald. Nashville, Tenn.: Vanderbilt University Press, 1970, pp. 3–48.

Buckley, Walter. *Sociology and Modern Systems Theory.* Englewood Cliffs, N.J.: Prentice-Hall, 1967.

Burns, T. and Stalker, G. M. *The Management of Innovation.* New York: Barnes & Noble, 1961.

Campbell, Donald. "Variation and Selection Retention in Socio-Cultural Evolution." *General Systems* 16 (1969): 69–85.

Campbell, John P. and Dunnette, Marvin D. "Effectiveness of T-Group Experiences in Managerial Training and Development." *Psychological Bulletin* 70, no. 2 (August 1968): 73–104.

Carey, Alex. "The Hawthorne Studies: A Radical Criticism." *American Sociological Review* 32, no. 3 (June 1967): 416.

Caro, Robert. *The Power Broker: Robert Moses and the Fall of New York.* New York: Random House, 1975.

Carroll, Glenn R. "Organizational Ecology." *Annual Review of Sociology* 10 (1984): 71–93.

Cates, Jerry R. *Insuring Inequality: Administrative Leadership in Social Security, 1935–54.* Ann Arbor, Mich.: University of Michigan Press, 1982.

Chandler, Alfred D. *Strategy and Structure.* Cambridge, Mass.: MIT Press, 1969.

———. *The Visible Hand: The Managerial Revolution in American Business.* Cambridge, Mass.: Harvard University Press, 1977.

Child, John. "Organizational Structure, Environment, and Performance: The Role of Strategic Choice." *Sociology* 6, no. 1 (January 1972): 1–22.

———. "Predicting and Understanding Organization Structure." *Administrative Science Quarterly* 18, no. 2 (June 1973): 168–185.

Clark, Burton. *Adult Education in Transition.* Berkeley: University of California Press, 1956.

———. *The Open Door Challenge: A Case Study.* New York: McCraw-Hill, 1960.

Clark, S. D. *The Church and Sect in Canada.* Toronto: University of Toronto Press, 1948.

Clarke, Lee. "Organizing Risk." Ph.D. dissertation, State University of New York at Stony Brook, 1985.

Clawson, Dan. *Bureaucracy and the Labor Process: The Transformation of U.S. Industry, 1860–1920.* New York: Monthly Review Press, 1980.

Clegg, Stewart and Dunkerley, David. *Organizations, Class and Control.* London: Routledge & Kegan Paul, 1980.

Clifford, James. "On Ethnographic Authority." *Representations* 1, no. 2 (1983): 118–146.

Coch, L. and French, J.R.P., Jr. "Overcoming Resistance to Change." *Human Relations* 1, no. 4 (1948): 512–532.

Cohen, Michael D., March, James C., and Olsen, Johan P. "A Garbage Can Model of Organizational Choice." *Administrative Science Quarterly* 17, no. 1 (March 1972): 1–25.

Collins, Randall. *The Credential Society: A Historical Sociology of Education and Stratification.* New York: Academic Press, 1979.

Committee on Small Business, U.S. House of Representatives. *Conglomerate Mergers—Their Effects on Small Business and Local Communities.* Washington, D.C.: U.S. Government Printing Office, House Document No. 96–343, October 2, 1980.

Coser, Lewis. *Greedy Institutions.* New York: Free Press, 1974.

———. "Publishers as Gatekeepers of Ideas." *The Annals, American Academy of Social Science* 421 (September 1975): 12–22.

———, Kadushin, Charles, and Powell, Walter W. *Books.* New York: Basic Books, 1982.

Cressey, Donald R. "Achievement of an Unstated Organizational Goal: An Observation on Prisons." *Pacific Sociological Review* 1 (1958): 43–49.

Crozier, Michel. *The Stalled Society.* New York: Penguin Books, 1974.

Cummings, L. L. and Scott, W. E. *Readings in Organizational Behavior and Human Performance,* rev. ed. Homewood, Ill.: Dorsey Press, 1973.

Cyert, Richard M. and March, James G. *A Behavioral Theory of the Firm.* Englewood Cliffs, N.J.: Prentice-Hall, 1963.

Dale, Ernest. *The Great Organizers.* New York: McGraw-Hill, 1971.

Dalton, Melville, *Men Who Manage.* New York: John Wiley & Sons, 1959.

Danielian, N. R. *AT&T, The Story of Industrial Conquest.* New York: Vanguard Press, 1939.

Davis, Nuel Pharr. *Lawrence and Oppenheimer.* New York: Simon & Schuster, 1968.

Davis, James W. and Dolbeare, Kenneth M. *Little Groups of Neighbors: The Selective Service System.* Chicago: Markham, 1968.

Demerath, N. J. and Peterson, Richard A., eds. *Systems, Change, and Conflict.* New York: Free Press, 1967.

Deutscher, Irwin. *What We Say/What We Do.* Glenview, Ill.: Scott, Foresman, 1973.

DiMaggio, Paul. "Structural Analysis of Organizational Fields," in *Annual Review of Research on Organizations,* vol. 8, edited by Barry Staw and L. L. Cummings. Greenwich Conn.: JAI Press, forthcoming.

———— and Powell, Walter W. "The Iron Cage Revisited: Institutional Isomorphism and Collective Rationality in Organizational Fields." *American Sociological Review* 48 (1983): 147–160.

Domhoff, G. William. *The Higher Circles.* New York: Random House, 1971.

————. *Who Rules America?* Englewood Cliffs, N.J.: Prentice-Hall, 1967.

Dore, Ronald. "Goodwill and the Spirit of Market Capitalism." *British Journal of Sociology* 34 (December 1983): 459–482.

Dornbush, Sanford and Scott, W. Richard. *Evaluation and the Exercise of Authority.* San Francisco: Jossey-Bass, 1975.

Drucker, Peter. *Concept of the Corporation.* New York: John Day, 1972.

Dubin, Robert. "Supervision and Productivity." In *Leadership and Productivity,* edited by Robert Dubin, George C. Homans, Floyd C. Mann, and Delbert C. Miller. San Francisco: Chandler, 1965.

Du Boff, Richard B. and Herman, Edward S. "Alfred Chandler's New Business History: A Review." *Politics and Society* 10, no. 1 (1980): 87–110.

Dunnette, Marvin, Campbell, John, and Argyris, Chris. "A Symposium: Laboratory Training." *Industrial Relations* 8, no. 1 (October 1968): 1–46.

Durkheim, Emile. *Division of Labor in Society.* New York: Free Press, 1960.

Eccles, Robert G. "Control with Fairness in Transfer Pricing." *Harvard Business Review* 61 (November–December 1983): 149–161.

————. "Transfer Pricing as a Problem of Agency." Harvard Business School, February 1984.

————. *The Transfer Pricing Problem: A Theory for Practice.* Lexington, Mass.: Lexington Books, 1985.

———— and White, Harrison. "Firm and Market Interfaces of Profit Center Control." Paper, Harvard University, February 1984.

Edwards, Richard. *Contested Terrain: The Transformation of the Workplace in the Twentieth Century.* New York: Basic Books, 1979.

Ehrenreich, Barbara and Ehrenreich, John. *The American Health Empire: Power, Profits, and Politics.* New York: Vintage Books, 1971.

Emery, F. E. and Trist, E. L. "The Causal Texture of Organizational Environments." In *Readings in Organization Theory—A Behavioral Approach,* edited by Walter A. Hill and Douglas Egan. Boston: Allyn and Bacon, 1966, pp. 435–447.

Etzioni, Amitai. *The Active Society.* New York: Free Press, 1968.

————. *A Comparative Analysis of Complex Organizations,* rev. ed. New York: Free Press, 1975.

————, ed. *Complex Organizations: A Sociological Reader.* New York: Holt, Rinehart & Winston, 1962.

———. *A Sociological Reader on Complex Organizations,* 2nd ed. New York: Holt, Rinehart & Winston, 1969.

Evan, William M. "The Organization-Set: Toward a Theory of Interorganizational Relations." In *Approaches to Organizational Design,* edited by J. D. Thompson. Pittsburgh: University of Pittsburgh Press, 1966, pp. 175–191.

Fama, Eugene F. "Agency Problems and the Theory of the Firm." *Journal of Political Economy* 88 (1980): 288–305.

——— and Jensen, Michael. "Separation of Ownership and Control." *Journal of Law and Economics* 26 (June 1983): 301–325.

Farberman, Harvey. "Criminogenic Market Structures: The Auto Industry." *Sociological Quarterly* 16 (1975): 438–457.

Federal Trade Commission. *Economic Report on Corporate Mergers.* Staff Report. Washington, D.C.: U.S. Government Printing Office, 1969.

Fiedler, Fred. "Engineer the Job to Fit the Manager." *Harvard Business Review* 43, no. 5 (1965): 115–122.

———. *A Theory of Leadership Effectiveness.* New York: McGraw-Hill, 1967.

Francis, Arthur. "Markets and Hierarchies: Efficiency or Domination?" In *Power, Efficiency and Institutions,* edited by Arthur Francis, Jeremy Turk, and Paul Willman. London: Heineman, 1983, pp. 105–116.

Francke, Richard Herbert and Kaul, James D. "The Hawthorne Experiments: First Statistical Interpretation." *American Sociological Review* 43 (1978): 623–643.

Friedson, Eliot, ed. *The Hospital in Modern Society.* New York: Free Press, 1963.

Freitag, Peter J. "The Cabinet and Big Business." *Social Problems* 23, no. 2 (December 1975): 137–152.

Friedland, Roger and Donald Palmer, "Park Place and Main Street: Business and Urban Power Structure." *Annual Review of Sociology* 10 (1984): 393–416.

Friedman, Milton. *Essays in Positive Economics.* Chicago: University of Chicago Press, 1953.

Gagnon, John H. and Simon, William. *Sexual Conduct: The Social Sources of Human Sexuality.* Chicago: Aldine, 1973.

Galbraith, John Kenneth. *The New Industrial State,* 2nd ed. Boston: Houghton Mifflin, 1971.

Gerth, Hans and Mills, C. Wright, eds. and trans. *From Max Weber: Essays in Sociology.* New York: Oxford University Press, 1946.

Classberg, Davita Silfen and Schwartz, Michael. "Ownership and Control of Corporations." *Annual Review of Sociology* 9 (1983): 311–332.

Goffman, Erving. *Asylums.* New York: Doubleday, 1961.

Goldberg, Victor P. "Bridges Over Contested Terrain. Exploring the Radical Account of the Employment Relationship." *Journal of Economic Behavior and Organization* 1 (1980): 249–274.

Goldner, Fred H. "The Division of Labor: Process and Power." In *Power in Organizations,* edited by Mayer Zald. Nashville, Tenn.: Vanderbilt University Press, 1970, pp. 97–144.

——— and Ritti, R. R. "Professionalization as Career Immobility." *American Journal of Sociology* 73 (March 1967): 491.

Goss, Mary E. W. "Patterns of Bureaucracy Among Hospital Staff Physicians." In *The Hospital in Modern Society,* edited by Eliot Freidson. New York: Free Press, 1963.

Gould, Stephen. "A Threat to Darwinism." *Natural History* 89, no. 4 (1975): 9.

Gouldner, Alvin. *Patterns of Industrial Bureaucracy.* New York: Free Press, 1954.

Graham, W. K. "Description of Leader Behavior and Evaluation of Leaders as a Function of LPC." *Personnel Psychology* 21 (Winter 1968): 457–464.

Granovetter, Mark. "Economic Actions and Social Structure: A Problem of Embeddedness." *American Journal of Sociology*, November 1985.

———. "The Idea of 'Advancement' in Theories of Social Evolution." *American Journal of Sociology* 88 (1979): 489–515.

———. "Labor Mobility, Internal Markets and Job Matching: A Comparison of the Sociological and Economic Approaches." Paper, State University of New York, Stony Brook, April 1983.

———. "Small Is Bountiful: Labor Markets and Establishment Size." *American Sociological Review* 49 (June 1984): 323–334.

———. "The Strength of Weak Ties." *American Journal of Sociology* 78 (May 1973): 1360–1380.

Guest, Robert. *Organizational Change.* Homewood, Ill.: Dorsey Press, 1962.

Gusfield, Joseph R. *The Culture of Public Problems: Drinking-Driving and the Symbolic Order.* Chicago: University of Chicago Press, 1981.

———. "Social Structure and Moral Reform: A Study of the Women's Christian Temperance Union." *American Journal of Sociology* 61 (1955): 221–232.

Hackman, J. Richard. "A Normative Model of Workteam Effectiveness." To appear in *Handbook of Organizational Behavior,* edited by Jay Lorsch. Chicago: Hall Publishing (forthcoming).

Hage, Jerald T. "Rejoinder." *Administrative Science Quarterly* 11, no. 1 (June 1966): 141–146.

———. "An Axiomatic Theory of Organizations." *Administrative Science Quarterly* 10, no. 3 (December 1965): 289–320.

——— and Aiken, Michael. "Routine Technology, Social Structure, and Organizational Goals." *Administrative Science Quarterly* 14, no. 3 (September 1969): 366–377.

Hagg, Ingemund and Johanson, Jan. *Firms in Networks—New Perspective on Competitive Power.* Stockholm, Sweden: Business and Social Research Institute, September 1983.

Hall, Richard. *Organizations, Structure, and Process,* rev. ed. Englewood Cliffs, N.J.: Prentice-Hall, 1977, pp. 104–119.

Hannan, Michael T. and Freeman, John. "The Population Ecology of Organizations." *American Journal of Sociology* 82, no. 5 (March 1977): 929–966.

———. "Structural Inertia and Organizational Change." *American Sociological Review* 49, no. 2 (1984): 149–164.

Hawley, Amos. "Human Ecology." In *The International Encyclopedia of the Social Sciences,* vol. 4, edited by David L. Sills. New York: Crowell-Collier and Macmillan, 1968, pp. 328–337.

———. *Human Ecology: A Theory of Community Structure.* New York: Ronald Press, 1950.

Hearn, Francis. *Domination, Legitimation, and Resistance: The Incorporation of the Nineteenth-Century English Working Class.* Westport, Conn.: Greenwood Press, 1978.

Herzberg, Frederick. *Work and the Nature of Man.* New York: T. Y. Crowell, 1966.

———, Mausner, B., and Snyderman, B. *The Motivation to Work,* 2nd ed. New York: John Wiley & Sons, 1959

Hickson, David et al. "Operations Technology and Organizational Structure: An Empirical Reappraisal." *Administrative Science Quarterly* 14, no. 3 (September 1969): 378–397.

———. "A Strategic Contingencies Theory of Intra-Organizational Power." *Administrative Science Quarterly* 16, no. 2 (June 1971): 216–229.

Hill, Walter A. and Egan, Douglas, eds. *Readings in Organizational Theory—A Behavioral Approach.* Boston: Allyn & Bacon, 1966.

Hirsch, Paul M. "Occupational, Organizational, and Institutional Models in Communication Research." In *Strategies for Communication Research,* edited by P. M. Hirsch et al. Beverly Hills, Calif.: Sage, 1977.

———. "Organizational Analysis and Industrial Sociology: An Instance of Cultural Lag." *The American Sociologist* 10, no. 1 (February 1975): 3–10.

———. "Organizational Effectiveness and the Institutional Environment." *Administrative Science Quarterly* 20, no. 4 (September 1975): 327–344.

———. "Processing Fads and Fashions: An Organization-Set Analysis of Cultural Industry Systems." *American Journal of Sociology* 77, no. 4 (January 1972): 639–659.

———. *The Structure of the Popular Music Industry.* Ann Arbor, Mich.: University of Michigan Survey Research Center, 1969.

Hirschorn, Larry. "The Post-industrial Labor Process." *New Political Science* 7 (Fall 1981): 11–33.

Homans, George. *The Human Group.* New York: Harcourt Brace Jovanovich, 1950.

Hopkins, Terence K. "Bureaucratic Authority: The Convergence of Weber and Barnard." In *Complex Organizations,* edited by Amitai Etzioni, New York: Holt, Rinehart & Winston, 1962, pp. 159–167.

House, Robert J. and Wigdor, Lawrence A. "Herzberg's Dual-Factor Theory of Job Satisfaction and Motivation: A Review of the Evidence and a Criticism." *Personnel Psychology* 20 (1967): 369–389.

Hulin, Charles L. and Blood, Milton R. "Job Enlargement, Individual Differences, and Worker Responses." *Psychological Bulletin* 69, no. 1 (1968): 41–55.

Institute for Research on Educational Finance and Governance (IFG). Policy Notes 4, no. 3. Stanford University, Summer 1983, pp. 1–7.

Jaco, E. G., ed. *Patients, Physicians, and Illness: Source Book in Behavioral Science and Medicine,* 2nd ed. New York: Free Press, 1972.

Jacobs, David. "Toward a Theory of Mobility and Behavior in Organizations." *American Journal of Sociology* 87, no. 3 (1981): 684–707.

Janowitz, Morris. *The Professional Soldier.* New York: Free Press, 1960.

Jensen, Michael C. "Organization Theory and Methodology." *The Accounting Review* 8, no. 2 (April 1983): 319–337.

——— and Meckling, William. "Theory of the Firm: Managerial Behavior, Agency Costs, and Ownership Structure." *Journal of Financial Economics* 3 (October 1976): 305–360.

Jones, S. H. R. "The Organization of Work: A Historical Dimension." *Journal of Economic Behavior and Organization* 3, no. 2–3 (1982): 117–137.

Jun, Jong S., and Storm, William B. *Tomorrow's Organizations.* Glenview, Ill.: Scott, Foresman, 1973.

Kahn, Robert L. "Human Relations on the Shop Floor." In *Human Relations and Modern Management,* edited by E. M. Hugh-Jones. Amsterdam, Holland: North-Holland, 1958, pp. 43–74.

Kanter, Rosabeth. *The Change Masters: Innovation for Productivity in American Corporations.* New York: Simon & Schuster, 1983.

———. *Men and Women of the Corporation.* New York: Basic Books, 1977.

Kaplan, Norman. "Professional Scientists in Industry." *Social Problems* 13 (1965): 88–97.

Kaplan, Robert S. "Accounting Lag: the Obsolescence of Cost Accounting Systems." Paper, Harvard University, March 1984.

———. "The Evolution of Management Accounting." *The Accounting Review* 49 (1984): 390–418.

Kasarda, John D. and Bidwell, Charles E. "A Human Ecological Theory of Organizational Structuring." In *Sociological Human Ecology: Contemporary Issues and Applications,* edited by Michael Micklin and Harvey Choldin. Boulder, Colo.: Westview Press, 1984, pp. 183–236.

Kast, Fremont and Rosenzweig, James. *Contingency Views of Organization and Management.* Palo Alto, Calif.: Science Research Associates, 1973.

Katz, Daniel et al. *Productivity, Supervision, and Morale in an Office Situation.* Detroit, Mich.: Darel Press, 1950.

——— and Kahn, Robert. *Social Psychology of Organizations.* New York: John Wiley & Sons, 1966.

Knightley, Phillip. *The First Casualty: From the Crimea to Vietnam—The War Correspondent as Hero, Propagandist, and Myth Maker.* New York: Harcourt Brace Jovanovich, 1976.

Koenig, Thomas, Gogel, Robert, and Sonquist, John. "Interlocking Directorates as a Social Network." *American Journal of Economics and Sociology* 40 (1981): 37–50.

——— et al. "Models of the Significance of Corporate Interlocking Directorates." *American Journal of Economics and Sociology* 38 (1978): 73–83.

——— and Sonquist, John. "Studying Interrelations Between Corporations Through Interlocking Directorates." In *Power and Hierarchical Control,* edited by Tom Burns and William Buckley. New York: Sage Publications, 1977.

Kolko, Gabriel. *The Roots of American Foreign Policy.* Boston: Beacon Press, 1970.

———. *Triumph of Conservatism.* New York: Free Press, 1977.

Korman, Abraham K. "Consideration, 'Initiating Structure,' and Organizational Criteria— A Review." *Personnel Psychology* 19, no. 4 (1966): 349–361.

Kornhauser, Arthur and Sharp, A. "Employee Attitudes, Suggestions from a Study in a Factory." *Personnel Journal* 10 (1943): 393–401.

Kornhauser, T., Dubin, R., and Ross, A. *Industrial Conflict.* New York: McGraw-Hill, 1954.

Kozol, Jonathan. *Illiterate America.* New York: Anchor/Doubleday, 1985.

Krupp, Sherman. *Patterns in Organizational Analysis.* New York: Holt, Rinehart & Winston, 1961.

Landau, Martin. "Redundancy, Rationality, and the Problem of Duplication and Overlap." *Public Administration Review* 29, no. 4 (July/August 1969): 346–358.

Landsberger, Henry. *Hawthorne Revisited.* Ithaca, N.Y.: Cornell University Press, 1958.

Langton, John. "The Ecological Theory of Bureaucracy: The Case of Josiah Wedgwood and the British Pottery Industry." *Administrative Science Quarterly* 29 (1984): 330–354.

Laumann, E. O. *Networks of Collective Action.* New York: Academic Press, 1976.

——— and Pappi, Franz U. "New Directions in the Study of Community Elites." *American Sociological Review* 38, no. 2 (April 1973): 212–230.

———, Verbrugge, Lois M., and Pappi, F. U. "A Casual Modelling Approach to the Study of a Community Elite's Influence Structure." *American Sociological Review* 39, no. 2 (April 1974): 162–174.

Lawler, Edward E. and Porter, Lyman W. "The Effect of Performance on Job Satisfaction." *Industrial Relations* 7, no. 1 (October 1967): 20–28.

Lawrence, Paul and Lorsch, Jay. *Organization and Environment.* Cambridge, Mass.: Harvard University Press, 1967.

Leatt, Peggy and Schneck, Rodney. "Technology, Size, Environment, and Structure in Nursing Subunits." *Organization Studies* 3, no. 3 (1982): 221–242.

Levine, Sol and White, Paul E. "Exchange as a Conceptual Framework for the Study of Interorganizational Relationships." *Administrative Science Quarterly* 5 (March 1961): 583–610.

Liebenstein, Harvey. *Beyond Economic Man: A New Foundation for Microeconomics.* Cambridge, Mass.: Harvard University Press, 1976.

Likert, Rensis. *The Human Organization.* New York: McGraw-Hill, 1967.

———. *New Patterns of Management.* New York: McGraw-Hill, 1961.

———. *New Ways of Managing Conflict.* New York: McGraw-Hill, 1975.

Lindsey, Robert. "Payola's Return to Records Reported." *New York Times,* March 6, 1985, p. A14.

Litwak, Eugene and Hylton, Lydia F. "Interorganizational Analysis: A Hypothesis on Coordinating Agencies." *Administrative Science Quarterly* 6, no. 4 (March 1962): 337–341.

Lorsch, Jay W. *Product Innovation and Organization.* New York. Macmillan, 1965.

Luthans, Fred and Kreitner, Robert. *Organizational Behavior Modification.* Glenview, Ill.: Scott, Foresman, 1975.

Lynch, Beverly P. "An Empirical Assessment of Perrow's Technology Construct." *Administrative Science Quarterly* 19, no. 3 (September 1974): 338–356.

Lynd, Robert S. "Review of Leadership in a Free Society." *Political Science Quarterly* 52 (1937): 590–592.

Macaulay, Steward. "Non-Contractual Relations in Business: A Preliminary Study." *American Sociological Review* 28, no. 1 (February 1963): 54–66.

Maniha, John and Perrow, Charles. "The Reluctant Organization and the Aggressive Environment." *Administrative Science Quarterly* 10, no. 2 (September 1965): 238–257.

Mann, Floyd C. *Leadership and Productivity,* edited by R. Dubin, G. C. Homans, Floyd C. Mann, and D. C. Miller. San Francisco: Chandler, 1965, pp. 68–103.

March, James G. "The Business Firm as a Political Coalition." *Journal of Politics* 24 (1962): 662–678.

———, ed. *The Handbook of Organizations.* Chicago: Rand McNally, 1965.

——— and Olsen, Johan P. *Ambiguity and Choice in Organizations.* Bergen, Norway: Universitetsforlaget, 1976.

——— and Simon, Herbert A. *Organizations.* New York: John Wiley & Sons, 1958.

Marcus, George E. and Cushman, Dick. "Ethnographies as Texts." *Annual Review of Anthropology* 11 (1982): 25–69.

Marglin, Steven. "What Do Bosses Do?" *Review of Radical Political Economics* 6, no. 2 (Summer 1974): 33–60.

Mariolis, Peter. "Bank and Financial Control Among Large U.S. Corporations." Ph.D. dissertation, State University of New York at Stony Brook, 1978.

———. "Interlocking Directorates and Control of Corporations." *Social Science Quarterly* 56 (December 1975): 425–439.

Marrow, Alfred J., Bower, David G., and Seashore, Stanley E. *Management by Participation.* New York: Harper & Row, 1967.

Maslow, Abraham. *Motivation and Personality,* 2nd ed. New York: Harper & Row, 1970.

———. *Toward a Psychology of Being.* New York: Van Nostrand Reinhold, 1968.

Massie, Joseph. "Management Theory." In *The Handbook of Organizations,* edited by James March. Chicago: Rand McNally, 1965, pp. 387–422.

May, Robert. *Stability and Complexity in Model Ecosystems.* Princeton, N.J.: Princeton University Press, 1973.

Mayo, Elton. *The Social Problems of an Industrial Civilization.* Cambridge, Mass.: Harvard University Press, 1945.

McGregor, Douglas. *The Human Side of Enterprise.* New York: McGraw-Hill, 1960.

McKelvey, Bill. *Organizational Systematics.* Berkeley, Calif.: University of California Press, 1982.

———— and Aldrich, Howard. "Populations, Natural Selection, and Applied Organizational Science." *Administrative Science Quarterly* 28 (March 1983): 101–128.

McNeil, Kenneth. "Understanding Organizational Power: Building on the Weberian Legacy." *Administrative Science Quarterly* 23, no. 1 (March 1978): 65–90.

———— and Miller, Richard. "The Profitability of Consumer Practices Warranty Policies in the Auto Industry." *Administrative Science Quarterly* 25 (1980): 407–426.

———— and Minihan, Edmond. "Regulation of Medical Devices and Organizational Behavior in Hospitals." *Administrative Science Quarterly* 22, no. 3 (September 1977): 475–490.

Mechanic, David. "Sources of Power of Lower Participants in Complex Organizations." *Administrative Science Quarterly* 7, no. 4 (December 1962): 349–364.

Melman, Seymour. *Pentagon Capitalism: The Political Economy of War.* New York: McGraw-Hill, 1970.

Messinger, Sheldon L. "Organizational Transformation: A Case Study of Declining Social Movement." *American Sociological Review* 20 (1955): 3–10.

Meyer, John W. and Rowan, Brian. "Institutionalized Organizations: Formal Structure as Myth and Ceremony." *American Journal of Sociology* 83, no. 2 (September 1977): 440–463.

————. "The Structure of Educational Organizations." In Marshall W. Meyer et al., *Environments and Organizations,* San Francisco: Jossey-Bass, 1978.

Meyer, John W. and Scott, W. Richard. *Organizational Environments: Ritual and Rationality.* Beverly Hills, Calif.: Sage, 1983.

Meyer, Marshall. "Two Authority Structures of Bureaucratic Organizations." *Administrative Science Quarterly* 13 (September 1968): 211–228.

———— and Brown, M. C. "The Process of Bureaucratization." *American Journal of Sociology* 83, no. 2 (September 1977): 364–385.

———— et al. *Environment and Organizations: Theoretical and Empirical Perspectives.* San Francisco: Jossey-Bass, 1978.

Michels, Robert. *Political Parties.* New York: Free Press, 1966.

Micklin, Michael and Choldin, Harvey, eds. *Sociological Human Ecology: Contemporary Issues and Applications.* Boulder, Colo.: Westview Press, 1984.

Miles, Raymond E. "Human Relations or Human Resources." *Harvard Business Review* 43, no. 4 (July/August 1965): 148–155.

Milner, Murray. *Unequal Care: A Case Study of Interorganizational Relations in Health Care.* New York: Columbia University Press, 1980.

Mindlin, Sergio E. and Aldrich, Howard. "Interorganizational Dependence: A Review of the Concepts and Reexamination of the Findings of the Aston Group." *Administrative Science Quarterly* 20, no. 3 (September 1975): 382–392.

Miner, John. *Theories of Organizational Structure and Process.* Chicago: Dryden Press, 1982.

Mintz, Beth. "The President's Cabinet, 1897–1972." *The Insurgent Sociologist* 5, no. 3 (Spring 1975): 531–548.

———— et al. "Problems of Proof in Elite Research." *Social Problems* 23, no. 3 (February 1976): 314–324.

———— and Schwartz, Michael. *Bank Hegemony.* Chicago: University of Chicago Press, 1985.

Mirrlees, James A. "The Optimal Structure of Incentives and Authority Within an Organization." *The Bell Journal of Economics* 7 (Spring 1976): 105–131.

Mischel, Walter. "Toward a Cognitive Social Learning Reconceptualization of Personality." *Psychological Review* 80, no. 4 (1973): 252–283.

Mizruchi, Mark S. *The American Corporate Network, 1904–1974.* Beverly Hills, Calif.: Sage Publications, 1982.

Moe, Terry. "The New Economics of Organization." *American Journal of Political Science* 28, no. 4 (November 1984): 739–777.

Moeller, Gerald H. and Charters, W. W. "Relations of Bureaucratization to Sense of Power Among Teachers." *Administrative Science Quarterly* 10, no. 4 (March 1966): 457.

Mohr, Lawrence. *Explaining Organizational Behavior: The Limits and Possibilities of Theory and Research.* San Francisco: Jossey-Bass, 1982.

———. "Organizational Technology and Organizational Structure." *Administrative Science Quarterly* 16, no. 4 (December 1971): 444–459.

Mollenkopf, John. "Theories of the State and Power Structure Research." *The Insurgent Sociologist* 5, no. 3 (Spring 1975): 245–264.

Montgomery, David. *Workers' Control in America: Studies in the History of Work, Technology, and Labor Struggles.* New York: Cambridge University Press, 1980.

Morris, Robert and Hirsch-Lescohier, Ilana. "Service Integration: To What Problems Is It the Presumed Solution?" In *The Management of Human Services,* edited by Rosemary C. Sarri and Yeheskel Hasenfeld. New York: Columbia University Press, 1978.

Nelson, Richard R. and Winter, Sidney G. *An Evolutionary Theory of Economic Change.* Boston: Belknap Press, 1982.

Newfield, Jack and DuBrul, Paul. *The Abuse of Power: The Permanent Government and the Fall of New York.* New York: Viking Press, 1977.

Noble, David. *America by Design.* New York: Alfred Knopf, 1977.

Nonet, Philippe. *Administrative Justice: Advocacy and Change in Government Agencies.* New York: Russell Sage Foundation, 1969.

Ouchi, William G. "Markets, Bureaucracies, and Clans." *Administrative Science Quarterly* 25 (March 1980): 129–141.

Overton, Peggy, Schneck, Rodney, and Hazlett, C. B. "An Empirical Study of the Technology of Nursing Subunits." *Administrative Science Quarterly* 22, no. 2 (June 1977): 203–219.

Owens, Arthur. "Can the Profit Motive Save Our Hospitals?" *Medical Economics* (March 1970): 77–111.

Palmer, Donald and Friedland, Roger. "Organization, Class and Space: A Model of the Spatial Structure of Corporate Production." Paper, Stanford University, 1983.

Palumbo, Dennis J. "Power and Role Specificity in Organization Theory." *Public Administration Review* 29, no. 3 (May/June 1969): 237–248.

Parsons, Talcott. "Introduction." In *Max Weber, Theory of Social and Economic Organization,* translated and edited by A. M. Henderson and Talcott Parsons. New York: Oxford University Press, 1947, pp. 58–60.

———. *Structure and Process in Modern Societies.* New York: Free Press, 1960.

Pennings, Johannes M. "Dimensions of Organizational Influence and Their Effectiveness Correlates." *Administrative Science Quarterly* 21, no. 4 (December 1976): 688–699.

——— and Goodman, Paul S. "Toward a Workable Framework." In *New Perspectives in*

Organizational Effectiveness, edited by Paul S. Goodman et al. San Francisco: Jossey-Bass, 1977, pp. 146–184.

Perrow, Charles. "The Bureaucratic Paradox: The Efficient Organization Centralizes in Order to Decentralize." *Organizational Dynamics* (Spring 1977): 2–14.

——. "Deconstructing Social Science." *New York University Educational Quarterly* 12, no. 2 (Winter 1981): 2–9.

——. "Demystifying Organizations." In *The Management of Human Services*, edited by Rosemary C. Sarri and Yeheskel Hasenfeld. New York: Columbia University Press, 1978, pp. 105–120.

——. "Departmental Power and Perspectives in Industrial Firms." In *Power in Organizations*, edited by Mayer Zald. Nashville, Tenn.: Vanderbilt University Press, 1970, pp. 59–70.

——. "The Effect of Technological Change on the Structure of Business Firms." In *Industrial Relations: Contemporary Issues*, edited by B. C. Roberts. London: Macmillan, 1968, pp. 205–219.

——. "A Framework for Comparative Organizational Analysis." *American Sociological Review* 32, no. 2 (April 1967): 194–208.

——. "Goals and Power Structures: A Historical Case Study." In *The Hospital in Modern Society*, edited by Eliot Freidson. New York: Free Press, 1963.

——. "Goals in Complex Organizations." *American Sociological Review* 26, no. 6 (December 1961): 854–865.

——. "Hospitals: Technology, Structure, and Goals." In *The Handbook of Organizations*, edited by James March. Chicago: Rand McNally, 1965, pp. 910–971.

——. "Is Business Really Changing?" *Organizational Dynamics* (Summer 1974): 31–44.

——. "Markets, Hierarchies and Hegemony: A Critique of Chandler and Williamson." In *Perspectives on Organization Design and Behavior*, edited by Andrew Van de Ven and William Joyce. New York: Wiley Interscience, 1981, pp. 371–386, and 403–404.

——. "Members as a Resource in Voluntary Associations." In *Organizations and Clients*, edited by W. Rosengren and M. Lefton. Columbus, Ohio: Charles E. Merrill, 1970, pp. 93–116.

——. *Normal Accidents: Living with High-Risk Technologies*. New York: Basic Books, 1984.

——. *Organizational Analysis: A Sociological View*. Belmont, Calif.: Wadsworth, 1970.

——. "The Organizational Context of Human Factors Engineering." *Administrative Science Quarterly* 28, no. 4 (1983): 521–541.

——. "Organizational Goals." *International Encyclopedia of the Social Sciences*, rev. ed. New York: Macmillan, 1968, pp. 305–311.

——. "Organizational Prestige: Some Functions and Dysfunctions." *American Journal of Sociology* 66, no. 4 (January 1961): 335–341.

——. *The Radical Attack on Business: A Critical Analysis*. New York: Harcourt Brace Jovanovich, 1972.

——. "Review of Organizational Intelligence." *Trans-action* 6 (January 1969): 60–62.

——. "Three Types of Effectiveness Studies." In P. S. Goodman, J. M. Pennings, and associates, *New Perspectives on Organizational Effectiveness*. San Francisco: Jossey-Bass, 1977, pp. 96–105.

—— and Pearson, David. "Complexity, Coupling and Nuclear Weapons." Paper, Yale University, 1984.

Perrucci, Robert and Pilisuk, Marc. "Leaders and Ruling Elites: The Interorganizational Bases of Community Power." Working paper no. 28, Institute for the Study of Social Change, Department of Sociology, Purdue University, n.d.

Peterson, Richard and Berger, David G. "Cycles in Symbol Production: The Case of Popular Music." *American Sociological Review* 40, no. 2 (April 1975): 158–173.

———. "Entrepreneurship in Organizations: Evidence from the Popular Music Industry." *Administrative Science Quarterly* 16, no. 1 (March 1971): 97–106.

Pfeffer, Jeffrey, *Power in Organizations.* Marshfield, Mass.: Pitman, 1981.

——— and Salanzick, Gerald, *The External Control of Organizations.* New York: Harper and Row, 1978.

Polanyi, Michael. *Personal Knowledge: Towards a Post-Critical Philosophy.* New York: Harper Torchbooks, 1962.

———. *The Tacit Dimension.* Garden City, N.Y.: Doubleday/Anchor, 1967.

Pollard, Sidney. *The Genesis of Modern Management: A Study of the Industrial Revolution in Great Britain.* Cambridge, Mass.: Cambridge University Press, 1965.

Powell, Walter W. *Getting into Print: The Decision Making Process in Scholarly Publishing.* Chicago. University of Chicago Press, 1985.

"Power to the Coalitions." *Modern Hospital* (April 1970), pp. 39–40d.

Pressman, Jeffrey L. and Wildavsky, Aaron. *Implementation.* Berkeley, Calif.: University of California Press, 1979.

Price, James L. "Continuity in Social Research: TVA and the Grass Roots." *Pacific Sociological Review* 1, no. 2 (Fall 1958): 63–68.

Putterman, Louis. "On Some Recent Explanations of Why Capital Hires Labor." *Economic Inquiry* 33 (April 1984): 171–187

Roethlisberger, F. J. and Dickson, William J. *Management and the Worker.* Cambridge, Mass.: Harvard University Press, 1947.

Rogers, David. *110 Livingstone Street.* New York: Random House, 1968.

Rony, Vera. "Bogalusa: The Economics of Tragedy." *Dissent* 13 (May/June 1966): 234–242.

Rosengren, W. and Lefton, M., eds. *Organizations and Clients.* Columbus, Ohio: Charles E. Merrill, 1970.

Rothschild, Emma. *Paradise Lost: The Decline of the Auto-Industrial Age.* New York: Random House, 1973.

Rothschild-Whitt, Joyce. "The Collectivist Organization: An Alternative to Rational Bureaucratic Models." *American Sociological Review* 44 (1979): 509–527.

———. "Worker Ownership: Collective Response to an Elite-Generated Crisis." *Research in Social Movements, Conflict and Change,* vol. 6. Greenwich, Conn.: JAI Press (forthcoming).

Rumberger, Russell W. "The Changing Skill Requirements of Jobs in the U.S. Economy." *Industrial and Labor Relations Review* 34 (1981): 578–590

———. *Overeducation in the U.S. Labor Market.* New York: Praeger, 1981.

Rushing, W. A. "Hardness of Material as Related to Division of Labor in Manufacturing Industries." *Administrative Science Quarterly* 13, no. 2 (September 1968): 229–245.

Sable, Charles and Piore, Michael. *The Second Industrial Divide.* New York: Basic Books, 1984.

Scherer, F. M. *Industrial Market Structure and Economic Performance,* 2nd ed. Chicago: Rand McNally, 1980.

Schumpeter, Joseph. *Capitalism, Socialism, and Democracy.* New York: Harper & Row, 1950.

———. *Imperialism and Social Classes.* Cleveland: Meridian Books, 1955.

Scott, Robert A. "The Selection of Clients by Social Welfare Agencies: The Case of the Blind." *Social Problems* 14, no. 3 (Winter 1967): 248–257.

Seashore, Stanley and Bowers, David. *Changing the Structure and Functioning of an Organization.* Ann Arbor, Mich.: Institute for Social Research, University of Michigan, 1963.

———— and Yuchtman, Ephraim. "Factorial Analysis of Organizational Performance." *Administrative Science Quarterly* 12, no. 3 (December 1967): 377–395.

Seeley, John R., Junker, Bulford H., and Jones, R. Wallace, Jr. *Community Chest.* Toronto: University of Toronto Press, 1957.

Selznick, Philip. "An Approach to a Theory of Bureaucracy." *American Sociological Review* 8 (1943): 47–54.

————. "Foundations of a Theory of Organizations." *American Sociological Review* 13 (1948): 25–35.

————. "Rejoinder to Wohlin." In *A Sociological Reader on Complex Organizations,* edited by Amitai Etzioni. New York: Holt, Rinehart & Winston, 1969, pp. 149–154.

————. *Law, Society, and Industrial Justice.* New York: Russell Sage Foundation, 1969.

————. *Leadership in Administration.* New York: Harper & Row, 1957.

————. *The Organizational Weapon: A Study of Bolshevik Strategy and Tactics.* New York: McGraw-Hill, 1952.

————. *TVA and the Grass Roots.* New York: Harper & Row, 1965.

Shapiro, C. and Stiglitz, J. "Equilibrium Unemployment as a Worker Discipline Device." *American Economic Review* 74, no. 3 (June 1984): 433–444.

Silberman, Charles E. "The Truth About Automation." *Fortune* 71 (January 1965), pp. 125–127.

————. "The Comeback of the Blue-Collar Worker." *Fortune* 71 (February 1965), pp. 153–155.

Sills, David. *The Volunteers.* New York: Free Press, 1957.

Simon, Herbert. *Administrative Behavior,* 3rd ed. New York: Free Press, 1976.

————. "The Architecture of Complexity." *Proceedings of the American Philosophical Society* 106 (1962): 467–482.

————. *Models of Man.* New York: John Wiley & Sons, 1956.

————. "On the Concept of Organizational Goal." *Administrative Science Quarterly* 9, no. 1 (June 1964): 1–22.

Skinner, B. F. *Beyond Freedom and Dignity.* New York: Bantam Books, 1971.

Sloan, Alfred P. *My Years with General Motors.* New York: Doubleday, 1972.

Smigel, Erwin O. *The Wall Street Lawyer,* rev. ed. Bloomington, Ind.: Indiana University Press, 1970.

Smith, H. L. "Two Lines of Authority: The Hospital's Dilemma." In *Patients, Physicians, and Illness: Source Book in Behavioral Science and Medicine,* 2nd ed., edited by E. G. Jaco. New York: Free Press, 1972.

Sproul, Lee, et al. *Organizing an Anarchy.* Chicago: University of Chicago Press, 1978.

Starbuck, William. "A Trip to View the Elephants and Rattlesnakes in the Garden of Aston," in *Perspectives on Organization Design and Behavior,* edited by Andrew H. Van de Ven and William F. Joyce. New York: Wiley, 1981, pp. 167–199.

Stinchcombe, Arthur L. "Bureaucratic and Craft Administration of Production." *Administrative Science Quarterly* 4 (1959): 168–187.

————. "Contracts as Hierarchical Documents." Work Report 65, Institute of Industrial Economics, Bergen, Norway, 1984.

Stogdill, R. M. and Coons, A. E., eds. *Leader Behavior: Its Description and Measurement.* Columbus, Ohio: Bureau of Business Research, 1957.

Stone, Katherine. "The Origins of Job Structures in the Steel Industry." *Radical America* 7, no. 6 (November/December 1973): 19–64.

Storing, Herbert J. "The Science of Administration: Herbert A. Simon." In *Essays on the Scientific Study of Politics,* edited by H. J. Storing. New York: Holt, Rinehart & Winston, 1962, pp. 63–105.

Strauss, Anselm L., et al. *Psychiatric Ideologies and Institutions.* New York: Free Press, 1964.

Strauss, George. "Human Relations, 1968 Style." *Industrial Relations* 7, no. 3 (May 1969): 262–276.

——. "Notes on Power Equalization." In *The Social Science of Organizations,* edited by Harold Leavitt. Englewood Cliffs, N.J.: Prentice-Hall, 1963.

Street, David, Vinter, Robert, and Perrow, Charles. *Organizations for Treatment.* New York: Free Press, 1966.

Sudnow, David. "Normal Crimes." *Social Problems* 12, no. 3 (Winter 1964): 255–275.

Sykes, A. J. "Economic Interest and the Hawthorne Researches: A Comment." *Human Relations* 18 (1965): 253–263.

Sykes, Gresham M. *The Society of Captives: A Study of a Maximum Security Prison.* Princeton, N.J.: Princeton University Press, 1971.

Tannenbaum, Arnold S. *Control in Organizations.* New York: McGraw-Hill, 1968.

—— et al. *Hierarchy in Organizations.* San Francisco: Jossey-Bass, 1974.

Tannenbaum, Robert, Weschler, I. R., and Massarik, F. *Leadership and Organization: A Behavioral Science Approach.* New York: McGraw-Hill, 1961.

Thompson, James. *Organizations in Action.* New York: McGraw-Hill, 1967.

Thompson, Victor A. *Modern Organization,* 2nd ed. University, Ala.: University of Alabama Press, 1977.

Turk, Herman and Lefkowitz, Myron J. "Toward a Theory of Representation Between Groups." *Social Forces* 40 (May 1962): 337–341.

Udy, Stanley H., Jr. "Bureaucracy' and 'Rationality' in Weber's Organization Theory." *American Sociological Review* 24 (1959): 591–595.

"The University Arsenal." *Look* (August 26, 1969), p. 34.

Useem, Michael. "Classwide Rationality in the Politics of Managers and Directors of Large Corporations in the United States and Great Britain." *Administrative Science Quarterly* 27 (1982): 199–226.

——. *The Inner Circle: Large Corporations and the Rise of Business Political Activity in the US and the UK.* New York: Oxford University Press, 1984.

Vickers, Sir Geoffrey. *Towards a Sociology of Management.* New York: Basic Books, 1967.

Vitich, Arthur J. and Bensen, Joseph. *Small Town in Mass Society.* Princeton, N.J.: Princeton University Press, 1958.

Vroom, Victor. *Work and Motivation.* New York: John Wiley & Sons, 1964.

—— and Arthur G. Jago. "On the Validity of the Vroom-Yetton Model." *Journal of Applied Psychology* 63, no. 2 (1978): 151–162.

Wallace, Anthony. *Culture and Personality,* 2nd ed. New York: Random House, 1970.

Wallerstein, Immanuel. *The Modern World-System: Capitalist Agriculture and the Origins of European World-Economy in the Sixteenth Century.* New York: Academic Press, 1974.

Walton, Clarence C. *Corporate Social Responsibilities.* Belmont, Calif.: Wadsworth, 1967.

Wamsley, Gary L. *Selective Service and a Changing America.* Columbus, Ohio: Charles E. Merrill, 1969.

Warren, Roland, Rose, Stephen, and Bergunder, Ann. *The Structure of Urban Reform.* Lexington, Mass.: Lexington Books, 1974.

Warwick, Donald P. *A Theory of Public Bureaucracy: Politics, Personality, and Organization in the State Department.* Cambridge, Mass.: Harvard University Press, 1975.

Weber, Max. *Economy and Society,* vols. 1 & 3, 4th ed., edited by G. Roth and C. Wittich. New York: Irvington Publications, 1968.

———. *The Theory of Social and Economic Organization,* translated and edited by A. M. Henderson and T. Parsons. New York: Oxford University Press, 1947.

Weick, Karl. "Educational Organizations as Loosely Coupled Systems." *Administrative Science Quarterly* 21, no. 1 (March 1976): 1–19.

———. *The Social Psychology of Organizing,* 2nd ed. Reading, Mass.: Addison-Wesley, 1979.

White, Harrison. "Agency as Control." Paper, Cambridge, Mass., Harvard University, 1983.

White, R. and Lippett, R. *Autocracy and Democracy.* Westport, Conn.: Greenwood Press, 1972.

Whitehead, T. N. *Leadership in a Free Society.* Cambridge, Mass.: Harvard University Press, 1936.

Whyte, William F. "Human Relations—a Progress Report." In *Complex Organizations,* edited by Amitai Etzioni. New York: Holt, Rinehart & Winston, 1962.

———. *Money and Motivation.* Westport, Conn.: Greenwood Press, 1977.

Wildavsky, Aaron. *Politics of the Budgetary Process,* 2nd ed. Boston: Little, Brown, 1974.

Wilensky, Harold L. "Human Relations in the Workplace." In Conrad Arensberg et al., *Research in Industrial Human Relations: A Critical Appraisal.* New York: Harper & Row, 1957.

———. *Organizational Intelligence: Knowledge and Policy in Government and Industry.* New York: Basic Books, 1969.

———. "The Professionalization of Everyone?" *American Journal of Sociology* 70 (September 1964): 137–158.

——— and Lawrence, Anne T. "Job Assignment in Modern Societies: A Re-Examination of the Ascription-Achievement Hypothesis." In *Societal Growth: Processes and Implications,* edited by Amos Hawley. New York: Free Press, 1979, pp. 202–248.

Wilensky, Harold L. and Lebeaux. Charles N. *Industrial Society and Social Welfare,* rev. ed. New York: Free Press, 1965.

Williamson, Oliver. "Franchise Bidding for Natural Monopolies—in General and with Respect to CATV." *Bell Journal of Economics* 7, no. 1 (Spring 1976): 73–104.

———. *Markets and Hierarchy: Analysis and Antitrust Implications.* New York: Free Press, 1975.

———. "Organizational Innovation: The Transaction-cost Approach." In *Entrepreneurship,* edited by J. Ronen. Lexington, Mass.: Heath Lexington, 1983, pp. 101–134.

———. "The Organization of Work: A Comparative Institutional Assessment." *Journal of Economic Behavior and Organization* 1 (1980): 5–38.

———. "Reply to Jones." *Journal of Economic Behavior and Organization* 4 (1983):57–68.

——— and Ouchi, William. "A Rejoinder." In *Perspectives on Organization Design and Behavior,* edited by Andrew Van de Ven and William Joyce. New York: Wiley Interscience, 1981, p. 390.

Wilson, William Julius. "The Urban Underclass, Social Dislocation, and Public Policy." In *American Minorities and Civil Rights: Where Now and Where Headed,* edited by Leslie Dunbar. New York: Pantheon, 1984.

Wolin, Sheldon. *Politics and Vision: Continuity and Innovation in Western Political Thought.* Boston: Little, Brown, 1960.

Woodward, Joan, ed. *Industrial Organization: Behavior and Control.* London. Oxford University Press, 1970.

———. *Industrial Organization: Theory and Practice.* London: Oxford University Press, 1965.

Woodward, Robert and Bernstein, Carl. *All the President's Men.* New York: Simon & Schuster, 1974.

Worthy, James C. "Organizational Structure and Employee Morale." *American Sociological Review* 15 (1950): 169–179.

Wright, Erik Olin. *Class Crisis and the State.* Schocken Books, 1978.

———. "To Control or Smash Bureaucracy: Weber and Lenin on Politics, the State and Bureaucracy." *Berkeley Journal of Sociology* 19 (1975): 69–108.

Wright, J. Patrick. *On a Clear Day You Can See General Motors.* New York: Avon Books, 1979.

Yago, Glen. *The Decline of Transit: Urban Transportation in German and U.S. Cities, 1900–1970.* New York: Cambridge University Press, 1984.

Zachariah, Mathew. "The Impact of Darwin's Theory of Evolution on Theories of Society." *Social Studies* 62, no. 2 (February 1971): 69–76.

Zald, Mayer N. "The Correctional Institution for Juvenile Offenders: An Analysis of Organization 'Character.' " *Social Problems* 8, no. 1 (Summer 1960): 57–67.

———. "Power Balance and Staff Conflict in Correctional Institutions." *Administrative Science Quarterly* 7 (June 1962): 22–49.

———, ed. *Power in Organizations.* Nashville, Tenn.: Vanderbilt University Press, 1970.

———. "The Social Control of Industries." *Social Forces* 57, no. 1 (September 1978): 79–102.

——— and Ash, Robert. "Social Movement Organizations: Growth, Decay, and Change." *Social Forces* 44, no. 3 (March 1966): 327–341.

——— and Denton, Patricia. "From Evangelism to General Service: The Transformation of the YMCA." *Administrative Science Quarterly* 8, no. 2 (September 1963): 214–234.

Zeitlin, Maurice. *American Society, Inc.* Chicago: Markham, 1970.

Zeitz, Gerald. "Structural and Individual Determinants of Organizations' Morale and Satisfaction." *Social Forces* 61, no. 4 (1983): 1088–1108.

Index

character of, 7; and society, 173–176; "society of," 255; and the state, 262–263; steepness of, 26–30; studies of morale and leadership in, 80, 85–96; technological model of, 140–146; as things in themselves, 167–169; as tools of management, 5–6, 71–73, 172, 196–197; as tools, 11–12; trivial, 172–173. *See also* Bureaucracy; Environmental theory; Human relations movement; Institutional analysis; Institutions; *names of specific organization theorists*
Organizations (March and Simon), 119, 120, 129, 155, 164, 220
Ouchi, William 236, 237

Pappi, Franz U., 199
Parsons, Talcott, 42, 46, 65, 140, 141, 210
Particularism: as aid to goal achievement, 10–13; clash with efficiency, 6–7; definition of, 6; reasons for rejection of, 6–9, 13–14; as tool for control, 11–12
Patent Office, U.S., 189
Patterns of Industrial Bureaucracy (Gouldner), 1
Pavlov's dogs, 96
"Payola," 183
Pentagon Capitalism (Melman), 166
Perrow, Charles, 161
Peterson, Richard, 182–184, 186
Pharmaceutical industry: governmental manipulations by, 189–190; influence on AMA by, 189–190
Polanyi, Michael, 217
Police departments, "cops and robbers" syndrome in, 17
Political ties, benefits of, 10–11
Population-ecology model of organizations (theory of social selection), 208–218
Porter, Lyman, 87
Powell, Walter W., 272
Power: definition of, 259; influence on distribution of risks and benefits, 259; non-zero-sum, 258–259; and organizations, 11; of the rich, 12; zero-sum, 259
Presley, Elvis, 187
Pressman, Lee, 139
Productivity: contingency theory of, 91–92; Hawthorne effect on, 79–80; impact of supportive behavior on, 104; role of job enlargement in, 90–91; role of

leadership in, 85–92; role of morale in, 80, 85–96
Professionals: adjustment of, to hierarchy, 42–46; debt collection practices of, 15–16; in organizations, 44–46; rationalization of services of, 16–17; rule consciousness of, 22–23; sale of practices by, 16
Professional services: and franchises, 16; rationalization of, 16; selling of, 16
Profit motive: 70–71; and cultural censorship, 181–182
Public data, 173
Public Speaking and Influencing Men in Business (Carnegie), 59
Pugh, Derek, 32
Putterman, Louis, 226
Pynchon, Thomas, 118

"Rabble hypothesis," 59
Radicalism, and profit, 181–182
Rationality: and model making, 121–123; myth of, in humans, 120–123; prescriptions for, 67–68, 75, 123
Reagan, Ronald, 164
Reinforcement, 96
Requisite variety, law of, 209
Rewards, for organizational service, 47–48
Rickenbacker, Eddie, 68
Risk and benefit distribution, influence of power on, 259
Risk taking, 29–30
Ritti, R. R., 45
Robber barons, 250
Rock music. *See* Music industry
Roethlisberger, F. J., 72, 73, 80–83
Roosevelt, Franklin D., 145
Roots of American Foreign Policy, The (Kolko), 166
Rose, Steven, 206, 208
Routines, as skills of organizations, 217–218
Rowan, Brian, 265–267, 271
Rules: as consequence of complexity, 21; and distribution requirements, 23–24; and expressive groups, 23, 27–29; good and bad types of, 25–26; interdepartmental, 23–24; and mechanization, 20–21; and professionalism, 22–23; reduction of, 20–23; for regulating interdepartmental contracts, 23–24; structural view of, 128–129; Weber's view of, 72n; in written form, 21–22

About the Author

Charles Perrow, Professor of Sociology at Yale University, is from Tacoma, Washington, and received his undergraduate education in fits and starts at the University of Washington; Black Mountain College, North Carolina; Reed College, Portland, Oregon; and the University of California at Berkeley. He received his B.A., M.A., and Ph.D. from Berkeley, all in sociology. He sees organizational phenomena at the root of social change in the last two centuries, leading to a "society of organizations" that can only be understood by examining organizations and their interaction. His research and teaching focus on organizations, social change, social movements, and accidents in high-risk systems, which he considers inevitable, even "normal." He is the author of five books and numerous articles and is currently working on an organizational interpretation of the U.S. Industrial Revolution and the subsequent crisis of our time.